STRENGTH FOR TODAY

STRENGTH FOR TODAY

John F. MacArthur

CROSSWAY BOOKS • WHEATON, ILLINOIS
A DIVISION OF GOOD NEWS PUBLISHERS

Strength for Today

Copyright © 1997 by John F. MacArthur

Published by Crossway Books
a division of Good News Publishers
1300 Crescent Street
Wheaton, Illinois 60187.

Cover photo: Dennis Flaherty

Jacket design: Cindy Kiple

First printing, 1997

Printed in the United States of America

All Scripture quotations in this book, except those noted otherwise, are from the *New American Standard Bible*, © 1960, 1962, 1963, 1968, 1971, 1972, 1973, 1975, and 1977 by The Lockman Foundation, and are used by permission.

Library of Congress Cataloging in Publication Data
MacArthur, John, 1939-
    Strength for today : daily readings for a deeper faith / John F.
MacArthur.
        p.   cm.
    Includes index.
    ISBN 0-89107-969-6
    1. Devotional calendars.   I. Title.
BV4811.M233 1997
242'.2—DC21   97-29635

07	06	05	04	03	02	01	00	99	98	97
15	14	13	12	11	10	9	8	7	6	5	4	3	2	1

To Jubilant Sykes—
whose love, loyalty, and majestic music
has ministered to me through the years

CONTENTS

INTRODUCTION

For many years I had the desire to produce a book that could be used as a daily devotional guide, yet offer significantly more than the typical thematic or topical anecdotes that make up the majority of devotionals. It would need to reflect what I am committed to: an in-depth approach to Bible exposition. Four years ago *Drawing Near* was published to fulfill that desire.

I was convinced the response to such a book would be good, but I was surprised by how overwhelming it was. Since that initial response, I am pleased that each year thousands more have been able to benefit daily from its brief but rich studies in God's Word.

Since *Drawing Near* was able to meet such an obvious need, it seemed logical to publish another devotional that could focus on some of the other key themes of Scripture that I wasn't able to cover in the first book. *Strength for Today* does just that, drawing from other important passages I have taught over the years.

This new devotional is designed like its predecessor—it should be used 365 days a year. Each month is devoted to the Scripture passages that teach about a particular theme, including such topics as assurance of salvation, humility, and how to deal with suffering. By the time you have spent a year studying this material, you will have gained a firm grasp of some of the important themes in the Bible.

But this is not simply an intellectual exercise. The real benefit of studying God's Word is the practical applications you draw from it. So while you are studying verse by verse through a passage, you'll find that each day stands on its own and makes direct application to your life.

As you use this book daily, you will learn how to approach Scripture on your own, developing the study skills you need to open up the Bible and discover its rich and marvelous truths for yourself. Such repeated exposure to God's Word trains you to think biblically, and that's what ultimately makes a difference in your spiritual life.

It is my prayer that you will continue to be "one who looks intently at the perfect law, the law of liberty, and abides by it, not having become a forgetful hearer but an effectual doer" (James 1:25). May this devotional be a wonderful encouragement in that pursuit!

DAILY READINGS

> *"I, therefore, the prisoner of the Lord,*
> *entreat you to walk in a manner worthy of the calling*
> *with which you have been called."*
> EPHESIANS 4:1

❖ ❖ ❖

Just as organizations have rules their members must follow,
God has standards Christians must live by.

When someone is part of a group, he or she is obligated to follow its laws or standards. American citizens are required to obey the laws of the United States. Employees must conform to the rules of their company. Athletic teams are expected to listen to their coach.

Most of us want to be part of a group because with belonging comes acceptance. This desire to conform can be quite strong, sometimes dangerously so. During Jesus' time, "many even of the rulers believed in Him, but because of the Pharisees they were not confessing Him, lest they should be put out of the synagogue; for they loved the approval of men rather than the approval of God" (John 12:42-43). Those rulers were so committed to their religious system that they damned their souls by rigidly adhering to its code.

Some people think belonging to the church is different though. They want the blessings, rights, and privileges of being a child of God, but they're unwilling to conform to biblical standards. But God expects Christians to live a certain way. Paul told the Corinthian believers to remove from their midst all who live immorally (1 Cor. 5:1-2). In 2 Thessalonians 3:6 he says, "Keep aloof from every brother who leads an unruly life and not according to the tradition which you received from us."

Since people can join athletic teams and businesses and follow the rules, since people can be so fearful of being cast out of their society that they forfeit their souls, since people can be so devoted to things that don't matter, shouldn't Christians make an even greater commitment to what matters most? In Ephesians 4:1-6 Paul tells us how we can "walk in a manner worthy of the calling with which [we] have been called" (v. 1). Let's commit ourselves to obey God as we learn what He requires of us.

❖ ❖ ❖

Suggestions for Prayer: Ask God to show you areas where your commitment to Him is lacking, and for help in strengthening those areas.

For Further Study: Read John 9. What were the parents of the man born blind most committed to? ❖ What effect did that commitment have on them?

"I, therefore, the prisoner of the Lord,
entreat you to walk in a manner worthy of the calling
with which you have been called."
EPHESIANS 4:1

✧ ✧ ✧

The Christian life is simply becoming
what Christ has already made you.

Suppose immediately after you were saved, the Lord stamped your forehead with the words, "Watch me. I'm a child of God." How would that affect your lifestyle?

We may not have a physical mark like that, but we do bear the name of Christ in this world. When we first put our trust in the Lord Jesus Christ, we became part of His family (Gal. 4:1-7). He "freely bestowed" His grace on us (Eph. 1:6). He "has blessed us with every spiritual blessing in the heavenly places in Christ" (1:3). And we have a rich, glorious inheritance in heaven (1:18). As God's children, we indeed have many rights, honors, and privileges, but He expects us to behave like His children. Just as a child honors his father by obeying him, we honor God by walking worthy of Him. Our actions must be actions He would approve. Our desires must be His desires. Our goals and objectives must be His goals and objectives.

One of my seminary professors once told me that the whole Christian life is simply becoming what you are. Because you are a child of God, you need to act like a child of God. In fact, the root of the Greek word translated "worthy" in Ephesians 4:1 speaks of equalization and balance. There ought to be perfect harmony between who you are and how you live. We lapse in our commitment to Christ when we fail to live that way.

Remember, though, that our obedience to God must not be a conformity to rules and regulations out of fear or legalistic pride. It is instead a conformity to righteousness out of gratitude and a deep love for Christ. Our desire to be worthy children is a result of understanding and appreciating all He has done for us.

Philippians 1:27 says, "Conduct yourselves in a manner worthy of the gospel of Christ." In other words, match your conduct to the gospel. The exalted reality of the gospel demands an exalted lifestyle.

✧ ✧ ✧

Suggestions for Prayer: Ask the Lord to help you act like His child.

For Further Study: Read 1 John 2:6. Christ is our supreme example of the worthy walk. ✧ Find examples in the Gospels where He demonstrates His commitment to the Father. ✧ How can you follow His example today?

> *"I, therefore, the prisoner of the Lord,*
> *entreat you to walk in a manner worthy of the calling*
> *with which you have been called."*
> EPHESIANS 4:1

❖ ❖ ❖

There can be no right living without right principles.

I magine someone saying, "I have some extra money lying around. I think I'll send a large check to the government." Absurd, isn't it? But every year, honest wage-earners fill out forms and give part of their income to the government. Why? It's not because they are generous but because there is a law—a doctrine—that says they have to.

Unless people know the reason for what they should do, it's unlikely they'll make a commitment to do it. Paul understood that, so he always taught doctrine before duty. "Therefore" in Ephesians 4:1 links the doctrine of chapters 1—3 to the duty of chapters 4—6. Doctrine and duty are inseparably linked; duty always flows out of doctrine. Right living is based on right principles.

Paul told the Colossian church, "We have not ceased to pray for you and to ask that you may be filled with the knowledge of His will in all spiritual wisdom and understanding" (1:9). For what purpose? "So that you may walk in a manner worthy of the Lord" (v. 10). Spiritual knowledge, wisdom, and understanding make up the pathway of a worthy walk.

When pastors teach duty without teaching doctrine, they weaken the Word of God because they've eliminated the motive. They may be able to stir up emotions, but that brings no long-term commitment. The pastor's responsibility is to teach the truth of God, and the hearer's responsibility is to obey it.

Of course, the source of God's truth is His Word: "All Scripture is inspired by God and profitable for teaching, for reproof, for correction, for training in righteousness; that the man of God may be adequate, equipped for every good work" (2 Tim. 3:16-17). Knowing the Bible well is our means of equipping ourselves for a righteous life.

As we think about our worthy walk, let's avoid emotionalism and legalism, and instead focus on living what we learn from a thorough and personal study of God's Word.

❖ ❖ ❖

Suggestions for Prayer: If you have neglected studying the Bible, confess that to God, and ask Him to give you a greater desire to learn His Word.

For Further Study: Read Ephesians 1—3 and list all we are or have in Christ. Knowing what God has given you, can you do any less than commit yourself to Him completely?

"I, therefore, the prisoner of the Lord,
entreat you to walk in a manner worthy of the calling
with which you have been called."
EPHESIANS 4:1

✧ ✧ ✧

Knowing and obeying God's Word helps us walk
worthy by protecting us from sin.

While we are discussing the importance of knowing right doctrine before right duty, let's see one way knowing the Bible helps us to walk worthy: it protects us from sin. From time to time you might hear people who have a fatalistic attitude toward sin saying, "I couldn't help myself" or "The Devil made me do it." Such excuses are foolish for Christians to make since God has given us the means to resist temptation.

The psalmist said, "Thy word I have treasured in my heart, that I may not sin against Thee" (Ps. 119:11). Without knowledge, we are defenseless and vulnerable. Knowing God's truth—by study and by application—enables us to say no to sin and yes to righteousness. Anyone who puts his faith in Jesus Christ but who does not keep God's Word constantly at the forefront of his mind will find himself entrapped in sin again and again.

Although we must know God's Word to defend ourselves against sin and to obey God's will, there is a danger. Once we know His truth, we are held accountable for what we know.

Second Peter 2:21 speaks of apostates, those who knew about Jesus Christ but returned to their former life without ever committing themselves to Him: "It would be better for them not to have known the way of righteousness, than having known it, to turn away from the holy commandment delivered to them." James 4:17 says, "To one who knows the right thing to do, and does not do it, to him it is sin."

So not knowing is better than knowing and not obeying. What's best, of course, is knowing the Word and obeying it, because it is our spiritual nourishment: "Like newborn babes, long for the pure milk of the word, that by it you may grow in respect to salvation" (1 Peter 2:2). For a Christian, neglecting the Word is spiritual starvation.

✧ ✧ ✧

Suggestions for Prayer: Ask forgiveness for times you have known the right thing to do but have not done it.

For Further Study: Read about a young man who gave in to temptation in Proverbs 7. Contrast him with Joseph in Genesis 39. What was the difference between them? ✧ Think about how Psalm 119:9 relates to them, and to you.

"I, therefore, the prisoner of the Lord,
entreat you to walk in a manner worthy of the calling
with which you have been called."
EPHESIANS 4:1

To mature in our faith, we must learn to
see things from God's perspective.

Paul was a prisoner of Rome. Why then did he call himself "the prisoner of the Lord"? Because he had the ability to see everything in terms of how it affected Christ. No matter what happened in his life, he saw it in relation to God. His questions were, "What does this mean, God?" and "How does this affect You?"

When a problem comes in life, we are prone to say, "Oh, woe is me!" and wonder how it will affect us: *Will it cause me pain? Will it cost me money?* Too often we think only on the earthly level. But like Paul, we should think on a heavenly level: *What is God trying to teach me? How can I glorify Him in this?* In fact, a good definition of Christian maturity is: automatically seeing things in light of the divine perspective.

This perspective, this God-consciousness, is the only right way for Christians to live. David said, "I have set the Lord continually before me; because He is at my right hand, I will not be shaken. Therefore my heart is glad, and my glory rejoices; my flesh also will dwell securely" (Ps. 16:8-9). Because David was always aware of God's presence, he found joy and security, and no trouble could disturb him for long.

Paul was the same way: he knew there was a reason for his imprisonment and that Christ would be glorified by it (cf. Phil. 1:12-14). Paul wasn't preoccupied with how it affected him, and thus he was able to rejoice, even in prison.

"God causes all things to work together for good to those who love God, to those who are called according to His purpose" (Rom. 8:28). Nothing happens outside of God's control. Let's trust that He knows what is best for us.

✧ ✧ ✧

Suggestions for Prayer: If you tend to get discouraged or complain when troubles come, ask God to forgive you and help you see troubles from His perspective. Acknowledge before Him that He is in control of everything.

For Further Study: Paul's attitude toward difficulties was cultivated by the experience he describes in 2 Corinthians 12:2-10. What did Christ teach him about troubles in verse 9, and how did that change Paul's outlook?

"I, therefore, the prisoner of the Lord,
entreat you to walk in a manner worthy of the calling
with which you have been called."

EPHESIANS 4:1

❖ ❖ ❖

A passion for Christ is what compels us
to live an exemplary life.

What do you think of when you hear the word *beggar*? You probably picture a haggard person in tattered clothes with an outstretched hand asking for money or food.

Would it surprise you to know that the apostle Paul was a beggar? He didn't beg for money, though, but for people to follow Christ. The word translated "entreat" in this verse means "to call out to someone with intensity" or "to plead with someone."

Paul pleaded with many people. He begged Herod Agrippa to hear the gospel (Acts 26:3). He told the church at Rome, "I urge you therefore, brethren, by the mercies of God, to present your bodies a living and holy sacrifice" (Romans 12:1). To the Corinthians he said, "We beg you on behalf of Christ, be reconciled to God" (2 Cor. 5:20). When Paul was committed to some principle of divine truth, he implored people to respond. He didn't approach the ministry with detachment or indifference.

Paul again feels compelled to beg in Ephesians 4:1: "I . . . entreat you to walk in a manner worthy of the calling with which you have been called." He doesn't just coldly say, "It is essential that you walk worthy." He begs them. Why? Because when you don't walk worthy, God is not glorified in your life, you are not fully blessed, the church cannot fully function, and therefore the world cannot see Jesus Christ for who He is. So much depends on our worthy walk. Paul pleads with us, to show how vital it is.

Paul's passion demonstrates an important truth: while knowledge is necessary in the Christian life, it is our desire to be like Christ that compels us toward righteousness. And when we have that desire, it will be natural for us to beg those around us to follow Christ as well.

❖ ❖ ❖

Suggestions for Prayer: Ask God to give you the heart of the apostle Paul who said, "We are ambassadors for Christ, as though God were entreating through us; we beg you on behalf of Christ, be reconciled to God" (2 Cor. 5:20).

For Further Study: Read Philippians 3:7-14. What characterized Paul's zeal?
❖ Which of these characteristics do you lack? Look for ways to bolster them as you daily work through this book.

*"I, therefore, the prisoner of the Lord,
entreat you to walk in a manner worthy of the calling
with which you have been called."*
EPHESIANS 4:1

✧ ✧ ✧

*A worthy lifestyle is possible only by
depending on God's resources.*

Walking is often used in Scripture as a symbol of the Christian life. It is simply a reference to your daily conduct or lifestyle—a day-by-day, step-by-step commitment to follow Christ. As Christians we "walk in newness of life" (Rom. 6:4). John wrote, "This is love, that we walk according to His commandments" (2 John 6). Paul said to walk in good works (Eph. 2:10) and to please God in our walk before Him (1 Thess. 4:1).

In Ephesians 4:1 Paul is saying, "Let your lifestyle be worthy of the calling to which you are called."

You may ask, "Is it possible to walk this way?" Yes, but only on this basis: you must devote yourself to be strengthened with the power of the Holy Spirit (Eph. 3:16), Christ's Word must dwell in your heart, His love must penetrate your life (vv. 17-19), and you must be "filled up to all the fulness of God" (v. 19), who "is able to do exceeding abundantly beyond all that we ask or think" (v. 20). We must live by the resources God has given us to walk the worthy walk. We'll never do it by just knowing the theology and then trying really hard.

Are you trying to live as a Christian without prayer, without studying the Bible, or even without giving much thought to Christ except on Sunday? Are you trying to be righteous without relying on the Holy Spirit? If you are, you will be frustrated in your efforts. You must commit every day and every moment to the Lord, trusting in His strength. Besides, why would you want to live on your own power when you can live by the power of God?

✧ ✧ ✧

Suggestions for Prayer: Thank God for giving you the Holy Spirit, who gives you the power to walk worthy before Him and others. ✧ Pray each day that the Holy Spirit will strengthen you to live in a way that pleases God.

For Further Study: Read Galatians 5:16-25. From your understanding of today's study, what does it mean to "walk by the Spirit"? ✧ What does walking by the Spirit protect you from?

> *"I, therefore, the prisoner of the Lord,*
> *entreat you to walk in a manner worthy of the calling*
> *with which you have been called."*
>
> EPHESIANS 4:1

✧ ✧ ✧

We didn't choose God; He chose us.

What is "the calling with which [we] have been called"? It is simply the position we have now as Christians. Paul said the Christians at Corinth were "saints by calling" (1 Cor. 1:2). Peter instructed his readers to make certain about God's calling and choosing them (2 Peter 1:10). Our calling is a high calling (Phil. 3:14), "a holy calling" (2 Tim. 1:9), and "a heavenly calling" (Heb. 3:1).

Who called us? Jesus has the answer: "No one can come to Me, unless the Father who sent Me draws him" (John 6:44). Jesus also said, "You did not choose Me, but I chose you" (15:16). Those "whom [God] predestined, these He also called; and whom He called, these He also justified; and whom He justified, these He also glorified" (Rom. 8:30). God called out to us, we responded in faith, and He saved us.

Suppose after investigating all the different religions of the world, a person chose Christianity. If Christianity were nothing more than a simple, personal choice to be saved, this person would have a certain level of commitment—that is, "Since I've decided to do it, it's worth doing." But if I'm a Christian because before the world began, the sovereign God of the universe chose me to spend eternity in His presence, that creates a much greater level of commitment.

If a single woman approached a bachelor, told him he had characteristics she admired, and asked him if he would be interested in marrying her, there would be something missing in that courtship. But suppose he approaches this woman first and says, "I have gone from one end of the world to the other, and your character and beauty surpass all others. Will you marry me?" We know then that nothing is missing.

Magnify that illustration by considering God's perspective. We didn't ask God if we could get in on a salvation deal. Out of all the people in the world, He chose us to receive His mercy! That's a high, holy, heavenly calling. Such a calling demands a response of commitment, doesn't it?

✧ ✧ ✧

Suggestions for Prayer: Thank God for His grace in choosing and calling you.*For Further Study*: Read Romans 8:29-39. How did Paul respond to the knowledge of God's calling for his life? ✧ How should God's calling affect your attitude?

"Walk . . . with all humility"
EPHESIANS 4:2

✧ ✧ ✧

Humility is fundamental to
spiritual growth and blessing.

It's no secret that family problems are on the rise. Husbands and wives can't get along. Children rebel against their parents. Unfortunately, most of the proposed solutions deal only with the peripheral issues instead of the central issue, which is pride. There will never be unity or happiness in a family without humility.

Humility is not only essential in families; it is also a basic ingredient for all spiritual blessing. The book of Proverbs is rich with such teaching. "When pride comes, then comes dishonor, but with the humble is wisdom" (11:2). "Before honor comes humility" (15:33). "The reward of humility and the fear of the Lord are riches, honor and life" (22:4). James tells us, "God is opposed to the proud, but gives grace to the humble" (4:6). Too often we forget how important humility is.

Did you know that pride was the first sin ever committed? An angel named Lucifer tried to exalt himself above God: "I will ascend to heaven; I will raise my throne above the stars of God, and I will sit on the mount of assembly in the recesses of the north. I will ascend above the heights of the clouds; I will make myself like the Most High" (Isa. 14:13-14). He said "I will" five times, and God said, "No, you won't" and cast him out of Heaven. Lucifer, "son of the morning," became Satan, "the accuser."

Every sin—whatever it is—has pride at its root, because all sin is defiance of God. What could be more prideful than saying, "I won't follow God's standard"? So in trying to overcome sin, we must also deal with our pride.

It is impossible to be saved without humility. God isn't impressed with credentials; you must come to God and say, "I am a sinner, and I realize I am worthy of nothing." There's no other way into God's family and no other way to walk once you're there.

Though you may have read your Bible, prayed, gone to church all your life, or even founded churches, if you aren't walking in humility, you aren't walking a worthy walk. The worthy walk begins with "all humility."

✧ ✧ ✧

Suggestions for Prayer: Consider how pride manifests itself in some areas of your life, confess those to God, and ask His forgiveness.

For Further Study: Read Luke 18:9-14. Compare the attitudes of the tax collector and the Pharisee. Which one pleased God and why?

"Let love of the brethren continue."
HEBREWS 13:1

❖ ❖ ❖

*To be a testimony to the world,
Christians need to live what they profess.*

The nineteenth-century preacher Alexander Maclaren once said, "The world takes its notion of God most of all from those who say they belong to God's family. They read us a great deal more than they read the Bible. They see us; they only hear about Jesus Christ." Sound biblical doctrine, as important a foundation as it is, is inadequate by itself to influence the world toward Christ's gospel.

Christians today could learn much from the early Christians, whose lives were such a rebuke to the immoral, pagan societies around them. Unbelievers in those cultures found it extremely difficult to find fault with Christians, because the more they observed them, the more they saw believers living out the high moral standards the church professed.

Christians in those days were obedient to Peter's instruction: "For such is the will of God that by doing right you may silence the ignorance of foolish men" (1 Peter 2:15). They also heeded Paul's advice to Titus: "In all things show yourself to be an example of good deeds, with purity in doctrine, dignified, sound in speech which is beyond reproach, in order that the opponent may be put to shame, having nothing bad to say about us" (Titus 2:7-8).

Jesus commanded His original disciples and us, "Let your light shine before men in such a way that they may see your good works, and glorify your Father who is in heaven" (Matt. 5:16). Of course, Jesus had in mind good works that were genuine and that came from a foundation of good teaching.

These verses ought to remind us, therefore, that doctrine and practice must go hand in hand. The author of Hebrews shifts naturally from doctrine and general exhortation to the specific admonitions of chapter 13. Love among believers is his starting point, and it should be ours as we seek to have a credible and worthy walk before the watching world.

❖ ❖ ❖

Suggestions for Prayer: Ask God to help you maintain a scriptural balance between doctrine and practice. ❖ Pray that He would correct specific areas in which you have been living out of balance.

For Further Study: Memorize James 1:25. Use a Bible with good cross references, and look up other verses that deal with "the law of liberty."

> *"Let love of the brethren continue."*
> **HEBREWS 13:1**

❖ ❖ ❖

Christianity's primary moral standard is love,
especially for fellow believers.

L ove of other believers is a natural outflow of the Christian life and should be a normal part of fellowship within the church. You can no doubt remember how after you were first saved it became very natural and exciting to love other Christians and to want to be around them. However, such an attitude is extremely difficult to maintain. This love, which is a gift from God's Spirit, must be nurtured or it will not grow—it may actually shrivel. That's why the apostle Peter urges us, "Since you have in obedience to the truth purified your souls for a sincere love of the brethren, fervently love one another from the heart, for you have been born again not of seed which is perishable but imperishable, that is, through the living and abiding word of God" (1 Peter 1:22-23).

Paul teaches us the same concept of nurturing and practicing love for one another when he writes: "Now as to the love of the brethren, you have no need for any one to write to you, for you yourselves are taught by God to love one another; for indeed you do practice it toward all the brethren who are in all Macedonia. But we urge you, brethren, to excel still more" (1 Thess. 4:9-10).

Paul also gives us the basic definition of brotherly love: "Be devoted to one another in brotherly love; give preference to one another in honor" (Rom. 12:10). Simply stated, brotherly love is caring for fellow Christians more than we care for ourselves. And such love presupposes that we will have an attitude of humility (Phil. 2:3-4).

So today's verse from Hebrews merely supports what Paul and Peter said elsewhere. The writer's admonition that we should let brotherly love continue tells us that this kind of love already exists. Our challenge today and each day is not to discover love for one another, but to allow it to continue and to increase.

❖ ❖ ❖

Suggestions for Prayer: Ask God to help you rekindle the love that used to be strong for a Christian friend, but perhaps isn't now.

For Further Study: Read 1 Samuel 18—20. What was so special about the love and friendship between David and Jonathan? ❖ What was the end result of that relationship (see especially 20:8-17)?

"Let love of the brethren continue."
HEBREWS 13:1

✧ ✧ ✧

Genuine love among Christians is a testimony
to the world, to ourselves, and to God.

The importance of brotherly love extends well beyond the walls of your local church or fellowship hall. In John 13:35 Jesus says, "By this all men will know that you are My disciples, if you have love for one another." In effect, God has made love for one another the measuring stick by which the world can determine if our Christian profession is genuine. That's why it's so important that we have a selfless attitude and sincerely place the interests of our brothers and sisters in Christ ahead of our own.

If you are a parent, you know what a delight it is when your children love and care for one another. Such harmonious relations make for a close-knit family and fulfill the words of the psalmist: "Behold, how good and how pleasant it is for brothers to dwell together in unity!" (Ps. 133:1). God is both pleased and glorified when Christian brothers and sisters love each other and minister together in harmony.

Neither the author of Hebrews nor the apostle John is equating love with a sentimental, superficial affection. As already suggested, practical commitment marks true brotherly love. If you do not have such commitment, it is fair to question your relationship to God (1 John 3:17). Refusing to help a fellow believer when you can, John reasons, reveals that you don't really love him. And if you don't love him, God's love can't be in your heart, which proves that you don't belong to Him. This logic is sobering and persuasive. It should motivate us all the more to see the importance of practicing brotherly love: "Let us not love with word or with tongue, but in deed and truth. We shall know by this that we are of the truth, and shall assure our heart before Him" (1 John 3:18-19).

✧ ✧ ✧

Suggestions for Prayer: Ask the Lord's forgiveness for times when you did not show brotherly love or when you were reluctant to help another Christian in need.

For Further Study: Read Luke 6:31-35 and notice how our duty to love extends even beyond the sphere of fellow believers. What kind of reward results?

*"Do not neglect to show hospitality to strangers, for by this
some have entertained angels without knowing it."*
HEBREWS 13:2

❖ ❖ ❖

*Hospitality should be a trait of all Christians,
because whenever we display it, we minister to the Lord.*

If you are a Christian, your responsibility to love others does not stop with
fellow believers. The apostle Paul is very explicit and direct about this:
"See that no one repays another with evil for evil, but always seek after that
which is good for one another and for all men" (1 Thess. 5:15). "All men"
includes even your enemies. The "strangers" mentioned in today's verse can
refer to unbelievers as well as believers. The writer of Hebrews is saying we
often won't know the full impact hospitality will have; therefore, we should
always be alert and diligent because our actions may even influence someone
toward salvation.

The last part of Hebrews 13:2, "some have entertained angels without
knowing it," further underscores the point that we can never know how significant or helpful an act of hospitality might be. Abraham had no idea that
two of the three men passing by his tent were angels and that the third was
the Lord Himself, but he still went out of his way to demonstrate hospitality
(Gen. 18:1-5). The primary motivation is still love, for the sake of those we
help and for the glory of God.

The Lord Jesus says, "Truly I say to you, to the extent that you did it to one
of these brothers of Mine, even the least of them, you did it to Me" (Matt.
25:40). As Christians, when we feed the hungry, take in the stranger, clothe
the naked, and visit someone in prison, we serve Christ. If we turn our backs
on people, believers or unbelievers, who have real needs, it is the same as turning our backs on Him (v. 45). Loving hospitality is therefore more than an
option—it is a command.

❖ ❖ ❖

Suggestions for Prayer: Pray that God would give you a greater desire to show
hospitality and that you could minister it to a specific person.

For Further Study: Read Genesis 18:1-15. Write down the positive ways in
which Abraham handled his opportunity to show love to strangers. ❖ How
well did Sarah handle this situation? ❖ How does the example of her attitude
relate to Hebrews 13:2?

*"Remember the prisoners, as though in prison
with them, and those who are ill-treated, since you
yourselves also are in the body."*
HEBREWS 13:2

❖ ❖ ❖

*Because we too are human beings, God makes it possible for us
to empathize with others who might be enduring hardship.*

The Apostolic Confession, an ancient church confession, says, "If any Christian is condemned for Christ's sake to the mines by the ungodly, do not overlook him, but from the proceeds of your toil and sweat, send him something to support himself, and to reward the soldier of Christ." You can see from this quote that the early church took seriously its responsibility to help people who were suffering persecution. To obtain money to free a fellow believer, some early Christians even sold themselves into slavery.

It's unlikely we'll ever have to face such extreme measures. But we can definitely learn from the heart attitude that prompted such an action. The point is, we should do whatever we can to understand what others are going through. We don't necessarily have to experience the same starvation, imprisonment, or harsh treatment that they are enduring in order to sympathize. Being human—"in the body," as today's verse says—and suffering our own hurts and hungers should be enough incentive for us to help others.

You can have loving empathy for someone in at least three ways. First, you can simply "be there" as a friend to encourage the other person when he is in trouble.

A second way to show empathy is by giving direct help. The Philippians shared with the apostle Paul in his affliction by financially supporting his ministry in other places (Phil. 4:14-16). In this way they also encouraged him spiritually.

Third, you can give empathy through prayer. Paul's closing words to the Colossians, "Remember my imprisonment" (Col. 4:18), were an appeal for prayer. It was the only means remaining by which the church could effectively support him.

If we have Christ's example, who is not "a high priest who cannot sympathize with our weaknesses" (Heb. 4:15), how can we possibly ignore the hurts of others, especially those of fellow believers? Instead, sincere empathy should be a regular part of our service for the Lord.

❖ ❖ ❖

Suggestions for Prayer: Pray for a greater alertness and sensitivity to those you know who might be hurting.

For Further Study: Based on the Good Samaritan story in Luke 10:29-37, what are the essential attitudes and actions of a good neighbor?

*"Let your way of life be free from the love of money,
being content with what you have."*
HEBREWS 13:5

✧ ✧ ✧

*If you are content with what God has given you,
you will not be a person who is covetous or a lover of money.*

I once had a man come into my church office and confess the sin of gluttony. When I told him he did not look overweight, he answered, "I know. It is not that I eat too much but that I want to. I continually crave food. It's an obsession."

Covetousness is very similar to that man's gluttonous attitude. You do not have to acquire a lot of things, or even anything at all, to be covetous. If you long to acquire things and are focusing all your attention on how you might get them, you are guilty of covetousness.

It is not wrong to earn or possess wealth. In the Old Testament, Abraham and Job had tremendous wealth. A number of faithful New Testament believers were also fairly wealthy. The problem comes when we have a greedy attitude that craves money above everything else. Paul warns us, "For the love of money is a root of all sorts of evil, and some by longing for it have wandered away from the faith, and pierced themselves with many a pang" (1 Tim. 6:10). Loving money is perhaps the most common form of covetousness; it is akin to lusting after material riches in various forms.

No matter how it appears, this kind of covetousness breeds the same spiritual result—it displeases God and separates us from Him. More income, a bigger house, nicer clothes, a fancier car can tempt all of us.

But the Lord wants you to be free from the materialism that so easily controls your non-Christian neighbors. Your earthly possessions are only temporary anyway. You will lose them all one day soon enough. So God tells you and me to be "content with what you have" (Heb. 13:5), realizing that we have "a better possession and an abiding one" (10:34) in our salvation.

✧ ✧ ✧

Suggestions for Prayer: Is there any covetousness or materialism in your life today? Confess it to the Lord, and pray that He would give you a renewed desire to trust Him rather than uncertain wealth.

For Further Study: Read Luke 12:13-34. Make a list of the things that illustrate how God cares for our material needs. ✧ How does the rich fool's attitude contrast with what Jesus teaches in verse 31?

> *"Let your way of life be free from the love of money,*
> *being content with what you have; for He Himself has said,*
> *'I will never desert you, nor will I ever forsake you,' so that we*
> *confidently say, 'The Lord is my helper, I will not be afraid.*
> *What shall man do to me?'"*
>
> HEBREWS 13:5-6

❖ ❖ ❖

Your relationship with God allows you
to enjoy genuine contentment.

In view of yesterday's lesson, you may be asking, "But how can I enjoy contentment and be satisfied with what I have?" You can begin by realizing God's goodness and believing that He will take care of you since you are one of His children. You can claim again the promise in Romans 8: "God causes all things to work together for good to those who love God, to those who are called according to His purpose" (v. 28).

Second, you should truly realize that God is omniscient—He knows all things and all your personal needs. He recognizes your individual needs long before you do and even before you pray about them. Jesus affirms, "Your Father knows that you need these things" (Luke 12:30).

You can also enjoy contentment by remembering that what you want or need is one thing; what you deserve is another. The patriarch Jacob confessed, "I am unworthy of all the lovingkindness and of all the faithfulness which Thou hast shown to Thy servant" (Gen. 32:10). Contentment will more likely be yours if you consider that God's smallest favor or blessing to you is more than you deserve.

Ultimately, however, real contentment will be yours if you have vital communion with God through Jesus Christ. Then, like the apostle Paul, temporal things will not matter so much: "I count all things to be loss in view of the surpassing value of knowing Christ Jesus my Lord, for whom I have suffered the loss of all things, and count them but rubbish in order that I may gain Christ" (Phil. 3:8).

❖ ❖ ❖

Suggestions for Prayer: God may or may not grant you some new blessing today or this week. In any case, pray that you would be content.

For Further Study: What do Ecclesiastes 2:24; 3:12-13; and 8:15 all say about contentment? ❖ What does Psalm 37:7 say our everyday attitude should be?

"Walk . . . with all . . . gentleness."
EPHESIANS 4:1-2

✧ ✧ ✧

The antidote to our vengeful, violent society is biblical gentleness.

A popular bumper sticker says, "Don't Get Mad—Get Even." People demand what they perceive to be their rights, no matter how the demand harms others. Some go to court to squeeze every last cent out of those who hurt them. More and more violent crimes are committed each year. We need a strong dose of biblical truth to cure these attitudes. The biblical solution is gentleness.

The world might interpret gentleness or meekness as cowardice, timidity, or lack of strength. But the Bible describes it as not being vengeful, bitter, or unforgiving. It is a quiet, willing submission to God and others without the rebellious, vengeful self-assertion that characterizes human nature.

The Greek word translated "gentleness" was used to speak of a soothing medicine. It was used of a light, cool breeze and of a colt that had been broken and tamed, whose energy could be channeled for useful purposes. It also describes one who is tenderhearted, pleasant, and mild.

Gentleness is not wimpiness though. It is power under control. The circus lion has the same strength as a lion running free in Africa, but it has been tamed. All its energy is under the control of its master. In the same way, the lion residing in the gentle person no longer seeks its own prey or its own ends; it is submissive to its Master. That lion has not been destroyed, just tempered.

Gentleness is one facet of the fruit of the Spirit (Gal. 5:23). It is also a key to wisdom. James asks, "Who among you is wise and understanding? Let him show by his good behavior his deeds in the gentleness of wisdom" (3:13). Verse 17 says, "The wisdom from above is first pure, then peaceable, gentle, reasonable, full of mercy and good fruits, unwavering, without hypocrisy."

Even if gentleness is not valued in our society, it is crucial to our godliness. Seek it diligently and prayerfully.

✧ ✧ ✧

Suggestions for Prayer: If you tend to be at all vengeful or unforgiving, ask God's forgiveness and His help to forgive those who hurt you. Seek to be gentle with them instead.

For Further Study: Throughout most of 1 Samuel, King Saul repeatedly tries to capture David and kill him. Read 1 Samuel 24. How did David demonstrate his gentleness in the face of his hostile enemy?

"Walk . . . with all . . . gentleness."
EPHESIANS 4:1-2

❖ ❖ ❖

Our anger must be under control
and should occur only for the right reason.

After the previous lesson, you might think that Christians must always be quiet and passive, never getting upset or angry about anything. Actually, believers do have the right to get angry, but only under certain conditions. Ephesians 4:26 says, "Be angry and yet do not sin; do not let the sun go down on your anger." So there is a certain kind of anger that isn't sinful. It must be under control, and it must be resolved expeditiously.

Proverbs 25:28 says, "Like a city that is broken into and without walls is a man who has no control over his spirit." Someone who is out of control is vulnerable. He falls into every temptation, failure, and weakness. On the other hand, "He who is slow to anger is better than the mighty, and he who rules his spirit, than he who captures a city" (16:32). One who rules his spirit has power and energy, but it's under control. That same power and energy out of control creates nothing but chaos and sinfulness. Those who are easily angered are not gentle.

Gentle people, on the other hand, control their energies and strengths, but they do have a tough side. They don't back away from sin or cease to condemn evil. Since the gentle person submits himself to God, he becomes angry over things that offend God, not himself. If someone offends him personally, he doesn't seek revenge. But when God is maligned, the lion in him roars. Such anger is called righteous indignation. Under God's control, anger reacts when it ought to react, for the right reason, and for the right amount of time.

❖ ❖ ❖

Suggestions for Prayer: Ask forgiveness if you are apt to get angry for the wrong reasons. Commit yourself to being gentle when you ordinarily would flare up in anger. ❖ If you don't get angry when you see evil, ask God to make you sensitive to what He hates.

For Further Study: At the very time Moses was receiving God's Law on Mount Sinai, the Israelites were involved in idolatry and debauchery. Read Exodus 32. What was Moses' reaction to their sin? ❖ Did he hold a grudge against them (vv. 31-32)? ❖ How can Moses' example be a pattern for your life?

"Walk . . . with all . . . gentleness."
EPHESIANS 4:1-2

✧ ✧ ✧

*Jesus is the greatest example of gentleness: He became angry when
God the Father was dishonored, but not when He, the Son, was.*

Jesus Christ is our supreme example of gentleness. Paul refers specifically
to this in 2 Corinthians 10:1. Jesus Himself said, "I am gentle and humble in heart" (Matt. 11:29).

Jesus showed righteous indignation when it was proper. When He found
the Temple filled with people selling exorbitantly priced sacrificial animals,
He drove them out, pouring out their money and overturning tables (Matt.
21:12). He told them, "It is written, 'My house shall be called a house of
prayer'; but you are making it a robbers' den" (v. 13). Jesus later said to the
scribes and Pharisees, "You serpents, you brood of vipers, how shall you
escape the sentence of hell?" (23:33). He did not stand idly by while the
Temple was defiled. He spoke out in judgment against hypocrites who dishonored God.

Even though Jesus became angry when God was maligned, He neither
retaliated against nor condemned those who attacked Him. "Christ also suffered for you, leaving you an example for you to follow in His steps, who
committed no sin, nor was any deceit found in His mouth; and while being
reviled, He did not revile in return; while suffering, He uttered no threats, but
kept entrusting Himself to Him who judges righteously" (1 Peter 2:21-23).
When God's Temple was defiled, Jesus cleaned it out. But when the temple
of His body was defiled, enduring the agony of the cross, with mockers all
around, all He said was, "Father, forgive them; for they do not know what they
are doing" (Luke 23:34). That's supreme gentleness—total selflessness.

It's so easy to strike back when someone criticizes or attacks us, but that's
not the way of the gentle Christian trying to walk worthy. The only time we
should let the lion in us roar is when God's honor is at stake. Jesus forgave
those who crucified Him. How can we do any less to those who hurt us?

✧ ✧ ✧

Suggestions for Prayer: We all fall short of Christ's example of gentleness.
Pray that God would help you each day to reflect more and more the gentleness of Christ.

For Further Study: Read the account of Christ's arrest and crucifixion in
Matthew 26:47—27:50. Did He have the power to strike back (26:53)? ✧ Find
all the instances you can in which Christ demonstrated His gentleness.

"Walk . . . with all . . . gentleness."
EPHESIANS 4:1-2

✧ ✧ ✧

To become more gentle,
begin by looking closely at your attitudes.

We've determined that gentleness is essential for those who want to walk worthy. How can you tell if you're gentle? I'll give you some practical questions so you can evaluate yourself honestly.

First of all, are you self-controlled? Do you rule your own spirit (Prov. 16:32), or does your temper often flare up? When someone accuses you of something, do you immediately defend yourself, or are you more inclined to consider whether there's any truth in what's being said?

Second, are you infuriated only when God is dishonored? Do you get angry about sin or when God's Word is perverted by false teachers?

Next, do you always seek to make peace? Gentle people are peacemakers. Ephesians 4:3 says they are "diligent to preserve the unity of the Spirit in the bond of peace." If someone falls into sin, do you condemn or gossip about that person? Galatians 6:1 instructs us to restore sinning brothers "in a spirit of gentleness; each one looking to yourself, lest you too be tempted." Gossip and condemnation divide believers; forgiveness and restoration unite them. Gentle people don't start fights; they end them.

Fourth, do you accept criticism without retaliation? Whether the criticism is right or wrong, you shouldn't strike back. In fact, you can thank your critics, because criticism can show you your weaknesses and help you grow.

Finally, do you have the right attitude toward the unsaved? Peter says, "Always [be] ready to make a defense to every one who asks you to give an account for the hope that is in you, yet with gentleness and reverence" (1 Peter 3:15). If we're persecuted, it's easy for us to think, *They can't treat me like that—I'm a child of God.* But God wants us to approach the unsaved with gentleness, realizing that God reached out to us with gentleness before we were saved (Titus 3:3-7).

Consider carefully your answers to these questions, and commit yourself to being characterized by gentleness. Remember that "a gentle and quiet spirit . . . is precious in the sight of God" (1 Peter 3:4).

✧ ✧ ✧

Suggestions for Prayer: If any of these questions have pointed out deficiencies in your gentleness, ask God to strengthen those areas.

For Further Study: Paul was often criticized by those who wanted to usurp his authority over the church. Study Paul's response to such people in 2 Timothy 2:24-26. ✧ Think about this passage's application to events in your life.

"Walk . . . with patience."
EPHESIANS 4:1-2

✧ ✧ ✧

Patient Christians endure negative circumstances, cope with difficult people, and accept God's plan for everything.

In our instant, microwave, drive-through, "I want it now" culture, patience is hard to come by. We get upset if we have to wait too long in the super-market line or get stuck behind the guy driving ten miles per hour under the speed limit.

But today's Scripture tells us that our lives need to be marked by patience. The Greek word translated "patience" literally means "long-tempered." A patient person doesn't have a short fuse or lose his temper.

There are three aspects to biblical patience. First, patience never gives in to negative circumstances, no matter how difficult. God told Abraham He would make him into a great nation and give Canaan to his descendants (Gen. 12:2, 7). When God made this promise, Abraham and Sarah had no children. They had to wait far past their childbearing years before God gave them a son. But Hebrews 6:15 says, "Having patiently waited, [Abraham] obtained the promise." "He did not waver in unbelief, but grew strong in faith, giving glory to God" (Rom. 4:20). He trusted God and patiently waited for Him to fulfill His promise.

A second aspect of patience is coping with difficult people. Paul tells us to "be patient with all men" (1 Thess. 5:14). This is applied gentleness—a spirit that refuses to retaliate. Our normal reaction is to be defensive when provoked. But a patient person bears insult, persecution, unfair treatment, slander, and hatred. You can't start a fight with a patient person. He defends God, not him-self, knowing that He will repay all wrongs at the right time.

Third, patience accepts God's plan for everything. It doesn't question God. A patient person says, "Lord, if this is what You have planned for me, that's all right." Romans 8:28 says, "We know that God causes all things to work together for good to those who love God, to those who are called according to His purpose." Since God is in control, we can be patient, waiting for Him to work out His will.

✧ ✧ ✧

Suggestions for Prayer: Ask God to help you recognize when you're apt to be impatient. When those times come, pray for strength to endure them.

For Further Study: James 5:10 says the prophets were examples of suffering and patience. Read what two prophets had to endure in Isaiah 6:9-12 and Jeremiah 1:5-19. ✧ How might they be examples to you as you seek to be faithful in the face of life's tests?

"Walk . . . with patience."
EPHESIANS 4:1-2

✧ ✧ ✧

Jesus is our greatest example of patience in all that
He endured to purchase our redemption.

Paul tells us here that the worthy walk is one of patience, and once again we see that Jesus modeled it for us. Throughout the Gospels, He repeatedly demonstrated the three aspects of patience we explored in the last lesson.

First, He endured negative circumstances. Before He came into the world, He was with the Father in the glory of Heaven, where the angels praised and worshiped Him continually. He left a place of total perfection and love and went to a place where He was mocked, hated, rejected, blasphemed, and crucified. He "endured the cross" (Heb. 12:2) even though He had the power to escape it.

Jesus also coped with difficult people. The night before His crucifixion, after three years of teaching about love and servanthood, His disciples were arguing about which of them was the greatest (Luke 22:24). Jesus didn't give up on them, however. More than that, He prayed for those who spit on Him and mocked Him at the cross: "Father, forgive them; for they do not know what they are doing" (23:34). He wanted His murderers to be forgiven so they could be with Him in Heaven forever.

In the Garden of Gethsemane, just hours before He was nailed to the cross, Jesus showed His willingness to accept the Father's plan. He prayed, "My Father, if it is possible, let this cup pass from Me; yet not as I will, but as Thou wilt" (Matt. 26:39). He was able to endure unimaginable suffering because He knew it was God's will.

We should be very thankful for Christ's "perfect patience" (1 Tim. 1:16), because our sin has offended Him time and time again. He could have sent us to Hell the first moment we sinned, but His Spirit patiently drew us to repentance. Because of His patience, we must commit ourselves to follow His perfect example.

✧ ✧ ✧

Suggestions for Prayer: Pray that God would daily give you strength to be patient in all things, just as Christ was.

For Further Study: Hebrews 12:3 tells us to "consider Him who has endured such hostility by sinners against Himself, so that you may not grow weary and lose heart." Christ's example of patience encourages us to endure when we suffer. Find other demonstrations of His patience in the Gospels, and consider how His example can affect your attitude during trials.

> *"Walk . . . with patience."*
> EPHESIANS 4:1-2

✧ ✧ ✧

Patience is crucial to our testimony.

The virtues of Ephesians 4:2-3 enable the church of Jesus Christ to have a powerful witness. Many think the key to evangelism is following a specific course or method, but according to Jesus, the greatest way to get people to believe the gospel is through our love and unity (John 17:21). Though evangelistic methods are important, often they aren't as effective as they could be because of the church's poor reputation among unbelievers. If the church were full of people who had genuine humility, gentleness, and patience, others would be more inclined to listen to what we say.

Sir Henry Stanley traveled to Africa in 1872 to find Dr. David Livingstone, the famous missionary and explorer, who had lost contact with the European community. After finding him, Stanley spent several months with Livingstone, who by that time was an old man. Apparently Livingstone didn't say much to Stanley about spiritual things—he just continued about his business with the Africans. Stanley observed that throughout the months he watched him, Livingstone's habits, especially his patience, were beyond his comprehension. Stanley could not understand Livingstone's sympathy for the pagan Africans, who had wronged Livingstone many times. For the sake of Christ and His gospel David Livingstone was patient, untiring, and eager. He spent himself for his Master.

In his account *How I Found Livingstone*, Stanley wrote, "His religion is not of the theoretical kind, but is a constant, earnest, sincere practice. It is neither demonstrative nor loud, but manifests itself in a quiet practical way, and is always at work. . . . In him religion exhibits its loveliest features; it governs his conduct not only towards his servants but towards the natives . . . and all who come in contact with him."

I'm not suggesting that you never talk about the gospel. But realize that what you say will have far greater effect when you live in harmony with what the gospel teaches. If the world could see a clear picture of Jesus Christ through the unity of the church and its humble, gentle, and patient people, our evangelism would be sped along on wings!

✧ ✧ ✧

Suggestions for Prayer: Pray that you would live in a way that glorifies God and attracts others to the Savior.

For Further Study: Read Matthew 5:13-16. What did Christ mean by being salt and light in the world? ✧ Think of specific ways you can obey the command in verse 16.

". . . Showing forbearance to one another in love."
EPHESIANS 4:2

❖ ❖ ❖

In order to walk worthy,
we must forgive our enemies and love them.

The term *forbearance* is not often used today and is therefore unfamiliar to many of us. The Greek word translated "showing forbearance" means "suppressing with silence." It carries the idea of throwing a blanket over sin. First Peter 4:8 says, "Love covers a multitude of sins," and Proverbs 10:12 declares, "Hatred stirs up strife, but love covers all transgressions." A forbearing person doesn't trumpet other people's sins but rather forgives them. Forbearance has room for the failures of others. A forbearing person also loves people in spite of the wrongs they might have done to him.

Agape, the word used for "love" in this verse, is the love that gives but never takes. It's the kind of love that seeks the highest good for another, no matter what the cost. God showed His *agape* by giving us His only Son (John 3:16). Jesus said, "Greater love [*agape*] has no one than this, that one lay down his life for his friends" (15:13). *Agape* is unconquerable benevolence and invincible goodness; it is completely selfless.

Perhaps the greatest description of forbearing love is the summary Jesus gives in Matthew 5:43-45: "You have heard that it was said, 'You shall love your neighbor, and hate your enemy.' But I say to you, love your enemies, and pray for those who persecute you in order that you may be sons of your Father who is in heaven." We were God's enemies before He saved us, but He was willing to send His Son anyway (Rom. 5:10). Since we are God's children, we must also seek our enemies' highest good, whatever it costs us. Such cost ought to include more than simply enduring slander and persecution from our enemies. Genuine forbearing love will assume the more difficult task of loving those who hate us.

❖ ❖ ❖

Suggestions for Prayer: Thank God that He showed forbearing love in sending Christ to die for undeserving sinners. ❖ Pray for your enemies and for strength to love them as you should.

For Further Study: Besides Christ, the clearest example of forbearing love is Stephen's attitude toward those who stoned him. Read his story in Acts 6—7, and note his love toward his executioners. ❖ Think about people you have a hard time loving, and pray that God would show you specific ways you can show love to them. Then follow through!

> *"Being diligent to preserve the unity of the Spirit*
> *in the bond of peace."*
> EPHESIANS 4:3

❖ ❖ ❖

The unity of the Spirit must be earnestly maintained
by humble, gentle, patient, loving Christians.

Today's Scripture spells out the goal of the worthy walk: the unity of the Spirit. Jesus prayed for Christians "that they may all be one; even as Thou, Father, art in Me, and I in Thee, that they also may be in Us; that the world may believe that Thou didst send Me" (John 17:21). Our witness to the world depends on our unity as believers.

The world is full of discord, animosity, bitterness, and resentment. If in the midst of the world there is an oasis of unity and harmony, people will wonder what we have. Then we have the opportunity to say, "This is what Christ can do." The world needs to see that the church is not just another social club, but an institution of God, supernaturally born, supernaturally sustained, with a supernatural destiny.

Our unity depends on the virtues we have been studying this month: gentleness, patience, and forbearing love. Without them, unity is impossible. In addition, our unity requires diligence. The word translated "diligent" in Ephesians 4:3 carries the ideas of both zeal and urgency: "Let's work on it, and work on it now." We need full dedication. But don't say first, "I'll head the committee" or "I'll make the posters." This is a personal passage, and if you want to hurry and start working on unity, you need to start in your heart. Commit yourself first to walking worthy by matching your life with your theology.

I am grieved by all the disunity and discord in the church today. One of the main causes is the focus on denominational distinctives—what divides us. We should instead focus on biblical distinctives—what unites us. We need to humble ourselves and learn to love each other. That won't happen by starting a global ecumenical movement, but it will happen when we become what God wants us to be. Working at unity is a full-time task that demands maximum dedication and obedience from every Christian.

❖ ❖ ❖

Suggestions for Prayer: Pray that God would unify His church around the world, and that He would begin with you.

For Further Study: Read about the unity of the early church in Acts 2:42-47 and 4:32-37. What characterized those believers? ❖ Which of their characteristics do you need to work on?

> *"Being diligent to preserve the unity of the Spirit*
> *in the bond of peace."*
> EPHESIANS 4:3

✦ ✦ ✦

The key to peace in the church is selfless love.

People often delude themselves that there is peace when there is no real peace (Jer. 8:11). However, we can show the world that Jesus is the true peacemaker if we have a community of peaceful, loving, united believers. Others will realize then that Christ must be sent from God, because only God can make true, lasting peace.

"The bond of peace" is what holds our unity together. The Greek word translated "bond" refers to a belt. It pictures the Body of Christ being wrapped with the belt of peace, a peace that is born of love.

Our bond of peace is vital to our testimony. As Christians, we have "peace with God" (Rom. 5:1) and "the ministry of reconciliation" (2 Cor. 5:18), the privilege of telling others how they may have peace with God. If we don't have peace among ourselves, why would unbelievers look to us to find peace with God?

The Corinthian church teaches us how *not* to have peace. Members would have a "love feast," followed by Communion. Apparently, though, those who brought food gorged themselves and became drunk, leaving the poorer believers to go hungry (1 Cor. 11:17-22). Those gluttons not only dishonored the Lord but also hurt their fellow believers, causing resentment and conflict.

During their worship services, everyone wanted attention. Paul laments, "Each one has a psalm, has a teaching, has a revelation, has a tongue, has an interpretation" (1 Cor. 14:26)—and they all wanted to speak at once. They weren't interested in building up each other, only in being heard. The result was a loud, confusing mess.

The Corinthians' disharmony was evident in different ways, but the root cause was the same: selfishness.

So where does peace come from? Self*less*ness, the primary characteristic of Christian love. Philippians 2:3 says, "Do nothing from selfishness or empty conceit, but with humility of mind let each of you regard one another as more important than himself." We must humble ourselves and focus on the needs of others. When that happens, there will be harmony and unity.

✦ ✦ ✦

Suggestions for Prayer: Confess any selfishness, and ask God to help you grow in selfless love.

For Further Study: What does Romans 8:6 equate peace with? Memorize this verse during the next few days.

> *"I . . . entreat you to walk in a manner worthy of the calling*
> *with which you have been called, with all humility and gentleness,*
> *with patience, showing forbearance to one another in love, being*
> *diligent to preserve the unity of the Spirit in the bond of peace."*
> EPHESIANS 4:3

✧ ✧ ✧

God is most concerned about who we are,
because who we are determines what we do.

Now that we've looked in depth at Ephesians 4:1-3, let's take a step back. These verses reveal a basic truth: the Christian life is not primarily about what we do but who we are. When Paul teaches about the worthy walk, about how we live each day, he never discusses actions, only attitudes.

It is possible to have what I call "action fruit"—such as praise (Heb. 13:15), giving (Phil. 4:17), evangelism (Rom. 1:13), and other good works (Col. 1:10)—without "attitude fruit," which is the fruit of the Spirit: "love, joy, peace, patience, kindness, goodness, faithfulness, gentleness, and self-control" (Gal. 5:22-23). Plenty of people can do good deeds without inner righteousness. But that's legalism; that's the hypocrisy that the Bible speaks so much about. The right path to true spirituality is to have proper attitudes first. The Holy Spirit works through our attitudes to produce right actions.

Unfortunately, many Christians miss this point. To them, being a Christian is primarily a list of do's—going to church, putting money in the offering, carrying a Bible—and don'ts—not cursing, not drinking, not murdering. They see external behavior as the fact of Christianity instead of the manifestation of it. They don't cultivate the inner graces.

Of course, God wants us to live righteous lives. But to those with merely external actions, Jesus said, "Woe to you . . . hypocrites! For you clean the outside of the cup and of the dish, but inside they are full of robbery and self-indulgence. . . . First clean the inside of the cup and of the dish, so that the outside of it may become clean also" (Matt. 23:25-26).

Don't let yourself become a slave to external religion. Make sure you do your good works out of love for God and others, as part of the overflow of the spiritual fruit in your life.

✧ ✧ ✧

Suggestions for Prayer: If you see hypocrisy in yourself, ask God to purge it. Pray for and diligently seek attitude fruit.

For Further Study: Jesus warned about internal sinfulness in Matthew 5:21-22, 27-30 and external righteousness in 6:1-18 and 7:1-5. How is Proverbs 4:23 an antidote to those?

> *"There is one body and one Spirit, just as also you were called*
> *in one hope of your calling; one Lord, one faith, one*
> *baptism, one God and Father of all who is over*
> *all and through all and in all."*
>
> EPHESIANS 4:4-6

❖ ❖ ❖

All Christians are part of the same Body,
with the same Spirit, who is our pledge of eternal life.

Everything God ever designed for the church is based on the unity of believers. Paul emphasizes that by listing seven "ones" in these verses. One is the key; it is the cause of the worthy walk.

How many bodies of Christ are there? There isn't a Presbyterian body, a Baptist body, and a Methodist body; nor is there a California body, a Utah body, and a Kansas body. There is just one Body, *the* church. "There is neither Jew nor Greek, there is neither slave nor free man, there is neither male nor female; for you are all one in Christ Jesus" (Gal. 3:28). Whatever your race, creed, nationality, or language, when you become a Christian, you become one with every other believer.

Paul's next point is that there is only one Spirit, who dwells in every believer. First Corinthians 6:19 says, "Do you not know that your body is a temple of the Holy Spirit who is in you?" We "are being built together into a dwelling of God in the Spirit" (Eph. 2:22). Individually we are the temple of the Spirit; collectively we are the dwelling of the Spirit.

We are also "called in one hope of [our] calling." We have only one eternal calling, only one eternal destiny, and the Holy Spirit guarantees our heavenly hope. "You were sealed in [Christ] with the Holy Spirit of promise, who is given as a pledge of our inheritance" (Eph. 1:13-14). He is our down payment, the first installment of our eternal inheritance.

Ephesians 4:4 focuses on the Holy Spirit's ministry to us: we are placed into one Body by the Spirit, one Spirit dwells in us, and our one hope is guaranteed by the Holy Spirit.

❖ ❖ ❖

Suggestions for Prayer: Thank God for the Holy Spirit's ministry in the church and in your life.

For Further Study: First Corinthians 12 has much to say about church unity. Read it carefully, noting in particular what the Spirit does in the Body and what our responsibility is as individual believers.

"One Lord, one faith, one baptism."

EPHESIANS 4:5

✧ ✧ ✧

All Christians have a common Lord, common beliefs,
and a common public testimony.

Yesterday we looked at what Christians have in common through the Spirit. Today's verse teaches us what we share through Christ.

Christians have only "one Lord," the Lord Jesus Christ. Acts 4:12 says, "There is salvation in no one else; for there is no other name under heaven that has been given among men, by which we must be saved." Paul says in Romans 10:12, "There is no distinction between Jew and Greek; for the same Lord is Lord of all."

Our "one faith" is simply the content of what the revealed Word of God tells us we are to believe. And the primary focus of the Scriptures is Christ. Though we have many denominations and congregations, there's only one true Christian faith. This faith is what Jude refers to in verse 3 of his epistle: "Contend earnestly for the faith which was once for all delivered to the saints."

Why then do churches differ so much in what they teach? Some of it comes from inadequate study or lack of diligence. Some is from unexamined tradition. The fundamental problem, though, is our humanness—we are fallen, fallible people, and that can color our understanding of Scripture. That's why it's so important we not hold too tightly to "our brand" of Christianity, but instead always think matters through biblically and discuss them courteously.

Christians also have "one baptism." This does not refer to Spirit baptism because that was implied in Ephesians 4:4 with the words "one body." (As 1 Corinthians 12:13 explains, we all were placed into the Body of Christ by the baptism of the Spirit.) "One baptism" in verse 5 refers to water baptism. When someone comes to believe in the only true Lord, he should be baptized as a public expression of his faith. Public baptism was an essential part of the early church's testimony to the world. It is no less essential today.

✧ ✧ ✧

Suggestions for Prayer: Thank God for our Lord Jesus Christ, for our common Christian faith, and for our baptism, by which we identify ourselves with Christ and His people.

For Further Study: The church at Corinth did not understand our oneness as believers. Read Paul's description of them in 1 Corinthians 1:10-17. What were the symptoms of their divisions? ✧ What did Paul command them to do? ✧ If there are divisions in your church, find ways that you can be a peacemaker.

> *"One God and Father of all who is over all*
> *and through all and in all."*
> EPHESIANS 4:6

✧ ✧ ✧

There is only one God, and we will have a strong testimony
by worshiping Him and holding on to what unites us.

The last point of Christian unity Paul mentions in Ephesians 4:4-6 is that Christians have "one God and Father." In Paul's day, people believed in many gods; so he emphasizes our God's uniqueness. No person or object can compare with God because He is "above all," which means He is the sovereign creator and controller of the universe; He is "through all," as the providential upholder of the universe; and He is "in all," which refers to His personal, indwelling presence.

Throughout the Old Testament, God emphasizes His uniqueness: "Know therefore today, and take it to your heart, that the Lord, He is God in heaven above and on the earth below; there is no other" (Deut. 4:39). "I am the Lord, and there is no other; besides Me there is no God" (Isa. 45:5). The Israelites were surrounded by nations that worshiped many gods, and God had to continually warn them about idolatry and judge them when they practiced it.

Israel's worship of the only true God was to be their central point of unity. It was to set them apart from the nations around them. By worshiping Him alone, they not only would remain strong as a nation, but would be a witness to the Gentiles of God's greatness.

As Christians, we have the same Father, and like Israel, our unity is founded on Him, as well as the other "ones" listed in Ephesians 4:4-6: one Body, one Spirit, one hope of our calling, one Lord, one faith, and one baptism. When we hold to these, we will be a powerful witness to the world.

✧ ✧ ✧

Suggestions for Prayer: Praise God for His uniqueness, that He alone is above all, through all, and in all.

For Further Study: The Psalms not only are rich with instruction about God but are also excellent means of praising Him. Read one psalm a day for the next several months, and write down what you learn about God. Whenever the psalmist praises God, let that be your prayer as well. When you have finished reading all the Psalms, you will know, honor, and love God more than ever.

> *"Walk in a manner worthy of the calling*
> *with which you have been called."*
> EPHESIANS 4:1

❖ ❖ ❖

Compared to walking worthy of Christ,
nothing else is really important.

Let's review what Paul has taught us from Ephesians 4:1-6. God has chosen and called us to be part of His family, and He expects us to act like His children. He wants us to walk worthy of Christ and be unified.

To follow God's will in this, we must, with His help, deal with our sin and develop godly virtues. Our lives must first be marked by "all humility" (v. 2). We become humble when we see ourselves as unworthy sinners and see the greatness of God and Christ. Pride will always be a temptation, but we can resist it if we remember that we have nothing to be proud about; every good thing we have is from God. He alone deserves the glory; we can take no credit.

Humility produces "gentleness," which is power under control. Gentle people willingly submit to God and others. They may become angry over what dishonors God, but they are forgiving to those who hurt them.

"Patience" flows from gentleness. A patient person endures negative circumstances, copes with difficult people, and accepts God's plan for everything.

We must "love" others with a forbearing love. Christian love is selfless, and forbearance keeps us from gossiping about the failures of others and causes us to love our enemies.

"Unity" (v. 3) is the goal of the worthy walk, and only diligent believers who pursue these virtues of the worthy walk will contribute to such unity. Because we have one Body, one Spirit, one hope, one Lord, one faith, one baptism, and one Father, we should behave as a unified people. Then we will have the effective testimony God wants for us.

Only one thing really matters from the moment you become a Christian until the day you see Jesus—that you walk worthy of Him. What you own, what you know, and what you do for a living are not all that important.

❖ ❖ ❖

Suggestions for Prayer: Ask God to give you the resolve to walk worthy every day.

For Further Study: Read Hebrews 11 and perhaps some related Old Testament passages, and note what was representative of the main characters' walks with the Lord.

> *"More than that, I count all things to be loss in view*
> *of the surpassing value of knowing Christ Jesus my Lord, for*
> *whom I have suffered the loss of all things, and count them*
> *but rubbish in order that I may gain Christ."*
> PHILIPPIANS 3:8

✧ ✧ ✧

God's greatest desire for us
is that we seek diligently to know Him.

To know God and all that He has revealed about Himself is the highest pursuit of life. "The fear of the Lord is the beginning of wisdom, and the knowledge of the Holy One is understanding" (Prov. 9:10). Such a realization should really be the starting point for all of life's other pursuits.

As David gave his throne to his son Solomon, his primary counsel was that Solomon know God: "As for you, my son Solomon, know the God of your father, and serve Him with a whole heart and a willing mind; for the Lord searches all hearts, and understands every intent of the thoughts. If you seek Him, He will let you find Him; but if you forsake Him, He will reject you forever" (1 Chron. 28:9).

Knowing God not only determines the quality of one's present life, but also the destiny of one's life in eternity. Jesus says, "And this is eternal life, that they may know Thee, the only true God, and Jesus Christ whom Thou hast sent" (John 17:3). Eternal life is simply knowing God in an intimate way for the rest of eternity. It begins here on earth when we believe in Christ and partake of His very nature and life.

How can we know God? The Lord says, "You will seek Me and find Me, when you search for Me with all your heart" (Jer. 29:13). Solomon teaches us, "For if you cry for discernment, lift your voice for understanding; if you seek her as silver, and search for her as for hidden treasures; then you will discern the fear of the Lord, and discover the knowledge of God" (Prov. 2:3-5). This pursuit of God must be our top priority in life. Otherwise, it is so easy to be distracted by the pursuit of money, career success, personal power and prestige, or any earthly endeavor that demands our time and energy.

✧ ✧ ✧

Suggestions for Prayer: Thank the Lord that you know Him personally.

For Further Study: Read 2 Peter 1:1-11. What are the benefits to those who know God? ✧ What qualities should be evident in your life?

*"You thought that I was just like you; I will reprove you,
and state the case in order before your eyes."*
PSALM 50:21

❖ ❖ ❖

*Idolatry is more than worshiping some inanimate object;
it is having an unworthy conception of God.*

Western society, with all its culture and scientific knowledge, is in the same satanic trap that governs the life of an aborigine bowing down to a rock. We all have our gods. Many worship the god of materialism—getting more stuff is their highest pursuit. Others worship the gods of sex or entertainment. Of course, behind all of this is the worship of self.

However, the essence of idolatry is possessing thoughts about God that are unworthy of Him. It may be creating a god, but it also may be making the true God into something He isn't, or thinking something about God that is untrue.

God said to the wicked in Psalm 50:21, "You thought that I was just like you." That's precisely what some have imagined about God. They have portrayed God after their own sinful mental image of Him. Careless Christians can do this also.

In *The Knowledge of the Holy* A. W. Tozer writes, "The history of mankind will probably show that no people has ever risen above its religion, and man's spiritual history will positively demonstrate that no religion has ever been greater than its idea of God. Worship is pure or base as the worshiper entertains high or low thoughts of God. For this reason, the gravest question before the church is always God Himself, and the most portentous fact about any man is not what he at a given time may say or do, but what he in his deep heart conceives God to be like."

As we learn about God this month, ask Him to remove misconceptions you may have about Him. Be diligent to learn what God says about Himself and not what you or others think He is like.

❖ ❖ ❖

Suggestions for Prayer: Praise God that He is the only God. ❖ Pray for forgiveness if you have been more committed to any other god or if you think thoughts about God that are unworthy of Him.

For Further Study: The ancient Greeks had hundreds of gods. Just for good measure the Athenians built an altar to the unknown god. Read Acts 17:16-34. How did Paul approach those who worshiped false gods? ❖ How can you use Paul's example as you witness to unbelievers today?

*"God is spirit, and those who worship Him
must worship in spirit and truth."*
JOHN 4:24

❖ ❖ ❖

God is a person,
but He has no physical characteristics.

As we begin our study of God, we must understand first of all that He is a person, not some unknowable cosmic force. In His Word, God is called Father, Shepherd, Friend, Counselor, and many other personal names. God is always referred to as "He," not "it." He also has personal characteristics: He thinks, acts, feels, and speaks.

We will learn three aspects of God's person in the next several days: God is spirit, God is one, and God is three. First, God has no physical body as we have: "God is spirit" (John 4:24), and "a spirit does not have flesh and bones" (Luke 24:39). Paul says He is "invisible" (1 Tim. 1:17). God represented Himself as light, fire, and cloud in the Old Testament and in the human form of Jesus Christ in the New Testament. But such visible revelations did not reveal the totality or fullness of God's nature.

You may wonder about verses like Psalm 98:1, "His right hand and His holy arm have gained the victory for Him," and Proverbs 15:3, "The eyes of the Lord are in every place." These descriptions are called anthropomorphisms, from the Greek words for "man" and "form." They picture God as though He were a man because God has chosen to describe Himself in a way we can comprehend. If He did not accommodate His revelation to our finite level, we would have no hope of understanding Him. You should not take anthropomorphisms literally, however. Otherwise you will have a false view of God that robs Him of His real nature and His true power. Look at Psalm 91:4: "Under His wings you may seek refuge." God is certainly not a bird, and "God is not a man" (Num. 23:19). He is spirit.

❖ ❖ ❖

Suggestions for Prayer: Thank God that He has enabled physical creatures like us to know Him.

For Further Study: Even though God is invisible, "since the creation of the world His invisible attributes, His eternal power and divine nature, have been clearly seen, being understood through what has been made" (Rom. 1:20). Read the response of a godly man to God's natural revelation in Psalm 104.

"Hear, O Israel! The Lord is our God, the Lord is one!"
DEUTERONOMY 6:4

✧ ✧ ✧

There is only one true God.

When God freed Israel to take her to the promised land, He said: "You shall have no other gods before Me" (Ex. 20:3). Later Moses told the Israelites, "The Lord, He is God; there is no other besides Him" (Deut. 4:35) and "The Lord is our God, the Lord is one!" (6:4). Israel was to believe in the one and only God.

But Jesus claimed to be God. Is He God number two? Not at all. In Mark 12:29-30, Jesus quoted Deuteronomy 6:4-5: "'Hear, O Israel! The Lord our God is one Lord; and you shall love the Lord your God with all your heart, and with all your soul, and with all your mind, and with all your strength.'" If Jesus were another God He might have said, "Split your allegiance between the two of us." But Jesus says we are to love God with undivided commitment. Therefore He agrees with Moses that there is only one God. However, He also says, "I and the Father are one" (John 10:30).

Paul also discusses the unity of God in 1 Corinthians 8. The pagan priests in Corinth would often sell the meat that had been sacrificed to idols. Some new Christians were offended when other Christians ate that meat. In response, Paul told them, "Concerning the eating of things sacrificed to idols, we know that there is no such thing as an idol in the world" (v. 4). Since an idol represented a nonexistent god, there was nothing wrong with eating the food. He continued, "There is no God but one. For even if there are so-called gods whether in heaven or on earth, as indeed there are many gods and many lords, yet for us there is but one God, the Father, from whom are all things, and we exist for Him; and one Lord, Jesus Christ, through whom are all things, and we exist through Him" (vv. 4-6). How can all things be from God the Father, for whom we exist, and by the Lord Jesus Christ, through whom we exist? Because they are one.

✧ ✧ ✧

Suggestions for Prayer: Praise God as David did: "For this reason Thou art great, O Lord God; for there is none like Thee, and there is no God besides Thee" (2 Sam. 7:22).

For Further Study: Read Ezekiel 6. What was God's response to Israel's idolatry? ✧ How does God feel about anything that might take first place in your heart instead of Him?

*"The grace of the Lord Jesus Christ, and the love of God,
and the fellowship of the Holy Spirit, be with you all."*
2 CORINTHIANS 13:14

✧ ✧ ✧

*Though there is only one God, He exists in three Persons:
God the Father, God the Son, and God the Holy Spirit.*

God is one, but He exists in three distinct Persons. We call this the Trinity, a contraction of "tri-unity," meaning "three in one." The word *Trinity* doesn't appear in the Bible, but God's existence as three Persons in one God is clear from Scripture.

Old Testament evidence of God's plurality can be found in the very first verse: "In the beginning God . . ." (Gen. 1:1). The Hebrew word used for God is *Elohim*, which is a plural noun. Isaiah 42:1 speaks of the Messiah: "Behold, My Servant, whom I uphold; My chosen one in whom My soul delights. I have put My Spirit upon Him; He will bring forth justice to the nations." The Messiah says in Isaiah 48:16, "The Lord God has sent Me, and His Spirit."

The New Testament is more explicit about God's triune nature. After Jesus' baptism, the Spirit of God descended upon Him as a dove, and the Father said, "This is My beloved Son, in whom I am well-pleased" (Matt. 3:17). The Father, Son, and Holy Spirit are together in the same scene.

Jesus says, "And I will ask the Father, and He will give you another Helper, that He may be with you forever; that is the Spirit of truth" (John 14:16-17). Paul closes 2 Corinthians by saying, "The grace of the Lord Jesus Christ, and the love of God, and the fellowship of the Holy Spirit, be with you all" (13:14). Peter declares that believers are chosen "according to the fore-knowledge of God the Father, by the sanctifying work of the Spirit, that you may obey Jesus Christ" (1 Peter 1:2).

So God is one, but God is three. This is a profound mystery that no human illustration can adequately describe and no scientific explanation can prove. The Trinity is something we have to take on faith, because God has taught it in Scripture.

✧ ✧ ✧

Suggestions for Prayer: Praise God that He is so far above our finite under-standing, yet has chosen to reveal Himself to us.

For Further Study: Read John 14—16. What does Jesus teach about His rela-tionship with the Father and the Spirit? ✧ What do you learn here about the different functions or ministries of each member of the Trinity?

"There is no one holy like the Lord."
1 SAMUEL 2:2

❖ ❖ ❖

*God's holiness means He transcends everything else
and is completely righteous and separated from evil.*

Holiness is arguably God's most significant attribute. The angels don't sing, "Eternal, eternal, eternal" or "Faithful, faithful, faithful" or "Mighty, mighty, mighty." Rather, they sing, "Holy, holy, holy, is the Lord God, the Almighty" (Rev. 4:8; compare Isa. 6:3). His holiness sums up all He is. The psalmist says, "Holy and awesome is His name" (Ps. 111:9). Moses sings, "Who is like Thee among the gods, O Lord? Who is like Thee, majestic in holiness, awesome in praises, working wonders?" (Ex. 15:11). And Hannah prays, "There is no one holy like the Lord, indeed, there is no one besides Thee, nor is there any rock like our God" (1 Sam. 2:2).

What does it mean that God is holy? The words translated "holy" in the Bible have the root meaning of "separation." God's being and character transcend everything else. He is not subject to the frailties and limitations of His creation. God is completely without sin. He does not just conform to a holy standard; He *is* the standard.

God's righteousness is related to His holiness. Holiness is the standard, and righteousness is its active fulfillment. Or you might say His holiness is His complete separation from all that is sinful, and His righteousness is the manifestation of that holiness.

David understood how holy and righteous God is. He says, "The Lord is righteous in all His ways" (Ps. 145:17), and "Thy righteousness, O God, reaches to the heavens, Thou who hast done great things; O God, who is like Thee?" (Ps. 71:19).

Sadly, many today completely misunderstand God's righteousness. If they really understood how holy God is, do you think they would live the way they do? But they ignore God's standard, thinking He won't really judge them because they're basically good people. But "God is a righteous judge, and a God who has indignation every day" toward the wicked (Ps. 7:11). Since God is holy, the penalty for any sin—however small that sin might seem—is death (Rom. 6:23).

Don't let the world corrupt your view of God. Don't treat your sin lightly. Instead, confess it, forsake it, and seek to please a holy God.

❖ ❖ ❖

Suggestions for Prayer: Ask that you would have the same righteous hatred of sin that God does.

For Further Study: Read the Book of Habakkuk. What are the prophet's questions? ❖ What are God's answers? ❖ Study in detail Habakkuk's response in chapter 3.

> *"The Lord is righteous in all His ways."*
> PSALM 145:17

❖ ❖ ❖

God's holiness is evident in everything He does,
particularly in creation, the law, judgment, and salvation.

The whole purpose of the Old Testament is to reveal the holiness and righteousness of God, who is utterly perfect and pure. In fact, the Hebrew word for "holy" is used more than 600 times in the Old Testament to indicate moral perfection.

What are some areas in which we see God's holiness? First, we see it in the original perfection of His creation: "God saw all that He had made, and behold, it was very good" (Gen. 1:31). All of creation was in tune with God's holy character.

Later God laid down His righteous, moral law for Israel. In it He gave rules about worship and society. He prescribed penalties for murder, adultery, and stealing. He condemned lying, coveting, and many other sins. There were many rules, but they revealed a God who is infinitely right and without error, flaw, or tolerance for sin. The law showed God's character: "The Law is holy, and the commandment is holy and righteous and good" (Rom. 7:12).

God's holiness will ultimately be demonstrated "when the Lord Jesus shall be revealed from heaven with His mighty angels in flaming fire, dealing out retribution to those who do not know God and to those who do not obey the gospel of our Lord Jesus. And these will pay the penalty of eternal destruction, away from the presence of the Lord and from the glory of His power" (2 Thess. 1:7-9). His judgment on sin is a reflection of His holiness; He must punish it.

Perhaps the supreme expression of God's holiness is seen in sending His Son to die on the cross (cf. Rom. 8:3-4). God paid the highest price, but it was the only price that could satisfy His holiness. Jesus Christ is Himself "the Holy and Righteous One" (Acts 3:14); so only He could "put away sin by the sacrifice of Himself" (Heb. 9:26). God's holiness is so infinite, and our unholiness is so great, that only the sacrifice of the God-man could pay for the enormity of our sin.

❖ ❖ ❖

Suggestions for Prayer: Thank God that He sent His Son to die for our sins, so we could be "holy and blameless before Him" (Eph. 1:4).

For Further Study: Some of God's laws for the Israelites are given in Exodus 21—23. Note in particular the penalties for breaking these laws. What does this passage teach you about God's character?

"But like the Holy One who called you,
be holy yourselves also in all your behavior;
because it is written, 'You shall be holy, for I am holy.'"
1 PETER 1:15-16

❖ ❖ ❖

God requires holiness and in Christ provides us the means to attain it.

As we have learned, God is holy, and absolute holiness is the standard for anyone who wishes to be in His presence. "God did not spare angels when they sinned, but cast them into hell and committed them to pits of darkness, reserved for judgment" (2 Peter 2:4). In the same way, men who reject God are sent "into the eternal fire which has been prepared for the devil and his angels" (Matt. 25:41).

How then can anyone become holy? There's only one way: through faith in Jesus Christ. It is through Christ's sacrifice for us that God can credit holiness to our account (2 Cor. 5:21). First Corinthians 6:11 says, "But you were washed, but you were sanctified [made holy], but you were justified in the name of the Lord Jesus Christ, and in the Spirit of our God." We are now called saints, and the Greek word for this in Scripture actually means "holy ones."

So, by God's grace we are positionally holy. By contrast, however, we are too often unholy in practice. But the Bible says, "Be holy yourselves also in all your behavior" (1 Peter 1:15) and "Let every one who names the name of the Lord abstain from wickedness" (2 Tim. 2:19). We need to be separate from the way the world lives. We need to let others know there is a difference in how Christians live.

When we live holy lives, we will have peace. "There is no peace . . . for the wicked" (Isa. 57:21), but God "disciplines us for our good, that we may share His holiness" (Heb. 12:10). And that discipline "yields the peaceful fruit of righteousness" (v. 11). If you lack peace, you may well have let sin come between you and God. If so, follow David's example in Psalm 51:9-10 and pray for a clean heart. You should also spend time with those who lead holy lives (Prov. 13:20; compare 1 Cor. 15:33).

❖ ❖ ❖

Suggestions for Prayer: Thank God again that He has made you positionally holy in Christ. ❖ Confess any sins you are aware of, and pray that you would live righteously today.

For Further Study: Answer the following questions, based on 2 Corinthians 5:14-21: What did Christ do for us on the cross? ❖ What happened to us when we were saved? ❖ How should we live as a result?

> *"Thou art the same,*
> *and Thy years will not come to an end."*
> PSALM 102:27

✧ ✧ ✧

God never changes, so He can be trusted to do what He says.

God alone is unchanging (or as the theologians say, immutable). The psalmist says, "Even [the heavens and earth] will perish, but Thou dost endure. . . . Thou art the same, and Thy years will not come to an end" (Ps. 102:26-27). Though Israel deserved destruction for its sin, God was faithful to His covenant with Abraham, saying, "I, the Lord, do not change; therefore you, O sons of Jacob, are not consumed" (Mal. 3:6). James calls God "the Father of lights, with whom there is no variation, or shifting shadow" (1:17).

What about those verses that say God changed His mind (e.g., Amos 7:3, 6; Jonah 3:10)? Let's look at an example. Jonah warned the wicked city of Nineveh of impending judgment. The city immediately repented, and "when God saw their deeds, that they turned from their wicked way, then God relented concerning the calamity which He had declared He would bring upon them. And He did not do it" (3:10). Who changed? The people of Nineveh! God's nature to punish evil and reward good remained the same, but the object changed.

You can't blame the sun for melting the wax and hardening the clay. The problem is in the substance of the wax and clay, not in the sun. In a similar way, our standing before God determines how God acts toward us.

What does God's unchanging character mean? To unbelievers, it means judgment. When God says, "The person who sins will die" (Ezek. 18:20) and "The wages of sin is death" (Rom. 6:23), He means it. When He says Hell is eternal (Matt. 25:46; Rev. 20:10, 13-15), then it is.

To Christians, His immutability means comfort. If He loved me in the past, He loves me now and forever. If He forgave and saved me, He did so forever. If He promised me anything, His promise stands forever. If the Bible says, "My God shall supply all your needs" (Phil. 4:19), we know the power that supplied Paul's needs is the same power that will supply ours. God told Israel, "I have loved you with an everlasting love" (Jer. 31:3), and His love for us is the same.

✧ ✧ ✧

Suggestions for Prayer: Praise God for His immutability, and thank Him for the comfort that brings you.

For Further Study: Find some promises God makes to His children in Scripture, and ask for faith to believe them, even when belief is difficult.

> *"But will God indeed dwell on the earth? Behold, heaven*
> *and the highest heaven cannot contain Thee."*
> 1 KINGS 8:27

✧ ✧ ✧

God is in all places; He is not confined by space.

No matter how big the universe is, God is bigger. His being fills up all of infinity. He is omnipresent—everywhere present. God says, "Do I not fill the heavens and the earth?" (Jer. 23:24). Solomon said at the dedication of the temple, "Will God indeed dwell on the earth? Behold, heaven and the highest heaven cannot contain Thee, how much less this house which I have built!" (1 Kings 8:27). There are no limits of time or space to His presence.

Some may object to the doctrine of omnipresence, saying, "Wouldn't the sin in the world defile an omnipresent God?" No. God is in the hearts of sinners convicting them of sin. He is also in Hell where He "is able to destroy both soul and body" (Matt. 10:28). Though God's essence is everywhere, He never mingles with impurity. In a similar way, Jesus lived among sinners and was "tempted in all things as we are, yet [He was] without sin" (Heb. 4:15).

Isaiah exhorts people to "call upon [God] while He is near" (55:6); yet Proverbs 15:29 says, "The Lord is far from the wicked." How can He be near some people and far from others when He is everywhere all the time? To answer this, we must distinguish between God's essence and His relation to people. He is everywhere in His essence, but with specific individuals He is far or near relationally. When we become Christians, Christ dwells in us. God can fill us with His fullness (Eph. 3:19), and the Spirit who lives in us can also fill us (1:13; 5:18). But before God's Spirit indwelt us relationally, His essence convicted us of sin and saved us.

The Old Testament tells us that God dwelt between the wings of the cherubim on the Ark of the Covenant. That location was a symbol of God's presence. Today the church represents God's presence on earth. In the Millennium, Christ's rule on the throne of David in Jerusalem will represent God's presence. In Heaven His presence will be represented by the throne of Revelation 4—5. Remember, though, that the symbol of God's presence never restricts His essence.

✧ ✧ ✧

Suggestions for Prayer: Praise God that He is omnipresent, and thank Him that He lives in you.

For Further Study: What does Psalm 139:7-18 teach about God's omnipresence? ✧ What was David's response (vv. 17-18)?

*"The Lord is near to all who call upon Him,
to all who call upon Him in truth."*
PSALM 145:18

✧ ✧ ✧

*Understanding God's omnipresence should encourage us in times of
distress and keep us from sinning.*

I t is a great comfort as a Christian to know that God is always present in
me both essentially and relationally. No matter what the trial, He is there.
Sometimes He might seem faraway, but He's really no further away than He's
ever been. His promise to us is, "I will never desert you, nor will I ever forsake you" (Heb. 13:5).

God is always with us to support our service to Him. When God called
Moses to proclaim His message and lead Israel out of slavery, Moses protested
because of his lack of speaking abilities (Ex. 4:10). But God said, "I . . . will
be with your mouth, and teach you what you are to say" (v. 12). Jesus commands us, "Go therefore and make disciples of all the nations . . . and lo, I am
with you always, even to the end of the age" (Matt. 28:19-20). If you doubt
you have the power to witness, remember that you have the same resource as
any evangelist—the presence and power of God!

God's continual presence is also a shield against sin. "No temptation has
overtaken you but such as is common to man; and God is faithful, who will
not allow you to be tempted beyond what you are able, but with the temptation will provide the way of escape also, that you may be able to endure it"
(1 Cor. 10:13). Nothing will ever tempt us without His giving us the strength
to resist.

The omnipresence of God should also motivate us to holiness. Most of us
prefer to sin with no one else watching. But when we sin—whether in
thought, word, or action—we sin in the presence of God. "The eyes of the
Lord are in every place, watching the evil and the good" (Prov. 15:3). "His
eyes are upon the ways of a man, and He sees all his steps. There is no darkness or deep shadow where the workers of iniquity may hide themselves" (Job
34:21-22). Don't do anything you wouldn't want God to see, because He'll
see it anyway!

✧ ✧ ✧

Suggestions for Prayer: Thank God for the comfort He brings to you through
His continual presence.

For Further Study: Hebrews 13:5 is a quote from Deuteronomy 31:6. Read
Deuteronomy 31:1-8. What was the basis for Moses' admonition to "be
strong and courageous"?

> *"Thine, O Lord, is the greatness and the power and the glory
> and the victory and the majesty, indeed everything that
> is in the heavens and the earth; Thine is the dominion, O
> Lord, and Thou dost exalt Thyself as head over all."*
>
> 1 CHRONICLES 29:11

✧ ✧ ✧

God has unlimited power and ultimate control over everything.

There is no limit to God's power. Revelation 19:6 says, "The Lord our God, the Almighty, reigns." In fact, one Hebrew name for God is *El Shaddai* (*El* means "God"; *Shaddai* means "almighty"). Another word for "almighty" is "omnipotent."

God can do anything effortlessly. It is no more difficult for Him to create a universe than it is for Him to make a butterfly. We get tired when we work, but God's infinite power never lessens: "The creator of the ends of the earth does not become weary or tired" (Isa. 40:28).

Not only does God have unlimited power but also the authority to use it. "Our God is in the heavens; He does whatever He pleases" (Ps. 115:3). But God's power, authority, and will are in harmony with His nature. He cannot sin, neither can He accept impenitent sinners. Such actions would contradict His holiness.

People often question what God does because they don't understand that He can do anything He wants. They ask, "Why did God do that?" I've often replied, "Because He wanted to." He showed His sovereignty—His ultimate control of everything—in showing mercy to some like Isaac and Jacob, while hardening the hearts of others like Pharaoh (Rom. 9:6-21). To those who object to God's right to control such things, Paul said, "Who are you, O man, who answers back to God? The thing molded will not say to the molder, 'Why did you make me like this,' will it? Or does not the potter have a right over the clay . . . ?" (vv. 20-21).

Never question God's use of His power. He is in control, and "The Lord is righteous in all His ways, and kind in all His deeds" (Ps. 145:17). We can trust that whatever He does, it's for the best.

✧ ✧ ✧

Suggestions for Prayer: Praise God for His infinite power and sovereignty.

For Further Study: Read Isaiah 40:21-31. How has God demonstrated His power? ✧ How has He demonstrated His sovereignty? ✧ What comfort should that bring to you?

"I pray that the eyes of your heart may be enlightened, so that
you may know . . . what is the surpassing greatness
of His power toward us who believe. These are in accordance
with the working of the strength of His might."
EPHESIANS 1:18-19

✧ ✧ ✧

God's power is seen in creation, preservation,
redemption, and resurrection.

Think of all the energy we get from the sun, and multiply that by the innumerable stars in space. But God by His great power created all the stars with no effort whatsoever: "By the word of the Lord the heavens were made, and by the breath of His mouth all their host" (Ps. 33:6). He just spoke, and they were made.

God's power also preserves the universe. Christ "upholds all things by the word of His power" (Heb. 1:3), and "in Him all things hold together" (Col. 1:17). Chaos would result unless His sustaining hands were directing the orderliness of creation (Ps. 104; Jer. 31:35-36).

God's power was beautifully demonstrated at the cross. Satan was subdued, death was conquered, and the penalty for our sins was paid. The gospel "is the power of God for salvation to every one who believes" (Rom. 1:16). When we were saved, God made each of us "a new creature" (2 Cor. 5:17). Not only that, but "He who began a good work in [us] will perfect it until the day of Christ Jesus" (Phil. 1:6). God's power saved us and gives us strength to live lives pleasing to Him.

The power of God is also made evident in resurrection. Did you know that someday God is going to resurrect every human being who ever lived? The righteous will be raised to eternal life, and the unrighteous to eternal damnation (John 5:28-29; Rev. 20:11-15). Billions of people, long dead, will be resurrected. What tremendous power!

✧ ✧ ✧

Suggestions for Prayer: Praise God for the power He has shown in His beautiful creation. ✧ Thank God that by His power He made you into a new creation and will someday raise you to eternal life.

For Further Study: Psalm 33 is a song of praise to God for His power and sovereignty. Examine what it teaches about God's power, and read it as your own prayer of praise.

> *"Yet those who wait for the Lord will gain new strength. . . .*
> *They will run and not get tired, they will walk and not become weary."*
> ISAIAH 40:31

✧ ✧ ✧

Relying on God's power gives us confidence to live as Christians.

What should be our response to God's power? First, we should worship Him. Our response should follow what God told Israel: "The Lord, who brought you up from the land of Egypt with great power and with an outstretched arm, Him you shall fear, and to Him you shall bow yourselves down, and to Him you shall sacrifice" (2 Kings 17:36).

Understanding God's power should also give us confidence: "I can do all things through Him who strengthens me" (Phil. 4:13). Because of His strength, we can live the Christian life each day with confidence. God "is able to do exceeding abundantly beyond all that we ask or think, according to the power that works within us" (Eph. 3:20).

Our eternal hope rests on the power of God. His power saved us and will "raise [us] up on the last day" (John 6:40). That day should be the great hope of the Christian, because whatever troubles we have on earth, our heavenly destiny is still secure.

When I'm tempted to worry, I'm comforted to remember that God's power is greater than any problem I have. The psalmist says, "I will lift up my eyes to the mountains; from whence shall my help come? My help comes from the Lord, who made heaven and earth" (Ps. 121:1-2). The God who made everything can certainly handle our troubles!

God's power also gives us spiritual victory. Paul instructs us to "be strong in the Lord, and in the strength of His might" (Eph. 6:10). When the adversary comes and you're on guard, you don't fight him; you go tell the commander, and he leads the battle. God will bring about the victory because "greater is He who is in [us] than he who is in the world" (1 John 4:4). Satan may be powerful, but he's no match for God.

Finally, understanding God's power gives us humility. Peter exhorts us, "Humble yourselves . . . under the mighty hand of God, that He may exalt you at the proper time" (1 Peter 5:6). Apart from God's gracious power we are nothing and can do nothing (John 15:5).

✧ ✧ ✧

Suggestions for Prayer: Thank God for each of these ways He uses His power for our benefit.

For Further Study: Read Psalm 121. In what ways does God demonstrate His power to us?

"Great is our Lord, and abundant in strength;
His understanding is infinite."
PSALM 147:5

✣ ✣ ✣

God knows everything, and so He knows our sin.

Our time in history has been called "the Information Age." Computers work around the clock storing the glut of information from all branches of knowledge. And this flood of data is growing bigger all the time. Without the help of advanced technology, we could process and interpret only a tiny fraction of it.

In contrast, God is omniscient; He knows everything. Our Scripture for today says, "His understanding is infinite." Isaiah asks, "Who has directed the Spirit of the Lord, or as His counselor has informed Him? With whom did He consult and who gave Him understanding? And who taught Him in the path of justice and taught Him knowledge, and informed Him of the way of understanding?" (40:13-14). The answer to all those questions is, "No one."

Since His knowledge is infinite, God never learns anything, nor does He forget anything. When you pray, you're not telling God something He doesn't know. He merely chooses to work through our prayers.

God knows every detail of our lives. Jesus says, "The very hairs of your head are all numbered" (Luke 12:7). God doesn't have to count them because He intrinsically knows how many there are. He also knows all our thoughts (Isa. 66:18). David says, "Even before there is a word on my tongue, behold, O Lord, Thou dost know it all" (Ps. 139:4). In that same psalm, David goes on to say, "Even the darkness is not dark to Thee" (v. 12). You can't hide anything from the knowledge of God.

God's omniscience should be a deterrent to our sinning. Think about some of the wrongs you did as a child when your parents weren't around. You never would have done those things in front of them because you didn't want to be punished. And you might have gotten away with a few things. But "God will bring every act to judgment, everything which is hidden, whether it is good or evil" (Eccles. 12:14). Even though the eternal penalty for sin has been paid by Christ, God still disciplines us when we sin (Heb. 12:5-11). Is there anything in your life you would be ashamed about if God knew? If so, repent, because He does know!

✣ ✣ ✣

Suggestions for Prayer: Praise God for His infinite knowledge.

For Further Study: Read David's praise for God's omniscience in Psalm 139:1-6. What specific areas of God's knowledge does he mention?

> *"And [Peter] said to Him, 'Lord, You know all things;*
> *You know that I love You.'"*
> JOHN 21:17

✧ ✧ ✧

Since God knows all things, He knows our struggles
and will help us through them.

It's comforting to know that in the vastness of the universe, I'm not lost in insignificance; God knows me personally. Have you ever wondered if He knows you're there? Some godly people in Malachi's time wondered that. Malachi spoke words of judgment against the wicked, but the faithful believers feared that God might forget them and that they too would be consumed by God's wrath. "Then those who feared the Lord spoke to one another, and the Lord gave attention and heard it, and a book of remembrance was written before Him for those who fear the Lord and who esteem His name. 'And they will be Mine,' says the Lord of hosts, 'on the day that I prepare My own possession, and I will spare them as a man spares his own son who serves him'" (Mal. 3:16-17). God has a book, and He doesn't forget who belongs in it. I know that God knows me and that I belong to Him.

David, too, found comfort in God's omniscience. He said, "Thou hast taken account of my wanderings; put my tears in Thy bottle; are they not in Thy book?" (Ps. 56:8). It was customary for hired mourners at funerals in David's time to catch their tears in a bottle, perhaps to prove they earned their money. David knew that none of his trials went unnoticed by God. Not only does He know about them, He cares about them too.

You might be frustrated sometimes in your Christian walk as you see sin in your life. But happily for us, God knows that we still love Him in spite of our failings. In John 21, Peter kept trying to convince Christ that he loved Him, although his words and actions didn't always prove it. Finally Peter said, "Lord, You know all things; You know that I love You" (v. 17). Peter appealed to the Lord's omniscience. We can do the same thing when we stumble.

✧ ✧ ✧

Suggestions for Prayer: Thank God for knowing and caring about your struggles.

For Further Study: Read Job 42:1-6. What did Job acknowledge about God? ✧ What did that lead him to do?

> *"The one who does not love*
> *does not know God, for God is love."*
> 1 JOHN 4:8

❖ ❖ ❖

God's love is unconditional and righteous.

We hear a lot today about love from books, magazines, TV, and movies. If you didn't know any better, you'd think that our society is the most loving on earth. Much of the "love," though, is nothing more than lust masquerading as love, or selfishness disguised as kindness. But today's verse tells us that "God is love"; the character of God defines love. To clear up any confusion about love, we need only to look at who God is. And then, of course, we need to seek to love others as God loves us.

First, God's love is unconditional and unrequited. "God demonstrates His own love toward us, in that while we were yet sinners, Christ died for us" (Rom. 5:8). God loved us when we were sinners, when we had no righteousness and we didn't—and couldn't—love Him back. God doesn't love us because we deserve it or because we love Him, but because it's His nature to love.

God's love doesn't mean He winks at sin, though. Just as earthly fathers discipline sinning children, "those whom the Lord loves He disciplines, and He scourges every son whom He receives" (Heb. 12:6). True love doesn't indulge unrighteousness, it confronts it. This kind of tough love isn't always fun, but it's for the best: "All discipline for the moment seems not to be joyful, but sorrowful; yet to those who have been trained by it, afterwards it yields the peaceful fruit of righteousness" (v. 11).

We'll study God's love more in the next lesson, but now it's only natural to examine how we ourselves are doing in demonstrating love. Is our love unconditional, or do we withhold love from those who hurt us? Do we love only those who love us back? Jesus says, "If you love those who love you, what credit is that to you? For even sinners love those who love them" (Luke 6:32). Loving those who love us is easy. Christ loved those at enmity with Him, and He expects us to love our enemies too.

❖ ❖ ❖

Suggestions for Prayer: Thank God for His great love toward us and for its greatest manifestation in the Person of Christ.

For Further Study: First John has much to say about God's love for us and our love for Him and others. Read the entire book, noting each instance of the word *love*.

"For God so loved the world
that He gave His only begotten Son,
that whoever believes in Him
should not perish, but have eternal life."

JOHN 3:16

✧ ✧ ✧

God's love is vicarious and sacrificial.

Today we continue a short study of a topic that brings joy to every Christian: God's love. Both Paul and John call His love "great" (Eph. 2:4; 1 John 3:1), because only great love would provide such a sacrifice as God did in Christ.

We have already seen that God's love is unconditional, unrequited, and righteous. God's love is also vicarious; it bears the pain of others. In a prophecy about Christ, Isaiah wrote: "Surely our griefs He Himself bore, and our sorrows He carried" (53:4). Christ bears our earthly sorrows, and, infinitely more significant, He bore the pain and punishment for our sins.

True love is a sacrificial love that gives without expecting anything in return. God gives so many good things to everyone, and He gave the greatest gift of all, His Son. As John 3:16 teaches, love was His motive for sending Christ to die; He wanted to provide salvation for us.

Again we must examine ourselves after seeing God's love. Galatians 6:2 says, "Bear one another's burdens, and thus fulfill the law of Christ." Are you encouraging and helping other Christians in difficulty? Also, ask yourself if you love regardless of the sacrifice. Some will "love" up to the point of pain or inconvenience but no further. However, Jesus commands us, "Love your enemies, and do good, and lend, expecting nothing in return; and your reward will be great, and you will be sons of the Most High; for He Himself is kind to ungrateful and evil men" (Luke 6:35). Love is not always easy, but it's always best.

So much more could be said about God's love. Countless books and hymns have been written about it. We can get only a basic understanding in these few paragraphs. But let this introduction serve as a starting point for a lifelong study of God's love. It's one of the greatest themes in the Bible; you can't miss it.

✧ ✧ ✧

Suggestions for Prayer: Pray for strength to bear the burdens of others and to love with sacrificial love.

For Further Study: Jesus talks about His love for us in John 15:9-17. In what ways should we respond to God's love? ✧ Based on these verses, think of specific ways you can demonstrate your love for God and others.

*"The Lord, the Lord God, [is] compassionate and gracious,
slow to anger, and abounding in lovingkindness and truth."*
EXODUS 34:6

❖ ❖ ❖

God's grace is His undeserved favor shown to sinners.

God's grace has always been a focus of praise for believers. Today's verse is quoted several times in the Psalms and elsewhere in Scripture (for example, Neh. 9:17, 31; Ps. 86:15; 103:8; 145:8). Paul is grateful for God's abundant grace in 1 Timothy 1:14, and John writes, "For of His fulness we have all received, and grace upon grace" (John 1:16). Today some of our favorite hymns are "Amazing Grace," "Marvelous Grace of Our Loving Lord," and "Wonderful Grace of Jesus."

What exactly is grace? It is simply God's free, undeserved, and unearned favor. It is a gift given by God not because we are worthy of it, but only because God, out of His great love, wants to give it.

Grace is evident to Christians in two main ways. The first is electing, or saving, grace. God "has saved us, and called us with a holy calling, not according to our works, but according to His own purpose and grace which was granted us in Christ Jesus from all eternity" (2 Tim. 1:9). "By grace [we] have been saved through faith" (Eph. 2:8). This is God's grace to sinners, for "where sin increased, grace abounded all the more" (Rom. 5:20).

Another grace in our lives is enabling, or sustaining, grace. We didn't just receive grace to be saved; we now live in grace. It is the grace of God that enables us to live the Christian life. When Paul asked that some debilitating "thorn in the flesh" (2 Cor. 12:7) be removed, the Lord told him, "My grace is sufficient for you, for power is perfected in weakness" (v. 9). Paul elsewhere says, "I can do all things through Him who strengthens me" (Phil. 4:13).

Remember, we have earned neither saving nor sustaining grace. Nothing we can do can make us worthy of one more bit of grace. God says, "I will be gracious to whom I will be gracious" (Ex. 33:19). This truth should make us all more grateful because He saved us and sustains us despite our sin. It should also make us humble because we have no worthiness to boast about (Eph. 2:9).

❖ ❖ ❖

Suggestions for Prayer: Thank God for His grace in saving and sustaining you.

For Further Study: Read Genesis 9:8-19. How did God extend grace to Noah and his family? ❖ What was the visible sign or symbol?

> *"Where sin increased,*
> *grace abounded all the more."*
> ROMANS 5:20

❖ ❖ ❖

God will lavish grace upon sinners who are truly repentant.

D id you ever sin so terribly that you felt, *I really blew it this time. There's no way God would want to forgive me now*? It's easy sometimes to let our past sins be a constant burden to us, even after we've confessed and repented. Paul has comfort for those who feel this way, and that comfort is founded on the power and measure of God's grace to us.

Before his conversion, Paul (then known as Saul) persecuted the church mercilessly (see Acts 8:3 and 9:1-2). He was "a blasphemer and a persecutor and a violent aggressor" (1 Tim. 1:13; see also Gal. 1:13). If anyone could be beyond grace, it was Paul.

But God intervened and saved him (Acts 9:3-19). Why? "For this reason," Paul says, "I found mercy, in order that in me as the foremost [sinner], Jesus Christ might demonstrate His perfect patience, as an example for those who would believe in Him for eternal life" (1 Tim. 1:16). If God would forgive Paul, He will forgive anyone who will confess their sins and repent. If He would show abundant grace to a violent unbeliever, He will also shower grace upon His penitent children.

God is not stingy with grace. Paul celebrates God's saving "grace, which He freely bestowed on us" (Eph 1:6), and "the riches of His grace, which He lavished upon us" (vv. 7-8). Speaking of sustaining grace, Paul says, "God is able to make all grace abound to you, that always having all sufficiency in everything, you may have an abundance for every good deed" (2 Cor. 9:8). Notice the words Paul uses: "*all* grace," "*abound*," "*all* sufficiency," "*everything*," "*abundance*," "*every* good deed." God's grace is inexhaustible and is given so freely that words cannot express it fully.

Great sins require great grace, but God will give super-abundant grace to those who seek forgiveness, for "where sin increased, grace abounded all the more" (Rom. 5:20). Don't let your past sins weigh you down; learn to rest upon God's super-abundant grace.

❖ ❖ ❖

Suggestions for Prayer: Ask God to teach you to understand His grace more fully and help you forget "what lies behind" (Phil. 3:13).

For Further Study: Read Romans 6. What is Paul's argument here? ❖ How are we to live now that we have received God's grace?

"Blessed be the God and Father of our Lord Jesus Christ,
who according to His great mercy has caused us to be born
again to a living hope through the resurrection of
Jesus Christ from the dead."
1 PETER 1:3

✧ ✧ ✧

Because of His mercy, God desires to lift sinners
out of their pitiful condition.

Several years ago I spent about a week in India. Each day I saw countless starving, diseased people with no home but a few square feet of filthy street. I could not help but feel compassion and pity on those people who lived in such misery.

In a spiritual sense, though, before God saved us, we were each even more pathetic than any beggar in India. Spiritually, we "were dead in [our] trespasses and sins . . . and were by nature children of wrath, even as the rest. But God, being rich in mercy, because of His great love with which He loved us, even when we were dead in our transgressions, made us alive together with Christ" (Eph. 2:1, 3-5). God saw our wretched condition and was moved to do something about it.

How does mercy compare with grace? Mercy has respect to man's wretched, miserable condition; grace has respect to man's guilt, which has caused that condition. God gives us mercy to change our condition; He gives us grace to change our position. While grace takes us from guilt to acquittal, mercy takes us from misery to glory.

Doesn't it give you great joy to know that God not only removed your guilt but looked at you and had compassion? And He's not through giving us mercy: "The Lord's lovingkindnesses indeed never cease, for His compassions never fail. They are new every morning; great is Thy faithfulness" (Lam. 3:22-23). We can always "draw near with confidence to the throne of grace, that we may receive mercy and may find grace to help in time of need" (Heb. 4:16).

✧ ✧ ✧

Suggestions for Prayer: Thank God for His great mercy, for the forgiveness and blessings you have as His child.

For Further Study: Luke 15:11-32 contains the well-known parable of the prodigal son, a moving illustration of God's loving compassion. What was the son's condition when he returned? ✧ What was his father's reaction? ✧ How does God respond to us when we turn to Him in repentance and humility?

> *"Be merciful, just as your Father is merciful."*
> LUKE 6:36

❖ ❖ ❖

*Since we have received mercy from God, we are obligated
to show mercy to those with physical or spiritual needs.*

Jesus demonstrated His mercy many times as He went about healing people and casting out demons. Two blind men cried out, "'Lord, have mercy
on us, Son of David!' . . . And moved with compassion, Jesus touched their
eyes; and immediately they regained their sight, and followed Him" (Matt.
20:30, 34). He was also deeply moved in spirit and wept when He saw the
sorrow that Lazarus's death caused (John 11:33-36).

His greatest mercy was shown, though, to those with spiritual needs. Not
only did He heal a paralytic, but He forgave his sins (Luke 5:18-25). He also
prayed for His executioners, saying, "Father, forgive them; for they do not
know what they are doing" (Luke 23:34).

We can show mercy by our physical acts. John says, "But whoever has the
world's goods, and beholds his brother in need and closes his heart against
him, how does the love of God abide in him? Little children, let us not love
with word or with tongue, but in deed and truth" (1 John 3:17-18).

We must also show mercy spiritually. Because we have experienced God's
mercy, we should have great concern for those who have not. We show spiritual mercy by proclaiming the saving gospel of Jesus Christ to the unsaved
and by praying that God would show His mercy to them.

We also demonstrate spiritual mercy by lovingly confronting sinning
Christians: "Brethren, even if a man is caught in any trespass, you who are
spiritual, restore such a one in a spirit of gentleness; looking to yourselves,
lest you too be tempted" (Gal. 6:1). Sinning Christians bring reproach on
Christ and His church and will fall under God's discipline. In such cases it is
wrong to say nothing and let the harm continue.

God has promised us in Matthew 5:7 that we will receive mercy from Him
if we are merciful to others. If we have received unlimited mercy from our loving God, if we have been lifted from our poor, sinful, wretched state to become
citizens of heaven, how can we withhold mercy from others?

❖ ❖ ❖

Suggestions for Prayer: Pray that you would be sensitive to opportunities to
show mercy today.

For Further Study: Read Matthew 23:37-39. What was Jerusalem's condition
in verse 37? ❖ How does that intensify the nature of Christ's compassion and
mercy toward His people?

> *"For the wrath of God is revealed from heaven against*
> *all ungodliness and unrighteousness of men, who*
> *suppress the truth in unrighteousness."*
>
> ROMANS 1:18

✧ ✧ ✧

God hates sin and will
judge unrepentant sinners.

We now come to a topic that is perhaps unpleasant to discuss, but it is essential if we are to have a right understanding of God: His wrath. The idea of a wrathful God goes against the wishful thinking of fallen human nature. Even much evangelism today speaks only of the joys and blessings of salvation without mentioning that those who are without God are under His wrath (Eph. 2:3).

God's attributes are balanced in divine perfection. If He had no righteous anger, He would not be God, just as He would not be God without His gracious love. He perfectly loves righteousness and perfectly hates evil (Ps. 45:7).

But God's wrath isn't like ours. The Greek word used for God's wrath in the New Testament refers to a settled, determined indignation. God does not "fly off the handle," whereas we tend to be emotional and uncontrolled in our anger.

Many times God expressed His wrath to sinful mankind in past ages. He destroyed all mankind except Noah and his family in the great Flood (Gen. 6—7). He destroyed Sodom and Gomorrah for their sins (Gen. 18—19). The Lord told unfaithful Israel, "Behold, My anger and My wrath will be poured out on this place, on man and on beast and on the trees of the field and on the fruit of the ground; and it will burn and not be quenched" (Jer. 7:20).

Some people today foolishly think the God of the Old Testament was a God of wrath and the New Testament God was a God of love, but His wrath is just as clearly taught in the New Testament. Jesus says, "He who believes in the Son has eternal life; but he who does not obey the Son shall not see life, but the wrath of God abides on him" (John 3:36). In the end-times Jesus will return "dealing out retribution to those who do not know God and to those who do not obey the gospel of our Lord Jesus" (2 Thess. 1:8). God is the same God, and He will always hate sin.

✧ ✧ ✧

Suggestions for Prayer: Praise God for His righteous hatred of sin.

For Further Study: Read more about God's wrath in Romans 1:18—2:16. What specifically causes His wrath? ✧ How does He display His wrath to the unrighteous?

"He who has received His witness has set
his seal to this, that God is true."
JOHN 3:33

✧ ✧ ✧

Since God is true in everything He does,
we can trust Him and His Word.

God's truthfulness is taught often in Scripture. Balaam, though no righteous man, got this right: "God is not a man, that He should lie, nor a
son of man, that He should repent; has He said, and will He not do it?" (Num.
23:19). Samuel said to King Saul that God "will not lie or change His mind;
for He is not a man that He should change His mind" (1 Sam. 15:29). Paul
tells us, "God . . . cannot lie" (Titus 1:2), and "Let God be found true, though
every man be found a liar" (Rom. 3:4). Jesus calls the Holy Spirit the "Spirit
of truth" (John 14:17; 15:26; 16:13).

Because God is true, and "all Scripture is inspired by God" (2 Tim. 3:16),
it follows that His Word is completely true. The psalmist says, "The sum of
Thy word is truth" (Ps. 119:160), and Jesus says, "Thy word is truth" (John
17:17).

The Bible, and therefore God Himself, is constantly under attack by critics. They say God doesn't exist. But the Bible says, "The fool has said in his
heart, 'There is no God'" (Ps. 14:1; 53:1). They say the world came into being
by itself. But Scripture says, "In the beginning God created the heavens and
the earth" (Gen. 1:1). They say the miracles in the Bible never happened. But
God's Word says that Jesus came "with miracles and wonders and signs which
God performed through Him" (Acts 2:22).

Always treat the Bible for what it is: the very words of God. Never deny its
truthfulness, neither in your thinking nor in your living. Instead, "be diligent
to present yourself approved to God as a workman who does not need to be
ashamed, handling accurately the word of truth" (2 Tim. 2:15).

✧ ✧ ✧

Suggestions for Prayer: Thank God that He and His Word are absolutely true
and trustworthy. ✧ If you have denied the truthfulness of the Bible, either in
your thoughts or in your life, pray for forgiveness and for understanding in
what the Bible has to say.

For Further Study: Read 2 Timothy 3:16-17. What useful qualities are inherent in God's Word? Meditate on these, and think of ways they can and should
affect your behavior.

> *"God is faithful, through whom you were called into*
> *fellowship with His Son, Jesus Christ our Lord."*
> 1 CORINTHIANS 1:9

✧ ✧ ✧

God is completely faithful to do what He has promised.

We live in a day of unfaithfulness, don't we? Some husbands and wives are unfaithful to their marriage vows. Children are often unfaithful to the principles taught by their parents. Parents are often unfaithful to meet the needs of their children. And all too frequently we are unfaithful to God.

Only God is always faithful, a fact often celebrated in Scripture: "Know therefore that the Lord your God, He is God, the faithful God" (Deut. 7:9). "Thy lovingkindness, O Lord, extends to the heavens, Thy faithfulness reaches to the skies" (Ps. 36:5). "Great is Thy faithfulness" (Lam. 3:23).

Let's look at several areas in which God is faithful to us. First, He's faithful in taking care of us. Peter says, "Let those also who suffer according to the will of God entrust their souls to a faithful Creator in doing what is right" (1 Peter 4:19). The word translated "entrust" is a banking term that speaks of a deposit for safekeeping. We're to give our lives to our "faithful Creator," who is best able to care for us because He created us. "My God shall supply all your needs according to His riches in glory in Christ Jesus" (Phil. 4:19).

God is also faithful in helping us resist temptation: "No temptation has overtaken you but such as is common to man; and God is faithful, who will not allow you to be tempted beyond what you are able, but with the temptation will provide the way of escape also, that you may be able to endure it" (1 Cor. 10:13). No believer can legitimately claim that he was overwhelmed by temptation or that "the Devil made me do it." When our faithfulness is tested, we have God's own faithfulness as our resource. "The Lord is faithful, and He will strengthen and protect you from the evil one" (2 Thess. 3:3).

✧ ✧ ✧

Suggestions for Prayer: Thank God for His faithfulness in taking care of you and protecting you from temptation.

For Further Study: God had promised Abraham a son, and He finally gave him Isaac. But God made a strange request. Read Genesis 22:1-18 and Hebrews 11:17-19. How did Abraham demonstrate his trust? ✧ In what areas do you have trouble trusting God?

"Faithful is He who calls you,
and He also will bring it to pass."
1 THESSALONIANS 5:24

✧ ✧ ✧

God is faithful in forgiving our sins and securing our salvation.

We have learned that God protects us from temptation, but what happens when we don't rely on God and give in to sin? John has the answer: "If we confess our sins, He is faithful and righteous to forgive us our sins and to cleanse us from all unrighteousness" (1 John 1:9). The Lord says in Jeremiah 31:34, "I will forgive their iniquity, and their sin I will remember no more." God has promised to forgive, and He is faithful to do so.

God's faithfulness stands out especially in His preserving His people for glory. He secures our salvation. Paul says, "For I am confident of this very thing, that He who began a good work in you will perfect it until the day of Christ Jesus" (Phil. 1:6). God will preserve us so that we may be "without blame at the coming of our Lord Jesus Christ" because He is "faithful" (1 Thess. 5:23-24).

There was once a boy whose dad left him on a downtown street corner and told him to wait there until he returned in about half an hour. But the father's car broke down, and he could not get to a phone. Five hours went by before the father managed to get back, and he thought his son would be in a state of panic. But when the father returned, the boy was standing in front of the corner dime store, looking in the window and rocking back and forth on his heels. The father threw his arms around him, apologized, and said, "Weren't you worried? Did you think I was never coming back?" The boy replied, "No, Dad. I knew you were coming. You said you would."

God is always faithful to His promises. The father in the story was unable to keep his promise because of circumstances out of his control. But God is able to overcome any circumstances to keep His word. With a simple faith like that boy's, we can always say, "I knew you would do it, God. You said you would."

✧ ✧ ✧

Suggestions for Prayer: Ask God for simple faith to trust Him whatever the situation.

For Further Study: David rejoices in God's faithfulness in Psalm 103. Make a list of all the ways God demonstrates His faithfulness in this psalm.

"The heavens are telling of the glory of God, and their expanse is declaring the work of His hands."

PSALM 19:1

✧ ✧ ✧

God's glory is the radiance of all He is.

In Isaiah's vision of Heaven, angels called out, "Holy, Holy, Holy, is the Lord of hosts, the whole earth is full of His glory" (Isa. 6:3). What exactly is the glory of God? It encompasses all that He is, the radiance of His attributes and divine nature.

Moses said to God, "I pray Thee, show me Thy glory!" (Ex. 33:18), and the Lord answered, "I Myself will make all My goodness pass before you, and will proclaim the name of the Lord before you; and I will be gracious to whom I will be gracious, and will show compassion on whom I will show compassion" (v. 19). Moses was not allowed to see God's face, which is the essence of His being: "You cannot see My face, for no man can see Me and live!" (v. 20). But Moses was allowed to see God's back, which represents the afterglow of His glory.

Perhaps God's afterglow is like the radiance of the sun. We only see the light that comes off the sun. If we got too close to it, we would be consumed. If the sun is so brilliant, what must God be like? His glory seen in creation is only a dim reflection of His character.

God displayed His glory many times in Scripture. He represented Himself as a great white cloud by day and a pillar of fire by night as He led Israel through the wilderness (Ex. 13:21). After the Tabernacle was built, "the cloud covered the tent of meeting, and the glory of the Lord filled the tabernacle" (Ex. 40:34). Years later, He filled the temple in a similar way (1 Kings 8:10-11). This manifestation of God's glory served as the focal point of worship for Israel.

God takes His glory very seriously. He said, "I will not give My glory to another" (Isa. 42:8). We must not steal God's glory by becoming proud and taking credit for the good things He has done. Instead of taking God's glory, say with David, "I will give thanks to Thee, O Lord my God, with all my heart, and will glorify Thy name forever" (Ps. 86:12).

✧ ✧ ✧

Suggestions for Prayer: Praise God for His glory and majesty.

For Further Study: Read Daniel 4, the story of a powerful man who did not give God the glory. What characterized Nebuchadnezzar in verses 30 and 37?

*"And the Word became flesh, and dwelt among us,
and we beheld His glory, glory as of the only begotten from
the Father, full of grace and truth."*

JOHN 1:14

✧ ✧ ✧

*Christ displayed God's glory on earth and will again
when He comes back. After seeing His glory in Scripture,
we should respond in worship and righteousness.*

From eternity past Christ had the glory of God. He "is the radiance of [God's] glory and the exact representation of His nature" (Heb. 1:3), and He prayed, "And now, glorify Thou Me together with Thyself, Father, with the glory which I ever had with Thee before the world was" (John 17:5).

Christ also displayed God's glory on earth. Most often He looked like an ordinary man, but one night He appeared in great glory to Peter, James, and John (Luke 9:28-36). "While He was praying, the appearance of His face became different, and His clothing became white and gleaming" (v. 29). Moses and Elijah came and spoke to Him, and the disciples "saw His glory" (v. 32).

When He comes again, He will come "on the clouds of the sky with power and great glory" (Matt. 24:30), to the joy of His people and to the terror of those who reject Him. His glory will fill the whole earth (Num. 14:21), and all creation will worship Him.

What should be our response to God's glory? Like the angels who sing, "Glory to God in the highest" (Luke 2:14), we should give Him praise. Also, as we see His glory we should change: "But we all, with unveiled face beholding as in a mirror the glory of the Lord, are being transformed into the same image from glory to glory, just as from the Lord, the Spirit" (2 Cor. 3:18). As we look at God, the Holy Spirit convicts us of sin and helps us grow and live righteous lives. As "children of God," we "appear as lights in the world" (Phil. 2:15).

The purpose of all creation is to glorify God. As a mirror reflects light, we are to reflect His glory to Him and to a sinful world. Seek to live a holy life so this reflection shines as brightly as possible, and make it your desire to glorify Him in everything you do.

✧ ✧ ✧

Suggestions for Prayer: Thank God for the hope of glory we have as we wait for Christ's return (Titus 2:13). ✧ Ask that your life would brightly reflect God's glory today.

For Further Study: Read about God's glory in Heaven in Revelation 21:1—22:5. How is His glory displayed?

> *"'Let him who boasts boast of this,*
> *that he understands and knows Me, that I am the Lord*
> *who exercises lovingkindness, justice, and righteousness on*
> *earth; for I delight in these things,' declares the Lord."*
>
> JEREMIAH 9:24

✧ ✧ ✧

Unless we have a personal relationship
with Him, we don't really know Him.

We have studied many truths about God this month, but just knowing the facts is not enough. Knowing facts about God doesn't necessarily mean knowing God, any more than knowing American history means you know Abraham Lincoln. Some of the most learned theologians in history, with great grasp of the facts about God, had no faith in God. They knew about God, but Christ will say to them on their day of judgment, "I never knew you; depart from Me" (Matt. 7:23).

The heart of knowing God is *relationship*. God is a relational being and has made us relational also, so that we might know Him. And like human relationships, knowing God requires time and commitment.

Of course, the first step in knowing God is salvation. When we were unsaved, we were enemies of God (Rom. 5:10), but now we are His friends (John 15:14-15). Once begun, this friendship is cultivated by studying the Bible and praying. God communicates His heart to us through His Word, and we communicate our hearts to Him in prayer.

Our fellowship with God is hindered by neglect. As a parallel, if you never spoke with your best friend, the friendship would suffer. Sin also harms our relationship with God because it moves us away from Him. We must remove whatever might hinder the relationship by continually confessing our sins (1 John 1:9), diligently studying His Word (Ezra 7:10), and devoting ourselves to prayer (Col. 4:2).

These things must be done with a fervent desire to know Him. We must have the heart of Paul who says, "I count all things to be loss in view of the surpassing value of knowing Christ Jesus my Lord" (Phil. 3:8), and of David who says, "Thy face, O Lord, I shall seek" (Ps. 27:8). Then we will "grow in the grace and knowledge of our Lord and Savior Jesus Christ" (2 Peter 3:18).

✧ ✧ ✧

Suggestions for Prayer: Pray that God would strengthen your desire to know Him.

For Further Study: Read Psalm 42. What was the psalmist's passion? ✧ What characterized his life despite his troubles?

*"He gives a greater grace. Therefore it says,
'God is opposed to the proud, but gives grace to the humble.'"*
JAMES 4:6

✧ ✧ ✧

*A person cannot be saved unless
he comes to God with a humble attitude.*

Today's verse is a challenge and a promise to anyone who is not sure about his salvation, or who thinks he is saved but does not measure up to the tests of faith in James's letter. Even the worst sinful character traits—relying on worldly wisdom, having enmity against God, lusting after fleshly and self-ish desires—are no match for God's abundant grace.

The kind of grace James is referring to here is simply God's saving grace—His undeserved favor of forgiveness and love bestowed on all sorts of sinners. Included within that favor is the Lord's promise of the Holy Spirit, an under-standing of God's Word, Heaven, and all spiritual blessings. Such grace is available to all who will come in faith to Christ. Nothing in this universe can prevent the truly humble and repentant person from receiving grace—not the strength of sin and depravity, not the might of Satan, not the pull of the flesh, not even the power of death.

Scripture often links humility with saving faith. That's why James quoted from Proverbs 3:34 ("God is opposed to the proud") to support his point in verse 6. In the Gospel of Matthew, Jesus tells us: "Truly I say to you, unless you are converted and become like children, you shall not enter the kingdom of heaven" (18:3).

If you are confused or doubtful regarding your salvation, just ask yourself, "Have I humbly submitted myself to God in faith and repentance?" If you have humbled yourself before God, rejoice! You are by definition a believer, one of the humble. Otherwise, you need to pray with the attitude of the tax gatherer in Luke 18:13, "God, be merciful to me, the sinner!" and receive His abundant grace.

✧ ✧ ✧

Suggestions for Prayer: Thank God for His continual grace, which He pours out to those who are humble before Him.

For Further Study: Read James 1—2. What tests of true faith are discussed there? ✧ How are we to respond to each of them? ✧ Reflect on your response to these issues in the past. How could you improve?

"Submit therefore to God."
JAMES 4:7A

✧ ✧ ✧

The truly humble will submit to God's authority.

Most people understand the basic requirements of military service. The first thing anyone experiences when he enlists is his rank within the chain of command under the commanding officer. Implicit in such lining up under the leadership of a superior is that the soldier, sailor, airman, or marine will obediently carry out all he is commanded to do.

However, the military is not the only context in which the concept of submission applies. James 4:7 uses the term "submit" in the far more important arena of our relationship to God. We are to submit to Him and come under the sovereign authority of the Lord Jesus Christ. This is the basic requirement for anyone who would be humble before God. Since Scripture often uses military terms to describe our service to God (Phil. 2:25; 2 Tim. 2:3), it is appropriate to see ourselves as enlisting in God's army, willingly obeying His commands, and following His leadership.

This kind of humble, willing submission to God's authority is what Jesus meant when He told the disciples, "If anyone wishes to come after Me, let him deny himself, and take up his cross daily, and follow Me" (Luke 9:23). This concept of submission simply means doing God's will from the heart, no matter what the cost.

The story of the rich young ruler provides a good measuring rod of our submissiveness to God. After the young man professed obedience to God's law, Jesus tested him further by commanding him to "go and sell all you possess, and give it to the poor, and you shall have treasure in heaven; and come, follow Me" (Mark 10:21). At that point the young man was not willing to obey Jesus. Instead, "his face fell, and he went away grieved, for he was one who owned much property" (v. 22).

How would you have reacted? Would you have willingly obeyed Jesus' command, or would you have allowed your pride to keep you from submitting to Him? If you have humbly lined up under God's authority, the proper response is not difficult.

✧ ✧ ✧

Suggestions for Prayer: Ask the Lord to remind you throughout this day of your need to submit all you do to His authority.

For Further Study: Read the Acts 9:1-22 account of the apostle Paul's conversion to Christ. What do you notice about his obedience and humility? ✧ What is noteworthy about Ananias' behavior?

"Resist the devil and he will flee from you."
JAMES 4:7B

✦ ✦ ✦

Anyone who possesses scriptural humility
will take an uncompromising stand against Satan.

The successful diplomat or politician is quite adept at the art of compromise and finding the middle ground on various issues. But such skill is a hindrance when it comes to determining your position before God. If you humbly, by faith and repentance, submit yourself to God's authority, you will immediately find yourself the enemy of Satan. You are either in God's kingdom and under His lordship, or you are in Satan's kingdom and under his lordship. It is impossible to have one foot in each kingdom and to be serving both kingdoms' rulers.

To "resist the devil" gives us insight into what it means to be an enemy of Satan. "Resist" means "to take a stand against" the person of Satan and his entire system, which includes everything he does and represents. Such resistance is the complete opposite of the position you had before you submitted to God. Ephesians 2:1-2 reminds us of what that position was: "You were dead in your trespasses and sins, in which you formerly walked according to the course of this world, according to the prince of the power of the air [Satan]." At that time, you had no power to resist the Devil and no desire to serve God, because you were slaves to Satan and his system (Heb. 2:14-15).

But all of that can and will change if you humbly switch your allegiance from Satan's kingdom to God's kingdom. In today's verse the apostle James is promising you that as a part of that changed loyalty, you will automatically be in a position to take a stand against Satan. The minute you forsake Satan's mastery he will flee from you.

Many Christians wrongly assume that Satan is much more powerful than he really is. But if you understand James's promise you will know you have abundant spiritual resources to handle Satan's empty threats. Being humble before God doesn't mean being weak before Satan. God enables you to stand firm and resist.

✦ ✦ ✦

Suggestions for Prayer: Thank God for the wealth of spiritual resources He provides for you to stand against the Devil.

For Further Study: Read Ephesians 6:10-18. Make a list of the spiritual weapons God has given us. ✦ Pick one of these, and do some additional reading and study to improve your application of it.

"Draw near to God."

JAMES 4:8

✧ ✧ ✧

The sincerely humble
will want a closer relationship with God.

The expression "draw near" was originally associated with the priesthood in Israel. Under the regulations of the Old Covenant, the priests represented the people before God. Prior to coming near God's presence, the priest had to be washed physically and be ceremonially clean. That meant he had to bathe, wear the proper garments, and offer sacrifices that made his own heart right with God. Then he could draw near to God on the people's behalf.

Eventually the Hebrew word for drawing near meant anyone who approached the presence of God in worship and prayer. The term became synonymous even of those whose hearts were far from God when they "worshiped" Him. For example, Isaiah 29:13 says, "This people draw near with their words and honor Me with their lip service, but they remove their hearts far from Me, and their reverence for Me consists of tradition learned by rote."

But the sincere believer, one who has truly humbled himself before God, knows that God wants worshipers to draw near with true and pure hearts: "Let us draw near with a sincere heart in full assurance of faith, having our hearts sprinkled clean from an evil conscience and our bodies washed with pure water" (Heb. 10:22). This applies the language of the Old Testament ceremonial system to us and says that as the priests prepared themselves to be near God, we also should prepare ourselves spiritually to worship Him.

So far this month we have seen that the humble person will come to God for salvation, submit to Him as Lord, and take a stand against the Devil. But the truly humble person will see that his relationship to God is inherently more than those actions. If you claim to be one of the humble, one who has a saving relationship to the Father through the Son, be sure you can also agree with the psalmist Asaph: "But as for me, the nearness of God is my good; I have made the Lord God my refuge, that I may tell of all Thy works" (Ps. 73:28).

✧ ✧ ✧

Suggestions for Prayer: Thank God for His grace and mercy in salvation that make it possible for us to have a close relationship with Him.

For Further Study: Read Hebrews 4. What sort of rest is the writer referring to? ✧ How does it compare to the rest that the people of Israel sought during Joshua's time?

"He will draw near to you."
JAMES 4:8

✧ ✧ ✧

God will come near to the truly humble,
who have by faith sought to be close to Him.

One of the greatest promises in the Bible is that God responds to the humble and draws near to them. Such people will yearn for a closeness to God by which they can know Him, love Him, learn His Word, praise Him, pray to Him, and fellowship with Him. In summary, the humble will be true worshipers, those who "worship the Father in spirit and truth" (John 4:23).

John 4:23 concludes with the statement, "for such people the Father seeks to be His worshipers." This strongly implies that God wants to have a relationship with the humble, which means He will respond to us. This idea of the Lord reaching out to us and responding to our humble obedience is also found in the Old Testament, when David instructed Solomon: "As for you, my son Solomon, know the God of your father, and serve Him with a whole heart and a willing mind; for the Lord searches all hearts, and understands every intent of the thoughts. If you seek Him, He will let you find Him; but if you forsake Him, He will reject you forever" (1 Chron. 28:9).

The principle of God's drawing near to the humble is illustrated by Jesus' parable of the prodigal son (Luke 15:11-32). First, the prodigal son manifests humility and repentance: "Father, I have sinned against heaven, and in your sight; I am no longer worthy to be called your son" (vv. 18-19). Next, his behavior pictures a longing to draw near to God: "he got up and came to his father" (v. 20). Finally, there is the picture of God drawing near to us: "while he was still a long way off, his father saw him, and felt compassion for him, and ran and embraced him, and kissed him" (v. 20).

You might not find yourself in the same predicament as the prodigal son did, but you will experience the same response from God if you have humbly drawn near to Him in faith and worshiped Him in spirit and in truth.

✧ ✧ ✧

Suggestions for Prayer: Pray that God would help you be a true worshiper of Him.

For Further Study: Read and meditate on Psalm 40. What things did David find true about God's nearness?

"Cleanse your hands . . . and purify your hearts."

JAMES 4:8

✧ ✧ ✧

Clean hands and a pure heart will always characterize the humble.

Hands represent our behavior, the pattern of our outward actions. Scripture uses that symbol when it encourages people to abandon their sinful behavior: "So when you spread out your hands in prayer, I will hide My eyes from you, yes, even though you multiply prayers, I will not listen. Your hands are full of bloodshed" (Isa. 1:15).

Today's verse uses "hands" in reference to the Jewish ceremonial requirements. The priests were required to wash their hands before they entered the presence of God in the tabernacle and temple (Ex. 30:19-21). Therefore, a call to have clean hands was not just a strange figure of speech for James's audience. As Jews, they would know that a person needed to go through a cleansing process and have a clean life if he wanted to be close to the Lord.

This cleansing process, however, includes more than correcting the outward behavior and lifestyle represented by the hands. The inward dimension of the heart must also be involved, which is why James 4:8 says, "Purify your hearts." The heart is what's inside a person—his thoughts, motives, and desires—the essence of his being. The apostle James is telling anyone who would be genuinely humble and want to be right with God that he must deal with his real self, the heart that is so corrupted and deceived by sin. The humble sinner will hear and obey words such as Ezekiel's: "Cast away from you all your transgressions which you have committed, and make yourselves a new heart and a new spirit!" (Ezek. 18:31).

Clean hands and a pure heart are essential traits for anyone who would be counted among the humble. If you have not submitted yourself to God, you won't have these traits, and you need to heed James's commands. If you are one of the humble, you will want to maintain a close relationship with the Lord. For you, therefore, it is crucial to remember what the apostle John promises in 1 John 1:9—"If we confess our sins, He is faithful and righteous to forgive us our sins and to cleanse us from all unrighteousness."

✧ ✧ ✧

Suggestions for Prayer: Pray that all your thoughts and actions today would be pure and pleasing to the Lord.

For Further Study: Read Isaiah 55. What does it say about the transformed heart and life? ✧ Commit verses 6-7 to memory.

"Be miserable and mourn and weep."

JAMES 4:9A

❖ ❖ ❖

Spiritual humility will be marked by a true sorrow over sin.

Modern culture does everything possible to avoid pain, to put off think-ing about unpleasant subjects, to maximize comfort, and to feel good about circumstances.

That philosophy is the reflection of a proud and self-centered attitude, not the humble and God-centered attitude we have been examining during the past week. Today we continue our look at humility in the Epistle of James. The apostle urges people to "be miserable" concerning their sin. The demands of the gospel begin at this point. James is not denying the joy that will come when the gospel is sincerely received. He is simply saying that sinners have to feel bad before they can feel good. The word *misery* in this sense refers to the inner feelings of shame over sin, the deep sorrow it causes, and the spirit of penitence the humbled sinner will have as a result.

The humble person will also mourn over his sin. This reminds us of what the Lord Jesus says in the Beatitudes: "Blessed are those who mourn, for they shall be comforted" (Matt. 5:4). Mourning is a brokenness of spirit that will cause the humble person's heart to ache when he realizes his total spiritual bankruptcy because of sin.

The word James uses for "mourn" is closely related to the concept of sor-row. But this sorrow is not just any ordinary sorrow or sadness that all peo-ple feel during the course of life. James uses a strong word that usually referred to the grieving over a loved one's death. James thus urges the hum-ble sinner to have a funeral mourner's lament or grief regarding his sinfulness.

Weeping is often the physical response that the sincerely humble mourner will have to his circumstances. Tears are God's gift to us that allow release for our aching hearts, as Peter discovered after he betrayed the Lord (Mark 14:72).

Misery, mourning, and weeping all point to a genuine sorrow over sin, what Paul calls "godly sorrow" (2 Cor. 7:10-11). If you are among the humble, this attitude will be yours as you enter God's kingdom (James 4:9) and as you live the Christian life (Matt. 5:3-4).

❖ ❖ ❖

Suggestions for Prayer: Pray that God would give you the proper sense of sor-row over all sin in your life—even over that which seems insignificant.

For Further Study: Read Hebrews 12:15-17. What was lacking in Esau's response (v. 17)? (Read Gen. 25:27-34 and 27:30-38 for background.)

> *"Let your laughter be turned into mourning,*
> *and your joy to gloom."*
> JAMES 4:9B

✧ ✧ ✧

The humble individual will come to see
that sin is not a laughing matter.

Humor has always had a place in popular culture. But in recent decades a more worldly side to humor has emerged. Situation comedies dominate the list of top-rated TV shows, but many are far from what's really best for people to view. The shows' contents so often pander to the immoral and tend to put down scriptural values. Meanwhile, the world also runs headlong after activities that stress fun and self-indulgence. Most people just want to enjoy life and not take anything too seriously.

God's Word acknowledges that there is a proper time and place for joy and laughter: "a time to weep, and a time to laugh; a time to mourn, and a time to dance" (Eccles. 3:4). The psalmist tells of one appropriate time for laughter and happiness: "When the Lord brought back the captive ones of Zion, we were like those who dream. Then our mouth was filled with laughter, and our tongue with joyful shouting" (Ps. 126:1-2).

But the Lord requires that anyone who would have a relationship with Him must begin on a sober, serious, humble note. In today's Scripture, James urges sinners to exchange worldly laughter and frivolity for godly mourning and gloom over their sin. The laughter spoken of here is the kind that indicates a leisurely indulging in human desires and pleasures. It pictures people who give no serious thought to God, to life, death, sin, judgment, or God's demands for holiness. Without mincing words, it is the laughter of fools who reject God, not that of the humble who pursue Him.

James's message is that saving faith and proper humility consist of a serious, heartfelt separation from the folly of worldliness as well as a genuine sorrow over sin. If these characteristics are present in your life, it is fairly safe evidence that you are one of the humble (see 1 John 2:15-17).

✧ ✧ ✧

Suggestions for Prayer: Seek forgiveness for any thoughts and actions that have kept you from a serious attitude in your walk with God.

For Further Study: Read 1 John 2:15-17. Think of several examples under each of the categories of worldliness in verse 16. Which of these are problems for you? ✧ What steps can you take, with God's help, to overcome them?

"Humble yourselves in the presence of the Lord,
and He will exalt you."
JAMES 4:10

✧ ✧ ✧

God graciously bestows every spiritual
blessing on the humble.

Those who are scripturally humble will recognize their unworthiness when they come before God. They will be like the prophet Isaiah who, in seeing God, cursed himself: "Woe is me, for I am ruined [damned]! Because I am a man of unclean lips, and I live among a people of unclean lips; for my eyes have seen the King, the Lord of hosts" (Isa. 6:5). Whenever you see who God really is—infinitely holy, sovereign, mighty, majestic, and glorious—all you can see about yourself is your own sin.

Every time Isaiah or any other person in the Old Testament came face to face with the reality of God's holy presence, he was overwhelmed with fear. A sinner in the presence of a holy God is overpowered by his sense of exposed sinfulness and has every reason to fear. It was the same in the New Testament, such as when the disciples were afraid after Jesus stilled the storm on the Sea of Galilee: "And they became very much afraid and said to one another, 'Who then is this, that even the wind and the sea obey Him?'" (Mark 4:41). If we are humble before the true God, we'll have the same response.

But God does not leave us bowed down in awe or cowering in fear. James promises us that the Lord will exalt the humble. And if we are humble in spirit and saved by grace, we will be sanctified and ultimately glorified. The apostle Paul summarizes this so well in Ephesians 2:4-7, "But God, being rich in mercy, because of His great love with which He loved us, even when we were dead in our transgressions, made us alive together with Christ (by grace you have been saved), and raised us up with Him, and seated us with Him in the heavenly places, in Christ Jesus, in order that in the ages to come He might show the surpassing riches of His grace in kindness toward us in Christ Jesus."

✧ ✧ ✧

Suggestions for Prayer: Thank God today for His holiness and His sovereign control over all things, especially how He is leading you to spiritual maturity.

For Further Study: Read Isaiah 6. What is the focal point of God's nature in this chapter? ✧ What could help you to be as willing as Isaiah was to serve God (v. 8)?

> *"Walk . . . with all humility."*
> EPHESIANS 4:1-2

❖ ❖ ❖

*Christ showed us humility by becoming a man
and living as a servant.*

Humility is not a very popular concept in our society, is it? We are taught to pursue honor and recognition from a young age. When my children were young, they stacked up trophies to the point of absurdity. Award shows are commonplace on television. We seem to have prizes for everything.

Humility is an elusive quality. The moment you think you are humble is the moment you forfeit it. But humility is the heart of the worthy walk; that's why Paul listed it here first. No matter how elusive it is, we must keep striving for it.

The Greek word for *humility* is a compound word. The first part means "low." In a metaphorical sense it was used to mean "poor" or "unimportant." The second part of the word means "to think" or "to judge." The combined meaning is to think of yourself as lowly or unimportant.

Did you know this word never appears in classical Greek? It had to be coined by Christians. The Greeks and Romans had no word for humility because they despised that attitude. They mocked and looked down on anyone who thought of himself as lowly.

In contrast, Christ taught the importance of humility and was our greatest example of that virtue. The exalted Lord Jesus was born in a stable. During His ministry He never had a place to lay His head. He owned only the garments on His body. He washed His disciples' feet, doing the job of a slave (John 13:3-11). When He died, He was buried in a borrowed tomb.

When the evangelical Moravian Brethren of Germany heard about slavery in the West Indies, they were told it was impossible to reach the slave population there because the slaves were separated from the ruling classes. In 1732 two Moravians offered to go and be slaves on the plantations and teach other slaves about Christ. They toiled at the sides of their fellow slaves, and the slaves listened because the two Moravians had humbled themselves. In a small way, that illustrates what Christ did for us: He humbled Himself by becoming a man so we could be saved.

❖ ❖ ❖

Suggestions for Prayer: Ask God to help you walk in Christlike humility.

For Further Study: Read about Christ's example of humility in Philippians 2:5-11. What was His attitude toward Himself, and how can you emulate His humility?

"Walk . . . with all humility."
EPHESIANS 4:1-2

❖ ❖ ❖

*The first step to humility
is understanding our sinfulness.*

I'll never forget a meeting I had at my house with some seminary students. One student asked me, very seriously, "John, how did you finally overcome pride?" I said jokingly, "Well, it was two years ago when I finally licked it, and it's never been a problem since then. It's so wonderful to be constantly humble." Of course, I have *not* completely overcome pride; it's a battle I face every day. Satan makes sure we always struggle with it.

Overcoming pride in even one area is difficult, but Ephesians 4:2 requires "all humility." Having some humility isn't enough. We must have total, complete humility in every relationship, every attitude, and every act.

So we all have a lot of work to do. But where do we start? How can we become humble?

Humility begins with self-awareness. We need to look at ourselves honestly. We can mask who we really are and convince ourselves that we're something wonderful. But we are sinners and need to confess our sins daily before God (cf. 1 John 1:9). Even Paul called himself the foremost of sinners (1 Tim. 1:15) and realized he had not yet reached the goal of Christlikeness (Phil. 3:12-14). Whenever you're tempted to be proud, remember you haven't arrived yet spiritually.

And don't fall into the trap of comparing yourself to others. Paul said, "We are not bold to class or compare ourselves with some of those who commend themselves; but when they measure themselves by themselves, and compare themselves with themselves, they are without understanding" (2 Cor. 10:12). If we're to be honest with ourselves and with God, we need to evaluate ourselves by an outside standard—God's standard. Humility starts when we take off the rose-colored glasses of self-love so we can see ourselves as unworthy sinners. We must recognize our faults and confess our sins daily.

❖ ❖ ❖

Suggestions for Prayer: Confess any known sins to God, and ask for help in overcoming them. ❖ Ask God to keep you from comparing yourself to others instead of to His perfect standard.

For Further Study: Many consider Paul to be the greatest Christian who ever lived, but he viewed himself very differently. Read 1 Timothy 1:12-17. How did he see himself? ❖ As he saw his sinfulness, what was his response to God?

"Walk . . . with all humility."
EPHESIANS 4:1-2

✧ ✧ ✧

*We are to walk as Christ walked. Our lack of conformity
to His standard ought to make us humble.*

What was your most humiliating experience? Life is full of embarrassing moments, but the most truly humbling experience I ever had was
preaching through the Gospel of John. For two years—eighty-eight sermons,
about one hundred hours of preaching, between two and three thousand hours
of study—I was constantly faced with the deity of Jesus Christ. Living with
the deity of Christ day after day and comparing yourself continually to Him
is one of the healthiest—and most humbling—things you can ever do.

That brings us to another step toward humility: Christ-awareness. When we
compare ourselves with ourselves, we get proud. But "the one who says he
abides in Him ought himself to walk in the same manner as He walked"
(1 John 2:6). When you can say, "I'm happy to announce that I now walk as
Jesus walked," then you'll have a right to be proud. But no one will believe
you.

Jesus was the perfect man. He was without sin. He gave all the right
answers and had the perfect attitude for every situation. He knew exactly how
to help everyone who needed help. Reading the Gospels, we see time after
time how Christ handled everything perfectly.

Even seeing His humanness, we realize how small we are. But when we
look at His deity, we feel still smaller. He created everything (Col. 1:16). He
turned water into wine, calmed storms, cast out demons, healed countless
people, and brought the dead to life. After His crucifixion, He rose from the
dead and sat at the Father's right hand (Eph. 1:19-20). Someday He will come
back, take His people home, and finally destroy all evil.

Despite Jesus' perfect deity and perfect humanity, He came to serve (Mark
10:45). How can we be proud if Jesus Christ humbled Himself? What righteous thing have we done that compares to His perfect life?

✧ ✧ ✧

Suggestions for Prayer: Pray that you might know Christ better and increasingly be more like Him.

For Further Study: Peter got a glimpse of Jesus' power in Luke 5:1-7. How
did Peter's sudden awareness of who Christ is affect him (v. 8)? ✧ What did
he do next (vv. 9-11)?

> *"Walk . . . with all humility."*
> EPHESIANS 4:1-2

❖ ❖ ❖

The more we comprehend the greatness of God,
the more humble we will become.

G od is not given proper respect today. He is often flippantly referred to as "the man upstairs"—more of a buddy than the eternal God. Many see Him as nothing more than a cosmic Santa Claus or an absent-minded grandfather who winks at sin.

Unfortunately, even Christians can be affected by these views. Such sin dishonors God and undermines the next step to humility: God-awareness. Instead of getting our ideas of God from the world, let's look at what the biblical writers say about Him.

David said, "O Lord, our Lord, how majestic is Thy name in all the earth, who hast displayed Thy splendor above the heavens!" (Ps. 8:1). As he contemplated the exalted position of God, it was only natural for him to say, "What is man, that Thou dost take thought of him? And the son of man, that Thou dost care for him?" (v. 4). We are so minuscule by comparison, it's a wonder He cares for us at all. But "though the Lord is exalted, yet He regards the lowly" (Ps. 138:6).

Isaiah 2:10 says, "Enter the rock and hide in the dust from the terror of the Lord and from the splendor of His majesty." When you compare yourself with God, you'll want to hide under a rock. Verse 11 gives the crux of the issue: "The proud look of man will be abased, and the loftiness of man will be humbled, and the Lord alone will be exalted in that day." Pride is the sin of competing with God. It lifts self up and attempts to steal glory from Him. But God says, "My glory I will not give to another" (Isa. 48:11). God will judge those who exalt themselves. God alone is worthy of exaltation.

As you seek humility, remember that you won't obtain it by sitting in a corner wishing for it. Rather, you'll gain humility by sitting in that same corner and reciting before God your sins, failures, and inadequacies, then opening the Scriptures and seeing God in all His majesty.

❖ ❖ ❖

Suggestions for Prayer: Pray that you would see God for who He really is, not how the world sees Him.

For Further Study: Read Job 38—41. What aspects of His greatness does God emphasize to Job? Make a list of the most prominent ones.

"Walk . . . with all humility."
EPHESIANS 4:1-2

✧ ✧ ✧

Satan will tempt us to be proud of our abilities and accomplishments,
but we must remember that every good thing we have is from God.

We've just studied three steps to humility. Let's look at the issue from another angle: What kinds of pride threaten to destroy our humility? Where will we struggle to be humble? There are several areas in which Satan will attack us.

The first area I call ability pride. We're often tempted to be proud of our strong points, not our weak ones. I've never been tempted to boast of my fantastic mathematical ability because I have none. But I am tempted to be proud of my preaching because it is my spiritual gift. Thankfully, the Lord helps me deal with such thoughts. It might come in the form of a letter saying, "I was in your church Sunday, and I violently disagree with everything you said." Or someone might tell me, "We came to hear you for the first time, but we like our pastor better." Times like those help me keep the proper perspective.

The key to overcoming ability pride is remembering that every gift you have is from God. All the credit belongs to Him. As Paul said to the Corinthians, "What do you have that you did not receive?" (1 Cor. 4:7).

Another temptation is verbal pride, or bragging. There is a tendency in human nature to tell people what good we have done or plan to do. People get into a conversation, and soon they're trying to top each other with their accomplishments. In contrast, Hannah asserts, "Boast no more so very proudly, do not let arrogance come out of your mouth; for the Lord is a God of knowledge; and with Him actions are weighed" (1 Sam. 2:3). God knows the truth about what you have done. Proverbs 27:2 instructs, "Let another praise you, and not your own mouth."

As a test, try to get through an entire week without talking about what you've done. Perhaps for a starter, try to last an afternoon. When people don't talk about themselves, the absence of boasting tells volumes about their character.

✧ ✧ ✧

Suggestions for Prayer: Repent of any pride in your own abilities or accomplishments.

For Further Study: The apostle Paul had tremendous advantages and abilities but refused to boast about them. Read Philippians 3:4-11. What were Paul's accomplishments? ✧ How did he consider them? ✧ What was most important to him?

"Walk . . . with all humility."
EPHESIANS 4:1-2

✧ ✧ ✧

Our possessions and positions in life are from God;
we can't take credit for them.

Many today take pride in their economic status. They boast about their riches and trust their money, thinking they must be great for acquiring all they have. But remember what Moses said to the Israelites before they entered the Promised Land: "You may say in your heart, 'My power and the strength of my hand made me this wealth.' But you shall remember the Lord your God, for it is He who is giving you power to make wealth" (Deut. 8:17-18). Everything you have, God gave to you. Don't parade your possessions as if you obtained them through your self-created abilities.

A related area is pride in one's class, which involves looking down on those in "lower" levels of society. Such people don't want lower-class people in their neighborhoods and certainly wouldn't invite them to dinner. If you are guilty of this sort of pride, keep in mind that God loves poor people. Jesus Himself was poor in this world and spent most of His time ministering to the poor.

Sometimes in moving up the social ladder, people may demand a certain kind of treatment. They expect the best of everything and get offended when they don't receive it. One of the things Jesus criticized the scribes and Pharisees for was this: "They love the place of honor at banquets, and the chief seats in the synagogues, and respectful greetings in the market places, and being called by men, Rabbi" (Matt. 23:6-7). Resist the temptation to seek worldly honor, glamour, and privileges.

Advertisers today continually entice us to draw attention to ourselves by what we wear. But undue attention to appearance can make people haughty, boastful, and indulgent, trying to show themselves as better than others. God hates that sin (Isa. 3:16-26).

John said, "Do not love the world, nor the things in the world. . . . The world is passing away, and also its lusts" (1 John 2:15, 17). Don't let the world tell you what you should seek or value. Remember instead that "the one who does the will of God abides forever" (v. 17).

✧ ✧ ✧

Suggestions for Prayer: Ask the Lord to give you contentment with your present status and to help you reach out to those not so blessed.

For Further Study: Read Luke 14:8-10; 1 Timothy 2:9-10; and James 2:2-8 and see if you are guilty of materialism or social pride.

March 16 THREATS TO HUMILITY: DOCTRINE AND HYPOCRISY

"Walk . . . with all humility."

EPHESIANS 4:1-2

❖ ❖ ❖

Avoid pride in your position, intelligence, or spirituality.

Years ago, when my children were young, my son Mark told my youngest child, Melinda, to take something out of the room. She said, "You're not my boss." Mark replied, "Dad is the boss of Mom, Mom is the boss of Matt, Matt is the boss of Marcy, Marcy is the boss of me, and I am the boss of you." So Melinda obeyed. After that, Melinda decided she was the boss of the dog, and the dog was boss of nobody. No one wants to be on the bottom rung of the ladder!

Everyone holds a certain position in life, and everyone is tempted to take advantage of it. Look at Herod in Acts 12:21-22: "Herod, having put on his royal apparel . . . began delivering an address to them. And the people kept crying out, 'The voice of a god and not of a man!'" He loved the attention. What happened? "Immediately an angel of the Lord struck him because he did not give God the glory, and he was eaten by worms and died" (v. 23).

Intellectual pride can also be a stumbling block. It's easy for Christians to think their theology is perfect and they have all the answers. But the more I study the Bible, the more I realize how little I know. I feel like a child who fills a pail in the ocean. My learning is only a small bucket of water compared to the vast sea of knowledge. I know very little, and I'm still learning.

The worst type of pride is external spirituality without internal holiness. Jesus reserved His greatest condemnations for those who had such pride: "Woe to you, scribes and Pharisees, hypocrites! For you are like whitewashed tombs which on the outside appear beautiful, but inside they are full of dead men's bones and all uncleanness. Even so you too outwardly appear righteous to men, but inwardly you are full of hypocrisy and lawlessness" (Matt. 23:27-28). You may look spiritual on the outside, going to church and acting "Christianly," but your heart may be full of sin.

❖ ❖ ❖

Suggestions for Prayer: Examine your heart, and confess any pride in your position, intelligence, or spirituality.

For Further Study: Read in Daniel 5 about what happened to a king who took pride in his position. Notice how God humbled him. Such sin wasn't trivial to God; it shouldn't be to us either.

> *"Do nothing from selfishness or empty conceit,*
> *but with humility of mind let each of you regard one another*
> *as more important than himself."*
> PHILIPPIANS 2:3

❖ ❖ ❖

Selfishness and conceit can prevent us from doing God's will.

Selfishness and conceit are all too common among people today. It seems there is hardly a prominent entertainer or sports figure who doesn't portray those characteristics to excess. Yet those traits are the very opposite of what should characterize the humble follower of Christ.

"Selfishness" in today's passage refers to pursuing an enterprise in a factional way. It involves an egotistical, personal desire to push your own agenda in a destructive and disruptive way. "Empty conceit" describes the force behind such overbearing behavior—personal glory. A person driven by such motivation thinks he is always right.

Paul's opening phrase in Philippians 2:3 has the force of a negative command: believers are never to act out of selfish ambition with the goal of heaping praise upon themselves. To do so inevitably leads to one of the common sin problems in our churches: factionalism, accompanied by jealousy, strife, disharmony, and partisanship. Paul knew what harm factionalism could do within a church. It was the primary problem he addressed in his letter of 1 Corinthians. The apostle summarized the Corinthian church's condition this way: "For since there is jealousy and strife among you, are you not fleshly, and are you not walking like mere men?" (1 Cor. 3:3). It is spiritually immature to be jealous of and to cause strife among fellow Christians, and it reveals a fleshly perspective.

Because our flesh (sinfulness) produces selfishness and conceit, it is vitally important to keep it under control (Gal. 5:16). Plans and agendas by themselves are valid, and they are not necessarily incompatible with humility in the Christian life. But if our goals and objectives are driven by selfishness, they become competitive and harmful. One key of dealing with selfishness is realizing that others also have goals and desires. Such a realization will help you go a long way toward killing the monster of selfishness in your life.

❖ ❖ ❖

Suggestions for Prayer: Pray that God's Spirit would rid your heart and mind of any attitudes of selfishness and conceit.

For Further Study: The beginning of 1 Corinthians deals with the subject of factionalism. Read chapter 1. What perspective does Paul have regarding church divisions? ❖ What does the second half of the chapter offer as a prime reason for divisions within the church?

"Do nothing from selfishness or empty conceit,
but with humility of mind let each of you regard one another
as more important than himself."
PHILIPPIANS 2:3

✧ ✧ ✧

One important way to prevent factionalism in the church is to regard
other members as more important than yourself.

Humility of mind" is a distinctive New Testament expression. There were similar terms in secular writings, but none that exactly fit the purposes of the New Testament writers. One form of the Greek word was used to describe the mentality of a slave. It was a term of derision, signifying anyone who was considered base, common, shabby, or low. Among pagans before Christ's time, humility was never a trait to be sought or admired. Thus the New Testament introduced a radically new concept.

In Philippians 2:3 Paul defines "humility of mind" simply as seeing others as more important than yourself. But how often do we really consider others that way? Frequently, even within the church, we think just the opposite of what Paul commands. For example, we are sometimes prone to criticize those with whom we minister. It is naturally easier for us to speak of their faults and failures than it is to refer to our own.

But Paul's attitude was different. He knew his own heart well enough to call himself the worst of sinners: "Christ Jesus came into the world to save sinners, among whom I am foremost of all" (1 Tim. 1:15). The apostle was also humble enough to realize that in his own strength he was not worthy of the ministry to which he had been called: "I am the least of the apostles, who am not fit to be called an apostle" (1 Cor. 15:9).

Your knowledge of others' sins and graces is based on their outward words and actions, not on what you can read from their hearts. But you, like Paul, do know your own heart and its sinful shortcomings (cf. Rom. 7). That ought to make it much easier to respect and honor others before yourself. And when you do that, you are helping prevent factionalism in your church and contributing to the edification of fellow believers.

✧ ✧ ✧

Suggestions for Prayer: Examine your life and ask God to help you turn from anything that would be keeping you from "humility of mind."

For Further Study: Read Genesis 13, and notice what happened between Abraham and his nephew Lot. How did God reassure Abraham after his graciousness toward Lot?

*"Do not merely look out for your own personal interests,
but also for the interests of others."*
PHILIPPIANS 2:4

✧ ✧ ✧

*The Lord wants us to have a general but sincere concern
for the ministry interests of fellow Christians.*

We live in a world that is preoccupied with special interests. On the national and international levels, interest groups push for public acceptance of their particular agendas. Likewise, on the local level most people care only about their own personal interests. They're concerned about their jobs, their families, their hobbies, and perhaps their favorite sports team. In addition to those, if you're a Christian, you will be concerned about your local church. But even there you can become focused only on your area of ministry.

In today's verse, the apostle Paul cautions us, "Do not merely look out for your own personal interests." He is warning first of all that we shouldn't see our personal activities and ministries as our only goals in life. When we become narrowly preoccupied with our own things, it can cause conflicts and other problems with people we know. Instead, God wants us to have a serious, caring involvement in some of the goals others are concerned about. And one way that will happen is if we take our eyes off ourselves and our often excessive concern for self-esteem in everything we do.

You may wonder exactly what Paul meant by the broad term "interests." It is a nonspecific word that has several meanings and implications. It includes legitimate goals and responsibilities you have as a Christian, but it also extends to the same kinds of concerns others in your church and family will have. Their needs, tasks, gifts, character qualities, and ministries should be considered equal in importance to yours.

Paul, by the Holy Spirit, is calling us to pursue a high standard of Christian living, but the standard is worth pursuing. The more we understand the importance of fellow believers and that they need our prayer and concern, the less our fellowships will be plagued by unscriptural competitiveness and pride of personal interest.

✧ ✧ ✧

Suggestions for Prayer: Ask the Lord to help you order your priorities today, so that you'll have time for involvement in the concerns of a Christian friend or relative.

For Further Study: Read Luke 10:38-42. What was Martha's attitude regarding the interests of her sister? ✧ What do Jesus' words to Martha say about where our ultimate interest should lie?

*"Have this attitude in yourselves which was also in Christ
Jesus, who, although He existed in the form of God, did not
regard equality with God a thing to be grasped."*

PHILIPPIANS 2:5-6

✧ ✧ ✧

Christ's coming to earth is the supreme example to us of humility.

We can usually identify with what someone else has experienced when
we have gone through the same thing. Even if we haven't been through
what the other person has, we can perhaps relate because we might someday
have a similar experience.

However, it is much harder to comprehend what Christ experienced when
He stooped from His lofty position at the right hand of God to come to earth
as a man. We'll never understand the magnitude of that descent because we
never were and never will be God. Nevertheless, today's passage presents, as
a pattern for us, Jesus' attitude in coming to this world.

As a Spirit-filled believer (Eph. 1:3-5, 13), the Lord has lifted you out of
your sin and given you the privilege of being His adopted child. He thereby
allows you to recognize and appreciate a little more what humility is all about.
Like Jesus, you will have to descend from an exalted level when you reach out
in humility to those who don't know Him.

Jesus further set the standard for us when He did not view His high position "a thing to be grasped." Loftiness of calling should never be something
we clench as a prized personal possession to exploit for our own benefit. That
is the attitude we would expect to see in worldly people of influence. But it
should not characterize those who claim to follow Jesus' standard.

In contrast, if you are Christ's disciple you will see more and more of His
humility in your life. That will occur as you continually exercise a selfless attitude toward the privileges and possessions He has given you. By not clinging
to these benefits, you will truly exemplify Jesus' attitude and more effectively
serve others: "Be devoted to one another in brotherly love; give preference to
one another in honor" (Rom. 12:10).

✧ ✧ ✧

Suggestions for Prayer: Pray that, starting today, God would grant you more
and more of a Philippians 2:5-6 attitude.

For Further Study: As Ephesians 1 spells out, you have much to be thankful
for as a child of God. Read the entire chapter, and list the many spiritual benefits Paul describes. Try memorizing several verses that are particularly striking to you.

*"But emptied Himself, taking the form of a bond-servant,
and being made in the likeness of men."*

PHILIPPIANS 2:7

✧ ✧ ✧

*As part of His humble descent from Heaven to earth,
Jesus set aside the exercise of His divine privileges.*

The next step in Jesus' pattern of humility as He came to earth and lived among mankind was His emptying of Himself. But Scripture is clear that while on earth our Lord claimed to be God: "He who has seen Me has seen the Father" (John 14:9). At no time did He stop being God.

The Greek word for "emptied" gives us the theological term *kenosis*, the doctrine of Christ's self-emptying. The *kenosis* basically reminds us of what we saw in yesterday's lesson: Jesus' humble refusal to cling to His advantages and privileges in Heaven. The Son of God, who has a right to everything and is fully satisfied within Himself, voluntarily emptied Himself.

We have already noted that Jesus did not empty Himself of His deity, but He did lay aside certain prerogatives. For one thing, He gave up His heavenly glory. That's why, in anticipation of His return to the Father, Christ prayed, "Glorify Thou Me together with Thyself, Father, with the glory which I ever had with Thee before the world was" (John 17:5).

Jesus also relinquished His independent authority and completely submitted Himself to the Father's will: "Not as I will, but as Thou wilt" (Matt. 26:39).

During His time on earth, Christ also voluntarily limited the use and display of His divine attributes. One good illustration of this concerned His omniscience, His knowledge of all things. In teaching about the end-times and His second coming, Jesus said, "But of that day and hour no one knows, not even the angels of heaven, nor the Son, but the Father alone" (Matt. 24:36).

Jesus' self-emptying demonstrates a wonderful aspect of the gospel. Unlike man-centered, works-oriented religions, the biblical gospel has God's Son willingly yielding His privileges to sacrifice Himself for sinners like us.

✧ ✧ ✧

Suggestions for Prayer: Pray that you would become more appreciative of the sacrificial humility Jesus Christ exercised on your behalf.

For Further Study: Scripture does not record a lot about Jesus' boyhood. But the account we do have verifies His emptying. Read Luke 2:39-52. What does verse 47 imply about Jesus' nature? ✧ How do verses 51-52 exemplify His emptying?

> *"Who, although He existed in the form of God, did not*
> *regard equality with God a thing to be grasped, but emptied*
> *Himself, taking the form of a bond-servant, and being*
> *made in the likeness of men."*
>
> PHILIPPIANS 2:6-7

✧ ✧ ✧

Jesus is the role model of the suffering servant.

J esus not only gave up His divine privileges when He emptied Himself, but He also became a servant. For us, this is the next phase in His supreme example of humility. Paul's phrase "the form of a bond-servant" can also be translated "the essence of a slave." Christ's servanthood was not just external—it extended to the essential, down-to-earth role of a bond-slave doing the will of His Father.

We would expect Jesus, the God-man, to be a servant only in the truest fashion. His servitude was not performed like a stage player putting on and taking off the costume of a servant. Jesus truly *became* a servant. He perfectly fulfilled everything Isaiah predicted about Him (52:13-14). Jesus was the Messiah who was a suffering servant.

Christ's entire earthly ministry is the yardstick by which we can measure servanthood. As God, He owned everything; as the servant, He had to borrow everything: a place to be born, a boat in which to cross the Sea of Galilee and preach from, a donkey (itself a symbol of humility and servitude) to ride into Jerusalem for His triumphal entry, a room to celebrate His final Passover in, and a grave to be buried in.

Our Savior acknowledged His role as a servant very simply: "I am among you as the one who serves" (Luke 22:27). And it was all done with love, with consistency, with humility, without the pretense of outward form.

As we continue to look to our Lord Jesus as the role model of humility, the challenge for us is to follow His attitude and practice. Paul instructs those who would be servants of Christ, "Let love be without hypocrisy. . . . Be devoted to one another in brotherly love; give preference to one another in honor; not lagging behind in diligence, fervent in spirit, serving the Lord" (Rom. 12:9-11).

✧ ✧ ✧

Suggestions for Prayer: Thank and praise the Lord that Jesus was such a humble but willing servant on your behalf.

For Further Study: Isaiah 52:13—53:12 is known as the Suffering Servant passage. As you read it, write down the various ways it describes Jesus' suffering. ✧ How is His humility in evidence?

*"... Emptied Himself, taking the form of a bond-servant,
and being made in the likeness of men. And being found
in appearance as a man, He humbled Himself by becoming
obedient to the point of death, even death on a cross."*

PHILIPPIANS 2:7-8

✧ ✧ ✧

*Except for sin, Jesus experienced the everyday things of a normal man;
but He was often not appreciated as the God-man.*

Jesus could understand what people around Him were dealing with because He lived under the same conditions. He can also identify with us today. It is true that He never married, never went to college, and never used a computer or a VCR. But He still has perfect knowledge about such things, and more. The point is, Christ knows firsthand about our basic physical and emotional needs because He actually lived and worked in a world affected by the Fall.

But there was one element of our world Jesus did not partake in: sin. The conclusion of Hebrews 4:15 says He was "tempted in all things as we are, yet without sin." Even though Jesus never sinned, He knows the struggles and temptations we face daily. Otherwise, He could not be the sympathetic High Priest that the first part of verse 15 mentions.

Although Jesus was a man who identified profoundly with those He came to serve, people around Him did not naturally see the most important thing about Him. Philippians 2:8 views Jesus from the perspective of those people. It says His human appearance was so authentic that most of them didn't know that He was also God. Many of them simply could not accept that a man like Jesus could also be higher than them: "Is not this Jesus, the son of Joseph, whose father and mother we know? How does He now say, 'I have come down out of heaven'?" (John 6:42).

Christ's close identification with mankind elicited a tragic response for people such as those in John 6. But for us, His humility is a great model and a heart-felt reassurance that He was perfectly man and perfectly God.

✧ ✧ ✧

Suggestions for Prayer: Thank God that you can freely approach Him in prayer through Jesus, who can identify so closely with all our struggles as human beings.

For Further Study: Read John 11:1-45, which describes the death and resurrection of Lazarus. How did Jesus demonstrate His humanity and deity to the disciples and other eyewitnesses?

"He humbled Himself by becoming obedient to
the point of death, even death on a cross."
PHILIPPIANS 2:8

❖ ❖ ❖

In His suffering and death, Jesus is our supreme example of humility.

We naturally react to injustice with deep hurt and an assertion of our rights. But Jesus' response to His accusers did not include one word of angry defensiveness. Matthew 27:12-14 tells us: "And while He was being accused by the chief priests and elders, He made no answer. Then Pilate said to Him, 'Do You not hear how many things they testify against You?' And He did not answer him with regard to even a single charge, so that the governor was quite amazed."

Later on, during His sham trial, Jesus continued to humble Himself. He accepted sinful men's abuse when they whipped Him, stripped off His robe, planted a crown of thorns on His head, mocked Him, spat on Him, and beat on Him with a reed. Christ did not even demand His rights when He was condemned to death and forced to walk to Calvary half-naked with a cross on His back.

Today's verse underscores the most shocking aspect of Christ's humiliation: the kind of death He died. He endured crucifixion, the cruelest form of death ever devised. The Romans used it to execute rebellious slaves and the worst criminals. Because He was King of the Jews, Jesus' death on the cross was seen as especially horrible by His people. The Jews had long known what the Law of Moses said: "He who is hanged [on a tree] is accursed of God" (Deut. 21:23). From everyone's standpoint, the Son of God suffered the ultimate in human degradation.

But in spite of the detestable treatment He suffered, Christ graciously and lovingly died for sinners like you and me. Such an example of selfless humility ought to motivate us, His followers, as we minister to others, "since Christ also suffered for you, leaving you an example for you to follow in His steps" (1 Peter 2:21).

❖ ❖ ❖

Suggestions for Prayer: Give thanks that Jesus' example of humility extended all the way to His willingness to redeem you.

For Further Study: Read one of the Gospel accounts of Jesus' suffering and death (Matt. 26—27; Mark 14—15; Luke 22—23; John 18—19). Record some observations about His general attitude during the ordeal. ❖ In what situations and ways does He show humility? ❖ If you have time, compare and contrast two of the accounts.

"Let your forbearing spirit be known to all men."
PHILIPPIANS 4:5

❖ ❖ ❖

Real humility will have a forbearance that is gracious toward others and content with its own circumstances.

Some Greek words have various meanings that are hard to translate into just one English word. This is true of "forbearing" in today's verse. It can refer to contentment, gentleness, generosity, or goodwill toward others. Some commentators say it means having leniency toward the faults and failures of others. Other scholars say it denotes someone who is patient and submissive toward injustice and mistreatment—one who doesn't lash back in angry bitterness. It reminds us very much of what we have been considering for the past week—humility.

The humble believer trusts God and does not hold a grudge even though others have unfairly treated him, harmed him, or ruined his reputation. Such a person does not demand his rights. Instead, he will pattern his behavior after his Lord Jesus, who in supreme humility manifested God's grace to us (Rom. 5:10).

If you are conscientiously following Christ, your behavior will go against the existentialism of modern society. Existentialism claims the right to do or say anything that makes one feel good. Today's existentialist unbeliever has a twisted logic that says, "If something makes you feel good but hurts me, you can't do it. But if something makes me feel good but hurts you, I can do it."

Unhappily, many believers have been caught up in that kind of thinking. They don't call it existentialism—self-esteem or positive thinking are the preferred terms—but the results are much the same. Such Christians do what satisfies their desires, often at the expense of other people. At its core, this kind of attitude is simply sinful self-love.

In contrast to such self-love, Philippians 4:5 exhorts us to exhibit humble forbearance and graciousness to others. Other Scriptures command us to love our enemies and show mercy to those who sin (Matt. 5:44; 1 Peter 4:8). Such qualities allowed the apostle Paul to say, "I have learned to be content in whatever circumstances I am" (Phil. 4:11). God wants us to be just as humble and content with our circumstances.

❖ ❖ ❖

Suggestions for Prayer: Ask the Lord to help you remain content in the midst of all that happens to you today.

For Further Study: Read Jesus' parable about mercy and compassion in Matthew 18:21-35. What parallels do you find between the parable and our study of forbearance? ❖ What kind of priority does Jesus give these issues?

> *"Then the mother of the sons of Zebedee came to*
> *Him with her sons, bowing down, and making a request*
> *of Him. And He said to her, 'What do you wish?' She said to*
> *Him, 'Command that in Your kingdom these two sons of mine*
> *may sit, one on Your right and one on Your left.'"*
>
> MATTHEW 20:20-21

✧ ✧ ✧

Use of the power play in our personal dealings
is incompatible with scriptural humility.

One of the most common tactics people use to get ahead is to draw upon the influence of family and friends. Even professing believers have not hesitated to "play politics" to get what they want. I know of a pastor some years ago who said that for his denomination's annual meeting he always booked a hotel room near the top leaders' rooms. He wanted to cultivate their friendships in hopes of receiving consideration for pastorates in larger churches.

Incredibly, today's passage has two of Jesus' closest disciples, James and John, coming with their mother to Jesus to ask a huge, unprecedented favor— that each brother be seated next to Him in His kingdom. It was even more amazing that this brazen, self-serving request came right after Christ predicted His imminent persecution and death. It's as though James and John each let Jesus' sobering words go in one ear and out the other. That's because they were so preoccupied with their own interests and plans.

The three probably were trying to exploit their family relationship with Jesus. By comparing John 19:25 with parallel passages, we know that the disciples' mother (Salome) was a sister of Mary, Jesus' mother. That would make James and John His first cousins and their mother His aunt.

So the three undoubtedly were relying on their kinship to Jesus as they made their selfish request for greater power and prestige within His kingdom. Obviously, they still had not grasped Christ's earlier promise from the Beatitudes: "Blessed are the gentle [meek, humble], for they shall inherit the earth" (Matt. 5:5). But such sublime teaching ought to be enough to convince us that the truly humble don't need power plays to achieve greatness. They already have it in Christ.

✧ ✧ ✧

Suggestions for Prayer: Thank the Lord for the many privileges you already enjoy as His child.

For Further Study: Read Matthew 23. What was Jesus' general attitude toward the Pharisees' motives and actions? ✧ List some specific characteristics you ought to avoid.

*"But Jesus answered and said, 'You do not know what
you are asking for. Are you able to drink the cup that I am
about to drink?' They said to Him, 'We are able.'"*

MATTHEW 20:22

❖ ❖ ❖

*Selfish ambition in spiritual things shows
that we are ignorant of the real path to God's glory.*

Yesterday we saw that James and John, with their mother, posed a bold power-play question to the Lord Jesus. Now, as He answers them, they display another attitude at odds with the humble spirit: selfish ambition.

If the brothers' power-play request was brazen, it was also very foolish. They did not have a clue about what was involved if Jesus granted their request. "The cup that I am about to drink" was His way of referring to His suffering and death. When He asked James and John if they were prepared to drink that cup, Christ was saying that if you are His disciple, you must be prepared for suffering and hardship.

In fact, Jesus' words "to drink the cup" indicate that something very difficult lay ahead. Not only do those words refer to the Savior's own painful suffering and death (Matt. 26:39), but they mean we must stay the course to the end, enduring whatever is necessary. James, John, and the other disciples initially did not have such staying power.

James and John, thinking they would always persevere, overconfidently declared, "We are able." Peter brashly promised never to forsake the Lord, and all the other disciples echoed that pledge. But Peter denied Jesus three times, and the ambitious brothers, along with the rest of the disciples, fled after Jesus' arrest.

The disciples eventually did finish well and shared in the "fellowship of His sufferings" (Phil. 3:10). James became the first martyred apostle, and John was exiled to the island of Patmos. But such faithfulness was not attained in their own strength, nor by their ambitious maneuvering, but by the Spirit's power. This is a strong reminder to us that no position in God's kingdom is rewarded because of selfish human ambition, but only by His sovereign choice of "those for whom it has been prepared" (Matt. 20:23).

❖ ❖ ❖

Suggestions for Prayer: Pray that God would give you a view of service in His kingdom that is unclouded by your own ambitions.

For Further Study: Read and compare Psalms 15 and 75. What do they say about pride and humility? ❖ Meditate on several verses that relate to that theme.

> *". . . That no one of you might become arrogant*
> *in behalf of one against the other."*
> 1 CORINTHIANS 4:6

✧ ✧ ✧

Genuine humility among Christians will leave
no room for arrogant partisanship.

The Corinthian church was a notorious illustration of the sin of partisanship among believers. Its partisanship—some members claimed allegiance to Paul, some to Apollos, and some to Cephas (Peter)—was essentially caused by pride. Paul, as author of 1 Corinthians, vigorously opposed such pride of divisions, as Apollos and Peter would have.

The Corinthian believers did have reason to be thankful to God for sending them such quality leaders. And it was right for those in Corinth to respect and honor their spiritual elders. Scripture says, "Appreciate those who diligently labor among you, and have charge over you in the Lord and give you instruction" (1 Thess. 5:12). However, the Corinthians went far beyond God's Word and exalted the leaders for the prideful sake of themselves, the followers, thus creating partisan sects.

Such partisan spirit, even on behalf of godly leaders, always leads to hostility toward other faithful servants of God. And the motivation behind all this is pride, which is essentially having an inflated (arrogant) view of yourself, one that says "I'm for me." When pride rules the operations of any church, humility is forgotten, and fellowship and harmony are inevitably torn apart.

You can help prevent or counteract partisanship simply by considering that all the daily benefits you take for granted—food, housing, clothing, job, family—are yours because of God's kind providence. And if you're a Christian, you have eternal life, God's Word, spiritual gifts, and many other blessings that are all of grace. The apostle James reminds us, "Every good thing bestowed and every perfect gift is from above, coming down from the Father of lights" (James 1:17).

So again we see that God gives us every reason to be humble and leaves no place for pride and partisanship. If you have a good pastor and good elders or deacons, humbly thank God for them. You and your leaders are all stewards of God, entrusted for a short while to serve Him with His resources.

✧ ✧ ✧

Suggestions for Prayer: Pray that the Lord would help you be a positive influence for humility and harmony, rather than for pride and partisanship.

For Further Study: Read Acts 14:8-18. How did the people of Lystra react to Paul and Barnabas? ✧ How difficult was it for Paul and Barnabas to correct the people's errors?

> *"Whoever wishes to become great among you*
> *shall be your servant, and whoever wishes to be*
> *first among you shall be your slave."*
> MATTHEW 20:26-27

✧ ✧ ✧

In God's sight, greatness is marked by a humble, servant's heart.

Bible commentator R.C.H. Lenski once wrote that God's "great men are not sitting on top of lesser men, but bearing lesser men on their backs." Jesus would have agreed with Lenski's observation, but He did not see it as wrong to desire greater usefulness to God. Those standards of usefulness, however, are much more demanding than any worldly ideals for self-serving, domineering leadership. For example, Paul lists for us the high standards God has for church overseers (1 Tim. 3:1-7). God considers men great who are among those willing to be servants.

In Matthew 20:26-27, Jesus was speaking of genuine servanthood, not the "public servant" who merely uses his position to gain power and personal prestige. The original Greek word for "servant" referred to a person who did menial labor and was the lowest level of hired help. Jesus could have used a more noble word to denote obedient discipleship, but He picked this one (from which we get *deacon*) because it best described the selfless humility of one who served.

But in verse 27, Jesus intensifies His description of God's way to greatness. He tells us if we want to be great in His kingdom, we must be willing to be slaves. Whereas servants had some personal freedom, slaves were owned by their masters and could go only where their masters allowed and do only what their masters wanted. The application for us as believers is that "whether we live or die, we are the Lord's" (Rom. 14:8).

If you desire real spiritual greatness, you will be willing to work in the hard place, the lonely place, the place where you're not appreciated. You'll be willing to strive for excellence without becoming proud, and to endure suffering without getting into self-pity. It is to these godly attitudes and more that Christ will say, "Well done, good and faithful slave . . . enter into the joy of your master" (Matt. 25:21).

✧ ✧ ✧

Suggestions for Prayer: Ask the Lord to help you cultivate a servant's heart.

For Further Study: Read 1 Timothy 3:1-7 and make a list of the qualifications for an overseer (elder). ✧ Meditate on the implications of each trait, and write down ways in which humility relates to these leadership qualities.

"He who plants and he who waters are one;
but each will receive his own reward according to his own
labor. For we are God's fellow-workers."
1 CORINTHIANS 3:8-9

❖ ❖ ❖

Humble teamwork in ministry gives God all the glory
and promotes humility.

Paul's agricultural illustration of planting and watering makes it clear that the ministry works best in a team concept and that all credit for results must go to God. Paul (the one planting) and Apollos (the one watering) had done their God-appointed work faithfully and well, but they had to wait on the Lord for whatever was accomplished.

Paul mentions just two kinds of ministry in today's passage: planting the seed of the gospel by evangelism and watering it by further teaching. However, the apostle's point applies to every kind of ministry you might engage in. You might be tempted to think that your ministry is glamorous or significant and that everything revolves around your efforts. Or you could be envious of another believer who has a more public ministry than you. But all God's work is important, and Paul is reminding us that whatever work He has called us to is the most important ministry we can have.

First Corinthians 3 also reminds us that all believers who minister are one in the Body of Christ. If you recognize and accept this fact, it is a sure guarantee that humility will be present as you serve God. Humility simply leaves no place for fleshly competitiveness or selfish jealousy toward other Christians.

God will be certain to recognize your individual, faithful work—"according to [your] own labor"—in His day of rewards. But Jesus also taught His disciples and us the parable of the laborers in the vineyard (Matt. 20:1-16) to keep our perspectives balanced regarding the corporate nature of ministry in God's kingdom. None of us should look with pride at our own service and see ourselves as deserving more reward than someone who worked less time or in a less prominent position. It is not our ministry, any more than it was Paul's or Apollos's. It is God's, and all the glory goes to Him, not us.

❖ ❖ ❖

Suggestions for Prayer: Pray that God would give you a greater sense of humble gratitude for whatever type of ministry opportunity you have.

For Further Study: Compare Matthew 19:27-30 with 20:1-16. Why could the disciples have been tempted to feel superior? ❖ What does the landowner's behavior in the parable suggest about the character of God?

> *"Owe nothing to anyone except to love one another; for he*
> *who loves his neighbor has fulfilled the law."*
> ROMANS 13:8

❖ ❖ ❖

If believers fulfill their constant debt of love, they will have
a continual attitude of sacrificial humility.

Origen, the early church father, wisely said, "The debt of love remains with us permanently and never leaves us. This is a debt which we pay every day and forever owe." The primary reason you and I can pay that debt is that "the love of God has been poured out within our hearts through the Holy Spirit who was given to us" (Rom. 5:5). God's own love to us and every other believer is the bottomless well from which we can draw and then share with others.

If we have this wonderful, supernatural resource of love through the Holy Spirit, it only follows that we must submit to the Spirit. When we do so, all the enemies and impediments to humility—pride, unjustified power-grabbing, selfish ambition, partisanship, hatred—will melt away. What an overwhelming thought to consider that such humility can be ours because God Himself, through His Spirit, is teaching us to love as we yield to Him (1 Thess. 4:9).

At every turn we see humility going hand in hand with godly love. Genuine love never turns its "freedom into an opportunity for the flesh" (Gal. 5:13). It will not do anything to cause another Christian to fall into sin or even be offended in his conscience (Rom. 14:21). Love that is from God will "be kind to one another, tender-hearted, forgiving each other, just as God in Christ also has forgiven [us]" (Eph. 4:32).

The greatest test of love and humility is the willingness to sacrifice for the good of others. As we have already seen in our study of humility, Jesus was the ultimate example of this (Phil. 2:5-8). Our supreme demonstration of humility is when we imitate Him: "We know love by this, that He laid down His life for us; and we ought to lay down our lives for the brethren" (1 John 3:16).

❖ ❖ ❖

Suggestions for Prayer: Pray for an occasion today to show some facet of biblical love to another person. ❖ If nothing develops today, keep praying that the Lord would make you alert for future opportunities.

For Further Study: First John 4 is a wonderful chapter on God's love and its meaning for believers. According to the apostle, how can we know truth from error? ❖ What benefits derive from God's love?

> *"After two days the Passover is coming, and the Son of Man
> is to be delivered up for crucifixion."*
> MATTHEW 26:2

❖ ❖ ❖

*Jesus adhered perfectly to God's timetable for His death,
which was part of the Father's larger plan of redemption.*

The history of redemption most definitely centers on the cross of Jesus Christ. Hymn writer John Bowring expressed this fact well:

> *In the cross of Christ I glory,*
> *Tow'ring o'er the wrecks of time.*
> *All the light of sacred story*
> *Gathers round its head sublime.*

The apostle Paul was so convinced of the central importance of Christ's death on the cross that he told the Corinthians, "I determined to know nothing among you except Jesus Christ, and Him crucified" (1 Cor. 2:2). Paul knew that without the cross of Christ there is no salvation and no true Christianity.

Jesus Himself knew the length of His earthly life was determined by God's sovereign timetable and that the time of His death could not be altered or thwarted. Concerning control over His life, He declared, "I have authority to lay it down, and I have authority to take it up again" (John 10:18). As the Son of God, Jesus was able to look forward to His death and even predict that it would be in Jerusalem and that He would rise on the third day (Matt. 16:21).

During Jesus' ministry, people such as the Jewish leaders unknowingly threatened God's timetable when they sought to kill Him. But all premature attempts to murder Christ failed because they did not fit into God's sovereign plan for how, when, and why Jesus should die on the cross (John 1:29; Acts 2:23-24).

But Jesus' reference to the Passover in Matthew 26:2 did fit into God's plan; our Lord's suffering and death was perfectly timed to coincide with that celebration. Passover was known by the Jews as the festival in which sacrificial lambs were slain, but now the death of the Lamb of God would forever replace Passover's importance. We can take great comfort in all this, knowing "Christ our Passover also has been sacrificed" (1 Cor. 5:7) and that Jesus the Lamb was "foreknown before the foundation of the world, but has appeared in these last times for the sake of [us]" (1 Peter 1:19-20).

❖ ❖ ❖

Suggestions for Prayer: Thank the Lord that His sovereign plan for Christ's sacrificial death could not be changed by man's will.

For Further Study: Read John 10:1-18, and select several verses for meditation and memorization. What does the passage say about the nature of salvation?

*"Peter answered and said to Him, 'Even though all may fall
away because of You, I will never fall away.'"*
MATTHEW 26:33

✧ ✧ ✧

*Prior to Jesus' death, Peter's trust in himself rather than God
distorted his judgment concerning loyalty to Jesus.*

L ike a self-willed child, Peter often heard and believed only what he
wanted to. He failed to grasp the Lord's warning that his faith would be
severely tested. At the Last Supper Jesus told Peter, "Simon, Simon, behold,
Satan has demanded permission to sift you like wheat" (Luke 22:31). But
Peter was unfazed by these words. Instead, he boasted, "Lord, with You I am
ready to go both to prison and to death!" (v. 33).

Christ in His divine wisdom knew that Peter's claim would not hold true.
Therefore, He went further and soberly predicted during the Supper that Peter
would soon not only desert His Lord but also deny Him three times. Now in
Matthew 26, following Peter's latest outburst of overconfidence, Jesus is constrained to repeat His prediction. Amazingly, Peter did not believe the thrust
of Jesus' words. He would rather fool himself and believe that Jesus was mis-
taken about his faithfulness and loyalty.

In reality, Peter's pride deceptively told him it was impossible for him to
deny the Lord. It also deceived him by filling him with a sense of superiority
over others and a supreme confidence in his own strength.

Like Peter, we often display our pride and ignorance when we brashly claim
great self-confidence about something that turns out just the opposite a short
time later. For example, we might presumptuously assert to Christian friends
that we always maintain our testimony, no matter what the situation. Then, to
our shame, the very next week we lie, cheat, or shade the truth to get ourselves
out of a difficult circumstance.

But what a reassurance to know that Jesus was willing to die for proud,
thoughtless disciples such as Peter and careless followers such as us.
Furthermore, our Lord is constantly in the business of forgiving and restoring those who stumble: "He is faithful and righteous to forgive us our sins and
to cleanse us from all unrighteousness" (1 John 1:9).

✧ ✧ ✧

Suggestions for Prayer: Pray that today and every day God would make you
more confident in His grace and power and less reliant on your own wisdom.

For Further Study: Read Matthew 16:13-28. What important principle in
verses 24-26 can help you avoid Peter's impulsive mistakes?

"Then Jesus came with them to a place called Gethsemane."
MATTHEW 26:36

❖ ❖ ❖

The agony of Jesus' death, beginning with His ordeal in the Garden of Gethsemane, is something finite believers will never fully comprehend.

C.H. Spurgeon, in an 1880s sermon, said this to his congregation: "It will not be enough for you to hear, or read [about Christ]; you must do your own thinking and consider your Lord for yourselves. . . . Shut yourself up with Jesus, if you would know him." However, even those who most conscientiously follow Spurgeon's admonition to meditate on Jesus' Person and ministry find the effort reveals much about Him that is beyond human understanding.

As we continue our study of the events leading up to the Lord's sacrificial death, we also realize that it's difficult to grasp the full meaning of many of them. Even with the aid of the Spirit's illumination, we find the weight of Jesus' agony and suffering more than our minds can completely fathom. As the sinless God-man, He could perceive the full scope of sin's horror in a way we never can.

Like every other aspect of Jesus' life, though, His agony in Gethsemane was part of God's foreordained plan of redemption. Christ's intense sorrow and mental wrestling in the face of His mission to take away the sin of the world fit perfectly with Scripture's portrait of Him. The prophet Isaiah predicted that He would be "a man of sorrows, and acquainted with grief" (Isa. 53:3). In John 11:35 "Jesus wept" at Lazarus' grave. Luke 19:41 tells us that at His triumphal entry into Jerusalem, "He saw the city and wept over it."

The Lord Jesus' experience in Gethsemane was the final accumulation of all the hardships, sorrows, and griefs He had to deal with in His earthly ministry. And our Lord, through His dark struggle in the Garden, is the best role model we will ever have of a godly response to trials and temptations. In view of His sacrificial death for us, His response to adversity should cause us to stand in awe of our great Savior and desire to follow His example.

❖ ❖ ❖

Suggestions for Prayer: Pray that the Lord would strengthen your resolve to follow His example in dealing with trials.

For Further Study: Read John 11:1-46, and list some parallels you see in verses 30-44 between Jesus' reactions to Lazarus's death and how He would respond to His own suffering and death.

"Then He said to them, 'My soul is deeply grieved, to the point
of death; remain here and keep watch with Me.'"
MATTHEW 26:38

✧ ✧ ✧

In His time of greatest distress, Jesus realized His human
weakness and His need to depend on the Father.

As Jesus entered the Garden of Gethsemane with Peter, James, and John, He experienced a more profound anguish over sin and death than ever before. His deep and desolate distress was made more severe when He considered the many personal disappointments that confronted Him. First, there was the betrayal by Judas, one of His own disciples. Then there would be the desertion by the Eleven and Peter's threefold denial of his Master. Jesus would also be rejected by His own people, Israel, whose leaders would subject Him to all kinds of injustices before His death.

It shouldn't surprise us, then, that Christ tells His three trusted disciples, "My soul is deeply grieved, to the point of death." A person can die from such heavy sorrow, which in God's providence did not happen to Jesus. However, the magnitude of Jesus' sorrow apparently caused the blood capillaries right under His skin to burst. As more and more capillaries burst from the extreme emotional pressures Jesus endured, blood escaped through His pores, "and His sweat became like drops of blood, falling down upon the ground" (Luke 22:44). Such sweating was just one outward result of what our Lord felt at the excruciating prospect of His having to *become* sin for us. His holiness was completely repulsed by such a thought.

It was because Jesus did keep watch and look to His Father in prayer that He endured and passed this test in the Garden. Right up to the end, Christ lived His earthly life in total, sinless submission to the Father. As a believer, you also will face times of severe testing and trial when only direct communion with God will give you the strength to prevail. And you also have the added encouragement of Jesus' example in Gethsemane, the climax of His experiences through which He became a High Priest who can fully "sympathize with our weaknesses" (Heb. 4:15).

✧ ✧ ✧

Suggestions for Prayer: Praise God today that Jesus was divinely enabled to withstand the trials and temptations that assaulted Him at Gethsemane.

For Further Study: Read Matthew 4:1-11. Write down several key differences between Jesus' encounter in the wilderness and His experience in Gethsemane. ✧ What similarities do you see in Christ's response to the two situations?

*"He went a little beyond them, and fell on His face
and prayed, saying, 'My Father, if it is possible, let this cup
pass from Me; yet not as I will, but as Thou wilt."*
MATTHEW 26:39

✧ ✧ ✧

*Jesus' prayer in the Garden of Gethsemane is a
perfect model of perseverance in seeking God's will.*

By humbly and submissively raising the option, "If it is possible, let this cup pass from Me," Jesus was not questioning the validity of God's plan of redemption or the Son's responsibility in it. The thought of His becoming sin for us was weighing heavier and heavier on Jesus, and He simply wondered aloud to God if there could be a way other than the cross to deliver men from sin. But as always, Jesus made it clear that the deciding factor in what was done would be the Father's will, not the Son's.

In contrast, while Jesus was wrestling earnestly in prayer before the Father, Peter, James, and John were oblivious to the struggle because they slept. The need for sleep was natural at such a late hour (after midnight), and their emotions—confused, frustrated, depressed—concerning Jesus' death may have induced sleep as an escape (Luke 22:45 says they were "sleeping from sorrow").

But even those "legitimate reasons" are inadequate to excuse the disciples' lack of vigilance in prayer. As is often true of us, the disciples did not accept Jesus' instructions and warnings at face value. His repeated predictions of His suffering and death, His forecast of the disciples' desertion, and His anticipation of the anguish in Gethsemane should have been more than enough incentive for the three men to stay alert and support Christ. But the disciples failed to heed Jesus' words or follow His prayerful example at a time of crisis.

For us today, the record of Scripture is the great motivation to follow the Lord's example. We can meditate on the written narrative of Gethsemane and rejoice in something the disciples didn't yet have before Jesus' death—the presence of the Holy Spirit, who continually helps us pray as we ought (Rom. 8:26-27).

✧ ✧ ✧

Suggestions for Prayer: Ask the Lord to grant you both sensitivity and perseverance as you seek His will during times of prayer.

For Further Study: Read Luke 11:5-10 and 18:1-8. What is the common theme of these two parables? ✧ What does Jesus' teaching suggest about the challenging nature of prayer?

*"He came to the disciples and found them sleeping, and said
to Peter, 'So, you men could not keep watch with Me for
one hour? Keep watching and praying, that you may not enter
into temptation; the spirit is willing, but the flesh is weak.'"*
MATTHEW 26:40-41

✧ ✧ ✧

*The need for spiritual vigilance by Christians is constant,
but it can't be achieved in the power of the flesh.*

Jesus must have been terribly disappointed in the Garden of Gethsemane when He found the three disciples sleeping. As He labored diligently in prayer before the Father, Peter, James, and John began their desertion of Jesus. They could not even stay awake and offer Him support during His time of greatest need.

Given all that was happening, the Lord's question, "So, you men could not keep watch with Me for one hour?" was not a harsh rebuke. In the spirit of a mentor, Jesus exhorted the three about their need for divine help: "Keep watching and praying, that you may not enter into temptation."

The phrase "keep watching and praying" indicates that all believers must have vigilance. Jesus wants all of us to anticipate temptation and seek God's help to resist the adversary, just as He did during His vigilant prayer in the Garden.

Our own best efforts to overcome Satan will certainly fail. The only way to deal with the Devil is to flee immediately from him into God's presence and prayerfully leave matters with Him.

But even when we know and seek to practice what Jesus told the disciples, it is often difficult to do what is right. Jesus saw His three dearest friends' reaction and was in the midst of His own spiritual struggle, so He acknowledged, "The spirit is willing, but the flesh is weak." The apostle Paul also knew the spiritual battle was real and very difficult (Rom. 7:15-23). But Paul was confident, too, that the only source of victory in our most intimidating spiritual challenges is obedience to the power of Jesus Christ: "Who will set me free from the body of this death? Thanks be to God through Jesus Christ our Lord!" (vv. 24-25).

✧ ✧ ✧

Suggestions for Prayer: Ask the Lord's forgiveness for any recent times when you have failed to be alert and diligent when praying.

For Further Study: Read 1 Peter 5:6-11. What is the first key to spiritual success? ✧ Why must we be alert for Satan? ✧ What makes faithfulness in suffering worthwhile?

". . . A great multitude with swords and clubs,
from the chief priests and elders of the people."
MATTHEW 26:47

❖ ❖ ❖

The crowd that captured Jesus at Gethsemane
illustrates the world's sinful, hateful rejection of Jesus Christ.

A crowd can have a positive, uplifting influence, as when a large group of neighbors bands together to help someone in need. But crowds can also have a negative impact, such as when they incite riots or heckle someone who is trying to give a speech.

The multitude that came to the Garden of Gethsemane to capture Jesus is a prime example of a crowd that formed for an evil purpose. That throng was not at all like the spontaneous groups of admirers that often sought the Lord. Instead, it was a carefully selected group whose only purpose was to arrest Jesus and ensure that He was executed.

Judas most likely rushed away from the upper room and informed the Jewish leaders that now was the time they had long waited for—an opportunity to seize Jesus, convict Him of rebellion against Rome, and force the Romans to put Him to death. By now the conspiracy against Jesus had grown very large and involved the Sadducees, the Pharisees, and the entire Sanhedrin. In their desire to guarantee Jesus' capture, the leaders gathered perhaps a thousand men that night.

This evil group was a prophetic portrait of the world's opposition to Christ through the ages. The crowd illustrated sinful disobedience by falsely accusing Him of crimes, by mindlessly and selfishly participating in His arrest (even without an informed opinion about Him), and by cowardly using the cover of darkness and the safety of an obscure location to implement the leaders' plot.

The unbelieving world has always disdained God's kingdom and the mission of His Son. Instead of coming in repentance and faith and reverently embracing Christ's work on the cross, the world wants to find any excuse to do away with the Savior. In contrast, believers are called to stand apart from any unbelieving crowd and defend the name of Jesus Christ.

❖ ❖ ❖

Suggestions for Prayer: Pray for the discernment and courage not to follow the mind-set of the world's crowd, but to rather be obedient to the Lord Jesus.

For Further Study: The large crowds that followed Jesus earlier in His ministry were not always sincere. Read John 6, and note the various ways the people misunderstood Jesus' message. ❖ How did He answer their objections and grumblings?

*"He who was betraying Him gave them a sign, saying,
'Whomever I shall kiss, He is the one; seize Him.' And immedi-
ately he came to Jesus and said, 'Hail, Rabbi!' and kissed Him.
And Jesus said to him, 'Friend, do what you have come for.'"*

MATTHEW 26:48-50

❖ ❖ ❖

*Judas Iscariot, in his attitudes and actions,
is a classic example of the false believer.*

As one of the Twelve, Judas was extremely disappointed at the kind of Messiah Jesus turned out to be. Instead of teaching the disciples how to conquer and control, Jesus taught them how to submit and serve. Any ambitions Judas might have had for gaining wealth, power, or prestige by being a close follower of Jesus were frustrated.

Judas' compulsive unbelief, combined with his relentless greed and ambition, found a perverse, temporal fulfillment when Satan entered him, and he struck a deal with the Jewish leaders to betray Jesus for money (Luke 22:3-6). As one possessed by the Devil, Judas's evil actions were no longer his own, though he was still responsible for them.

Judas could have chosen any of several ways to identify Jesus to the mob, but under Satan's direction he selected a kiss. This kiss was normally given as a sign of affection between close friends or between pupil and teacher. In the context of Judas' scheme, however, the kiss could hardly have been more despicable because he twisted its meaning so cynically. It is hard to imagine what grief Jesus must have felt when the one who had been treasurer for the Twelve brashly came forward, said "Hail, Rabbi!" and kissed his Master.

Judas' situation was unique, but his basic attitude is typical of all false believers. The church has always had those who hypocritically profess allegiance to Christ but at heart are really His enemies. Whether it is to advance their business or profession, gain social acceptance, or salve a guilty conscience, hypocrites identify with the church for various reasons. But like Judas, their basic motivation is sinful self-interest.

May God give us the courage to examine our hearts and repent of such traits, and the discernment to deal biblically with false believers in the church.

❖ ❖ ❖

Suggestions for Prayer: Ask God to graciously protect the integrity and purity of your local church.

For Further Study: Read the Epistle of Jude, and list the key traits of false teachers. ❖ What should you know and do regarding such people (vv. 17-23)?

*"Then Jesus said to him, 'Put your sword back into its place;
for all those who take up the sword shall perish by the sword.'"*
MATTHEW 26:52

❖ ❖ ❖

*It is wrong to violently take justice into our own hands,
even to defend or promote the name of Christ.*

The Body of Christ does not grow and strengthen itself by physical warfare. Every time it has endeavored to do so, the name and cause of Jesus
Christ have been harmed. Such wars as the Crusades in the Holy Land or later
religious wars between Catholics and Protestants in Europe served no scriptural purpose. As Jesus taught many times, and as Paul reiterated to the
Corinthians, "The weapons of our warfare are not of the flesh, but divinely
powerful for the destruction of fortresses" (2 Cor. 10:4).

Peter, in his usual headstrong fashion, had not yet understood this principle the night of Jesus' arrest. That's when Peter used his sword and cut off the
ear of one of the high priest's prominent slaves. But the impulsive disciple's
reaction was all wrong. Peter no doubt took Christ's earlier statement, "Let
him who has no sword sell his robe and buy one" (Luke 22:36) much too literally. Our Lord was actually speaking of preparedness for spiritual, not physical, warfare.

Jesus therefore had to instruct Peter to put away his weapon. In effect, He
was saying, "Peter, no matter how unjust My arrest is, you must not respond
with vigilante action. If you do that and kill someone else, your own life will
justly be forfeited as punishment."

Christ's power has been demonstrated many times—in person to Peter and
through Scripture to us. It is incredible that any of us should think He needs the
puny help of a sword, a gun, or any other human device. Christ's battles are won
in the strength of His sovereign power alone, as He pointed out to Peter: "Do you
think that I cannot appeal to My Father, and He will at once put at My disposal
more than twelve legions [72,000] of angels?" (Matt. 26:53).

❖ ❖ ❖

Suggestions for Prayer: Ask God's forgiveness for times when you've been
too quick to seek your own justice during arguments or conflicts.

For Further Study: Read 2 Kings 19:14-37. How did King Hezekiah respond
when God's people and land were threatened? ❖ How did the prophet Isaiah
support Hezekiah's actions? ❖ How did God finally respond to the Assyrians'
threat?

"Then all the disciples left Him and fled."
MATTHEW 26:56

❖ ❖ ❖

*In defecting from Christ in an hour of crisis,
the eleven disciples displayed certain marks of faithlessness.*

Sometimes no amount of truth and logic will ever persuade someone to change their mind. We all know that is true from times we have debated another person on a particular topic. Nothing we say will convince them that their plans may be wrong or their opinions unsound. Jesus knew that far better than us as he continued to face the hostile crowd in Gethsemane.

As the Son of God, Jesus could confidently tell the crowd that "All this has taken place that the Scriptures of the prophets may be fulfilled" (Matt. 26:56). The Son knew that, completely apart from the armed mob's evil motives and intentions, the Father was sovereignly using the situation to accomplish His righteous and gracious purposes.

But Jesus' words to the crowd obviously gave little comfort or reassurance to His own disciples. They finally realized Christ was going to be seized. Fear and panic gripped them when they further realized they might have to risk suffering and death with Him. Therefore, each of the eleven "left Him and fled."

The disciples' faithless desertion reveals several common characteristics of weak commitment. First, any believer who neglects God's Word and prayer will be unprepared and unfaithful when testing comes. Second, a weak disciple is likely to be impulsive, like Peter, and respond to a crisis with faulty human discernment. Third, a defective disciple tends to be impatient, like Jesus' men, refusing to listen to His promises and unwilling to wait for His deliverance.

It's easy to criticize Jesus' disciples for their faithless lack of resolve in letting Him down and running away when things became difficult. But if you are an honest follower of Christ, you know that you have sometimes compromised or run away when your faith was tested. As a result, you need to confess your failings and lean more than ever on God's Word, prayer, and the strength of the Holy Spirit to help you stay the course (Eph. 5:15-21).

❖ ❖ ❖

Suggestions for Prayer: Commit yourself today to be faithful to Christ, no matter what circumstance confronts you, and pray for strength.

For Further Study: John 14 comes from a section of the Gospels called the Upper Room Discourse. Read this chapter, and identify the verses in which Jesus promises peace. ❖ What additional Helper does He promise to send believers? ❖ What is the key to obedience (vv. 23-24)?

> *"The chief priests and the whole Council kept trying*
> *to obtain false testimony against Jesus, in order*
> *that they might put Him to death."*
> MATTHEW 26:59

❖ ❖ ❖

The only evidence of guilt against Jesus was man-made and contrived.

The essence of the Jews' ancient legal system is found in the Lord's words to Moses and Israel: "You shall not distort justice; you shall not be partial" (Deut. 16:19). Therefore, it is truly amazing to consider what twisted measures the Jewish leaders resorted to in their trial of Jesus.

The Council, or Sanhedrin, was authorized to judge only those cases in which charges already had been brought. But in Jesus' case, with no formal charges yet made and with the Jews' rush to judgment, the Council had to act illegally as a prosecuting body to keep the chief priests' murder plot moving forward.

As the sinless Son of God, Jesus was innocent of any wrongdoing. Therefore, the only way for the Jews to convict Him was to obtain false testimony against Him. And to do that, the leaders had to pervert the very heart of their judicial system and endorse the words of liars.

But the Jews quickly found it was not easy even to manipulate and assemble false charges. As is so often the case with liars, what they testified to was not only false but inconsistent. Mark's Gospel notes that even the two witnesses' more usable charges about Jesus and the destruction of the temple were not consistent (14:57-59).

It is one of the strongest affirmations in the Bible to Christ's moral and spiritual perfection that not a single human witness could make an accusation that would convict Him of a crime. After all the desperate maneuvering by the Jews to come up with even the flimsiest testimony against the Lord, He stood innocent of any violation of God's moral or spiritual law. Instead, it is the unjust, hateful group of men that will one day stand before God condemned for their sinful actions in falsely accusing the Savior.

❖ ❖ ❖

Suggestions for Prayer: Pray for wisdom and integrity in the judges who make decisions in today's courtrooms.

For Further Study: Read Deuteronomy 16:18-20 and 19:15-20. How do these passages show that Jesus' trial before the Sanhedrin was based on wrong principles (list several factors)?

"'Behold, you have now heard the blasphemy; what do you think?' They answered and said, 'He is deserving of death!'"
MATTHEW 26:65-66

❖ ❖ ❖

Like many through the centuries, members of the Sanhedrin rejected Jesus Christ without fairly judging all the evidence.

Lynching is an activity we don't hear much about today. But during earlier generations, the heinous crime occurred quite regularly. Innocent people, or those merely presumed guilty (prior to any trial), were tortured and killed, usually by angry, hateful mobs. Often the person lynched was a victim of racial or political prejudice or some other irrational fear held by the perpetrators.

The members of the Sanhedrin certainly held blind prejudices against Jesus. No amount of evidence would open their eyes to the truth of who He was. Those unbelieving leaders of Israel discounted Jesus' claims to deity long before they placed Him on trial. He had even pleaded with them, "If I do not do the works of My Father, do not believe Me; but if I do them, though you do not believe Me, believe the works, that you may know and understand that the Father is in Me, and I in the Father" (John 10:37-38).

In today's passage the high priest Caiaphas reacts forcefully to Jesus' agreement that He is God's Son and the Messiah (see Matt. 26:64). Caiaphas's mind was made up; he was convinced that Jesus had blasphemed, and he was determined to rush forward with this "evidence" to condemn Jesus to death. Caiaphas and the Council could barely wait to render a verdict. The high priest asked for their opinion on Jesus' guilt, and immediately the Council members asserted, "He is deserving of death!"

The irony of the Jewish leaders' condemnation of Jesus was their blind insistence that He was a blasphemer when in reality they were the blasphemers for their rejection of the Lord and His message. Even more sobering is that every person who has ever finally rejected Christ is also guilty of blasphemy and will suffer the same fate as the chief priests and elders: "He who does not obey the Son shall not see life, but the wrath of God abides on him" (John 3:36).

❖ ❖ ❖

Suggestions for Prayer: Pray for someone you know who has been closed to the gospel. Ask God to open his or her heart and grant him or her repentance.

For Further Study: Read Hebrews 3—4. What spiritual attitude do these chapters warn of? What Old Testament parallel does the writer make?

*"Peter remembered the word which Jesus
had said, 'Before a cock crows, you will deny Me three
times.' And he went out and wept bitterly."*

MATTHEW 26:75

✧ ✧ ✧

Even when a believer sins greatly, God is there to forgive and restore.

Peter's denial of the Lord Jesus was a great tragedy. But Peter had already taken a number of steps toward denial before uttering a single word that repudiated Christ. First, he presumptuously boasted that he would never fall away (Matt. 26:33). Second, Peter was insubordinate to Jesus and blatantly refused to accept the Lord's prediction of his disloyalty (v. 35). Third, he was prayerless in the Garden of Gethsemane (vv. 40-41). Fourth, he foolishly and unnecessarily wielded the sword to defend Jesus (vv. 51-52). Finally, Peter compromised himself and willfully went to a place (the high priest's court-yard) of spiritual danger (v. 69), where his faith could be tested beyond its endurance.

As Peter tried to wait inconspicuously in the high priest's courtyard, on three occasions he was confronted by other bystanders and accused of being one of Jesus' followers. Peter's reaction showed he had lost all sense of real-ity and awareness of God. Each accusation was a bit more incriminating and provoked a more vehement denial by Peter. After the third denial, according to the Lord's providence, Peter's slide was halted. A penetrating look from Jesus Himself (Luke 22:61) and his remembering of Jesus' prediction that he would deny Him three times were enough to bring Peter to his senses. As our verse explains it, "he went out and wept bitterly."

Peter's tears were not merely tears of remorse—they indicated a true sor-row and turning from sin. It was not until he saw Christ's face and remem-bered His words that Peter grasped the seriousness of his sin and repented. This is a profound lesson for you and me. Peter's sin itself did not cause him to repent; his forgiveness and restoration came only when he turned from sin to God. After His resurrection, Jesus affirmed Peter's restored love three times (John 21:15-17). This gift of restored fellowship through God's gracious for-giveness is available to all believers (1 John 1:7, 9).

✧ ✧ ✧

Suggestions for Prayer: Commit your thoughts and plans to God throughout the day so that you may avoid the kind of compromising situation Peter was in.

For Further Study: Read Psalm 51. How does David's dealing with sin par-allel what we saw about Peter's coming to his senses? ✧ What verses from this psalm are especially helpful in seeing this parallel?

> *"Father, forgive them; for they do not know*
> *what they are doing."*
> LUKE 23:34

❖ ❖ ❖

As Jesus forgave others (including us),
we should extend forgiveness to those who wrong us.

Jesus had a forgiving heart right up to the end, even after He had experienced a lifetime of mankind's worst treatment. He came down to a world He had created, but that world rebuffed Him. Its inhabitants' eyes were blinded by sin, and they could not see any beauty in Jesus. Almost immediately after His humble birth in a stable, King Herod sought to have Him killed (Matt. 2:13, 16-18). And the Jewish leaders on various occasions contested Christ's teachings and looked for opportunities to seize Him and kill Him. The cross was just the culmination of a lifetime of persecution against Jesus.

Jesus' death by crucifixion was one of the most humiliating, painful forms of execution the world has ever known. From a human perspective, we would have expected Him to plead with God the Father for mercy or to be enraged at God and denounce Him for allowing Him to be crucified. If we had written the original script for Jesus' crucifixion scene, we probably would have had Him screaming threats of retaliation at His killers. But our Savior did none of those things. Instead, He asked His Father to forgive His enemies.

The Lord Jesus prayed for the most important need His executioners would ever have. They would never be able to enter the presence of a holy God if their sins were not forgiven. Christ was concerned that His opponents, who were ignorantly putting Him to death, have an opportunity to be forgiven rather than endure God's vengeance.

Such an attitude of love and mercy should also be ours. We, unlike Jesus, are sinners ourselves who need constant forgiveness. Therefore, when we are wronged, our primary concern ought to be that God would forgive the one who has sinned against us. An excellent model of this attitude is Stephen, who prayed as he was being stoned to death, "Lord, do not hold this sin against them!" (Acts 7:60). He followed Christ's own example of love and forgiveness, and so should we.

❖ ❖ ❖

Suggestions for Prayer: Pray that you may have a more consistently forgiving attitude toward others who wrong or offend you.

For Further Study: Read Matthew 18:21-35. What is implied in Jesus' figurative expression "seventy times seven" (v. 22) regarding forgiving others? ❖ Ultimately, how much does it matter that we maintain a forgiving attitude (vv. 32-35)?

"Truly I say to you, today you shall be with Me in Paradise."
LUKE 23:43

✧ ✧ ✧

*The circumstances are never too adverse, nor the hour too late,
to offer the gospel of Christ to someone.*

Jesus was crucified between two criminals (thieves)—one on each side of His cross. At first the two men both joined the onlookers in hurling unbelieving rhetoric at the Lord (Mark 15:32). But one of the thieves obviously had a change of heart as the hours elapsed. He rebuked the other thief by pointing out Jesus' sinlessness (Luke 23:40-41) and then expressed his need of salvation: "Jesus, remember me when You come in Your kingdom!" (v. 42). And Jesus graciously answered the thief's request.

The dying thief's conversion is an extraordinary story. At Calvary there was nothing convincing or favorable about Jesus. From man's vantage point He was dying because He had been completely rejected; even the disciples had deserted Him. Jesus appeared weak, disgraced, and ashamed. When the thief uttered his plea for help, no one was pointing to Jesus and saying, "Behold, the Lamb of God who takes away the sin of the world!" (John 1:29).

Given the circumstances, it is difficult to comprehend how Christ could be concerned with the immediate salvation of a wretched thief who was justly being executed for his crimes. But our Lord cared very much about the destiny of that man's soul. Jesus' desire to see sinners saved was constant, because He came to seek and save the lost (Luke 19:10). His concern for the unsaved is the supreme example and motivation to us in reaching out to others.

The thief's salvation is also a clear illustration of the sovereignty of God in redemption. So often the church wants to attribute someone's salvation to human cleverness in presenting a well-crafted message at just the right time and in the most appropriate place. But salvation is always the direct result of God's intervening grace. The sovereign work of God's Spirit, not circumstances, gave the thief a saving understanding about who Jesus was and what His death was accomplishing.

✧ ✧ ✧

Suggestions for Prayer: Ask God for the courage to reach out with the good news of salvation no matter what the circumstances.

For Further Study: Read John 4:1-42. What excuses could Jesus have used for not talking to the woman? ✧ How did He keep His focus during His conversation with her?

"When Jesus therefore saw His mother, and the disciple
whom He loved standing nearby, He said to His mother,
'Woman, behold, your son!'"
JOHN 19:26

✧ ✧ ✧

No matter what trials we have, it is still possible
to be concerned for others' needs.

As the time for Jesus' death grew closer, His mother's well-being was on His heart and mind. His concern is consistent with what we have already seen in our brief study of some of Jesus' last words on the cross—our Lord was faithful in ministry no matter what the cost.

Here the object of Jesus' focus shifted to a small group of five friends at the foot of His cross. And out of this sympathetic band, which included the disciple John, Salome (John's mother), Mary the wife of Clopas, and Mary Magdalene, Christ's attention drew especially toward His mother.

Mary, the mother of our Lord, was perhaps the neediest person of any in that cluster that stood beneath the cross. She was most likely a widow by this time; otherwise, Jesus would not have shown so much special concern for her future welfare. Mary was also seeing and feeling the fulfillment of Simeon's prophecy that her soul would be pierced because of Jesus (Luke 2:34-35). Drawn to the place of her son's execution by loving concern and sorrow, Mary stood with the others but undoubtedly felt very alone as she suffered quietly.

At that moment Jesus graciously intervened and reminded Mary that she needed to regard Him not primarily as her son but as her Savior. When Jesus called Mary "Woman," He was using a title of respect. His intent was simply to commit Mary into John's care.

At Calvary, Christ experienced the agony of the cross, the weight of the world's sin, and the wrath of God the Father. Yet through all His ordeal, which is beyond our comprehension, Jesus took some moments to show compassion to others who were hurting. That's a pattern we are to follow. We should never be so overwhelmed with our own pain and trials—and certainly not life's routine, daily cares, and burdens—that we lose sight of others' needs.

✧ ✧ ✧

Suggestions for Prayer: Thank God for Jesus' incredible example of compassion in the midst of the most adverse circumstances.

For Further Study: Read Matthew 27:46; John 19:28; John 19:30; and Luke 23:46. What additional traits do these reveal about Jesus? ✧ Look for at least one example you can apply to your life.

> *"Now from the sixth hour darkness fell upon*
> *all the land until the ninth hour."*
> MATTHEW 27:45

❖ ❖ ❖

The darkness over the land while Jesus bore our sin
was an indicator that the cross was a place of divine judgment.

The biblical phenomenon of light was not associated with Christ's death. Instead, as today's verse says, "Darkness fell upon all the land until the ninth hour [3:00 P.M.]."

Scripture says little about that darkness. Ancient historical reports mention an unusual, worldwide darkness that seemed to coincide with the date of Christ's death. Astronomical records indicate that the sun and moon were too far apart that day for a normal solar eclipse. Therefore, the darkness had to be caused by God's intervention.

But you may still ask, "Why did God intervene like this when Jesus died?" Again, sources outside Scripture provide a reasonable clue. For many years the Jewish rabbis taught that a darkening of the sun meant judgment from God for an especially heinous sin. Many passages in Scripture make the link between darkness and God's judgment. Jesus spoke several times of divine judgment in terms of "outer darkness," where "there shall be weeping and gnashing of teeth" (Matt. 8:12; 22:13; 25:30).

In sending darkness over the whole earth for three hours, God presents us with an object lesson concerning His attitude on the day Jesus died. The darkness was God's sign of judgment against mankind for the gross sin of rejecting and murdering His beloved Son. It is also a sign of God's reaction to sin as a whole. Darkness is a graphic portrayal of the cross as the focal point of God's wrath, a place of His immense judgment, where sin was poured out on His Son Jesus, our Savior. This twofold object lesson ought to be a constant, fresh reminder to us of how seriously God views sin and how vital it was that the Lord Jesus die on our behalf.

❖ ❖ ❖

Suggestions for Prayer: Thank God that He can use aspects of nature to illustrate spiritual truth for our finite minds. ❖ Pray that the Lord will never let you take for granted the awesome seriousness of the events at Calvary.

For Further Study: Read Exodus 10:12-29. How did the plague of darkness differ from the plague of locusts? ❖ What was Pharaoh's ultimate response to these two plagues? ❖ How does this preview the onlookers' reaction to seeing darkness at the cross?

"My God, My God, why hast Thou forsaken Me?"
MATTHEW 27:46

✧ ✧ ✧

*God always must turn His back on sin, even if that meant
for a short time severing fellowship with His Son.*

The Reformer Martin Luther is said to have gained no insight at all when he secluded himself and tried to understand Jesus' temporary alienation from the Father at Calvary. But in the secrets of divine sovereignty, the God-man was separated from God at Calvary as the Father's wrath was poured out on the innocent Son, who had become sin for all those who believe in Him.

Forsaken means that a person is abandoned, cast off, deserted; he feels alone and desolate. Jesus must have had all those feelings and more. His cry from the cross could be restated this way: "My God, My God, with whom I have had eternal, unbroken fellowship, why have You deserted Me?" Against that backdrop of uninterrupted intimacy, Jesus' being forsaken by God becomes an even more crushing experience for Him. Sin did what nothing else had done or could do—it caused Christ's separation from His Heavenly Father.

Jesus' separation does not in any sense mean He stopped being God or the Son. It does mean that for a while Jesus ceased to know intimate fellowship with the Father, similar to how a child might for a time cease to have fellowship with his human father.

God had to turn His back on Jesus while the Son was on the cross because God could not look upon sin (Hab. 1:13), even in His own Son. Christ, in going to the cross, took upon Himself "our transgressions . . . our iniquities" (Isa. 53:5) and became "a curse for us" (Gal. 3:13) and "the propitiation for our sins" (1 John 4:10).

Our fallen minds, like Luther's, are unable to grasp all the significance of today's verse. But as our Lord experienced anguish over the separation sin caused, we ought to grieve over how our sins break off the fellowship God wants to have with us.

✧ ✧ ✧

Suggestions for Prayer: Pray that God would give you the discernment to see the seriousness of sin and the motivation to repent of and shun any besetting sin in your life.

For Further Study: Read John 3:18-20, 36. What do these verses say about the basic seriousness of sin? ✧ What is the only remedy for sin's evil effects?

> *"Now the centurion, and those who were with him . . . became*
> *very frightened and said, 'Truly this was the Son of God!'"*
>
> MATTHEW 27:54

✧ ✧ ✧

The testimony of the soldiers after Jesus' crucifixion
demonstrates the sufficiency of His death for all sinners.

M ost of the time our daily activities are dictated by the routine respon-sibilities of our jobs. That's how it was for the Roman soldiers who stood at the foot of the cross when Jesus gave up His life. They were there simply out of duty, to make sure the crucifixion was carried out properly and without interference.

The soldiers probably had little knowledge of Judaism and had not heard of Jesus before, unless it was by hearsay. Therefore, they really had no idea why the Jewish leaders and most of the crowd were so intent on killing Him. To these anonymous soldiers, Christ's claims to be the Son of God and a king seemed equally ludicrous and harmless.

The darkness and the earthquake, however, radically changed their attitudes. Their emotional fear produced by those events quickly turned to reverential awe for who Jesus was. They sensed that the natural phenomena had a supernatural origin and suddenly realized that Jesus was indeed the Son of God.

Jesus' gracious and profound words, spoken from the cross and before Pilate, and His humble, selfless demeanor worked on the soldiers' hearts. But it was the ministry of the Holy Spirit that ultimately convinced them to con-fess Christ's deity.

The declaration "Truly this was the Son of God!" proclaimed by the centu-rion (see also Mark 15:39) on behalf of himself and his men, was for the sol-diers a profession of faith in Christ. Although that testimony was uttered by someone else after Jesus had died, it became in essence His final testimony from the cross. It also offers us compelling proof that His grace can extend to all sin-ners, even to those who helped put Him to death. In John 12:32 Jesus announced, "And I, if I be lifted up from the earth, will draw all men to Myself."

✧ ✧ ✧

Suggestions for Prayer: Pray for someone today who needs salvation—per-haps someone whom you quit praying for because you thought it unlikely they would ever respond to the gospel.

For Further Study: Read Mark 10:17-27. The young man was outwardly a prime candidate for salvation, in contrast to the Roman soldiers. What kept him outside the kingdom? ✧ What do verses 26-27 teach about the nature of salvation?

"And many women were there looking on from a distance, who
had followed Jesus from Galilee, ministering to Him."
MATTHEW 27:55

✧ ✧ ✧

The women who supported Jesus' ministry all the way
to the cross are fine examples of compassionate loyalty.

C aring, consistent loyalty is a wonderful characteristic of godly women. This trait is probably more evident in them than it is in godly men. The women by the cross were the main group of believing eyewitnesses to Jesus' crucifixion. They also showed incredible loyalty in the face of ridicule and danger. This courage contrasted with the disciples who, except for John, had fled in fear the night before Jesus was crucified.

We saw in a lesson earlier this month that some of the women, including our Lord's mother, had been watching the crucifixion from the foot of the cross (John 19:25-27). But in today's verse the women are described as "looking on from a distance." They had not suddenly become afraid of the Roman soldiers or the Jewish leaders. Neither had they become ashamed of being known as Jesus' followers. They withdrew because their grief was deep and their hope shattered at the impending death of their Master. The women's endurance, however, was undaunted.

Throughout His ministry, devoted women such as those at the cross ministered generously to Jesus and the disciples. Luke 8:2-3 says, "Mary who was called Magdalene . . . Joanna the wife of Chuza . . . Susanna, and many others . . . were contributing to their support out of their private means." It is probable that most of the meals Jesus and the Twelve ate were prepared by faithful women.

The women who followed Jesus set the standard for faithful service and compassionate loyalty that Paul later outlined for godly women: "a reputation for good works . . . washed the saints' feet . . . assisted those in distress, and . . . devoted herself to every good work" (1 Tim. 5:10). Such self-giving acts of practical service are marks of excellence and spiritual maturity that ought to be evident in the lives of all believers.

✧ ✧ ✧

Suggestions for Prayer: Is there a Christian friend to whom you can affirm your loyalty? Pray for an opportunity to serve that person in a practical way.

For Further Study: Read John 13:3-17. How did Jesus demonstrate the theme of today's study? ✧ What impact did Jesus' example have on Peter?

> *"Do not be afraid; for I know that you are looking for*
> *Jesus who has been crucified. He is not here, for*
> *He has risen, just as He said."*
> MATTHEW 28:5-6

✧ ✧ ✧

The fact of Jesus' resurrection is the culmination of redemptive history
and the essential basis of the Christian faith.

Without the Resurrection, our Christian faith would just be a lot of wishful thinking, no better than human philosophies and speculative religions. In fact, the noted seventeenth-century philosopher John Locke, some of whose ideas were incorporated into the Declaration of Independence, wrote, "Our Saviour's resurrection is truly of great importance in Christianity, so great that His being or not being the Messiah stands or falls with it."

From its very early accounts, Scripture has contained the message of resurrection hope. Death has never been the end for the believer, but simply a gateway to eternal life in Heaven. Abraham was ready to sacrifice his only son Isaac because in faith "he considered that God is able to raise men from the dead" (Heb. 11:19). The Lord assured Daniel that believers "will awake . . . to everlasting life" (Dan. 12:2).

The Resurrection was the focal point of Christ's teaching to the disciples about His sufferings and death: "The Son of Man must suffer many things and be rejected by the elders and the chief priests and the scribes, and be killed, and after three days rise again" (Mark 8:31). It is therefore completely understandable that Matthew and the other three Gospel writers all included an historical account of Jesus' resurrection in their narratives.

Paul knew that without the Resurrection our salvation could not have been possible. He was also convinced that the truth of the Resurrection must be believed or else salvation cannot be received: "If you confess with your mouth Jesus as Lord, and believe in your heart that God raised Him from the dead, you shall be saved" (Rom. 10:9).

It's no wonder that Paul, the other apostles, and every leader in the early church continually proclaimed Christ's resurrection as the culmination of His ministry. Those men were so captivated by the significance of the Resurrection that they could not help but preach it. And that should be our attitude today.

✧ ✧ ✧

Suggestions for Prayer: Thank God for the truth of John 11:25, which gives us the hope of resurrection in Jesus' own words.

For Further Study: Read Acts 2:14-36 or 3:12-26. What is the focal point of Peter's evangelistic sermons? ✧ How does he prove his theme?

*"Now I make known to you, brethren, the gospel which I preached
to you, which also you received, in which also you stand."*
1 CORINTHIANS 15:1

❖ ❖ ❖

The true church has consistently testified
to the power of the Resurrection.

Kenneth Scott Latourette observed in his *History of the Expansion of
Christianity*: "It was the conviction of the resurrection of Jesus which
lifted his followers out of the despair into which his death had cast them and
which led to the perpetuation of a movement begun by him."

This statement was true for the church at Corinth, even with its many problems. The apostle Paul opens his well-known chapter on the Resurrection in
1 Corinthians 15 by implicitly affirming the Corinthians' testimony to that
doctrine. Simply by receiving the gospel and having their lives transformed,
the believers at Corinth demonstrated the reality of Jesus' resurrection. And
that resurrection is what empowered the gospel. Paul did not need to explicitly remind the Corinthians of Christ's rising to life until verse 4, "He was
raised on the third day." The apostle was confident at the outset that the
Corinthians had already believed in the truth of the Lord's resurrection.

The fact that the Corinthian church continued to exist, though beset with
problems of immaturity and other weaknesses, was a solid witness to the
power of the gospel of the risen Christ. Only a living Savior could have converted some of the hardened sinners of Corinth—extortioners, idolaters, the
sexually immoral—into a community of the redeemed. Paul was concerned
and distressed about many of the things that did and did not happen in the
church at Corinth, but he did not hesitate to call the core group of members
there "brethren."

In spite of many challenges from skepticism, persecution, heresy, and
unfaithfulness, the church through the centuries has continued to testify to the
reality of Christ's resurrection. The true church celebrates that truth often, not
just on Easter Sunday. Actually, because the church gathers on Sunday, the
Lord's Day, the first day of the week (when Jesus rose), we remember the
Resurrection every week. Praise the Lord for that reminder the next time you
worship on the Lord's Day.

❖ ❖ ❖

Suggestions for Prayer: Thank God that His church was faithful in the past
to testify to the truth of the Resurrection.

For Further Study: Read Acts 4, and list some things that suggest a testimony
to the power of the Resurrection.

> *"And last of all, as it were to one untimely born,*
> *He appeared to me also."*
>
> 1 CORINTHIANS 15:8

✧ ✧ ✧

The resurrection power of Christ
transformed Paul into a preacher of the gospel.

Throughout history, reliable eyewitness testimony about a person or event has been one of the most accepted forms of courtroom evidence. The apostle Paul appeals to the eyewitness record as an important confirmation of the Resurrection's reality. He cites the examples of Peter, the apostles (twice), 500 believers, and James (1 Cor. 15:5-7). And with today's verse, Paul presents himself as a special eyewitness to the fact of Jesus' resurrection.

Paul's case was unique. He was not among the original apostles, nor the 500 other believers, all of whom had opportunities to be with the Lord during His earthly ministry and/or see Him soon after He arose. Paul was not even a Christian during his early life and career but was rather the leader of those who persecuted the early church.

Furthermore, Paul's situation was different because Christ's appearance to him was not only post-resurrection but post-ascension. The Lord's dramatic manifestation to the apostle was probably several years after the forty-day period of His many other appearings.

Paul genuinely viewed the timing of Jesus' appearance to him as coming "to one untimely born." We know he greatly rejoiced in his conversion, but if he had not seen the risen Savior then or some other time, Paul could not have become an apostle. In other words, by gracious, sovereign provision God chose Paul to be an apostle because "He [Jesus] appeared to me also." The longtime opponent of the church was now like the Twelve—he had seen the risen Christ.

The power of the Resurrection is always strong enough to change a life. It transformed Paul's life in three major ways. First, he recognized his sin and saw how far removed external religion was from internal godliness. Second, his character was revolutionized. He went from a self-righteous hatred of the things of Christ to a self-giving love for the truth. Finally, Paul's personal energy and motivation were completely redirected. He went from being a zealous opponent of Christians to one who fervently served and supported the church.

✧ ✧ ✧

Suggestions for Prayer: Ask God to help your testimony always show forth the power of the risen Christ.

For Further Study: What common elements were present in Paul's experiences in Acts 18:9-10; 23:11? Note some things that were more unusual about Paul's experience in 2 Corinthians 12:1-7.

*"How do some among you say
that there is no resurrection of the dead?"*
1 CORINTHIANS 15:12

✧ ✧ ✧

*Without the truth of bodily resurrection,
the Christian faith would not make sense.*

Even though Paul and the other apostles made the resurrection of Christ and His followers from the dead a central part of the gospel message, some new Gentile converts (the Corinthians especially) had difficulty accepting the idea of bodily resurrection. That struggle resulted mainly from the effects of Greek dualism, which viewed the spiritual as inherently good and the physical as inherently bad. Under that belief, a physical resurrection was considered quite repulsive.

The only way for the doubting Gentiles to accommodate their dualism was to say that Jesus was divine but not truly human. Therefore, He only *appeared* to die, and His appearances between the crucifixion and ascension were manifestations that merely *seemed* to be bodily. But Paul knew that was bad doctrine. He wrote to the Romans, "Concerning His Son . . . born of the seed of David according to the flesh . . . declared with power to be the Son of God by the resurrection from the dead" (Rom. 1:3-4).

To deny the actual, bodily resurrection of Christ creates some very significant doctrinal problems. Without His resurrection, the gospel is an empty message that doesn't make sense. Without the Resurrection, Jesus could not have conquered sin and death, and thus we could not have followed in that victory either.

Without physical resurrection, a life of faith centered on the Lord Jesus is worthless. A dead savior cannot provide any kind of life. If the dead do not rise bodily, Christ did not rise, and neither will we. If all that were true, we could not do much more than conclude with Isaiah's Servant, "I have spent My strength for nothing and vanity" (49:4). But the glorious reality is that we can affirm with Job, "I know that my Redeemer lives, and . . . .without my flesh [after death] I shall see God" (Job 19:25-26).

✧ ✧ ✧

Suggestions for Prayer: Thank God that the truth of the Resurrection makes our theology credible and the gospel powerful.

For Further Study: Sometimes Jesus' closest followers have doubts about the Resurrection. Read John 20:19-29. How did Jesus prove to the disciples that it was really Him? ✧ What else did Jesus implicitly appeal to when He confronted Thomas's doubts?

"If we have only hoped in Christ in this life,
we are of all men most to be pitied."
1 CORINTHIANS 15:19

✧ ✧ ✧

Without Christ's resurrection, our individual
Christian lives would be pathetic exercises in futility.

In ancient times the strongest swimmer among the sailors on a ship was called the *archegos*, a Greek word that means "front-runner" or "pioneer." If as the ship approached shore, it got caught in waves so strong that a safe landing was doubtful, the *archegos* would fasten one end of a long rope to the ship, tie the other end around himself, jump into the water, and guide the ship to land. Once on land, he would secure the rope to a rock or tree. Then the other passengers could disembark and use the rope as a safety tether to reach the shore.

Jesus is our *archegos*. If He didn't overcome death and make a way possible for us to do the same, we would have nothing more to look forward to than life on earth, which would leave us with no brighter hope than the typical unbeliever (Rom. 6:23).

The *archegos* illustration shows us once again the crucial importance of Christ's rising from the grave. Without the Resurrection, Christianity loses its doctrinal strength, as we saw in yesterday's study. Furthermore, the Christian life would become futile and pathetic if we could not point to the truth of the Resurrection. If our Lord were still in the tomb, He could not help us regarding eternity or our earthly ministry. We would have nothing to justify our efforts in Bible study, preaching, teaching, witnessing, or any activity of Christian service.

However, God the Father did raise "Jesus our Lord from the dead, He who was delivered up because of our transgressions, and was raised because of our justification" (Rom. 4:24-25). Because Christ lives, we too shall live (John 14:19). This great certainty should give us all the confidence and motivation we'll ever want or need as we serve our Lord and risen Savior, Jesus Christ.

✧ ✧ ✧

Suggestions for Prayer: Based on the reality of the Resurrection, ask God today to give you fresh incentive to be His faithful servant.

For Further Study: Read Luke 24:1-12. What immediate effect did knowledge of Jesus' resurrection have on Mary Magdalene and the other women? ✧ How did their reaction differ from most of the disciples'?

> *"What will those do who are baptized for the dead? If the dead
> are not raised at all, why then are they baptized for them?"*
> 1 CORINTHIANS 15:29

✧ ✧ ✧

*The fact of the Resurrection often is a powerful
testimony to draw people to saving faith in Christ.*

The apostle Paul knew that believers who face death with joy and hope can present powerful testimonies to unbelievers. The prospect of life in Heaven and a reunion with loved ones is a strong motive for people to hear and receive the gospel. When believers die, their spirits go immediately to be with the Lord. And one day in the future their glorified bodies will rejoin their spirits, and Christians will worship and enjoy God for all eternity.

First Corinthians 15:29 uses the term "baptized" to refer to those who were testifying that they were Christians. Although the mere act of baptism does not save a person, anyone who is an obedient Christian will be baptized. In Paul's day, the church assumed that any believer would have been baptized, and people were not baptized unless the church was confident their profession of faith was genuine.

"The dead" in 1 Corinthians 15:29 could also include believers, those who have died and whose lives were persuasive testimonies to the life, death, and resurrection of Jesus Christ. People were being saved (baptized) in Corinth because of ("for") the faithful witness of deceased believers.

The Resurrection is still a powerful incentive to salvation. In my years as a pastor I have seen people come to Christ after the death of a believing spouse or parent. Those husbands and wives, sons and daughters could not bear the thought of never seeing their loved one again. Those converted survivors were unknowingly touched and changed by the reunion hope that already sustains believers. That hope, based on the promise of resurrection, upheld David after the death of his infant son: "I shall go to him, but he will not return to me" (2 Sam. 12:23).

✧ ✧ ✧

Suggestions for Prayer: Ask the Lord's forgiveness for times when your testimony has been weak and the resurrection hope in your life has not been evident.

For Further Study: Read Matthew 22:23-33. What did the Sadducees' hypothetical story demonstrate about their belief concerning resurrection? ✧ How important was the doctrine of resurrection to Jesus? ✧ To what did He appeal in correcting the Sadducees?

*"If from human motives I fought with wild beasts at Ephesus,
what does it profit me? If the dead are not raised,
let us eat and drink, for tomorrow we die."*

1 CORINTHIANS 15:32

✧ ✧ ✧

*The truth of the Resurrection is an incentive for believers
to persevere in service for Jesus Christ.*

Certainly Paul's statement in today's verse is an extraordinary one, but it reiterates that the truth of Christ's resurrection and the hope of believers' resurrection are definite incentives for Christian service. It allows us to look more closely at what motivated Christians like Paul, and how we also should be motivated for service.

The apostle may have fought with literal wild animals at Ephesus. Or he may be speaking figuratively of the wild Ephesian mob that opposed him in Acts 19. But whatever the case, Paul knows that no mere human motives were compelling him to engage in such battles or continually risk his safety in other ways. He would not have put up with so many difficulties had his purposes and objectives been only temporal and worldly.

Paul and all Christians throughout history have been willing to labor under adversity, suffer, be persecuted, and continue diligently in the Lord's service because they were convinced God's kingdom extends beyond the frailties and limits of this life (Rom. 8:18). If our ministry on earth were an end in itself, then it would make sense to "eat and drink, for tomorrow we die."

However, you can praise God today that your life does not have to end simply with sensual pleasures and comforts. The hope and motivation in all your service for Christ can be identical to faith's giants in Hebrews 11 who earnestly served, that they "might obtain a better resurrection" (v. 35).

✧ ✧ ✧

Suggestions for Prayer: Pray that God would use the truth of the Resurrection to motivate you toward more faithful service in a difficult area of ministry or in a ministry in which you have been inconsistent.

For Further Study: Memorize 1 Corinthians 15:58. What does the "therefore" refer to? Make this verse a constant reminder of the incentive you should have for serving the Lord.

"Do not be deceived: 'Bad company corrupts good morals.'
Become sober-minded as you ought, and stop sinning; for some
have no knowledge of God. I speak this to your shame."
1 CORINTHIANS 15:33-34

✧ ✧ ✧

Trusting in the fact of Christ's resurrection and looking forward to our
own rising from the dead ought to stimulate us toward sanctification.

Like any essential teaching of Scripture, the doctrine of the Resurrection can be studied and discussed from an academic standpoint only. When that happens, we usually acquire a factual understanding of the topic and perhaps some appreciation of how the doctrine supports our faith—but that's as far as we go.

However, our studies on the Resurrection have already taught us some of the implications this Bible truth ought to have for our conduct. The hope of the Resurrection can give everyone an incentive to be saved and believers an incentive for service. This hope also provides a third incentive: the motivation toward sanctification.

The apostle Paul knew that those in the Corinthian church were being exposed to the heretical theology that there is no real resurrection from the dead. This false teaching was having a bad influence on the Corinthians' behavior. That's why Paul tells them in today's verse, "Bad company corrupts good morals." It is impossible to be around evil people and not be contaminated both by their ideas and their habits. The apostle goes on to urge those believers who hoped in a resurrection to be a positive influence on others and lead them to the truth.

This glimpse at the situation in Corinth proves that sound doctrine matters and does affect how people live. We see all around us today what results when there is no belief in a resurrection. People become short-sighted and live as they please because ultimately nothing keeps them accountable. This is all the more reason for us to hold firm to the truth of the Resurrection, live in its hope, and proclaim it to others.

✧ ✧ ✧

Suggestions for Prayer: How is the pursuit of holiness coming in your life? Pray that the Lord would increase your diligence and help you especially in an area of weakness.

For Further Study: Read 1 Peter 1. List all the verses that refer to God's plan for Christ's death and resurrection. ✧ How does the existence of such a divine plan strengthen your hope? ✧ Write a theme sentence for the chapter.

> *"Just as we have borne the image of the earthy,*
> *we shall also bear the image of the heavenly."*
> 1 CORINTHIANS 15:49

✧ ✧ ✧

All believers can look forward to one day
receiving new bodies and new images.

Jesus' post-resurrection appearances present a glimpse of the greatness, power, and wonder that our own resurrection bodies will have. Our Lord appeared and disappeared at will and always reappeared in other places. He was able to go through walls and doors, but He could also eat, drink, sit, talk, and be seen by others. Jesus was remarkably the same as before His death, yet He was even more remarkably changed. The body the disciples and other followers saw after the Resurrection was the same one we'll see when we go to be with Him. Christ will also appear in the same form when He returns to earth (Acts 1:11).

As it was with Jesus, our perishable, natural, and weak bodies will be raised imperishable, spiritual, and powerful. No longer will they limit us in our service to God. In Heaven we'll blaze forth the magnificent glory that God so graciously gives to His own (Matt. 13:43). Christ promises to "transform the body of our humble state into conformity with the body of His glory, by the exertion of the power that He has even to subject all things to Himself" (Phil. 3:21).

The future resurrection of believers to the glories of Heaven has always been a blessed hope and motivation for the church through the centuries—and it should be for you and me. No matter what our present bodies are like—healthy or unhealthy, beautiful or plain, short-lived or long-lived, pampered or abused—they are not our permanent bodies. One day these natural, created bodies will be re-created as supernatural. Even though the Bible gives us just a glance at what those new bodies will be like, it is a precious assurance to know that "we shall be like Him" (1 John 3:2).

✧ ✧ ✧

Suggestions for Prayer: Pray for an opportunity to share insights from this study with a Christian friend, especially if he or she has been discouraged recently.

For Further Study: Read Luke 24:33-53. What do verses 37-43 verify about Jesus' new body? ✧ Write down other things from the entire passage that describe how Jesus had changed from the way He was prior to the cross. How had He remained the same?

"'Death is swallowed up in victory. O death, where is your victory? O death, where is your sting?' . . . but thanks be to God, who gives us the victory through our Lord Jesus Christ."
1 CORINTHIANS 15:54-55, 57

✧ ✧ ✧

The Resurrection seals what we could not: victory over death.

Death is the great enemy of mankind. It comes to everyone without exception. It violates our dominion of God's creation, breaks apart relationships, disrupts families, and causes us to grieve the loss of loved ones. However, Christ's resurrection has broken the power of death for Christians because "death no longer is master over Him" (Rom. 6:9).

In today's passage the apostle Paul reminds us of the final victory over death that results once we have been transformed into our resurrection bodies. To make his point, Paul quotes from the Old Testament prophets Isaiah and Hosea. In using Hosea's sting of death metaphor, Paul implies that death left its sting in Christ, as a bee leaves its stinger in its victim. On the cross Jesus bore all of death's sting (sin), so we wouldn't have to bear any of it. When sin's penalty has been removed, death merely interrupts our earthly life and ushers us into the heavenly realm, where we will worship and praise God forever.

Paul concludes (v. 57) by thanking God, who provided us the triumph over sin and death. We also should be thankful to God who, through Christ's redeeming work, gave us what we could never have obtained by ourselves. God promises to all believers the heavenly in exchange for the earthly, and the immortal in exchange for the mortal.

With Jesus Christ's triumph over death, we have no reason to fear what death can do to us. Instead, we should rejoice concerning the Lord's promise to us about the next life: "Death and Hades were thrown into the lake of fire . . . and He shall wipe away every tear from their eyes; and there shall no longer be any death; there shall no longer be any mourning, or crying, or pain" (Rev. 20:14; 21:4).

✧ ✧ ✧

Suggestions for Prayer: Thank God that in His sovereign wisdom and power He has defeated death and removed all reasons for the believer to be afraid of it.

For Further Study: Read 2 Kings 2:9-14 and 4:18-37. What do these passages preview about Jesus' control over death, His own and ours? ✧ Do they remind you of any particular New Testament stories?

"For man is born for trouble, as sparks fly upward."
JOB 5:7

✧ ✧ ✧

Because they are sinners, still living in a sinful world,
Christians should expect to encounter difficulties.

I t all depends on how you look at it." That may be a cliché, but it is very applicable for believers as they deal with trials and sufferings. Any trial can be a joyous experience for a Christian if he looks at it from the proper, biblical perspective. Or, as with Jonah (Jonah 4) and Elijah (1 Kings 19:1-14), trials can be frustrating times of self-pity if believers lose their focus on what God is doing.

For some of us, the first hurdle to overcome is the very notion that trials and sufferings will be a part of the Christian life. But Job 5:7 reminds us that trouble is inevitable. If we imagine an ideal world where everything is just right all the time for believers, we are setting ourselves up for profound disappointment. Jesus Himself tells us we must expect significant difficulties in our lives: "In the world you have tribulation" (John 16:33).

All of us, to a greater or lesser extent, need to be prepared for testings and tribulations. And these troubles will be different for each of us. For some, the trial might be a financial crisis, accompanied by the loss of personal savings or investments. For some, it could be the loss of employment, with the anxiety of not being able to find another job anytime soon. Perhaps for others, the severe trial will be a serious illness or injury in their family, a fatal car accident, or being devastated by a major crime like murder or burglary.

In God's purpose and plan, trials and sufferings are real and should not catch us by surprise or leave us angry and perplexed. If we recognize the Lord's sovereign role in all these things, we will be able to affirm these words from an old hymn:

Whate'er my God ordains is right:
Holy His will abideth;
I will be still whate'er He doth,
And follow where He guideth.

✧ ✧ ✧

Suggestions for Prayer: Ask God for wisdom to better understand and accept the truth that He is sovereign over all areas of life. ✧ Pray for a friend or family member who might be currently in the midst of a trial.

For Further Study: Read 1 Kings 19:1-14. Who and what did Elijah focus on more than God? ✧ What events from chapter 18 did the prophet quickly forget?

*"If the world hates you, you know that it has hated Me
before it hated you. If you were of the world, the world would
love its own; but because you are not of the world, but I chose
you out of the world, therefore the world hates you."*

JOHN 15:18-19

✧ ✧ ✧

*Because they are not part of the world's system,
Christians should expect it to hate and oppose them.*

I f you've been a Christian for a while, you doubtless remember how soon
you realized that you were no longer in step with the world's culture. You
were no longer comfortable with its philosophy. You no longer had the
world's desires and yearnings. You no longer felt good about doing some of
the things the world takes for granted. In fact, you even felt constrained to
speak out against such things and urge unbelievers to turn from their sins and
embrace Christ. All that opposition to worldliness, when added up, can and
will result in hatred toward us from people in the world.

In John 15, the Greek word translated "world" (*kosmos*) refers to the
world's system of sin, which is devised by Satan and acted out by sinful people. The Devil and his angels sometimes make it even more difficult for us by
subtly presenting their "religion" as if it were true. Such deception can lull us
into complacency and leave us spiritually weak when persecution comes.

Because of the world's relentless opposition to God's kingdom, it is crucial that we remember Christ's call to stand for Him in our sinful society. The
apostle Paul exhorts us to be "children of God above reproach in the midst of
a crooked and perverse generation" (Phil. 2:15).

If we take Scripture seriously and prayerfully spend time in it daily, we will
not be caught off guard when our faith is opposed. Instead, we will be heart-
ened by Jesus' words, "You are the light of the world. A city set on a hill cannot be hidden" (Matt. 5:14).

✧ ✧ ✧

Suggestions for Prayer: Ask the Lord to strengthen you today and to remind
you that even though you are not of the world, you are to be a light to it.

For Further Study: Read the account of John the Baptist's death in Mark 6:14-
29. How did John suffer before he was killed? ✧ What character differences
do you see between John and Herod?

> *"All these things they will do to you for My name's sake,*
> *because they do not know the One who sent Me."*
> JOHN 15:21

✧ ✧ ✧

The world, in its general hatred of the truth
and ignorance of God, will also hate believers.

The religious leaders of Jesus' time hated Him intensely. If we are committed to following Him wholeheartedly today, we can't expect to avoid persecution and hardship any more than He did. In John 15:20 our Lord tells us what to expect: "Remember the word that I said to you, 'A slave is not greater than his master.' If they persecuted Me, they will also persecute you."

If our perspective is right, however, this expectation should actually make us happy and even provide a certain sense of security. Receiving persecution from the world because we are Christ's representatives means we have an opportunity to experience what Paul called "the fellowship of His sufferings" (Phil. 3:10). As one commentator has said, Christian suffering "is the very means God uses to transform us into the image of His Son." Troubles and pains can be great reassurances that we have been united with Christ.

As we saw yesterday, it's no surprise that the world hates us. It despises our general opposition to its system, but aside from that, the world hates believers simply because it doesn't know God.

This basic ignorance of God usually appears in one of two ways. Either it shows up as apathy and religious superstition (Acts 17:22-23) or as more glaring actions and attitudes of moral and spiritual deviation (Romans 1:18—2:2). Whatever the case, people in the world are just doing what is natural for them because of their sin and depravity.

As a Christian, what should your response be? You should not be indifferent or accommodate the serious challenges you'll face from the world. Instead, you ought to, by faith, realistically accept the truth of John 15:21, comfortably rest in the teaching of Philippians 3:10, and confidently seek to minister to the world "because the foolishness of God [the gospel] is wiser than men, and the weakness of God [the cross] is stronger than men" (1 Cor. 1:25).

✧ ✧ ✧

Suggestions for Prayer: Ask the Lord to help you begin grasping what it means to partake in "the fellowship of His sufferings."

For Further Study: Read Acts 5:17-42. How is the world's attitude toward the gospel displayed in this passage? ✧ What did the apostles appeal to when faced with severe opposition?

*"By faith Abraham, when he was tested, offered up Isaac;
and he who had received the promises was offering up
his only begotten son."*
HEBREWS 11:17

✧ ✧ ✧

*The main reason God allows trials in the lives
of Christians is to test the strength of their faith.*

The memorable example in Genesis 22 of Abraham's testing is perhaps the severest trial any human being has ever faced. When God told Abraham to offer his only son Isaac as a burnt offering on one of the mountains of Moriah (Gen. 22:1-2), Abraham no doubt was stunned. In terms of God's nature, His plan of redemption, His promise to Abraham, and His love for Isaac, the entire concept was utterly inconceivable and unprecedented.

But in the face of all that, Abraham showed remarkable faith in dealing with this trial (Gen. 22:3-8). He did not second-guess God, as many of us would, but rather obeyed immediately (v. 3) and displayed the confidence that he and Isaac would return (v. 5) and that God would supply a lamb for the offering (v. 8). Then Abraham showed he was ready to obey completely. Genesis 22 tells us he "bound his son Isaac, and laid him on the altar on top of the wood. And Abraham stretched out his hand, and took the knife to slay his son" (vv. 9-10). What unbelievable faith, and what a dramatic moment when God spared Abraham from the full cost of obedience (vv. 11-12)! The story clearly shows us the nature of true faith (Gen. 15:6) and why Abraham was later called the father of the faithful (Rom. 4:11-12; Gal. 3:6-7).

As heirs to Abraham and his extraordinary trust in God, we can also endure the most difficult trials and pass tests of faith that seem unimaginably severe at the time. God might want us to offer our own loved ones to Him and let them go His way rather than tightly holding on to them for our own purposes. However, if we look to God as Abraham did (Heb. 11:17-19), we can be confident in any trial and know with certainty that our faith has passed the test.

✧ ✧ ✧

Suggestions for Prayer: Pray that God would strengthen your faith even in the smallest of daily trials.

For Further Study: Read 2 Kings 20:1-11 and 2 Chronicles 32:24-31. What was at the heart of Hezekiah's difficulties (2 Chron. 32:25)? ✧ Why did God test him (v. 31)?

> *"To keep me from exalting myself, there was given me a thorn
> in the flesh, a messenger of Satan to buffet me."*
> 2 CORINTHIANS 12:7

✧ ✧ ✧

God sometimes uses trials to humble believers.

Professional athletics, as a whole, makes up one of the least humble sectors in modern American society. Players with multi-million dollar salaries and extravagant benefits have replaced those who played because they loved their sport and had great community loyalty.

One such noble model from the past was Lou Gehrig, the Hall of Fame first baseman with the New York Yankees, whose career ended in 1939 after he was stricken with a rare and always fatal neuromuscular disease. Throughout his ordeal, Gehrig conducted himself with dignity and humility, all of which culminated on July 4, 1939, before a capacity crowd at Yankee Stadium, with millions more listening on the radio. He concluded his special remarks on "Lou Gehrig Day" with this amazing statement: "Today, I consider myself the luckiest man on the face of the earth." He died approximately two years later.

Shouldn't those who seek to serve and glorify God react in similar fashion if confronted by the same kind of trial? They will if they remember that He sometimes sends trials to humble His children and remind them they are not to be overconfident in their own spiritual strength (Rom. 12:3).

Today's verse tells us God allowed Paul to be plagued by some sort of chronic, painful problem, "a messenger of Satan." This likely refers to a man who led the opposition to Paul at the church in Corinth. When we are greatly blessed spiritually—Paul saw the risen Christ several times and was even taken up into the third heaven—the Lord sometimes allows "a thorn in the flesh" to afflict us, that we might remain humble. Whenever we are besieged by such trials and come to the point where all strength seems gone, God's Word reminds us, as it did Paul, "'My grace is sufficient for you, for power is perfected in weakness.' Most gladly, therefore, I [Paul] will rather boast about my weaknesses, that the power of Christ may dwell in me" (2 Cor. 12:9).

✧ ✧ ✧

Suggestions for Prayer: Ask the Lord to remind you throughout the day of your humble dependence on Him, whether or not you are going through a trial.

For Further Study: Read James 4:6-10 and 1 Peter 5:5-7. What do these passages say is the key to genuine humility?

*"Considering the reproach of Christ greater
riches than the treasures of Egypt . . ."*
HEBREWS 11:26

✧ ✧ ✧

*Trials can show that material things are inadequate
to meet our deepest needs.*

We rely every day on material possessions—cars, computers, pagers, telephones, microwaves, radios, and TVs. These familiar conveniences make us feel as though it's quite a hardship to cope without them. Therefore it's difficult to avoid the pitfall Jesus warned about in Matthew 6:24, "No one can serve two masters; for either he will hate the one and love the other, or he will hold to one and despise the other. You cannot serve God and mammon [riches]."

Materialism can exert such a powerful influence on us as believers that the Lord will sometimes subject us to trials just so He can remove us from the grip of the world's devices and riches. Various trials and sufferings will almost invariably reveal how inadequate our possessions are to meet our deepest needs or provide genuine relief from the pains and stresses of life. And this realization ought to become more and more true of you as you grow in the Christian life. I have observed that mature believers, as time goes by, become less and less attached to the temporal items they've accumulated. Such stuff, along with life's fleeting experiences, simply fades in importance as you draw closer to the Lord.

Moses is a wonderful example of someone who learned through trials these important lessons about materialism (Heb. 11:24-26). He spent forty years in Pharaoh's household and was brought up to be an Egyptian prince. But he was willing to leave a position of prestige and power so he could experience something of the sufferings of his fellow Israelites, who were living as slaves in Egypt. God in effect made Moses a participant in Israel's trials, content to rely on Him, not on the comforts and advantages of materialism: "By faith he left Egypt, not fearing the wrath of the king: for he endured, as seeing Him who is unseen" (Heb. 11:27).

The Lord might need to get our attention in similar fashion, so that we learn one of the key lessons from life's trials: to rely on His unlimited spiritual wealth, not on our finite and fading material possessions.

✧ ✧ ✧

Suggestions for Prayer: Ask the Lord to make you more willing to rely on His strength and less willing to lean on material things.

For Further Study: Read 1 Timothy 6:6-11. According to Paul, what does contentment involve?

> *"For now I know that you fear God, since you have not*
> *withheld your son, your only son, from Me."*
> GENESIS 22:12

❖ ❖ ❖

Trials from the Lord will reveal to believers
what they love and appreciate the most.

A big part of the reason for the Lord's testing Abraham at Moriah was to show him what he valued most in life. The question God wanted Abraham to answer was, "Do you love Isaac more than Me, or do you love Me more than Isaac?" And the Lord was prepared for the drastic test of taking Abraham's son's life if that's what was necessary for Abraham to give God first place in everything.

God also tries the sincerity of those today who claim to love Him (see Deut. 13:3; Matt. 22:36-37). Jesus was so concerned that we have our priorities right that He made this radical statement: "If anyone comes to Me, and does not hate his own father and mother and wife and children and brothers and sisters, yes, and even his own life, he cannot be My disciple" (Luke 14:26). Christians must love Christ so much that by comparison they will seem to hate their families and themselves. In order to test this first love, God might in some dramatic fashion ask us to renounce the many tugs and appeals from family and place His will and affections first in our life.

That kind of radical obedience, which is what Abraham had, always leads to God's blessings. Jesus Himself was a perfect example of this principle. Because He was fully human as well as fully God, our Lord did not escape ordinary pain and hardship while on earth. As the Suffering Servant (Isa. 53), He learned completely what it means to obey through pain and adversity, all the way to His crucifixion (Heb. 5:7-9). As a result, the Son was exalted by the Father (Phil. 2:8-9).

God sometimes makes our path of obedience go through the experiences of trials and sufferings. But if we are faithful to His Word and will, those difficulties will teach us to value and appreciate God's many blessings.

❖ ❖ ❖

Suggestions for Prayer: Pray that your priorities each day would stay in line with God's.

For Further Study: Read Deuteronomy 6:1-9. What must be the top priority for all believers?

*"To obtain an inheritance which is imperishable and undefiled
and will not fade away, reserved in heaven for you."*

1 PETER 1:4

✧ ✧ ✧

*We can rejoice after enduring a trial because
our hope in Heaven will be renewed.*

The joy a Christian experiences as a result of trials can be the best kind he will ever know. But so often we allow the everyday stress and strain of financial difficulties, health problems, unrealized goals, and many other trials to rob us of our joy in Christ. True joy stems from spiritual realities that are much greater than temporal circumstances.

In today's verse Peter gives us one strong reason for rejoicing—the confident hope that as Christians we have inherited a place in Heaven. This confidence can be so powerful that Peter, who was writing to believers suffering persecution, describes it as a truth we ought to "greatly rejoice" in (v. 6). This expressive, intense word is always used in the New Testament in relation to the joy of knowing God, never of shallow, temporal relationships.

Jesus' disciples had a difficult time seeing that trials could be related to the certainty of going to Heaven. In teaching them about His upcoming death, Christ told the Twelve, "Therefore you, too, now have sorrow; but I will see you again, and your heart will rejoice, and no one takes your joy away from you" (John 16:22). And that is exactly what happened when they saw the risen Savior and understood the impact of His work.

We can have two responses to trials, just like passengers riding a train through the mountains. We can look to the left and see the dark mountainside and be depressed. Or we can look to the right and be uplifted by the beautiful view of natural scenery stretching into the distance. Some believers even compound their sadness by continuing to look to the mountain shadows of their trial after life's train has moved away from the threatening peaks. But they would not forfeit their joy if they simply looked ahead to the brightness and certainty of their eternal inheritance.

Nothing in life can take away the wonderful promise of Heaven's glory: it was reserved by God, bought by Christ, and guaranteed by the Spirit (see Eph. 1:11-13).

✧ ✧ ✧

Suggestions for Prayer: Ask the Lord to help you meditate today on the glories promised for you in the future.

For Further Study: Read Revelation 21 and note the primary living conditions that will be true of Heaven.

> *"And after you have suffered for a little while, the God*
> *of all grace . . . will Himself perfect, confirm,*
> *strengthen and establish you."*
> 1 PETER 5:10

✧ ✧ ✧

Successful endurance of present trials leads
to greater focus on glorifying God in the future.

Sufferings and trials teach us patience. However, in Heaven we won't need to have patience, and therefore it is not the major long-term lesson God wants us to learn from trials. He is far more pleased if we grasp the truth that what we suffer now is directly related to our ability to glorify Him in eternity. Worshiping God will be our role in Heaven (Rev. 4—5), and Paul reminds us that "if we endure, we shall also reign with Him" (2 Tim. 2:12). In other words, if we learn to endure trials and tribulations now, we can expect to receive great reward in eternity. I believe that reward is primarily the capacity to glorify God; and therefore the greater our present endurance, the greater will be our capability to glorify Him in the future.

At one point during Jesus' ministry with the disciples, two of them—brothers James and John—desired that He appoint them to the two positions of greatest prestige in His kingdom—seats at His right and left hands (see Matt. 20:20-23). James and John recognized the concept of eternal rewards, but they did not understand how it works. Thus Jesus asked them if they were ready to endure the cup of suffering and death (as He was) prior to occupying such powerful positions in His kingdom (v. 22). This implies again that endurance in trials and advancement in future glory are correlated. (Jesus endured the greatest suffering on the cross, and He was raised to the highest position, at the Father's right hand.)

The application for us from all this is clear: the Lord wants us to realize that the end of every trial contains much satisfaction and joy because we are building up our future capacity to glorify Him. At the same time, we are comprehending more and more about the value of persevering through all sorts of pain and tribulation (see Rev. 2:10).

✧ ✧ ✧

Suggestions for Prayer: Ask God to give you the desire to see the benefits of trials from an eternal perspective.

For Further Study: Read Revelation 4—5. What attributes of God do you see, directly or indirectly, that are worthy of eternal praise?

*"Blessed be the God and Father of our Lord Jesus Christ,
the Father of mercies and God of all comfort; who comforts
us in all our affliction so that we may be able to comfort those
who are in any affliction with the comfort with which we
ourselves are comforted by God."*

2 CORINTHIANS 1:3-4

❖ ❖ ❖

*God entrusts comfort to us, often through trials,
so that we may comfort others.*

The nation of Ireland is nicknamed the "Emerald Isle" for good reason—it contains some of the greenest countryside of any location on earth. In visiting there I have noticed that abundant mist and fog, which often shroud the rolling landscape, help produce the rich green grass and trees. That phenomenon is much like the Christian life. Many times when our life is obscured by the sufferings and sorrows of trials, it has a refreshing beauty of soul that is not always readily seen. As the apostle Paul's life demonstrates, sensitive and merciful hearts are the products of great trials.

Difficulties beset us so that God might bestow much comfort on us. But such comfort is not merely for our own benefit. The Lord entrusts His comfort to us that we might share it with others, as verse 4 of today's passage indicates. And He comforts us in direct proportion to the number of trials we endure, which means the more we suffer, the more God comforts us; and the more He comforts us, the more we can comfort others who are hurting.

When we do experience real comfort in the wake of a trial, perhaps the most precious result is the sense of Christian partnership we feel. If God's comfort helps us to comfort others, then it's clear that other believers are positively affected by what we learn from our trials. The entire process lifts us beyond ourselves and shows us that as part of a local fellowship or the greater Body of Christ we are not alone and do not have to undergo various trials in a vacuum.

The comfort we receive and the sense of partnership that results is a great incentive for any of us to be encouraged through trials and sufferings, knowing that such experiences enable us to minister as integral parts of the Body of Christ (see 1 Cor. 12:26; 2 Cor. 1:6-7).

❖ ❖ ❖

Suggestions for Prayer: Thank God for His unlimited supply of comfort.

For Further Study: Read Isaiah 40:1; 49:13; 51:3; 61:2. What promise does each verse have in common?

> *"But where can wisdom be found? And where is the*
> *place of understanding? Man does not know its value,*
> *nor is it found in the land of the living."*
>
> JOB 28:12-13

❖ ❖ ❖

God's wisdom is our source for understanding life and all its trials.

The supernatural wisdom believers need in order to understand their trials is simply not available from our society. During Job's ordeal he soon learned the utter inadequacy both of his reason and his friends' misguided advice. That led him to the profound conclusion that the Lord's wisdom is the only source for comprehending life and all its difficulties.

Wisdom in general has always been among the highest, most respected virtues believers can have. The Lord was greatly pleased when Solomon asked for wisdom rather than riches or power (1 Kings 3:5-13), and Solomon later set forth the basic importance of God's wisdom: "For the Lord gives wisdom; from His mouth come knowledge and understanding" (Prov. 2:6).

God's wisdom puts things in the right perspective during trials and helps us endure them. But as we have already noted, it is not something we will have automatically. The apostle James, in the context of a passage about trials, says we must ask for wisdom: "If any of you lacks wisdom, let him ask of God, who gives to all men generously and without reproach, and it will be given to him" (James 1:5).

In keeping with our series on trials' lessons, it's crucial that as we experience difficult tests, we ask God for wisdom to persevere according to His Word. Without a practical understanding of how to live according to His will and Word, we will not see His sovereign hand of providence at work in our trials. And we will miss one of God's most important purposes in bringing sufferings and trials to us—that we would become more dependent on Him.

Once we have the Lord's wisdom and realize that we have become more and more dependent on Him, we'll be like Job, who received this answer to his earlier questions: "'Behold, the fear of the Lord, that is wisdom; and to depart from evil is understanding'" (28:28).

❖ ❖ ❖

Suggestions for Prayer: Pray that you would be more diligent in gleaning wisdom from your study of Scripture.

For Further Study: Read 1 Kings 3:5-13. What does Solomon's request reveal about his character? ❖ What rewards and closing promise did God give to him as a result?

*"But let the brother of humble circumstances glory in his high
position; and let the rich man glory in his humiliation,
because like flowering grass he will pass away."*
JAMES 1:9-10

❖ ❖ ❖

*God does not exempt any believer, rich or poor,
from trials and suffering.*

There is a basic principle of life that we all know to be true—namely, that trials and sufferings do not exclude privileged people. This is a humbling truth that we don't always like to acknowledge, yet it operates before us regularly in such things as natural disasters. No one can deny that large-scale floods, hurricanes, or earthquakes affect both rich and poor, young and old, educated and uneducated; all races and classes are susceptible to pain, hardship, and even death during such events. After a major earthquake, for example, nearly everyone feels the effects of disruptions in transportation and communication. And the ground's violent shaking can damage or destroy both modest bungalows and expensive mansions.

The realization that God does not show favoritism in sending trials and difficulties is also quite sobering and humbling for those in the Body of Christ. As today's first verse suggests, the challenge for poor believers is in realizing that they can rejoice in their exalted spiritual position as Christians (1 Peter 1:3-6), no matter how lowly their earthly status might be. Current economic hardship does not diminish the glories of our future inheritance (see Eph. 1:11-14).

The challenge for wealthier believers is to accept the "humiliation" that trials bring, remembering that such tests will make them more dependent on God and His grace rather than on earthly riches. Such wealth is only temporary, and it fades away like the grass of the field.

Once we grasp the truth of this equalizing factor, we will be more inclined to declare with sincerity, "My resources are in God." The divine impartiality revealed through trials also has a wonderful unifying effect on the church. The commentator R.C.H. Lenski summarized it this way: "As the poor brother forgets all his earthly poverty, so the rich brother forgets all his earthly riches. The two are equals by faith in Christ."

❖ ❖ ❖

Suggestions for Prayer: Ask the Lord to give you a better appreciation for His evenhandedness in bringing trials our way.

For Further Study: Read Hebrews 12:3-13. What are some parallels between this passage and what we have been studying about trials? ❖ Does God exempt any believer from correction?

"God has not given us a spirit of timidity [fear],
but of power and love and discipline."
2 TIMOTHY 1:7

✧ ✧ ✧

The true follower of Christ has no reason
to fear potential sufferings and trials.

Concerning frustration and fear at the 1992 Winter Olympics, speed skater Dan Jansen said, "What happened was I skated a race that I can only describe as tentative. I looked good. I didn't slip. Yet something kept me from going flat out." The favored Jansen, haunted by well-publicized failures to win medals in 1988 or 1992, finally overcame his fear and triumphed in 1994 in the 1,000-meter speed-skating event.

Believers' can also react with intense fear and painful disappointment to life's trials if they are not prepared for the possibility of difficulties. But many centuries ago Proverbs 29:25 encouraged God's followers not to be afraid: "The fear of man brings a snare, but he who trusts in the Lord will be exalted." Paul exhorted Timothy in a similar way when he wrote the words of today's verse.

In Matthew 10:29-31, the Lord Jesus provides a wonderful reason for His disciples not to serve Him under a cloud of fear. The point of His common-sense illustration is simple. If the Father cares for small birds and numbers each hair on our heads, He is certainly concerned about our physical and spiritual welfare and the ultimate good of our souls. No matter how bad the situation is or how prolonged the trial may seem, God is able to sustain us.

Later Jesus provided an excellent summary of His teaching on fear with these familiar words to the Twelve: "Peace I leave with you; My peace I give to you; not as the world gives, do I give to you. Let not your heart be troubled, nor let it be fearful" (John 14:27). With such a strong promise and reassurance that the Holy Spirit will always be present, how can any of us who profess Jesus Christ make room for debilitating fear, no matter what tough tests and persecutions may yet face us?

✧ ✧ ✧

Suggestions for Prayer: If you have a particular situation or person in your life that causes you much fear and anxiety, pray that God would strengthen you and remove the cause of that fear.

For Further Study: Read Psalm 118:5-9. Memorize verse 6 or another one in this brief passage that will be a helpful resource should you face persecution.

*"And the rain descended, and the floods came,
and the winds blew, and burst against that house; and yet it
did not fall, for it had been founded upon the rock."*
MATTHEW 7:25

✧ ✧ ✧

*Faithfulness in discipleship will mean we are prepared
for the worst possible adversity and trial.*

People are often unprepared for life's unexpected upheavals. This was vividly illustrated by the once-in-500-year floods that struck the Northern Plains of the United States in the spring of 1997. One community on the Red River in North Dakota was especially devastated by the surprising events.

After working diligently for days to fortify levees against the swelling river, people in Grand Forks were hopeful. But one early morning in mid-April 1997, the relentless Red River broke through the earthen and sandbag flood barriers and inundated the entire town of 50,000. Few deaths or serious injuries occurred, but practically the entire population had to abandon homes and property to the muddy waters. It was one of the largest mass evacuations in the history of American disasters, and it will take many months, even years, before Grand Forks and surrounding towns can repair all the flood damage.

For believers, facing such an utterly unexpected trial can help them learn to grow closer to the Lord. And they can prepare themselves by resting in the truth of the prophet's words: "The steadfast of mind Thou wilt keep in perfect peace, because he trusts in Thee. Trust in the Lord forever, for in God the Lord, we have an everlasting Rock" (Isa. 26:3-4).

Jesus emphasized the need for total self-denial by His followers and complete preparedness to face any challenge, even death (Matt. 10:38-39). If we are living daily as His disciples, no trial will catch us totally unprepared. We might be temporarily surprised and feel inadequate initially, but we won't remain that way. We already know from our studies this month that a sovereign God has the right to bring certain trials and tribulations into our lives, and He is also more than able to give us every resource we need to endure (Phil. 4:11-13; 1 Peter 5:6-7).

✧ ✧ ✧

Suggestions for Prayer: Thank God for the strength and wisdom He gives through His Word so that you may be prepared for whatever trial He sends.

For Further Study: Read 1 Peter 5:6-11, and spend some extra time meditating on or memorizing one or two of the verses. ✧ Write down one key thought that relates to being spiritually prepared for trials.

> *"Be anxious for nothing, but in everything by prayer*
> *and supplication with thanksgiving let your*
> *requests be made known to God."*
> PHILIPPIANS 4:6

✧ ✧ ✧

Genuine believers will react thankfully to trials and suffering.

Preventive spiritual maintenance is very important. If we are disciplined believers, we'll practice it and prepare ourselves for any kind of trials and hardships. Then when the unexpected happens, we'll be able to respond in a godly manner and truly appreciate what the Lord is teaching us.

The attitude expressed in today's verse is basic and is one of the strongest antidotes to fear and lack of preparation in the face of trials. The apostle Paul affirms an attitude that allows us to call upon God for help in difficulties but does not leave room for doubt, blame, or second-guessing. Those responses reveal an absence of faith and a lack of acceptance of what God has for us.

A prayerful and grateful reaction to God's tests in our lives, no matter how painful, unexpected, or difficult to understand at the time, results in our receiving His unsurpassed peace. A careful look at Philippians 4:6, along with verse 7—"the peace of God, which surpasses all comprehension, shall guard your hearts and your minds in Christ Jesus"—proclaims that God's chief concern for us is not so much specific answers to our every request, but that we know His supernatural peace. We can also glean this principle from the long series of questions Job asked God about Himself. God chose not to answer Job's questions per se (see Job 38—41) because His purpose was simply that Job know God's sovereignty and submit to it.

That may be His purpose for us as well. Therefore, the Lord wants us to be prepared for trials and sufferings with a faith-filled, grateful response, one that recognizes He has an ultimate purpose for us (1 Peter 5:10) and remembers His promise that we will receive no trial or temptation we can't bear (1 Cor. 10:13).

✧ ✧ ✧

Suggestions for Prayer: Ask God to help you stay faithful in your reading and study of Scripture so that the preventive maintenance of your soul will be strong. ✧ Thank the Lord for His peace that is available even in the most difficult circumstances. ✧ Praise Him for a specific time when that peace was especially comforting to you.

For Further Study: Read Ephesians 2:14-15; 6:15; and 1 Thessalonians 5:23. What important components characterize peace?

*"We know that God causes all things to work together
for good to those who love God, to those who
are called according to His purpose."*

ROMANS 8:28

✧ ✧ ✧

*We will be better prepared for what God teaches us through
trials if we have a basic understanding of His providence.*

I believe it is vital that all Christians have an essential awareness of God's providence if they want to be fully prepared to cope with life's adversity. Providence is how He orchestrates, through natural means and processes, all things necessary to accomplish His purposes in the world. It is the most frequent way He works and controls the daily course of human events. The only other means the Lord uses to intervene in the flow of history is miracles. But He does not perform miracles in the same way now as He did during the days of Christ, the apostles, and the prophets. However, God has *continuously* used providence from eternity past to coordinate the infinite variety of factors necessary to accomplish His perfect purpose.

Think about it. The vast scope and endless outworking of divine providence, in which God draws together millions of details and circumstances to achieve His will each day, is a far greater miracle than the relatively uncomplicated, one-time supernatural occurrences that we usually term miracles. Belief in God's providence is, therefore, one of the greatest exercises of faith we can have and a major contributor to our general preparedness and peace of mind as we encounter trials and hardships.

Paul trusted wholeheartedly in the providence of God, no matter how easy or challenging life was (Phil. 4:11). Joseph the patriarch stated his confidence in providence this way: "You [his brothers] meant evil against me, but God meant it for good in order to bring about this present result, to preserve many people alive" (Gen. 50:20). Until we come to a similar acceptance of God's providential control of everything, we will not fully realize the rich lessons He wants to teach us through trials, and we will not be able to apply the truth of Romans 8:28.

✧ ✧ ✧

Suggestions for Prayer: Thank the Lord that His providence is always at work for your benefit. If this concept is new to you, ask Him to help you understand it better through His Word.

For Further Study: Read more about Joseph in Genesis 39—50. Jot down some of his positive character traits. ✧ What events in the narrative were possible only because of providence?

> *"Your adversary, the devil, prowls about like a roaring lion,*
> *seeking someone to devour. But resist him, firm in your faith,*
> *knowing that the same experiences of suffering are being*
> *accomplished by your brethren who are in the world."*
>
> 1 PETER 5:8-9

❖ ❖ ❖

All of Satan's involvement in our sufferings and trials is under God's control,
which means our success against him is also in God's sovereign hands.

During the past twenty-five years, there has been a tremendous upsurge of interest in the occult, Satan worship, and evil supernatural influences. Such unwise fascination has had an impact on the church and led to an overemphasis on spiritual warfare in some circles. But such unbiblical emphases give us an unbalanced perspective on the role Satan plays in our trials and persecutions.

On the other hand, 1 Peter 5:8-9 places Satan's activities in the proper context. Peter urges us to watch our surroundings and be alert to possible temptations. But as we do, we can be encouraged that Jesus Christ has already defeated Satan, and therefore the evil one can have no long-term victories in our lives (1 John 4:4).

Peter goes on to admonish us that we need to resist Satan, which simply means we must "stand up against" him with our spiritual feet solidly planted on the objective truth of the Word (see also James 4:7). The Devil is a liar and a deceiver, and the surest way to deflect his onslaughts is with the infallible, revealed truth of Scripture.

In the biblical accounts of Satan's participation in the trials, persecutions, or sufferings of God's servants, God is always the one in control (see Job 1:1—2:8; Matt. 4:1-11). Therefore, our responsibility as we prepare for possible satanic attacks is to recall that our own grand strategies of spiritual warfare, however relentless and innovative they might be, will not provide the vigilance Peter speaks of. Paul gives us a further example of the right kind of preparation when he describes the essence of spiritual warfare as "taking every thought captive to the obedience of Christ" (2 Cor. 10:5). If we heed the implications of those words, there's really nothing else we need to have or do in combating the Devil.

❖ ❖ ❖

Suggestions for Prayer: Ask God to give you a biblical, balanced approach to dealing with Satan and his many subtle temptations.

For Further Study: Read Mark 9:14-29. What does this passage affirm about Jesus' authority? ❖ What basic lesson did the disciples need to be reminded of?

> *"Beloved, do not be surprised at the fiery ordeal among you,*
> *which comes upon you for your testing, as though some*
> *strange thing were happening to you."*
> 1 PETER 4:12

✧ ✧ ✧

We can be certain of God's love for us, no matter
how unexpected or difficult any trial might be.

Reassuring words are vital as we strive to deal in a godly fashion with trials and sufferings in our Christian lives. In today's verse, Peter opens with a pastoral term ("beloved") that conveys tenderness, love, and concern for his audience. It reinforces in a single word the concepts of fervent love for one another and love that covers sin (1 Peter 4:8). Such love is a welcome reality to lean on whenever anyone is undergoing suffering or persecution.

Trials can easily tempt us to be discouraged and doubt God's love. That likely was happening to believers in Peter's time. For example, the emperor Nero coated many, including children, in pitch and used them as human torches. With such cruel persecution going on, we can see why Peter wrote to fellow Christians—which includes us—to reassure them of God's love.

Peter's expression "fiery ordeal," which can refer to many different types of difficulties, provides reassurance that troubles and trials come for a purpose. In the Greek translation of the Old Testament, "fiery" referred to a smelting furnace that refined metals of their foreign, unwanted elements. That process is pictured in verses such as Psalm 66:10, "For Thou hast tried us, O God; Thou hast refined us as silver is refined." So "fiery ordeal" represents the various sufferings God allows in our lives to purify us.

Peter closes by assuring us that trials are not out of the ordinary, or "some strange thing." We should not be surprised at them as if each was some bizarre occurrence, coming at us simply by chance. Trials, therefore, should be seen as part of life. They might catch us off guard at first, but we can confidently deal with them, knowing that God's loving care for us never fails.

✧ ✧ ✧

Suggestions for Prayer: Thank the Lord that no trial, no matter how unusual it seems at first, needs to catch you by surprise.

For Further Study: Jesus taught the disciples about the inevitability of sufferings, trials, and disappointments. What warnings did He give in John 15—16? ✧ What major resource did He promise?

*"But to the degree that you share the sufferings of Christ,
keep on rejoicing; so that also at the revelation of His glory,
you may rejoice with exultation."*
1 PETER 4:13

✧ ✧ ✧

*We should rejoice in trials and persecutions,
not for their own sake, but for the benefits that result.*

The late D. Martyn Lloyd-Jones, in his classic book *Studies in the Sermon on the Mount*, made the following careful distinction on what it means to rejoice in persecution: "The Christian is, in a sense, one who must feel his heart breaking at the effect of sin in others that makes them do this [persecute believers]. So he never rejoices in the fact of persecution as such."

We can draw from this, then, that 1 Peter 4:13 and other verses (notably Matt. 5:11-12), while they encourage the positive attitude of rejoicing in trials, do not mean we should have a masochistic or elitist view of suffering. The joy we are to have should go beyond the pain and heartache of the suffering itself and focus on the ramifications of what God is doing in our life.

Peter begins our verse by asserting that one of those ramifications is enjoying the fellowship of Christ's sufferings. That means we can share, for His sake, in the same kind of suffering and rejection He endured. We should be ready for such persecution whenever we share the gospel or generally identify with Him. The apostles learned this lesson soon after Jesus departed— "rejoicing that they had been considered worthy to suffer shame for His name" (Acts 5:41). We will increasingly embrace such suffering as a privilege if we heed Peter's exhortation.

The apostle goes on to give us more motivation for rejoicing. "The revelation of His glory" is a reference to Jesus' second coming, which in itself ought to bring tremendous joy to all believers. If we have faithfully endured all the persecutions, sufferings, trials, and problems of this life, when our Lord returns we will have genuine reason to rejoice all the more. And it will be with an intense and joyous outburst that exceeds any we've had before (see Luke 6:22-23).

✧ ✧ ✧

Suggestions for Prayer: Ask God to give you the right motivation to rejoice in the midst of suffering.

For Further Study: Matthew 5:11-12 contains some of the most challenging truth in all the Bible. Commit these verses to memory, and look for opportunities in which they can become real in your experience.

*"If you are reviled for the name of Christ, you are blessed,
because the Spirit of glory and of God rests upon you."*
1 PETER 4:14

❖ ❖ ❖

***The indwelling Holy Spirit allows us to rejoice,
no matter how greatly we suffer or are persecuted.***

One of the greatest scientific breakthroughs of the past half century has been the discovery of the DNA molecule, which carries unique and essential genetic information about all living beings. The most well-known practical application of DNA has been the "fingerprinting" technique in which genetic information from one DNA sample is compared with that of another. If the information matches, it's highly probable, but not absolutely certain, that the samples identify the same individual.

While discoveries about DNA's ability to more precisely determine physical identity have been newsworthy, God long ago established His infallible truth regarding spiritual identity. The apostle Paul gives us the basic criterion by which we can know if we are believers: "However you are not in the flesh but in the Spirit, if indeed the Spirit of God dwells in you. But if anyone does not have the Spirit of Christ, he does not belong to Him" (Rom. 8:9). This reinforces Jesus' teaching to Nicodemus about being born again (John 3:3-6). Therefore, all genuine believers will know the Holy Spirit's indwelling presence.

The Spirit's presence in our lives is one final reason we have to rejoice in trials and sufferings. Peter calls the Holy Spirit "the Spirit of glory" because as deity the Spirit has glory as an essential attribute. Although that glory doesn't manifest itself today as it did in the Old Testament (e.g., the cloud in the tabernacle), the Spirit's indwelling a Christian is nonetheless real for any who are undergoing a trial.

First Peter 4:14 is referring to a special grace that goes beyond the normal indwelling of the Spirit. It is much like the extraordinary power that Stephen realized before and during his stoning (see Acts 6:15; 7:55-60). God's Spirit gave him amazing composure and strength and lifted him above normal pain and fear. The Holy Spirit also blesses us with abundant grace, specially suited to our times of need. Therefore, it should be hard for us to react with any attitude but rejoicing, no matter how difficult our trials.

❖ ❖ ❖

Suggestions for Prayer: Thank God for the presence and power of the Holy Spirit, who ministers daily in your life.

For Further Study: Read Exodus 3:1-6. What was unique about the bush? ❖ How did Moses react to God's glory?

"By no means let any of you suffer as a murderer, or thief,
or evildoer, or a troublesome meddler."
1 PETER 4:15

✧ ✧ ✧

We must not presume that God blesses every possible kind
of suffering a Christian may become involved in.

I t's quite obvious that some sufferings and trials are not part of God's plan
for us. Believers should never suffer because they've murdered, robbed, or
done evil. But in today's verse Peter mentions a fourth category—"a troublesome meddler"—whose meaning is not as apparent and whose application
might be more in dispute.

"A troublesome meddler" interferes with everyone else's business, and
Paul says we should avoid such persons (1 Thess. 4:11; 2 Thess. 3:14; 1 Tim.
5:13). But I believe Peter also uses the term to refer to a political agitator,
someone who actively tries to disrupt the normal function of the government.
If this understanding is correct, then Peter is commanding Christians to be
good citizens in their non-Christian cultures (cf. Rom. 13:1-7). We are to go
to work, live peacefully, witness to others, and exalt Christ.

Believers are not to act like radicals who are intent on overthrowing existing authority or imposing Christian standards on society. Getting into trouble
with your employer or being fired by him because of disruptive activities, even
those done in the name of Christ, is not honorable but disgraceful.

Most believers would never even consider the possibility of being involved in
militia groups that are engaged in separatist activities and are violently opposed
to all legitimate governmental authority. Yet some Christians wrongly see validity in strategies of civil disobedience and violence as they oppose some govern-
ment-sanctioned acts, specifically abortion. They are not satisfied with simply
providing biblical counsel or material and educational assistance at a local pro-
life agency, as many believers have done over the past twenty-five years.

Therefore, if we would seek to promote what is right and redress injustices,
we must use scriptural discernment regarding which strategies to implement
or support. Similarly, the Lord wants us to evaluate all our trials and sufferings and be sure they are placing us in the center of His will. Otherwise, we
can claim to suffer righteously when we are not and merely be "a troublesome
meddler," which is not pleasing to God.

✧ ✧ ✧

Suggestions for Prayer: Pray that your church would always have biblical reasons for supporting any efforts at redressing social wrongs.

For Further Study: What areas does Peter include in 1 Peter 2:11-19 when he
encourages obedience to authority?

> *"Therefore, let those also who suffer according to the will of God*
> *entrust their souls to a faithful Creator in doing what is right."*
> 1 PETER 4:19

❖ ❖ ❖

The final attitude we should have in facing trials
and sufferings is that of entrusting ourselves to God.

Geoffrey Bull epitomizes the modern-day believer who entrusts his entire soul to God's will in the middle of terrible suffering. Bull was punished with solitary confinement, brainwashing, many kinds of intimidation, and starvation during more than three years of imprisonment by the Communist Chinese forty years ago. During his affliction he prayed that God would help him remember Scriptures, realize His peace, and triumph over doubt, fear, loneliness, and fatigue. The final two lines of a poem he wrote summarize Bull's complete trust in God's plan and purpose:

> *And Thy kingdom, Gracious God,*
> *Shall never pass away.*

The term "entrust" is a banker's expression meaning "to deposit for safe-keeping." Peter encourages all believers who experience trials and tribulations to give over their very lives ("souls") to God's care. The Lord is indeed "a faithful Creator" who made us. Therefore we can and should trust Him fully as the only one who is able to care for all our needs.

By this point Peter has assumed that his original readers, since many had endured persecution, knew what suffering was like. Therefore, he could also present the Lord as a sovereign God who could be trusted to do "what is right." Because it is God's will to allow sufferings and trials in the lives of all believers, it is only logical that Peter exhort us to entrust ourselves to Him during such times.

Peter's instruction is also related to Romans 12:1, "I urge you therefore, brethren, by the mercies of God, to present your bodies a living and holy sacrifice, acceptable to God, which is your spiritual [or rational] service of worship." Paul reminds us that it is much easier to react as we should to trials if we have already resolved, with God's help, to entrust everything to Him. Then we can face with calm and confidence, rather than worry and fear, whatever God allows.

❖ ❖ ❖

Suggestions for Prayer: Review your commitment to God, and ask Him to bring to mind anything that you need to entrust wholly to Him; then by faith take that step.

For Further Study: Psalm 25 describes David's desire to trust in God. Read it and pick out several verses or a paragraph to meditate on.

*"And they chose Stephen, a man full of faith
and of the Holy Spirit."*
ACTS 6:5

✧ ✧ ✧

***Stephen's excellent character teaches us much
about responding to suffering and death.***

S tephen, the first Christian martyr, is one of the most inspiring biblical
examples of faithfulness in life and ministry. But his personal excellence
shines forth most through the familiar account of his death by stoning.

As one of the first deacons in the church, Stephen was recognized early on
as a man of great faith and spirituality (Acts 6:5). And a few verses later Luke
describes him as "full of grace and power" (v. 8). That was a grace of lovingkindness toward others, which he displayed in a most powerful way just before
his death.

In Acts 7:60, as the Jews were pelting him with rocks, Stephen was able to
look up to Heaven and say, "Lord, do not hold this sin against them!" That
kind of faith-filled, grace-filled reaction to those who were hatefully killing
him was possible only because Stephen believed in God's sovereign control
over his life and death.

At the very start of his encounter, Stephen manifested another amazing
response to his horribly unjust treatment: his enemies "saw his face like the
face of an angel" (Acts 6:15). It's impossible for us to know precisely what
such an expression would have been like, but it denoted a supernatural tran-
quility and joy that comes from being enveloped by the Lord's glorious presence. Stephen's awesome expression must have been an extremely forceful
rebuke to the Jewish leaders who claimed to know God.

The typical reaction from many of us in the same situation would have
been to exhibit much anxiety, stress, and anger. But Stephen demonstrated no
such response. Instead, he is a role model for how any believer ought to
behave during the most challenging trial. He had more than adequate grace
to cope well in every circumstance (cf. 2 Cor. 12:9; James 4:6), which is true
of all genuine Christians—those "full of faith and of the Holy Spirit."

✧ ✧ ✧

Suggestions for Prayer: Thank the Lord for Christian friends who are role
models to you. ✧ Pray that your behavior today would be special and Spirit-
filled, not ordinary and man-centered.

For Further Study: Read Exodus 33:7-11, 17-23; 34:29-35. What does Moses'
experience reveal about the power of God's glory?

> *"But being full of the Holy Spirit, he gazed intently*
> *into heaven and saw the glory of God, and*
> *Jesus standing at the right hand of God."*
>
> ACTS 7:55

❖ ❖ ❖

Because Stephen was so consistently Spirit-filled, it was natural
for him to react in a godly way to persecution and death.

The cliché "Garbage in, garbage out" provides a good clue to the essence of the Spirit-filled Christian life. Just as computers respond according to their programming, we respond to what fills our minds. If we allow the Holy Spirit to program our thought patterns, we'll be controlled and renewed by Him and live godly lives. And that's exactly how Stephen consistently and daily lived his life.

The expression "being full" is from a Greek verb (*pleroo*) that literally means "being kept full." Stephen was continuously filled with the Holy Spirit during his entire Christian life. This previewed Paul's directive in Ephesians 5:18, "but be filled with the Spirit." These words don't mean believers are to have some strange mystical experience, but simply that their lives ought to be fully controlled by God's Spirit.

Stephen gave evidence of his Spirit-filled godliness as He was about to die from stoning. Acts 7:55-56 says he looked to Jesus and let his adversaries and any witnesses know that he saw Christ standing at the right hand of God. Stephen did not focus on his difficult situation but fixed his heart on the Lord, which is what all believers must do: "Keep seeking the things above, where Christ is, seated at the right hand of God. Set your mind on the things above, not on the things that are on earth" (Col. 3:1-2).

Stephen's spiritual sight was incredible and enabled him to see the risen Christ and be certain of his welcome into Heaven the moment he died. We won't have that kind of vision while we're still on earth, but if we are constantly Spirit-filled like Stephen, we will always see Jesus by faith and realize His complete presence during the most trying times (John 14:26-27; Heb. 13:5-6).

❖ ❖ ❖

Suggestions for Prayer: Pray that God would direct your mind away from mundane distractions and toward Him throughout this day.

For Further Study: Stephen established a magnificent pattern during his short ministry in Acts 6. Read that chapter, and jot down several positive things you see about how he did things.

> *"Rejoice in the Lord always; again I will say, rejoice!"*
> PHILIPPIANS 4:4

✧ ✧ ✧

The apostle Paul was a model believer
who did not let his troubles steal His joy in the Lord.

According to today's verse, believers should never let a negative outlook replace our joy, no matter how bad life seems to be. The apostle Paul set an example that was far different. He wrote to the Philippians that in spite of being imprisoned in Rome, he was still rejoicing. Even though Paul was restricted under trying and harsh conditions, he was glad because the gospel message was being declared, even among the prison guards. Paul was not so concerned about his own hardships but that others hear the saving good news of Jesus Christ (see 1 Cor. 9:16).

Paul saw himself as a prisoner for the sake of Christ and the gospel. Therefore, he never gave in to any temptation to indulge in self-pity but rather focused on his duty of telling others about his Lord and Savior. Some of Paul's other letters also mention his imprisonment (see Eph. 3:1; Col. 4:10) but always positively, because the apostle never forgot that being a prisoner was merely part of the role he was called to as an ambassador for God's kingdom.

Paul's Roman imprisonment resulted in his joyful attitude extending out in evangelism: "My imprisonment in the cause of Christ has become well-known throughout the whole praetorian guard and to everyone else" (Phil. 1:13). However, Paul's ultimate impact on the guards and others was not just from his outward expressions of happiness. Rather, those who heard him were changed because they saw an attitude of joy and a message of truth deeply fixed in a man experiencing great trials and afflictions.

What a profound example Paul is for you and me today. For instance, we can make difficult witnessing opportunities easier by exhibiting Christlikeness and godly joy no matter how events are pressing us down. Such attitudes, so different from what people naturally expect, will give us many chances to testify of God's grace (see 1 Peter 3:15).

✧ ✧ ✧

Suggestions for Prayer: Ask the Lord to help you look above and beyond your problems and focus on what He has done for you.

For Further Study: A very striking example of Paul's rejoicing in the midst of suffering happened at the Philippian dungeon. Read Acts 16:22-34. What did he and Silas do to make the best of that trial?

> *"Whether in pretense or in truth, Christ is proclaimed;*
> *and in this I rejoice, yes, and I will rejoice."*
> PHILIPPIANS 1:18

❖ ❖ ❖

It is possible to maintain your joy even while dealing with criticisms and irritating distractions.

The dictionary definition of *detraction* is "the uttering of material (as false or slanderous charges) that is likely to damage the reputation of another." A detractor wants to undermine and destroy the good name and credibility of another. Great statesmen, such as President Abraham Lincoln during the American Civil War, often have been the targets of contentious political opponents and stinging detractions by the press.

For the church, the most difficult criticism has arisen from within, from false professors who once claimed to support it and its leaders. Paul came to know the disappointment and distress of being torn down when his detractors at Philippi assailed him even while he sat in prison. But he is a model of how one can rise above such pain and discouragement.

Paul's main detractors (Phil. 1:15) were his fellow preachers who proclaimed the same gospel as he did. They were not at odds with him over doctrine but over personal matters. Paul's detractors were envious of his ministry gifts and the way God had blessed his efforts with many converts and numerous churches.

Contending with the detractors at Philippi was not a completely new trial for Paul. He had previously learned patience in dealing with the letdowns caused by other supposed supporters (see 2 Tim. 1:15; 4:16). Now his opponents were testing his patience to the extreme as they sought to destroy his credibility with his supporters.

The detractors' tactics might have unsettled the faith of some in the churches, but not Paul's confidence. He stood up to all the unpleasantness with joy because, as our verse indicates, he knew the cause of Christ was still being advanced.

Paul's exemplary behavior under fire provides an obvious lesson for us: no amount of false and unfair criticism should steal our joy in Christ and His gospel. And we can keep rejoicing if we, like Paul, stay devoted to our top priority, proclaiming and glorifying the name of Christ.

❖ ❖ ❖

Suggestions for Prayer: Thank the Lord that the gospel and its power are strong enough to overcome any amount of jealous detraction. Pray that you would stay focused on gospel priorities.

For Further Study: Read Nehemiah 4—6. How did Nehemiah deal with the detractors to his work? ❖ What was the eventual outcome (6:16)?

"For to me, to live is Christ, and to die is gain."
PHILIPPIANS 1:21

❖ ❖ ❖

*We can count on Scripture to give us
confidence in the face of death.*

A few years ago my radio ministry heard from a listener who was exhibiting exactly the right attitude in the face of a terminal illness. A teenager from the Midwest sent a prayer request concerning her recently diagnosed Lou Gehrig's disease. That Christian young woman, who by now is probably with the Lord, accepted her condition with grace and optimism. Here is part of what she wrote to us: "I love the Lord very much and feel the Lord is using my condition to work in different peoples' lives. Please pray with me that He would continue to use me no matter what the outcome."

Her sentiments were right in step with Philippians 1:21, in which the apostle Paul proclaims his joy and confidence at the possibility of death. What enabled him to rejoice was his complete confidence in the Word of God.

Earlier Paul had articulated his trust in God's promises when he wrote these familiar words in Romans 8:28, "We know that God causes all things to work together for good to those who love God, to those who are called according to His purpose." Now he shared verbatim with the Philippians from Job 13:16, "For I know that this shall turn out for my deliverance" (Phil. 1:19). That too was a trustworthy promise from the Word, and it made Paul confident that his current trials would have a positive outcome.

Whether suffering was of long or short duration, Paul knew that the righteous would be delivered from their temporal trials. That was certainly borne out when God restored Job from his difficult, lengthy ordeal of testing.

Knowing all this, and realizing that all of God's written Word is available to us, we can certainly have Paul's type of confidence as we consider the inevitability of death. And we can "keep on rejoicing" (1 Peter 4:13), even if it's the Lord's will that we experience an early departure from this life.

❖ ❖ ❖

Suggestions for Prayer: Thank God for the provision of His Word, which is such an infallible guide as you deal with the uncertainties of death. ❖ Pray for someone you know at your church or in your neighborhood who may be facing death right now.

For Further Study: Read Psalm 34:17, 19; 37:39-40; 91:3; 97:10. What theme runs through these verses that would help you deal as you ought with trials and sufferings?

"For to me, to live is Christ, and to die is gain."
PHILIPPIANS 1:21

❖ ❖ ❖

*In addition to Scripture, God has given us more than
adequate spiritual resources to meet suffering and death.*

Wall Street, the name synonymous with the American stock market and
financial investing, is a place where confidence can rise and fall with
great force and unpredictability, right along with the rising or sinking level of
stock prices. Prices always seem to even out, but who can be certain about
how they will behave in the future?

The apostle Paul's spiritual confidence was not based on the changeable-
ness of financial markets but on truths that are stable and reliable. Yesterday
we saw his confidence in God's Word, and today we'll look at three more reasons Paul could confront death confidently.

First, Paul had confidence in the prayers of other believers. But it was not
a presumptuous confidence because he believed in asking others to pray (see
Rom. 15:30). Paul was convinced that "the effective prayer of a righteous man
can accomplish much" (James 5:16).

Second, Paul was confident that the Holy Spirit would supply all necessary
resources to sustain him through any suffering, even death. All Christians can
have that same confidence: "The Spirit also helps our weakness; for we do
not know how to pray as we should, but the Spirit Himself intercedes for us
with groanings too deep for words" (Rom. 8:26).

Third, Paul had the utmost confidence in Christ's promises. The apostle was sure
that God had called him to a specific ministry (Acts 26:16) and that if he was faithful, he would never suffer shame (Mark 8:38). Jesus never abandons His sheep, no
matter how bleak and frustrating their circumstances seem (John 10:27-28).

Our verse from Philippians summarizes Paul's confidence and joy in spite of
possible death. As long as he was serving Jesus Christ, he'd just as soon die because
death frees the believer from the burdens of earth and lets him glorify Christ in eternity. We can rely on the same promises and provisions as Paul did and have his kind
of joy. Jesus "is the same yesterday and today, yes and forever" (Heb. 13:8).

❖ ❖ ❖

Suggestions for Prayer: Confess any ways in which you have a misplaced
confidence. ❖ Ask the Lord to reinforce in your heart a Pauline confidence that
rejoices no matter what.

For Further Study: Read Romans 8, and list as many spiritual resources and
reasons for rejoicing as you can from the chapter.

"For momentary, light affliction is producing for us an eternal weight of glory far beyond all comparison."
2 CORINTHIANS 4:17

❖ ❖ ❖

Believers are far more blessed when they concentrate on the spiritual rather than physical aspects of life.

Concerning endurance, Paul is again our role model. One reason he was able to endure pain and trials was that he knew the physical was far less important and lasting than the spiritual. He realized that our physical bodies are naturally aging and therefore not permanent. He was probably aware of this more than most people because his rigorous ministry with its travel demands hastened his own aging process. And surely he also aged more rapidly than others because of all the physical and emotional persecution he endured from his enemies.

Paul was able to accept physical suffering and aging because he knew his inner man (his spiritual self, his new creation) was being renewed daily (2 Cor. 4:16). It's not easy for us to follow Paul's example; yet he urges believers to "set your mind on the things above, not on the things that are on earth" (Col. 3:2). Many of the trials and sufferings the Lord brings to us compel us to obey Paul's words, look away from ourselves, and experience the spiritual growth that is so directly the result of suffering (see 1 Peter 5:10).

God's Word assures us that He will provide all the strength we need to endure. In closing, consider the prophet's words:

> *Do you not know? Have you not heard? The Everlasting God, the Lord, the Creator of the ends of the earth does not become weary or tired. His understanding is inscrutable. He gives strength to the weary, and to him who lacks might He increases power. Though youths grow weary and tired, and vigorous young men stumble badly, yet those who wait for the Lord will gain new strength; they will mount up with wings like eagles, they will run and not get tired, they will walk and not become weary.*

—ISAIAH 40:28-31

❖ ❖ ❖

Suggestions for Prayer: As you go through this day, pray that the Lord would help you focus on the spiritual rather than the physical.

For Further Study: Read Hebrews 11:1-16. What common ingredient allowed those in this passage to look beyond the physical toward the spiritual?

*"For momentary, light affliction is producing for us an
eternal weight of glory far beyond all comparison."*
2 CORINTHIANS 4:17

❖ ❖ ❖

*It is far easier to endure trials when we
value the future over the present.*

A few years ago the popular *Back to the Future* movies dealt rather whim-
sically with the possibility of time travel, which always involved entering the future. The recurring theme was that with all the complications of
tampering with the future, it was better to live in the present. Viewers could
infer that, ultimately, it is not worth it to dwell a lot on the future.

That is just the opposite of the apostle Paul's attitude about the future. He
dealt with the profound certainties of what awaits all believers in the life to
come. For Paul, the value of the future was another important reason he could
endure life's sufferings and trials. The temporal pain for him and us is incon-
sequential compared to what awaits us in Heaven (Rom. 8:18).

Trials are inevitable, and the pain associated with them can be very intense,
but when compared to what we will enjoy in the future, they hardly matter.
Paul saw them as light afflictions, or literally "weightless trifles." He knew that
their real significance is only in how they contribute to our eternal glory.

That contribution is anything but trivial. Rather, it produces "an eternal
weight of glory." Concerning this expression, it's as if Paul envisioned an old-
fashioned two-sided scale that was being tipped in favor of the future by the
cumulative mass ("eternal weight of glory") of his individual sufferings. Paul
could endure the pain of present trials when he was certain that they con-
tributed positively to his life in Heaven.

The amount of trials and suffering you and I endure now is also directly
linked to our eternal rewards. Those rewards are not external bonuses such as
fancier crowns, better robes, or bigger heavenly mansions. Instead they refer
to our increased capacity to praise, serve, and glorify God. That fulfilled
Paul's greatest desire and enabled him to joyfully persevere in trials, and it
should do the same for us.

❖ ❖ ❖

Suggestions for Prayer: Ask God to give you a perspective that sees every
trial as trivial in light of eternal rewards.

For Further Study: Read Romans 8:18-25. How far do the effects of sin and
suffering extend? ❖ What does Paul say about hope in this passage?

"And while being reviled, He did not revile in return;
while suffering, He uttered no threats, but kept entrusting
Himself to Him who judges righteously."
1 PETER 2:23

✧ ✧ ✧

Jesus Christ, as the sinless sufferer, is the only model
we need as we endure life's trials.

Prior to his death in 1555, the English Reformer and martyr Hugh Latimer expressed his convictions this way: "Die once we must; how and where, we know not. . . . Here is not our home; let us therefore accordingly consider things, having always before our eyes that heavenly Jerusalem, and the way thereto in persecution." Latimer knew much about how to face suffering, but he knew that Jesus Himself was the final model regarding how to deal with suffering and death.

That model is summarized in today's verse, which is a quote from the Suffering Servant passage in Isaiah 53. All the horrible physical and verbal abuse Christ endured just prior to the cross, along with the evil tearing down of His perfectly virtuous character, was unjustified, and yet He did not strike back. As the Son of God, Jesus had perfect control of His feelings and powers.

Jesus found the strength to endure such an abusive final trial when He "kept entrusting Himself to Him who judges righteously." Literally, Jesus kept handing Himself and all His circumstances, climaxing with His death on Calvary (Luke 23:46), over to the Father. The Son had complete trust in God, the just and fair Judge of the entire earth (see Gen. 18:25).

We can follow His example and endure persecution and unjust suffering without answering back, whether it be in the workplace, among relatives, or in any social setting. The key is simply entrusting our lives, by faith, to a righteous God who will make everything right and bring us safely into His glory (1 Peter 5:6-10).

Stephen and Paul are notable role models for how we can triumph over life's persecutions and hardships, even death. But those great men were themselves merely "fixing [their] eyes on Jesus, the author and perfecter of faith" (Heb. 12:2). We must do the same.

✧ ✧ ✧

Suggestions for Prayer: As you daily experience life's normal difficulties and challenges, ask God to help you better remember the perfect example Jesus set in facing the worst of pain and suffering.

For Further Study: Read Hebrews 1:1-2 and 4:14-16. Compare and contrast what these passages tell us about Christ's deity and humanity. ✧ What do they reveal about the superiority of His example?

"O Lord, who may abide in Thy tent? Who may dwell on Thy holy hill? He who walks with integrity, and works righteousness, and speaks truth in his heart."

PSALM 15:1-2

✧ ✧ ✧

To love Christ and to be characterized by ever-increasing fidelity to biblical truth is the heart of true integrity.

Christian integrity has been defined as the absence of compromise and the presence of biblical convictions. In the words of the psalmist, it is to work righteousness and to speak truth from the heart (Ps. 15:2).

Many people in Scripture demonstrate exemplary integrity. For example, Jesus spoke of Nathanael as an Israelite "in whom is no guile" (John 1:47). To be without guile is to be truthful and unpretentious, which is another way of saying Nathanael had integrity. What a wonderful commendation!

Like Nathanael, Daniel was a man of uncompromising integrity, and in our studies this month Daniel's example will demonstrate the power, characteristics, and blessings of biblical integrity. You will also see how God uses even the most difficult circumstances to test and refine your integrity.

This is an especially timely topic for our day because the spirit of compromise is flourishing all around us: in politics, in sports, in business, and sadly, even in the church. But Scripture calls us to an uncompromising standard that reflects the integrity of Christ Himself. As the Apostle John said, "The one who says he abides in [Christ] ought himself to walk in the same manner as He walked" (1 John 2:6).

This month you will see some of the challenges that await those who refuse to compromise their biblical convictions, as well as the blessings that come to them. As you do, I pray that the Lord will strengthen and encourage you, and that you will be one who truly "walks with integrity, and works righteousness, and speaks truth in his heart."

✧ ✧ ✧

Suggestions for Prayer: Make King David's prayer yours today: "Guard my soul and deliver me; do not let me be ashamed, for I take refuge in Thee. Let integrity and uprightness preserve me, for I wait for Thee" (Psalm 25:20-21).

For Further Study: Read Daniel 1, 3, and 6 in preparation for our studies this month. Make a list of the character traits you see in Daniel, Shadrach, Meshach, and Abed-nego that are worthy of imitation.

"In the third year of the reign of Jehoiakim king of Judah,
Nebuchadnezzar king of Babylon came to Jerusalem and besieged
it. And the Lord gave Jehoiakim king of Judah into his hand,
along with some of the vessels of the house of God; and he
brought them to the land of Shinar, to the house of his god, and
he brought the vessels into the treasury of his god."

DANIEL 1:1-2

❖ ❖ ❖

Integrity shines brightest against
the backdrop of adversity.

Our passage today tells of the tragic time in Israel's history when God chastened her severely by allowing King Nebuchadnezzar and the wicked nation of Babylon to march against her and take her captive. God never coddles His people, nor does He wink at their sin. Israel's chastening illustrates the principle that "judgment [begins] with the household of God" (1 Peter 4:17). But as severe as His discipline can be, it is always aimed at producing greater righteousness and godly integrity in His children (Heb. 12:5-11).

The Babylonian captivity set the stage for a truly uncommon display of integrity from Daniel and his three Hebrew friends. In the days ahead we will examine their character in some depth. For now, however, be encouraged that adversity of any kind—even chastening for sin—is God's way of providing the rich soil for nourishing and strengthening the spiritual fruit of integrity. Without the adversities of Babylon, Daniel's integrity and that of his friends would not have shone as brightly as it did and would not have had the significant impact it had on King Nebuchadnezzar and his entire kingdom.

Perhaps you are currently experiencing adversities that are especially challenging, and you may not yet understand what God is accomplishing through them. But like Daniel and his friends, you can pray for the wisdom to understand His will and the faith to trust Him through the process. And you can be assured He will never fail you.

❖ ❖ ❖

Suggestions for Prayer: Each day your integrity is tested in many ways. Ask the Lord to help you be aware of those times and to make choices that honor Him.

For Further Study: Read 1 Kings 9:3-5. What kind of integrity did God require of Solomon? ❖ What promises did He make if Solomon obeyed?

"Then the king ordered Ashpenaz, the chief of his officials, to bring in some of the sons of Israel, including some of the royal family and of the nobles, youths in whom was no defect, who were good-looking, showing intelligence in every branch of wisdom, endowed with understanding, and discerning knowledge, and who had ability for serving in the king's court; and he ordered him to teach them the literature and language of the Chaldeans. . . . Now among them from the sons of Judah were Daniel, Hananiah, Mishael and Azariah."

DANIEL 1:3-4, 6

✧ ✧ ✧

Man values physical beauty and superior human capabilities, whereas God values spiritual character.

As King Nebuchadnezzar was besieging Jerusalem, he received word that his father had died. So he returned to Babylon, leaving Jehoiakim, king of Judah, in power. To ensure the king's loyalty, Nebuchadnezzar instructed Ashpenaz, the chief of his officials, to take some hostages from among the royal families of Israel. Among those selected were Daniel, Hananiah, Mishael, and Azariah.

Nebuchadnezzar's plan was to train these young hostages in the ways of the Babylonians (Chaldeans), then press them into service as his representatives among the Jews. There were an estimated fifty to seventy-five hostages, each of whom was young (probably in his early teens), handsome, and without physical defect. In addition, each had superior intellect, education, wisdom, and social graces.

Being among such a select group of people could have led to pride in Daniel, Hananiah, Mishael, and Azariah. But self-glorification meant nothing to them. Their priority was to serve their God with humility, integrity, and fidelity. Nebuchadnezzar could look on them favorably, train them in the ways of the Chaldeans, and offer them power and influence in his kingdom, but he could never incite their pride or diminish their allegiance to the Lord.

Like Babylon, our society is enamored with physical beauty and human capabilities. However, let your focus be on spiritual character and using for God's glory the talents and abilities He has given you.

✧ ✧ ✧

Suggestions for Prayer: Thank the Lord for the special gifts He has given you. ✧ Prayerfully guard your heart against subtle pride, which undermines spiritual character.

For Further Study: Read Daniel 4:28-36. How did God deal with King Nebuchadnezzar's pride? ✧ What was the king's response (see v. 37)?

> *"Now among them from the sons of Judah were Daniel,*
> *Hananiah, Mishael and Azariah. Then the commander of the*
> *officials assigned new names to them; and to Daniel he*
> *assigned the name Belteshazzar, to Hananiah Shadrach,*
> *to Mishael Meshach, and to Azariah Abed-nego."*
>
> DANIEL 1:6-7

✧ ✧ ✧

You can't always prevent personal loss,
but you can respond to it in ways that glorify God.

It was a quiet January morning in the San Fernando Valley of Southern California until suddenly and without warning the earth shook with such a violent force that many department stores, apartment houses, homes, and freeway overpasses crumbled under the strain. Within minutes the 1994 Northridge earthquake left scars upon lives and land that in some cases may never heal. Such catastrophic events remind us of just how difficult dealing with personal loss can be.

Daniel, Hananiah, Mishael, and Azariah understood personal loss. Perhaps in our day only those who have suffered as prisoners of war or as refugees from war's ravages can fully appreciate the deep sense of loss those men must have felt after being cut off from family, friends, and homeland.

Their loss included even their own names. When taken captive, each of them had a Hebrew name that reflected his godly upbringing. But in an apparent effort to remove that influence and to exalt the pagan deities of Bel (or Baal) and Aku, Nebuchadnezzar's commander changed their names from Daniel (which means "God is judge") to Belteshazzar ("Bel provides" or "Bel's prince"), from Hananiah ("the Lord is gracious") to Shadrach ("under the command ofAku"), from Mishael ("Who is what the Lord is?") to Meshach ("Who is what Aku is?"), and from Azariah ("the Lord is my helper") to Abed-nego ("the servant of Nebo [the son of Baal]").

Daniel and his friends couldn't prevent their losses, but they could trust God and refuse to let those losses lead to despair or compromise. That's an example you can follow when you face loss.

✧ ✧ ✧

Suggestions for Prayer: Ask the Lord for the wisdom to see your losses through His loving eyes, and for the grace to respond appropriately. ✧ Pray for those whom you know who have suffered loss recently.

For Further Study: Read Job 1:13-22. How did Job respond to his losses? ✧ What can you learn from his example?

"And the king appointed for them a daily ration from the king's choice food and from the wine which he drank, and appointed that they should be educated three years, at the end of which they were to enter the king's personal service. . . . But Daniel made up his mind that he would not defile himself with the king's choice food or with the wine which he drank; so he sought permission from the commander of the officials that he might not defile himself."

DANIEL 1:5, 8

✧ ✧ ✧

*Godly integrity is built upon
the foundation of biblical authority.*

From the world's perspective, King Nebuchadnezzar had much to offer his Hebrew captives: the best food, the best education, and high positions in his kingdom. But Daniel's perspective was quite different. He did not object to receiving a pagan education because God had given no direct prohibition against that, and a Babylonian education had much to offer in the areas of architecture and science. But as with anyone receiving a secular education, Daniel would have to exercise discernment in sorting out the true from the false and the good from the bad.

It was when Daniel was asked to violate a direct command from God that he drew the line and took his stand on biblical principle. That's the character of godly integrity. It bases decisions on the principles from God's Word, not on mere preference, intimidation, or peer pressure. Seemingly Daniel had every reason to compromise: he was young, away from home, and facing severe consequences if he defied the king's order. Yet he was unwavering in his obedience to God.

Although Daniel couldn't obey the king's order, he handled the situation in a wise and respectful manner by seeking permission to abstain from eating what God had forbidden. From his example we learn that standing on principle will sometimes put us at odds with those in authority over us, but even then we can love and respect them.

✧ ✧ ✧

Suggestions for Prayer: Pray for those in authority over you who may want you to do things that would displease the Lord. ✧ Pray for wisdom and grace to maintain a loving attitude toward them while still standing on biblical principles.

For Further Study: Read Acts 5:17-29. How did the apostles respond to the authorities who commanded them to stop preaching the gospel?

> *"Now God granted Daniel favor and compassion*
> *in the sight of the commander of the officials."*
>
> DANIEL 1:9

❖ ❖ ❖

God's favor is the rich reward of obedience.

G od delights in granting special grace and favor to those whose hearts are set on pleasing Him. For example, "Noah found favor in the eyes of the Lord" and was spared the ravages of the Flood (Gen. 6:8). Joseph found favor in His sight and was elevated to prominence in Egypt (Gen. 39—41). God granted Moses and the children of Israel favor in the sight of the Egyptians, and they were able to plunder Egypt in the Exodus (Ex. 11:3; 12:36).

When Daniel chose to obey God by not defiling himself with the king's special diet (Dan. 1:8), he demonstrated great courage and integrity. God responded by granting him favor and compassion in the sight of Ashpenaz, the commander of the king's officials. The Hebrew word translated "favor" speaks of goodness or kindness. It can also include a strong affection from deep within. "Compassion" means a tender, unfailing love. Together these words tell us that God established a special relationship between Ashpenaz and Daniel that not only protected Daniel from harm in this instance, but also helped prepare him for his future role as a man of enormous influence in Babylon.

Today God's favor is the special grace He grants His children in times of need. It is especially evident when their obedience brings persecution. The apostle Peter wrote, "This finds favor [grace], if for the sake of conscience toward God a man bears up under sorrows when suffering unjustly. . . . If when you do what is right and suffer for it you patiently endure it, this finds favor [grace] with God" (1 Peter 2:19-20).

Daniel knew that refusing the king's special diet could lead to serious consequences, but he was more interested in obeying God's Word than avoiding man's punishment. He had the right priorities, and God honored his obedience, just as He will honor yours.

❖ ❖ ❖

Suggestions for Prayer: Let the prayer of Moses be yours today: "Let me know Thy ways, that I may know Thee, so that I may find favor in Thy sight" (Ex. 33:13).

For Further Study: Read Genesis 39. What were the results of God's favor upon Joseph?

*"The commander of the officials said to Daniel, 'I am
afraid of my lord the king, who has appointed your food and
your drink; for why should he see your faces looking more
haggard than the youths who are your own age? Then you would
make me forfeit my head to the king.' But Daniel said to
the overseer whom the commander of the officials had appointed
over Daniel, Hananiah, Mishael and Azariah, 'Please test
your servants for ten days, and let us be given some vegetables to
eat and water to drink. Then let our appearance be observed
in your presence, and the appearance of the youths who are eating the king's choice food; and deal with your servants
according to what you see.' So he listened to them in this
matter and tested them for ten days."*

DANIEL 1:10-14

❖ ❖ ❖

*People of biblical integrity tend also to be people
with unashamed boldness.*

I love to read the biographies of great missionaries and other godly people whose lives reflect an uncommon commitment to Christ and whose boldness in the face of difficulties sets them apart from their peers. Daniel was such a man. From his youth he delighted in doing God's will and proclaiming God's Word with boldness. He shared David's perspective in Psalm 40:8-9, "I delight to do Thy will, O my God; Thy Law is within my heart. I have proclaimed glad tidings of righteousness in the great congregation; behold, I will not restrain my lips, O Lord."

In stark contrast to Daniel's boldness was Ashpenaz's fear. Although he thought kindly of Daniel, Ashpenaz feared for his life if Daniel and his friends were to appear pale and malnourished after he granted them exemption from the king's special diet. So with characteristic wisdom and boldness, Daniel suggested a simple test designed to relieve Ashpenaz's fears and prove God's faithfulness. Tomorrow we will see the results of that test (v. 15). But for today I pray that you will have the boldness of Daniel as you take every opportunity to proclaim God's Word.

❖ ❖ ❖

Suggestions for Prayer: Like Daniel you may be facing a situation that requires a special measure of boldness. If so, ask the Lord to strengthen you as you set your heart on doing His will.

For Further Study: Read Ephesians 6:19-20; Philippians 1:19-20. What was the source of Paul's boldness?

> *"So [the king's overseer] listened to [Daniel and his friends*
> *in this matter and tested them for ten days. And at the end of ten*
> *days their appearance seemed better and they were*
> *fatter than all the youths who had been eating the king's choice*
> *food. So the overseer continued to withhold their choice food and*
> *the wine they were to drink, and kept giving them vegetables."*
>
> DANIEL 1:14-16

❖ ❖ ❖

All spiritual commitment will be tested.

When God wants to prove the quality of one's commitment, He tests it. The test may come directly from Him, as with Abraham when God asked him to sacrifice his son Isaac (Gen. 22:1-2), or it may come through difficult circumstances, as with the Israelites during their wilderness wanderings (Deut. 8:16), or it may even come from Satan himself, as God permitted with Job (Job 1:12; 2:6). Regardless of its source, every test is designed by God to produce greater spiritual fruit in His children (1 Peter 1:6-7).

Daniel, Shadrach, Meshach, and Abed-nego's tests came at the hands of their Babylonian captors. Separation from family, friends, and homeland must have been an extremely difficult test for them, but through it all their commitment to the Lord remained unshakable. Now they faced a test to determine whether or not they could remain undefiled. For ten days they would eat only vegetables and drink only water, while their fellow captives ate the king's special diet.

Normally such a brief period of time would make no noticeable change in one's physiology, but God must have intervened because at the conclusion of just ten days, these four young men were clearly healthier and more vigorous than their peers. The results were so convincing that their overseer allowed them to remain on a vegetarian diet throughout their entire three-year training period. God honored their uncompromising spirit.

When you are tested, remember that God is working on your spiritual maturity and that He will never test you beyond what you are able to endure and will always provide a means of victory (1 Cor. 10:13).

❖ ❖ ❖

Suggestions for Prayer: Pray for wisdom and strength to meet each test in your life with courage and victory.

For Further Study: Read Psalm 26:1-3. What did King David request of God? ❖ How does he describe a person of integrity?

*"As for [Daniel, Shadrach, Meshach, and Abed-nego],
God gave them knowledge and intelligence in every branch of
literature and wisdom; Daniel even understood
all kinds of visions and dreams."*

DANIEL 1:17

❖ ❖ ❖

*Godly wisdom guards against the
influences of a godless society.*

From the beginning of human history Satan has tried to confuse and confound God's purposes by corrupting man's thinking. In the Garden of Eden he succeeded by calling God's character into question and convincing Eve that her disobedience would have no consequences. To this day he continues to deceive entire civilizations by blinding "the minds of the unbelieving, that they might not see the light of the gospel of the glory of Christ" (2 Cor. 4:4).

Daniel and his friends were captives of a pagan king who wanted to dilute their allegiance to God by reprogramming their thinking. However, unlike Eve, they were determined not to be overcome by the evil influences around them. God honored their integrity and taught them everything they needed to know to be productive in Babylonian society and to influence it for righteousness.

Babylon was the center of learning in its day, boasting of advanced sciences, sophisticated libraries, and great scholars. God gave these young men the ability to learn and retain that level of knowledge, and the wisdom to apply it to their lives. Furthermore, He gave Daniel the ability to interpret dreams and receive visions—gifts that would prove crucial later in his life as God elevated him to a position of prominence in Babylon and revealed the plan of history to him (see chapters 7—12).

Surely Daniel, Shadrach, Meshach, and Abed-nego didn't understand all that God had in store for them or why He would allow them to be tested so severely at such a young age. But when they chose to love and trust Him despite their circumstances, they demonstrated the kind of wisdom that protects God's children from the influences of a godless society. As we do the same, God uses us in significant ways. Also, we find that God never calls us to a challenge that He won't equip us to handle.

❖ ❖ ❖

Suggestions for Prayer: King David prayed, "Teach us to number our days, that we may present to Thee a heart of wisdom" (Ps. 90:12). Make that your prayer as well.

For Further Study: Read Colossians 1:9-12. What are the results of being filled with "spiritual wisdom and understanding"?

> *"Then at the end of the days which the king had specified for*
> *presenting them, the commander of the officials presented*
> *them before Nebuchadnezzar. And the king talked with them, and out*
> *of them all not one was found like Daniel, Hananiah, Mishael and*
> *Azariah; so they entered the king's personal service. And as for every*
> *matter of wisdom and understanding about which the king consulted*
> *them, he found them ten times better than all the magicians*
> *and conjurers who were in all his realm."*
>
> DANIEL 1:18-20

❖ ❖ ❖

God always equips you for the tasks He requires of you.

Daniel and the other young men deported in 606 B.C. received three years of intense training under the watchful eye of the commander of King Nebuchadnezzar's officials. At the conclusion of their training, they were presented to the king for his personal evaluation. The results were impressive indeed. Of all those who were trained, none compared to Daniel, Hananiah, Mishael, and Azariah. Beyond that, they were found to be ten times better than all the wise men in the entire kingdom of Babylon! Consequently, at the age of only seventeen or eighteen, they were made the king's personal servants.

Why were these young men so superior to their peers? It wasn't simply their training, because each man had received the same education. The difference was their character and the faithful provisions of their God, who granted them special knowledge, intelligence, and wisdom (v. 17). They were so righteous and wise that even those who did not believe in their God were compelled to acknowledge the quality of their lives. That's the impact every believer should have on those around them!

God wants you to live the kind of life that silences those who would seek to malign you or your God (1 Peter 2:15), and He has provided every spiritual resource for you to do so (2 Peter 1:3). Therefore, when you live with integrity, you prove to others that God really does accomplish His work in those who love Him.

❖ ❖ ❖

Suggestions for Prayer: Make a list of spiritual resources that are yours in Christ, then praise Him for each of them.

For Further Study: Read Psalm 119:97-104. What are the psalmist's attitudes toward God's Word (His "law")? ❖ What steps did he take to ensure that godliness would be evident in his life?

> *"And Daniel continued until
> the first year of Cyrus the king."*
> DANIEL 1:21

❖ ❖ ❖

People of integrity are people of significant spiritual influence.

When King Nebuchadnezzar took Daniel as one of his personal servants, it was just the beginning of a ministry that would last for seventy years. Daniel 2:48 records that soon afterward "the king promoted Daniel and gave him many great gifts, and he made him ruler over the whole province of Babylon and chief prefect over all the wise men of Babylon." At Daniel's request, the king also appointed Shadrach, Meshach, and Abed-nego to positions of authority, thereby providing an even stronger voice for righteousness in Babylon.

Years later, Nebuchadnezzar's son, Belshazzar, "clothed Daniel with purple and put a necklace of gold around his neck, and issued a proclamation concerning him that he now had authority as the third ruler in the kingdom" (Dan. 5:29). Following Belshazzar's death and the fall of Babylon to the Medes and Persians, Darius the Mede appointed Daniel as one of only three men in the kingdom to have oversight over all his governors (Dan. 6:1-2). As the Lord continued to bless Daniel, and as he distinguished himself among Darius' leaders, the king appointed him as prime minister over the entire kingdom. Daniel therefore "enjoyed success in the reign of Darius and in the reign of Cyrus the Persian" (Dan. 6:28).

Daniel's life was one of enormous influence, which began when he was a youth who chose commitment over compromise. He was faithful with little, and the Lord gave him much. Perhaps few Christians will have the breadth of influence Daniel enjoyed, but every Christian should have his commitment. Remember, the choices you make for Christ today directly impact the influence you will have for Him tomorrow. So live each day to hear the Lord's "Well done, good and faithful [servant]; you were faithful with a few things, I will put you in charge of many things; enter into the joy of your master" (Matt. 25:23).

❖ ❖ ❖

Suggestions for Prayer: Ask the Lord to guard your integrity, so that your influence for Him will be strong and ever-increasing.

For Further Study: Read the prayer of Jabez in 1 Chronicles 4:10. What did Jabez request of God? ❖ What was God's response?

*"Nebuchadnezzar the king made an image of gold, the
height of which was sixty cubits and its width six cubits; he set it
up on the plain of Dura in the province of Babylon. Then
Nebuchadnezzar the king sent word to assemble the satraps, the
prefects and the governors, the counselors, the treasurers,
the judges, the magistrates and all the rulers of the provinces to
come to the dedication of the image that Nebuchadnezzar
the king had set up. Then the satraps, the prefects and the governors, the counselors, the treasurers, the judges, the magistrates
and all the rulers of the provinces were assembled for the
dedication of the image that Nebuchadnezzar the king had set up;
and they stood before the image that Nebuchadnezzar had set up."*

DANIEL 3:1-3

❖ ❖ ❖

*People are incurably religious and will worship
either the true God or a false substitute.*

Scripture teaches that a double-minded man is "unstable in all his ways" (James
1:8). That certainly was true of King Nebuchadnezzar, who shortly after
declaring that Daniel's God "is a God of gods and a Lord of kings" (Dan. 2:47),
erected a huge image of himself and assembled all his leaders for its dedication.

The image was ninety feet tall and was probably constructed of wood over-
laid with gold. Because the plain of Dura was flat, the statue would have been
visible for a great distance. The gold idol was a magnificent sight as it reflected
the bright sunlight of that region.

The king's plan was to have all his leaders bow down to the image, thereby
bringing glory to himself, verifying their loyalty, and unifying the nation
under one religion. But he was soon to learn that three young men with spiritual integrity would never abandon worship of the true God, regardless of the
consequences.

Worshiping the true God or a false substitute is the choice that everyone
must make. Sadly, millions of people who wouldn't think of bowing to a tan-
gible image nevertheless worship useless gods of their own imaginations.
Even Christians can be lured into self-love and covetousness, which are forms
of idolatry (Col. 3:5). That's why you must always guard your heart diligently.

❖ ❖ ❖

Suggestions for Prayer: Thank the Lord for the privilege of knowing and worshiping the true God.

For Further Study: According to Romans 1:18-32, what are the spiritual and
moral consequences of idolatry?

*"Then the herald loudly proclaimed: 'To you the command
is given, O peoples, nations and men of every language, that at
the moment you hear the sound of the horn, flute, lyre,
trigon, psaltery, bagpipe, and all kinds of music, you are to fall
down and worship the golden image that Nebuchadnezzar
the king has set up. But whoever does not fall down and worship
shall immediately be cast into the midst of a furnace of
blazing fire.' Therefore at that time, when all the peoples heard
the sound of the horn, flute, lyre, trigon, psaltery, bagpipe,
and all kinds of music, all the peoples, nations and men of every
language fell down and worshiped the golden image
that Nebuchadnezzar the king had set up."*

DANIEL 3:4-7

✧ ✧ ✧

The choices you make reveal the convictions you embrace.

After King Nebuchadnezzar had gathered all his leaders to the dedication of his golden image, he issued a proclamation that at the sound of his orchestra they were to fall down and worship the image. Those leaders were the most influential and respected people in Babylon, so you might expect them to be people of strong convictions and personal integrity. Sadly, that was not the case, and with only three exceptions they all lacked the courage to say no.

Granted, punishment for disobeying the king's decree would be severe indeed. But even the threat of a fiery death could not intimidate Shadrach, Meshach, and Abed-nego. Instead, it simply revealed the depth of their commitment to God. That's what makes them such remarkable role models. As young men barely twenty years old, they demonstrated tremendous courage and conviction.

Each day Christians face considerable pressure to compromise spiritual integrity and to adopt standards of thought and behavior that are displeasing to the Lord. Young people especially are vulnerable to negative peer pressure and intimidation. Shadrach, Meshach, and Abed-nego show us that young people can be spiritual leaders who are strong in their faith and exemplary in their obedience. May that be true of you as well, regardless of your age.

✧ ✧ ✧

Suggestions for Prayer: Remember to pray often for the young people in your church, and do what you can to encourage them in their walk with the Lord.

For Further Study: Read Joshua 1:1-9. How did God encourage Joshua as he faced the intimidating task of leading the nation of Israel?

"For this reason at that time certain Chaldeans came forward
and brought charges against the Jews. . . . 'There are certain
Jews whom you have appointed over the administration of the
province of Babylon, namely Shadrach, Meshach, and Abed-
nego. These men, O king, have disregarded you; they do not serve
your gods or worship the golden image which you have set up.'"

DANIEL 3:8-12

✧ ✧ ✧

Expect spiritual opposition.

H ave you noticed that whenever you take a public stand for righteousness you feel the reaction of the world more strongly? Even something
as noble as doing your work with integrity and diligence can bring ridicule,
rejection, or even open hostility. But that shouldn't surprise you. Jesus said,
"'A slave is not greater than his master.' If they persecuted Me, they will also
persecute you" (John 15:20). The apostle Paul warns that "indeed, all who
desire to live godly in Christ Jesus will be persecuted" (2 Tim. 3:12).

Shadrach, Meshach, and Abed-nego were well-acquainted with spiritual
opposition, and in today's passage they are targets of envious Chaldeans who
want to see them put to death. The accusations brought against them were not
entirely true because they had not disregarded the king. On the contrary, they
were model citizens and exemplary leaders. They had attended the king's cer-
emony and fulfilled all their other civil duties insofar as those duties did not
violate their responsibility to God.

Their accusers weren't motivated by loyalty to the king or by their personal
allegiance to his religious views. They were jealous and resentful because they
hated having Jewish captives ruling over them (see Dan. 2:49).

Sometimes Christians today will do their work excellently and be promoted over their peers, only to incur the displeasure of jealous workmates
who criticize or bring false and discrediting accusations against them. If ever
you are in that situation, you need to be especially diligent to do your work
as unto the Lord (Col. 3:23), to guard your own attitude, and to let the Lord
be your defender.

✧ ✧ ✧

Suggestions for Prayer: In obedience to the Lord, "Love your enemies, do
good to those who hate you, bless those who curse you, pray for those who
mistreat you" (Luke 6:27-28).

For Further Study: Read Daniel 6. What parallels do you see between
Daniel's situation and our current passage? ✧ How did God prove Himself
faithful in each?

*"Then Nebuchadnezzar in rage and anger gave orders
to bring Shadrach, Meshach, and Abed-nego; then these men
were brought before the king. Nebuchadnezzar responded and
said to them, 'Is it true, Shadrach, Meshach and Abed-nego,
that you do not serve my gods or worship the golden image that
I have set up? Now if you are ready, at the moment you hear the
sound of the horn, flute, lyre, trigon, psaltery, and bagpipe, and
all kinds of music, to fall down and worship the image that I
have made, very well. But if you will not worship, you will immediately be cast into the midst of a furnace of blazing fire; and
what god is there who can deliver you out of my hands?'"*

DANIEL 3:13-15

✧ ✧ ✧

God humbles the proud but gives grace to the humble.

When King Nebuchadnezzar asked Shadrach, Meshach, and Abed-nego "What god is there who can deliver you out of my hands?" he showed the extent to which a person can be blinded by sinful pride and arrogance. It is sheer folly to pit one's power against God's, but that's precisely what he did.

Nebuchadnezzar's attitude reflects that of Satan himself, who boasted that he would ascend into Heaven and make himself like the Most High God (Isa. 14:13-14). God is quick to correct such foolish notions. Later in his life Nebuchadnezzar learned that "everyone who is proud in heart is an abomination to the Lord; assuredly, he will not be unpunished" (Prov. 16:5). After being severely chastened by God, the king came to his senses and proclaimed, "I Nebuchadnezzar praise, exalt, and honor the King of heaven, for all His works are true and His ways just, and He is able to humble those who walk in pride" (Dan. 4:37).

Although they may not be as openly defiant as Nebuchadnezzar was, everyone who willfully disobeys God's Word is following his example by exalting their own will over God's and challenging His authority in their lives.

✧ ✧ ✧

Suggestions for Prayer: Ask the Lord to keep you humble and to forgive any subtle pride you may be harboring in your heart.

For Further Study: Read Psalm 31:23-24 and James 4:13-16. How does the psalmist encourage the humble? ✧ What is James's caution to those who live as if they are not accountable to God?

> *"Shadrach, Meshach and Abed-nego answered and said*
> *to the king, 'O Nebuchadnezzar, we do not need to give you an*
> *answer concerning this. If it be so, our God whom we serve*
> *is able to deliver us from the furnace of blazing fire; and He will*
> *deliver us out of your hand, O king. But even if He does not, let it*
> *be known to you, O king, that we are not going to serve your gods*
> *or worship the golden image that you have set up.'"*
>
> DANIEL 3:16-18

✧ ✧ ✧

Unconditional obedience is the
trademark of mature faith.

In Matthew 13 Jesus speaks of people who hear the gospel and initially respond with joy, only to turn away when persecution arises. Tragically, that's a common occurrence today that is caused by preachers who promise health, wealth, prosperity, and special miracles to all who believe. People who embrace such error are not prepared for the cost of discipleship (cf. Matt. 16:24; John 15:20).

Shadrach, Meshach, and Abed-nego understood what it meant to serve God unconditionally. They knew He could move in their defense if it pleased Him to do so, but their faith was not dependent on miracles or any other special benefits they might receive from Him. They stood on convictions and deferred to His will even when doing so brought the threat of a fiery death. Their attitude was that of Christ Himself as He faced the agony of the cross and prayed, "Father . . . not as I will, but as Thou wilt'" (Matt. 26:39).

Their response to King Nebuchadnezzar's ultimatum may sound arrogant or disrespectful, but they were simply acknowledging that they had nothing to say in their own defense. They had served him faithfully as far as they could, but serving his gods and bowing down to his image was out of the question. God forbids any form of idolatry, and they would not be coerced or intimidated into disobeying Him.

Like Shadrach, Meshach, and Abed-nego, your faith in God isn't measured by whether or not He rescues you from a difficult situation, but by your willingness to trust and obey Him unconditionally.

✧ ✧ ✧

Suggestions for Prayer: Express your love to the Lord and your desire to serve Him faithfully despite the circumstances.

For Further Study: Read Matthew 13:1-23. What response does each soil represent?

> *"Then Nebuchadnezzar was filled with wrath, and his facial*
> *expression was altered toward Shadrach, Meshach and*
> *Abed-nego. He answered by giving orders to heat the furnace*
> *seven times more than it was usually heated. And he*
> *commanded certain valiant warriors who were in his army*
> *to tie up Shadrach, Meshach and Abed-nego, in order*
> *to cast them into the furnace of blazing fire."*
>
> DANIEL 3:19-20

❖ ❖ ❖

Persecution is the world's futile attempt
to silence the voice of godly integrity.

King Nebuchadnezzar was a brilliant and powerful man who had built an enormous empire by bringing entire nations under his control. Yet when three youths refused to compromise their devotion to God, he lost rational control and flew into such an intense rage that his face became visibly distorted.

Wanting to vent his wrath upon Shadrach, Meshach, and Abed-nego, Nebuchadnezzar ordered that the furnace be heated seven times hotter than usual. You might expect him to have turned the fire down, thereby punishing them more severely by prolonging their pain. But the king was reacting emotionally, not logically, which often is the case when sinful people are confronted by righteousness.

We see the same pattern throughout Scripture. For example, King Herod's wife hated John the Baptist and had him beheaded for confronting her sinful marriage to the king (Mark 6:19ff.). Those who couldn't cope with the wisdom and spirit of Stephen stirred up the Jews against him, which eventually led to his death by stoning (Acts 6:9 ff.). The Old Testament prophets and the Lord Himself were killed by those who were hostile to God. Similarly, the Thessalonian and Judean Christians endured angry persecution from their own countrymen (1 Thess. 2:14-15).

The opposition we face today may be more subtle, but it all has its source in Satan, who "was a murderer from the beginning" (John 8:44). So don't be surprised if subtle opposition suddenly erupts into murderous wrath. But be encouraged, knowing that even when it does, it can never thwart God's plans or overcome His sustaining grace.

❖ ❖ ❖

Suggestions for Prayer: Pray for boldness to speak the truth in love and never to fear the world's reaction.

For Further Study: Read 2 Thessalonians 1:3-10. Why does God allow Christians to suffer persecution? ❖ When and how will God deal with those who persecute His children?

*"Then [Shadrach, Meshach, and Abed-nego] were tied up in
their trousers, their coats, their caps and their other clothes,
and were cast into the midst of the furnace of blazing fire. For
this reason, because the king's command was urgent and the
furnace had been made extremely hot, the flame of the fire slew
those men who carried up Shadrach, Meshach and Abed-nego.
But these three men, Shadrach, Meshach and Abed-nego, fell
into the midst of the furnace of blazing fire still tied up."*

DANIEL 3:21-23

❖ ❖ ❖

*When God doesn't deliver you from a trial,
He refines you through the trial.*

When facing excommunication at the Diet of Worms, Martin Luther
wrote to the Elector Frederick, "You ask me what I shall do if I am
called by the emperor. I will go down if I am too sick to stand on my feet. If
Caesar calls me, God calls me. If violence is used, as well it may be, I commend my cause to God. He lives and reigns who saved the three youths from
the fiery furnace of the king of Babylon, and if He will not save me, my head
is worth nothing compared with Christ. This is no time to think of safety. I
must take care that the gospel is not brought into contempt by our fear to confess and seal our teaching with our blood."

Luther was willing to risk even death for the sake of Christ. Like Shadrach,
Meshach, and Abed-nego before him, he valued integrity above his own life,
and in his loneliest hour drew encouragement from their experience.

Often we pray to avoid trials when God wants to use them for our greater
good. But trials test the genuineness of our faith and purge us of sin and shal-
lowness like a refiner's fire purges gold. The process may be painful, but the
result is more precious than the purest gold (1 Peter 1:7).

❖ ❖ ❖

Suggestions for Prayer: Pray that you might face each trial with wisdom,
patience, and a clear sense of the Lord's presence.

For Further Study: Read Acts 20:22-24. What was the apostle Paul's perspective on the persecution that awaited him in Jerusalem? ❖ What was his
ultimate goal?

"Then Nebuchadnezzar the king was astounded and stood up
in haste; he responded and said to his high officials,
'Was it not three men we cast bound into the midst of the
fire?' They answered and said to the king, 'Certainly,
O king.' He answered and said, 'Look! I see four men loosed
and walking about in the midst of the fire without harm, and
the appearance of the fourth is like a son of the gods!'"

DANIEL 3:24-25

✧ ✧ ✧

God will never leave His children alone.

King Nebuchadnezzar was livid with rage when he had Shadrach, Meshach, and Abed-nego bound and cast into the fiery furnace. But his rage quickly turned to astonishment when he saw four men loosed and walking around unharmed by the flames. Clearly something supernatural and beyond his control was occurring.

Although he described the fourth person as being "like a son of the gods," he did not have the Son of God in mind. As a pagan he would not have understood an Old Testament appearance of Christ, such as occurred to Abraham in Genesis 18. But he understood enough to believe that God had "sent His angel and delivered His servants who put their trust in Him" (v. 28).

I believe Nebuchadnezzar was correct. God sent an angelic messenger to comfort those young men and to explain that they would not be harmed by the fire. God would turn their darkest hour into their greatest triumph. Others in Scripture have been similarly encouraged by special angels from the Lord. God honored Elijah, for example, by having angels personally serve him food at an especially discouraging time in his life (1 Kings 19:4-7).

If you are a Christian, God has promised never to leave you or forsake you (Heb. 13:5). He will be with you in every circumstance. When necessary, He will dispatch His angels to minister to you in special ways (Heb. 1:14). Let that truth encourage you today, especially if you are undergoing a trial.

✧ ✧ ✧

Suggestions for Prayer: Praise the Lord for the protection and encouragement He has given you in the past and for His promise of similar blessings in the future.

For Further Study: According to 1 Peter 2:18-23 and 4:12-16, how should Christians respond to persecution?

> *"Then Nebuchadnezzar came near to the door of the furnace*
> *of blazing fire; he responded and said, 'Shadrach, Meshach and*
> *Abed-nego, come out, you servants of the Most High God, and*
> *come here!' Then Shadrach, Meshach and Abed-nego came out of*
> *the midst of the fire. And the satraps, the prefects, the governors*
> *and the king's high officials gathered around and saw in regard to*
> *these men that the fire had no effect on the bodies of these men*
> *nor was the hair of their head singed, nor were their trousers*
> *damaged, nor had the smell of fire even come upon them."*
>
> DANIEL 3:26-27

❖ ❖ ❖

A righteous life attracts people to God.

When Jesus said, "Let your light shine before men in such a way that they may see your good works, and glorify your Father who is in Heaven" (Matt. 5:16; compare v. 14), He was teaching that what we believe as Christians must be evident in the way we live. When it is, others will be drawn to God and honor Him.

Shadrach, Meshach, and Abed-nego were powerful witnesses for God because they lived according to their convictions. Nebuchadnezzar had done everything he could to intimidate them into compromise, and when that failed he called for their death. But God's protection of them was so thorough that the intense flames didn't even singe their hair or scorch their clothing. In fact, they emerged from the furnace without so much as the smell of smoke on them.

So powerful was the integrity of these young men and the hand of God upon their lives that within just a few short verses Nebuchadnezzar went from defying God to exulting Him as "the Most High God." That phrase doesn't mean he had abandoned his traditional worship of many gods (apparently that comes in Daniel 4), but he was placing the God of Shadrach, Meshach, and Abed-nego at the top of the list.

So it is when your life impacts others for Christ. They may not yet fully believe, but God uses your faithfulness as a foundation for His future work in their lives.

❖ ❖ ❖

Suggestions for Prayer: Ask the Lord to use you to witness to someone today.

For Further Study: We have seen the impact of a consistently godly life, but according to Romans 2:17-24, what is the impact of a hypocritical life?

*"Nebuchadnezzar responded and said, 'Blessed be the God
of Shadrach, Meshach, and Abed-nego, who has sent His angel and
delivered His servants who put their trust in Him, violating
the king's command, and yielded up their bodies so as not to serve
or worship any god except their own God. Therefore, I make
a decree that any people, nation or tongue that speaks anything
offensive against the God of Shadrach, Meshach and Abed-nego
shall be torn limb from limb and their houses reduced to a
rubbish heap, inasmuch as there is no other god who is able to
deliver in this way.' Then the king caused Shadrach, Meshach and
Abed-nego to prosper in the province of Babylon."*

DANIEL 3:28-30

✧ ✧ ✧

God is honored when you are faithful.

When a well-known National Football League coach was asked why he
always had a Christian minister on the sideline with his team, he
explained, "I'm not even sure if I believe in God, but in case there is one, I
want Him on my side." King Nebuchadnezzar seems to have had a similar attitude when he blessed the God of Shadrach, Meshach, and Abed-nego and
decreed that anyone speaking an offense against Him would be torn to pieces
and have their homes reduced to rubbish.

Nebuchadnezzar believed that certain peoples or nations had their own
gods, and even though he didn't believe that the God of the Hebrews was the
one true God, he had just witnessed dramatic proof that He was more powerful than the gods of Babylon. Therefore, he acknowledged Him as the
supreme God and took steps to ensure that no one would offend Him. No
doubt he also reasoned that having a God like that on his side would be a definite advantage.

Regardless of Nebuchadnezzar's motives, his decree glorified God by
exalting Him over Babylon's false gods. More important, Shadrach, Meshach,
and Abed-nego's integrity glorified God by demonstrating the power and
influence of an uncompromising life. When the king caused them to prosper
in Babylon, the name of the Lord prospered with them.

✧ ✧ ✧

Suggestions for Prayer: Pray daily to live as Shadrach, Meshach, and Abed-
nego lived and to be used as they were used.

For Further Study: According to Ephesians 3:20, what is God able to accomplish through you when you live with integrity? Are you trusting Him to do so?

*"It seemed good to Darius to appoint 120 satraps over the
kingdom, that they should be in charge of the whole kingdom,
and over them three commissioners (of whom Daniel was
one), that these satraps might be accountable to them, and
that the king might not suffer loss. Then this Daniel began
distinguishing himself among the commissioners and satraps
because he possessed an extraordinary spirit, and the king
planned to appoint him over the entire kingdom."*

DANIEL 6:1-3

✧ ✧ ✧

*Nations come and go, but God's plans
continue through people of biblical integrity.*

As we come to Daniel 6, King Nebuchadnezzar is gone; Belshazzar, his
son and successor to the throne, has been slain; the great Babylonian
Empire has fallen to the Medo-Persians; and a king identified only as "Darius"
(probably another name for Cyrus) is ruling the Medo-Persian Empire. But
amidst all those changes, two things remain constant: Daniel distinguishes
himself among his peers, and God exalts him.

Daniel served in Babylon for seventy years under three kings, each of
whom recognized him as a man of unique wisdom and integrity. King
Nebuchadnezzar "made him ruler over the whole province of Babylon and
chief prefect over all the wise men of Babylon" (Dan. 2:48). King Belshazzar
"clothed [him] with purple and put a necklace of gold around his neck, and
issued a proclamation concerning him that he now had authority as the third
ruler in the kingdom" (Dan. 5:29).

Now King Darius is about to appoint Daniel as prime minister over the entire
kingdom, and within a year the king will issue a decree for the Jews to return to
Judah, thereby ending the seventy-year Babylonian captivity (Ezra 1:1-3). I
believe Cyrus made that decree because of Daniel's wisdom and influence.

Through Daniel's faithfulness we learn that God is sovereign and will accomplish His plans regardless of human authorities. So despite any political, social, or
economic changes that may come, remain faithful to Christ and He will use you
in ways that are exceeding abundantly beyond all you ask or think (Eph. 3:20).

✧ ✧ ✧

Suggestions for Prayer: Pray that true Christianity will flourish in America
and that our nation's leaders will come to love the Lord and govern with biblical wisdom.

For Further Study: According to Isaiah 40:7-8, 15-17, how does God view the
nations?

> *"Then the commissioners and satraps began trying to find a
> ground of accusation against Daniel in regard to government
> affairs; but they could find no ground of accusation or evidence
> of corruption, inasmuch as he was faithful, and no negligence or
> corruption was to be found in him. Then these men said, 'We
> shall not find any ground of accusation against this Daniel
> unless we find it against him with regard to the law of his God.'"*
>
> DANIEL 6:4-5

❖ ❖ ❖

Live so as to silence your critics.

Whenever God exalts a righteous person, there will be those who are jealous and who criticize. Sometimes, as in Daniel's case, the jealousy turns to bitter opposition. But Daniel's accusers had a problem: try as they may, they could find no ground of accusation against him. He was blameless and above reproach in his character and political dealings. Their only option was to somehow indict him for being totally committed to God. What a wonderful testimony to his faithfulness!

When an individual has served in office as long as Daniel had and his enemies can bring no charges of wrongdoing against him, he or she must be a person of great integrity and personal purity. That was the strength of Daniel's character, and God wants you to have that kind of character as well.

There will always be those who want to discredit you. Even if they aren't jealous of your position, they'll resent your Christian faith and will scrutinize your attitudes and actions in an attempt to tarnish your reputation. How will your character hold up under that kind of scrutiny?

The apostle Peter wrote, "Keep your behavior excellent among the Gentiles, so that in the thing in which they slander you as evildoers, they may on account of your good deeds, as they observe them, glorify God in the day of visitation" (1 Peter 2:12). That means you must live the kind of life that silences your critics and refutes their accusations. When you do, some of them might even come to Christ.

❖ ❖ ❖

Suggestions for Prayer: Ask the Lord to guard your testimony and to minister saving grace to anyone who might seek to discredit you.

For Further Study: Read Philippians 1:12-18. What was the apostle Paul's perspective on those who were envious of him? Do you share his perspective?

> *"Then these commissioners and satraps came by agreement to*
> *the king and spoke to him as follows: 'King Darius, live forever!*
> *All the commissioners of the kingdom, the prefects and*
> *the satraps, the high officials and the governors have consulted*
> *together that the king should establish a statute and enforce*
> *an injunction that anyone who makes a petition to any god or man*
> *besides you, O king, for thirty days, shall be cast into the lions'*
> *den. Now, O king, establish the injunction and sign the document so*
> *that it may not be changed, according to the law of the Medes*
> *and Persians, which may not be revoked.' Therefore King*
> *Darius signed the document, that is, the injunction."*

DANIEL 6:6-9

✧ ✧ ✧

Integrity is more precious than flattery.

King David once prayed:

> *O Lord, lead me in Thy righteousness because of my foes; make*
> *Thy way straight before me. There is nothing reliable in what they*
> *say; their inward part is destruction itself; their throat is an open*
> *grave; they flatter with their tongue. Hold them guilty, O God . . .*
> *for they are rebellious against Thee. But let all who take refuge in*
> *Thee be glad, let them ever sing for joy; and mayest Thou shelter*
> *them, that those who love Thy name may exult in Thee. For it is*
> *Thou who dost bless the righteous man, O LORD, Thou dost sur-*
> *round him with favor as with a shield.*

—PSALM 5:8-12

That could have been Daniel's prayer as well, being surrounded by men who were rebellious against God who and flattered Darius so they could have Daniel put to death. By their own devices they would fall, but not before Daniel's integrity was tested.

Darius yielded to deceitful flattery, decreeing that he alone could grant petitions. (His ego is reminiscent of Nebuchadnezzar's [Dan. 3:12].) Daniel, on the other hand, was unyielding in his convictions, and God literally surrounded him with favor as with a shield.

✧ ✧ ✧

Suggestions for Prayer: Pray that when your faith is tested, you will stand firm and have the assurance that God is surrounding you with His favor.

For Further Study: Psalm 5:12 says that God blesses the righteous man. According to Psalm 64:10 and Psalm 92:12-15, what are some of those blessings?

> *"Now when Daniel knew that the document was signed,*
> *he entered his house (now in his roof chamber he had windows*
> *open toward Jerusalem); and he continued kneeling on his knees*
> *three times a day, praying and giving thanks before his God,*
> *as he had been doing previously. Then these men came by*
> *agreement and found Daniel making petition and*
> *supplication before his God."*
>
> DANIEL 6:10-11

✧ ✧ ✧

There is a direct link between prayer and integrity.

It is no coincidence that those whom God uses most effectively are those who are most fervent in prayer. David, for example, called upon the Lord in the morning, at noon, and at night, and the Lord heard his prayers (Ps. 55:17). Daniel followed the same pattern, praying three times a day from his roof chamber, where he could look out above the rooftops of Babylon toward Jerusalem.

Houses in Babylon often had latticework over their windows to allow ventilation, and Daniel would be visible through that latticework as he faced Jerusalem, prayed for its restoration, and gave thanks to God. He knew that Darius had issued a decree making it illegal to pray and that violating the decree would give his enemies opportunity to accuse him, but he would not forsake prayer or compromise his convictions. He would continue to call upon the Lord and leave any consequences to Him.

That was a bold decision for Daniel to make, especially in light of the punishment he would face. Would you be as bold if you knew that your prayers would lead to persecution and possible death? Perhaps more important, are you that committed to prayer even when you aren't facing persecution? I trust that you are. The seriousness of the spiritual battles you face requires faithfulness in prayer. That's why Paul said, "Devote yourselves to prayer, keeping alert in it with an attitude of thanksgiving" (Col. 4:2).

✧ ✧ ✧

Suggestions for Prayer: Are you devoted to prayer? If not, begin today to set aside a specific time daily to commune with the Lord and meditate on His Word. You might try keeping a written record of your prayer requests, noting the specific ways God answers them.

For Further Study: What was our Lord's pattern of prayer, and how did He instruct His disciples to pray (see Luke 5:16; 6:12; Matt. 6:5-13)?

"Then they approached and spoke before the king about the king's injunction, 'Did you not sign an injunction that any man who makes a petition to any god or man besides you, O king, for thirty days, is to be cast into the lions' den?' The king answered and said, 'The statement is true, according to the law of the Medes and Persians, which may not be revoked.' Then they answered and spoke before the king, 'Daniel, who is one of the exiles from Judah, pays no attention to you, O king, or to the injunction which you signed, but keeps making his petition three times a day.' Then, as soon as the king heard this statement, he was deeply distressed and set his mind on delivering Daniel; and even until sunset he kept exerting himself to rescue him. Then these men came by agreement to the king and said to the king, 'Recognize, O king, that it is a law of the Medes and Persians that no injunction or statute which the king establishes may be changed.' Then the king gave orders, and Daniel was brought in and cast into the lions' den. The king spoke and said to Daniel, 'Your God whom you constantly serve will Himself deliver you.' And a stone was brought and laid over the mouth of the den; and the king sealed it with his own signet ring and with the signet rings of his nobles, so that nothing might be changed in regard to Daniel."

DANIEL 6:12-17

✧ ✧ ✧

When human resources have been exhausted,
God has only begun to work.

The ink had barely dried on Darius' decree when Daniel's enemies reappeared to accuse him of disregarding the order. Only then did Darius realize the grave consequences of his actions.

In his deep distress the king exhausted every legal effort to save Daniel, but to no avail. Even he could not revoke the death sentence he had unwittingly placed on his loyal and trusted servant. In his grief and humility he confessed that God Himself would deliver Daniel. He was right!

✧ ✧ ✧

Suggestions for Prayer: What are you praying for that only God can do, so that when He does it, He alone will get the glory?

For Further Study: Read 2 Corinthians 12:9-10. What was the apostle Paul's attitude toward his own weaknesses?

"Then the king went off to his palace and spent the night fasting, and no entertainment was brought before him; and his sleep fled from him. Then the king arose with the dawn, at the break of day, and went in haste to the lions' den. And when he had come near the den to Daniel, he cried out with a troubled voice. The king spoke and said to Daniel, 'Daniel, servant of the living God, has your God, whom you constantly serve, been able to deliver you from the lions?' Then Daniel spoke to the king, 'O king, live forever! My God sent His angel and shut the lions' mouths, and they have not harmed me.'"

DANIEL 6:18-22A

❖ ❖ ❖

When circumstances seem darkest,
we can see God's hand most clearly.

It is obvious that King Darius cared deeply for Daniel and that he had some degree of faith in Daniel's God. Although he believed that God could deliver Daniel (v. 16), he spent a distressing and sleepless night anxiously awaiting dawn, so he could see if his belief was true. At the crack of dawn he hurried to the lions' den and called out to Daniel. Imagine his relief to hear Daniel's voice and to learn about how the angel had shut the lions' mouths.

Why did Darius think God would deliver Daniel? I'm sure he learned of God from Daniel himself. Surely Daniel talked about Shadrach, Meshach, and Abed-nego's deliverance from the fiery furnace and about other marvelous things God had done for His people. The king's response shows that Daniel's testimony was effective and that his integrity had lent credibility to his witness.

But suppose God hadn't delivered Daniel from the lions. Would He have failed? No. Isaiah also believed God, but he was sawn in half. Stephen believed God but was stoned to death. Paul believed God but was beheaded. Trusting God means accepting His will, whether for life or death. And for Christians, "to live is Christ, and to die is gain" (Phil. 1:21).

❖ ❖ ❖

Suggestions for Prayer: Pray for those Christian leaders today who influence kings and presidents throughout the world. Ask the Lord to give them boldness and blameless integrity.

For Further Study: How does God view the death of His children (see Ps. 116:15 and John 21:18-19)?

*"Then Daniel spoke to the king, 'O king, live forever! My God
sent His angel and shut the lions' mouths, and they have not
harmed me, inasmuch as I was found innocent before Him;
and also toward you, O king, I have committed no crime.' Then
the king was very pleased and gave orders for Daniel to be
taken up out of the den. So Daniel was taken up out of the den,
and no injury whatever was found on him, because he had
trusted in his God. The king then gave orders, and they brought
those men who had maliciously accused Daniel, and they cast
them, their children, and their wives into the lions' den; and
they had not reached the bottom of the den before the lions
overpowered them and crushed all their bones."*

DANIEL 6:21-24

✧ ✧ ✧

God will always vindicate His people.

One of the challenges of the Christian life is to react properly when being
unjustly accused. Our natural inclination is to defend ourselves, which
is appropriate at times. But there are other times when we must remain silent
and trust the Lord to defend us.

Apparently Daniel said nothing in his own defense when he was charged
with disregarding the king's decree to stop praying. Of course the charge itself
was true, but his motives were righteous, and he knew he was innocent before
God. Therefore, like Jesus Himself before His accusers, Daniel chose to
remain silent and entrust himself to God, who "judges righteously" (1 Peter
2:22-23).

Vindication doesn't always come quickly, but in Daniel's case it did. God
affirmed his innocence by protecting him from the hungry lions. King Darius
affirmed his innocence by putting his accusers to death. That was swift and
decisive judgment.

Never lose heart or feel that God has abandoned you when evil people
seem to prevail. The day will come when God will vindicate you. When He
does, His judgment will also be swift and decisive.

✧ ✧ ✧

Suggestions for Prayer: Pray for a loving attitude toward those who unjustly
accuse you.

For Further Study: Read James 5:7-11. What encouragement does James give
to those who suffer at the hands of evil people? ✧ Who does he use as an
example of someone who suffered with patience? ✧ At what point in time will
God's people be vindicated?

"Then Darius the king wrote to all the peoples, nations, and men of every language who were living in all the land: 'May your peace abound! I make a decree that in all the dominion of my kingdom men are to fear and tremble before the God of Daniel; for He is the living God and enduring forever, and His kingdom is one which will not be destroyed, and His dominion will be forever. He delivers and rescues and performs signs and wonders in heaven and on earth, who has also delivered Daniel from the power of the lions.'"

DANIEL 6:25-27

❖ ❖ ❖

It doesn't take a lot of people to make an impact for Christ; it merely takes the right kind.

Today's passage proclaims the sovereignty and majesty of the living God and calls on everyone throughout the nation to fear and tremble before Him. Those verses could have been written by King David or one of the other psalmists, but they were written by a pagan king to a pagan nation. His remarkable tribute to God's glory was the fruit of Daniel's influence on his life.

God doesn't really need a lot of people to accomplish His work; He needs the right kind of people. And Daniel shows us the impact one person can have when he or she is sold out to God. That's how it is throughout Scripture. For example, Noah was God's man during the Flood, Joseph was God's man in Egypt, Moses was God's man in the Exodus, and Esther was God's woman in the days of King Ahasuerus. So it continues right down to the present. When God puts His people in the right place, His message gets through.

As a Christian, you are God's person in your family, school, or place of employment. He has placed you there as His ambassador to influence others for Christ. That's a wonderful privilege and an awesome responsibility.

❖ ❖ ❖

Suggestions for Prayer: Thank the Lord for His marvelous grace in your life and for the opportunities He gives you each day to share His love with others.

For Further Study: The key to Daniel's fruitfulness, and to yours as well, is given in Psalm 1. Memorize that psalm, and recite it often as a reminder of God's promises to those who live with biblical integrity.

"So this Daniel enjoyed success in the reign of Darius
[even] in the reign of Cyrus the Persian."
DANIEL 6:28

✧ ✧ ✧

True success is more a matter
of character than of circumstances.

By anyone's standards Daniel was a remarkably successful man. After entering Babylon as one of King Nebuchadnezzar's young Hebrew hostages, he quickly distinguished himself as a person of unusual character, wisdom, and devotion to his God. Within a few years Nebuchadnezzar had made him ruler over the province of Babylon and chief prefect over all the wise men. Many years later Nebuchadnezzar's son, Belshazzar, promoted him to third ruler in his kingdom, and later King Darius made him prime minister over the entire Medo-Persian Empire.

As successful as Daniel was, being successful in the world's eyes was never his goal. He wanted only to be faithful to God. And because he was faithful, God honored and exalted him in Babylon. But God's plans for Daniel extended far beyond Babylon. Daniel's presence in Babylon opened the door for the Hebrew people to return to Jerusalem (Ezra 1:1-3), and it also paved the way for the Magi's visit to Bethlehem centuries later (Matt. 2:1-12). Those wise men heard of the Jewish Messiah through Daniel's prophecies (Daniel 9).

God used Daniel in marvelous ways, but Daniel was just one part of a much bigger picture. Similarly, God will use you and every faithful believer in marvelous ways as He continues to paint the picture of His redemptive grace. As He does, He may exalt you in ways unimaginable, or He may use you in humble ways. In either case, you are truly successful if you remain faithful to Him and use every opportunity to its fullest for His glory.

✧ ✧ ✧

Suggestions for Prayer: Thank the Lord for Daniel, Shadrach, Meshach, and Abed-nego and for the principles we have learned this month from their lives. Pray daily that your life, like theirs, will be characterized by godly integrity and that God will use you each day for His glory.

For Further Study: Memorize Joshua 1:8 and 1 Corinthians 4:1-2. What key to success did God give Joshua? ✧ How does the apostle Paul describe a successful servant of Christ? ✧ Would your friends and relatives characterize you as a truly successful person?

"Be all the more diligent to make certain about
His calling and choosing you."
2 PETER 1:10

❖ ❖ ❖

Every true Christian should enjoy the reality of salvation.

A sad fact of contemporary Christianity is that many in the church greatly misunderstand what the Bible teaches about the assurance of one's salvation. As a result many genuine believers struggle with doubts about the reality of their salvation, while many professing believers are confident they are saved when in truth they are headed for Hell.

Such a misunderstanding is unnecessary since Scripture makes it abundantly clear that believers should not only enjoy assurance of their salvation but *cultivate* it as well. That's why the apostle Peter said, "Be all the more diligent to make certain about His calling and choosing you."

Peter's command establishes the need for self-examination. Only by testing one's assurance by God's Word can anyone know for sure if he is saved or not. Yet most preaching today minimizes or ignores assurance altogether, encouraging people to view any doubts about their salvation as attacks by the enemy. The unfortunate result is a false assurance that the Lord categorized as follows: "Not everyone who says to Me, 'Lord, Lord,' will enter the kingdom of heaven; but he who does the will of My Father who is in heaven. Many will say to Me on that day, 'Lord, Lord, did we not prophesy in Your name, and in Your name cast out demons, and in Your name perform many miracles?' And then I will declare to them, 'I never knew you; depart from Me'" (Matt. 7:21-23). What a terrifying and haunting pronouncement!

Because a clear understanding of one's salvation is so vital, Scripture encourages true believers with the promise of full assurance, while making false professors uncomfortable by seeking to destroy their false sense of security. A true believer's sense of assurance should not ebb and flow with the emotions; it is meant to be an anchor even in the midst of life's storms. But a false professor has no right to assurance. For the next month, we'll look at what God's Word teaches about assurance and how you can have it.

❖ ❖ ❖

Suggestions for Prayer: Thank God that He not only grants you salvation but also gives you His Word as a mirror to reflect and confirm the transformation He has made in your life.

For Further Study: Read John 10 and 17. Make a list of the verses that reflect the security every true believer has in Christ.

*"Test yourselves to see if you are in
the faith; examine yourselves!"*

2 CORINTHIANS 13:5

❖ ❖ ❖

**True believers will see the glory of Christ reflected in their lives
when they examine the genuineness of their salvation.**

A ssurance of one's salvation has been a key issue throughout the history of the church, especially the Reformers' reaction to the Roman Catholic Church's assertion that since salvation is a joint effort between man and God, the outcome is in doubt until the end. John Calvin, the leading sixteenth-century Reformer, taught that believers can and should be assured of their salvation. He made the grounds for assurance objective, urging believers to look to the promises in God's Word to gain a sense of personal assurance.

Later Reformed theologians (including the seventeenth-century English Reformers known as Puritans), however, recognized that genuine Christians often lacked assurance. So they emphasized the need for practical evidences of salvation in a believer's life. Thus they tended to emphasize a subjective means of establishing assurance, counseling people to examine their attitudes and actions for evidence of their election.

The question is: Should Christians derive assurance through the objective promises of Scripture or through subjective self-examination? The Bible teaches that both will lead to assurance. The objective basis for salvation is the finished work of Christ on our behalf, including the promises of Scripture (2 Cor. 1:20). The subjective support is the ongoing work of the Holy Spirit in the lives of Christians, including His convicting and sanctifying ministries. Romans 15:4 refers to both aspects of assurance: "Whatever was written in earlier times was written for our instruction, that through perseverance [subjective] and the encouragement of the Scriptures [objective] we might have hope."

The Holy Spirit applies both grounds of assurance to believers: He "bears witness with our spirit that we are children of God" (Rom. 8:16). Are you sure of your salvation? Ask yourself the objective question: "Do I believe?" If you truly believe, you can be sure you are saved (John 3:16; Acts 16:31). The subjective question is: "Is my faith real?" That's why Paul said, "Test yourselves to see if you are in the faith; examine yourselves!" (2 Cor 13:5). Use the remaining days of this month as an opportunity to take the test.

❖ ❖ ❖

Suggestions for Prayer: Ask God to reveal your true heart attitude toward Him. Make Psalm 139:23-24 your prayer.

For Further Study: Read 2 Corinthians 3:18. How might this be considered part of Paul's test? ❖ What should true believers be looking for in their lives?

*"Therefore having been justified by faith, we have peace
with God through our Lord Jesus Christ."*
ROMANS 5:1

❖ ❖ ❖

*Peace with God is the first link in the chain that
securely binds a true believer to Jesus Christ.*

Perhaps the most significant attack Satan wages against Christians is raising doubt about the reality and security of their salvation. He continually
promotes the destructive notion of a works-righteousness system as a means
of salvation, thus making the preservation of one's salvation totally dependent
upon the believer's faithfulness.

To counteract such a misguided interpretation of what the Bible teaches
about salvation, the apostle Paul wrote Romans 3 and 4 to establish that salvation comes only on the basis of God's grace working through man's faith.
Quoting Genesis 15:6, Paul said, "'Abraham believed God, and it was reck-
oned to him as righteousness'" (Rom. 4:3).

Because some might have questioned if good works, which offer no security at all, were then the conditions under which a person preserved salvation,
Paul wrote Romans 5:1-11 to further cement in believers' minds that our hope
as Christians is not in ourselves but in our great God (cf. 2 Tim. 2:13; Heb.
10:23). Six links bind us to our Lord and Savior, and our passage for today
describes the first: peace with God.

It's hard to imagine that we were ever enemies of God, but the sad fact is
that all unbelievers are at war with God and He is at war with them (Rom.
8:7; Eph. 5:6). Yet every individual who has been justified by faith in Christ
receives reconciliation with God, which also brings peace with Him. And this
peace is permanent and irrevocable because Christ "always lives to make
intercession for them" (Heb. 7:25).

Not only did Jesus Christ establish eternal peace between us and God the
Father, but also "He Himself is our peace" (Eph. 2:14). That emphasizes Christ's
atoning work as the basis for our assurance. Such absolute and objective facts are
what allow you to stand firm under Satan's attacks. They free you from focusing
on your own goodness and merit and allow you to serve the Lord with the confidence that nothing can separate you from your Heavenly Father (Rom. 8:31-39).

❖ ❖ ❖

Suggestions for Prayer: Thank God for saving you and establishing peace
between you and Him. ❖ Ask Him to guide you into opportunities of service.

For Further Study: Read Romans 3—4. What verses establish that salvation
is solely the work of God? Keep a list for reference when Satan may attack
your faith.

> *"Through [Christ] also we have obtained our introduction*
> *by faith into this grace in which we stand."*
> ROMANS 5:2

✧ ✧ ✧

It is God's grace, not the believers' faith, which
enables them to stand firm in their salvation.

In Old Testament times, the notion of having direct access or "introduction" to God was unthinkable, because if anyone was to look at Him they would surely die. After the tabernacle was built, only the high priest could enter the holy of holies, where God would manifest His divine presence, and only once a year for just a brief time.

But Christ's atoning sacrifice on the cross ushered in a New Covenant that made access to God possible for any person, Jew or Gentile, who trusts in His sacrifice. All of us who believe can now "draw near with confidence to the throne of grace, that we may receive mercy and find grace to help in time of need" (Heb. 4:16).

Because of our faith in Him, Christ escorts us "into this grace in which we stand." The Greek word for "stand" refers to permanence, standing firm and immovable. Certainly faith is necessary for salvation, but it is God's grace and not our faith that has the power to save us and maintain that salvation. What God did initially through grace, we cannot preserve through our efforts. That would be a mockery of God's grace and an indication of our lack of trust in His desire and power to preserve our salvation. Paul said, "I am confident of this very thing, that He who began a good work in you will perfect it until the day of Christ Jesus" (Phil. 1:6).

In spite of our effort to avoid it, all of us will fall into sin, but our sin is not more powerful than God's grace. Jesus paid the penalty for all our sins. If the sins we committed prior to our salvation were not too great for Christ's atoning death to cover, surely none of those we have committed since then or will commit are too great for Him to cover (Rom. 5:10). A dying Savior ushered us into God's grace; we all need to depend on the fact that a living Savior will keep us in His grace.

✧ ✧ ✧

Suggestions for Prayer: Thank God for His preserving grace. ✧ Confess any distrust in His power to preserve your salvation.

For Further Study: Read Romans 8:31-34. Why is God worthy of your trust? ✧ How does Christ support that truth?

> *"We exult in hope of the glory of God. And not only this, but*
> *we also exult in our tribulations, knowing that tribulation*
> *brings about perseverance; and perseverance, proven character;*
> *and proven character, hope; and hope does not disappoint."*
>
> ROMANS 5:2-5

❖ ❖ ❖

God promises all believers that one day
they will receive Christ's glory.

The security that every believer desires in his or her salvation is founded on the very fact that God is the author of salvation—every aspect of it is solely His work, and thus it cannot be lost. The final piece of God's great work is the ultimate glorification of every Christian: "Whom [God] foreknew, He also predestined to become conformed to the image of His Son, that He might be the first-born among many brethren; and whom He predestined, these He also called; and whom He called, these He also justified; and whom He justified, these He also glorified" (Rom. 8:29-30).

This third link in the chain that eternally binds believers to Christ completes the three aspects of salvation. Paul already established that salvation is anchored in the *past* because Christ made peace with God. It is anchored in the *present* because Christ continually intercedes for every believer and establishes our standing in grace. Here Paul proclaims that salvation is also anchored in the *future* because God promises His children that one day they will be clothed with the glory of His Son.

The Greek word for "exult" in Romans 5:2 refers to jubilation and rejoicing. Every believer ought to rejoice in the future rather than fearing it, because Jesus Christ secured the hope that his ultimate destiny is to share in the very glory of God. Christ is the guarantee of our hope because He Himself is our hope (1 Tim. 1:1).

We also have another reason to rejoice in the hope of glory: our tribulations contribute to our present blessing and ultimate glory. Paul states in Romans 5:3-5 that our afflictions for Christ's sake produce increasing levels of maturity in handling the trials of life. As you continue to pursue holiness, the more you will be persecuted and troubled, but the greater will be your hope as you see God sustain you through His all-powerful grace.

❖ ❖ ❖

Suggestions for Prayer: Ask God to give you His perspective on your trials and show you how to focus on your future glory in the process.

For Further Study: Read Matthew 5:10-12; Romans 8:18; 2 Corinthians 4:17; and 1 Peter 4:19. How should you view your trials? ❖ When they come, what should you do?

*"The love of God has been poured out within our hearts
through the Holy Spirit who was given to us. For while we
were still helpless, at the right time Christ died for the
ungodly. For one will hardly die for a righteous man; though
perhaps for the good man someone would dare even to die.
But God demonstrates His own love toward us, in that
while we were yet sinners, Christ died for us."*

ROMANS 5:5-8

✧ ✧ ✧

*Salvation ushers believers into a love relationship
with God that lasts throughout eternity.*

The eighteenth-century hymn writer William Cowper wrote in "There Is a Fountain":

*E'er since by faith I saw the stream
Thy flowing wounds supply,
Redeeming love has been my theme
And shall be till I die.*

Perhaps the most overwhelming concept in all Christianity is that God loved us so much "that He gave His only begotten Son, that whoever believes in Him should not perish, but have eternal life" (John 3:16). And more than that, God even graciously imparts His love to us—He pours it "out within our hearts through the Holy Spirit who was given to us" (Rom. 5:5). Paul here reveals that in Christ we are given subjective evidence of salvation. God Himself implants that evidence deep within us. As a result, we love the One who first loved us (1 John 4:7-10).

The idea that God "poured out" His love refers to a lavish outpouring. God didn't just squeeze out His love in little drops—He poured it out in immeasurable torrents. And that is seen in perhaps the greatest manifestation of God's love in all eternity: when we were ungodly sinners totally incapable of bringing ourselves to God, He sent His Son to die for us who were completely unworthy of such love.

Think of how God's love impacts your assurance. Now that you are saved, you can never be as wretched as you were before your conversion, and He loved you totally then. Because God loved you so completely, you can be secure in your salvation.

✧ ✧ ✧

Suggestions for Prayer: Confess those times you have taken for granted God's love for you, then meditate on Romans 5:8.

For Further Study: Read Ephesians 3:14-19. How does the Holy Spirit help us to "know the love of Christ"?

> *"Much more then, having now been justified by His blood,*
> *we shall be saved from the wrath of God through Him.*
> *For if while we were enemies, we were reconciled to God*
> *through the death of His Son, much more, having*
> *been reconciled, we shall be saved by His life."*
>
> ROMANS 5:9-10

❖ ❖ ❖

Jesus Christ delivers His brethren not only from sin and its judgment,
but also from uncertainty and doubt about that deliverance.

God is a God of wrath. But the wrath due to be poured out on all mankind, Christ took on Himself. That's what the apostle Paul meant when he said that those who put their faith in Him have been "justified by His blood" and are assured of being "saved from the wrath of God through [Christ]" (Rom. 5:9). As a result of Christ's atoning work, all Christians are identified with Christ, are adopted as God's children through Him, and are no longer "children of wrath" (Eph. 2:3).

But Paul doesn't stop there because the ongoing intercessory work of Christ has great significance for every believer and the security of his salvation. In Romans 5:10 Paul argues from the greater to the lesser to show that it was a much greater work of God to bring sinners to grace than to bring them to glory. Since God brought us to Himself when we were enemies, we will be reconciled continually now that we are His friends. When God first reconciled us, we were wretched, vile, and godless sinners. Since that was not a barrier to His reconciling us then, there is nothing that can prevent the living Christ from keeping us reconciled.

This truth has great ramifications for our assurance. If God already secured our deliverance from sin, death, and future judgment, how could our present spiritual life possibly be in jeopardy? How can a Christian, whose past and future salvation are guaranteed by God, be insecure in the intervening time? If sin in the greatest degree could not prevent our becoming reconciled, how can sin in lesser degree prevent our staying reconciled? Our salvation can't be any more secure than that.

❖ ❖ ❖

Suggestions for Prayer: Ask God to reveal to you how you might even now be insecure about your salvation. Then ask Him to make the intercessory work of Christ more real to you each day.

For Further Study: Read John 5:26; 10:28-29; 14:19; Romans 8:34-39; Colossians 3:3-4; Hebrews 7:25; and Revelation 1:18. List all the securities you can find. ❖ How does Christ save you by His life?

"We also exult in God through our Lord Jesus Christ,
through whom we have now received the reconciliation."
ROMANS 5:11

✧ ✧ ✧

The final link in the chain that eternally binds
believers to Christ is their joy or exultation in God.

Perhaps nowhere outside of Scripture has Christian joy been expressed more beautifully than in these stanzas from Charles Wesley's hymn "O For a Thousand Tongues to Sing":

O for a thousand tongues to sing
My great Redeemer's praise,
The glories of my God and King,
The triumphs of His grace!

Hear Him, ye deaf; His praise, ye dumb,
Your loosened tongues employ;
Ye blind, behold your Savior come;
And leap, ye lame for joy!

Galatians 5:22 says that "joy" is one aspect of the fruit of the Spirit, and as such it is one of the great securities of salvation. The Greek for "joy" means "to exult," "to rejoice jubilantly," or "to be thrilled." What is our motivation to be so thrilled? Paul says it's because we received reconciliation from Christ. God gives us abundant joy both in our salvation and ultimately for who God is. Thus our present sense of internal joy is an additional guarantee of our future salvation.

One of the reasons David was a man after God's own heart was his rejoicing in the Lord for the Lord's own sake. He said, "O magnify the Lord with me, and let us exalt His name together" (Ps. 34:3). Other psalmists echoed that same joy. One wrote, "For our heart rejoices in Him, because we trust in His holy name" (Ps. 33:21), while another said, "Then I will go to the altar of God, to God my exceeding joy; and upon the lyre I shall praise Thee, O God, my God" (Ps. 43:4). As you make God the focus of your joy, He will grant you an assurance only He can give.

✧ ✧ ✧

Suggestions for Prayer: How often do you exult in what God has accomplished for you? Ask God to give you a greater joy in Him as you learn more about Him from His Word.

For Further Study: Look up "joy" in a concordance and determine the percentage of the references that refer to joy in one's salvation. ✧ What significant application can you make from those verses?

*"These things I have written to you who believe
in the name of the Son of God, in order that you may
know that you have eternal life."*

1 JOHN 5:13

✧ ✧ ✧

*The apostle John presents eleven objective and
subjective tests for assurance of salvation.*

The New Testament epistles are filled with enough material on assurance to fill volumes of commentaries. Yet there is one small epistle, 1 John, that was written to deal exclusively with the issue of assurance. The apostle John states his reason for writing this letter in our verse for today: "These things I have written to you who believe in the name of the Son of God, *in order that you may know that you have eternal life*" (emphasis added). John did not want his readers to doubt their salvation; he wanted them to have full assurance of it.

Certainly what John wrote in this epistle will not disturb genuine believers, but it will alarm anyone who has a false sense of assurance. In fact, he directed his letter to those who have placed their faith in Christ, which is the bedrock of all assurance: "I have written to you who believe." There is no place for self-examination outside of faith in Christ. That's why everything John says about assurance is predicated on faith in Christ and the promises of Scripture.

Throughout his epistle, John maintains a delicate balance between the objective and subjective grounds of assurance. The objective evidence makes up a doctrinal test, while the subjective evidence provides a moral test. John moves in and out between the two kinds of tests as he presents a total of eleven criteria that will indicate whether one possesses eternal life.

As you study through these tests for the next eleven days, they will confirm for you, if you are a genuine believer, the reality of your salvation. But if you have been given a false assurance, you will know where you stand and what you need to do.

✧ ✧ ✧

Suggestions for Prayer: If you are a true believer, ask God to use these upcoming days to give you a greater love for Him. If you're not sure if you truly know our great Lord and Savior, ask Him to reveal Himself to you so that these next few days will be life-changing ones.

For Further Study: Read John 20:31. How would reading through the Gospel of John also provide assurance of salvation? Begin such a reading plan.

> *"What we have seen and heard we proclaim to you also, that*
> *you also may have fellowship with us; and indeed our fellow-*
> *ship is with the Father, and with His Son Jesus Christ."*
>
> 1 JOHN 1:3

✧ ✧ ✧

Enjoying communion with both God and Jesus Christ
is solid proof that one's salvation is real.

When we hold baptisms in the church I pastor, invariably every person who gives their testimony will describe the overwhelming sense of forgiveness they now feel and the new purpose they have for their lives. They are expressing a wonderful result of salvation in Christ, of which Jesus said, "I came that they might have life, and might have it abundantly" (John 10:10). By saying that life could be *abundant*, Jesus was saying that salvation would result in more than a change of position—it is a change of experience! The Christian life is a rich life in which we are meant to experience joy, peace, love, and purpose.

The abundant life in Christ begins with a close communion and fellowship with the living God and the living Christ. The apostle Paul says, "God is faithful, through whom you were called into fellowship with His Son, Jesus Christ our Lord" (1 Cor. 1:9). In Galatians 2:20 Paul describes what that fellowship meant to him personally: "I have been crucified with Christ; and it is no longer I who live, but Christ lives in me; and the life which I now live in the flesh I live by faith in the Son of God, who loved me, and delivered Himself up for me." Great intimacy with Christ belongs to all genuine believers.

Have you experienced communion with God and Christ? Have you sensed Their presence? Does your love for Them draw you into Their presence? Have you experienced the exhilarating joy of talking in prayer to the living God? And have you experienced the thrill of discovering a new truth in His Word? If you have, then you have experienced the abundant life that Jesus promised to all who put their trust in Him.

✧ ✧ ✧

Suggestions for Prayer: Much like God asked Israel to recount the great works He had done for them, meditate on the many ways God has made your life richer as a result of knowing Him.

For Further Study: Read Romans 8:15; 2 Corinthians 1:3; Ephesians 5:19; Philippians 4:19; Hebrews 4:16; and 1 Peter 5:10. What does each verse teach about your relationship with God? ✧ In what ways is your life abundant as a result?

*"If we say that we have fellowship with Him and yet walk
in the darkness, we lie and do not practice the truth. But if we
walk in the light as He Himself is in the light, we have fellowship
with one another, and the blood of Jesus His Son cleanses
us from all sin. If we say that we have no sin, we are deceiving
ourselves, and the truth is not in us. If we confess our sins, He is
faithful and righteous to forgive us our sins and to cleanse us
from all unrighteousness. If we say that we have not sinned,
we make Him a liar, and His word is not in us."*

1 JOHN 1:6-10

✧ ✧ ✧

True believers are sensitive to their sin and confess it.

Throughout Scripture, light is used as a metaphor for truth—both intellectual and moral truth (cf. Ps. 119:105, 130; Prov. 6:23). When the apostle John writes, "God is light, and in Him there is no darkness at all" (1 John 1:5), he is stating that the Lord is absolutely sinless since light and darkness cannot coexist.

Some claim to have fellowship with God (v. 6), to have no sin (v. 8), and even to have never sinned (v. 10). But they are living in darkness; it is characteristic of unbelievers to be oblivious to the sins in their lives. But that is not true of genuine believers. They have a right sense of sin: they "walk in the light as He Himself is in the light" (v. 7), and they "confess [their] sins" (v. 9). True believers know that if they want to commune with God, they need to confess their sins and turn to Christ as their "Advocate" before God (2:1).

The apostle Paul was very sensitive to the sinful realities of his life (Rom. 7:14-25). What about you? Are you aware of the spiritual battle raging within you? Do you realize you must live a holy life to have fellowship with God? Are you willing to confess and forsake any sin in your life? Do you realize you can choose not to sin? Are you weary of doing battle with the sin in your life (cf. Rom. 7:24)? If these things are true of you, rejoice in the assurance of your salvation.

✧ ✧ ✧

Suggestions for Prayer: Confess any known sin to God right now, then forsake it.

For Further Study: Read Romans 7:14-25. Make a list of all the ways Paul was sensitive to his sin. ✧ How many of those can you relate to? ✧ How should you respond?

> *"By this we know that we have come to know Him,*
> *if we keep His commandments."*
>
> 1 JOHN 2:3

✧ ✧ ✧

True believers obey God's commandments.

Before Jesus ascended to Heaven after His resurrection, He gave the following Great Commission to His disciples: "Go therefore and make disciples of all the nations, baptizing them in the name of the Father and the Son and the Holy Spirit, teaching them to observe all that I commanded you" (Matt. 28:19-20). Notice that a true disciple was to observe, or obey, all of Christ's commands.

The apostle John understood well the Lord's instruction. He knew that obedience to the commands of God produces assurance—the confidence of knowing for sure "that we have come to know Him" (1 John 2:3). The Greek word for "keep" in that verse refers to watchful, careful, thoughtful obedience. It is not an obedience that is only the result of external pressure; it is the eager obedience of one who "keeps" the divine commandments as if they were something precious to guard. Such obedience is motivated by love, as John indicates in verse 5: "Whoever keeps His word, in him the love of God has truly been perfected. By this we know that we are in Him." That's supported by the word translated "commandments," which refers specifically to the precepts of Christ rather than laws in general. Legal obedience demands perfection or penalty, while 1 John 2:3 is a call to gracious obedience because of the penalty Christ has already paid.

However, those who claim to know God and yet despise His commandments John calls liars: "The one who says, 'I have come to know Him,' and does not keep His commandments, is a liar, and the truth is not in him" (v. 4). "They profess to know God, but by their deeds they deny Him, being detestable and disobedient, and worthless for any good deed" (Titus 1:16).

How can you determine if you are a true Christian? Not by sentiment, but by obedience. If you desire to obey God out of gratitude for all Christ has done for you, and if you see that desire producing an overall pattern of obedience, you have passed an important test indicating the presence of saving faith.

✧ ✧ ✧

Suggestions for Prayer: If you have found your obedience is predicated more on the act of obedience than on gratitude for God, confess that now and seek to change your attitude.

For Further Study: Memorize 1 Samuel 15:22 as motivation for the right spirit of obedience.

*"Do not love the world, nor the things in the world. If anyone
loves the world, the love of the Father is not in him."*
1 JOHN 2:15

✧ ✧ ✧

*Genuine believers love God and reject
the world and all its philosophies.*

As the "god of this world" (2 Cor. 4:4), Satan has designed a system that the Bible simply calls "the world." The Greek term (*kosmos*) refers to a system encompassing false religion, errant philosophy, crime, immorality, materialism, and the like. Of it the apostle John wrote, "All that is in the world, the lust of the flesh and the lust of the eyes and the boastful pride of life, is not from the Father, but is from the world. And the world is passing away, and also its lusts; but the one who does the will of God abides forever" (1 John 2:16-17). While the world and its fleshly preoccupations are but temporary realities, the true believer has eternal life and will abide forever.

When someone becomes a Christian, he acquires a new set of goals and motivations; the world and its lusts no longer attract but repel him. He no longer loves "the world, nor the things in the world" (v. 15). At times he may be lured into worldly pursuits, but he is doing not what he loves but what he hates (cf. Rom. 7:15). That's because new life in Christ gives the believer a love for God and the things of God.

Jesus said those who follow Him are not of the world, just as He was not of the world. We still move about in it to do His will, but we are not of it. That's why Jesus specifically asked the Father to keep us from the evil one (John 17:14-16). We're vulnerable to being sucked into this evil world's system now and then, but our love is toward God. That love is what will redirect our focus toward heavenly priorities.

Do you reject the world and its false religions, damning ideologies, and godless pursuits? Instead, do you love God, His truth, His kingdom, and all that He stands for? If you reject the world and its devilish desires, that is a strong indication you have new life in Christ.

✧ ✧ ✧

Suggestions for Prayer: Ask God to reveal to you ways you may still be clinging to the world. When He does, sever those connections.

For Further Study: Read 2 Corinthians 4:4; Ephesians 2:1-3; and James 4:4. What is Satan's ultimate goal in pulling people into his system?

"Beloved, now we are children of God, and it has not appeared as yet what we shall be. We know that, when He appears, we shall be like Him, because we shall see Him just as He is. And everyone who has this hope fixed on Him purifies himself, just as He is pure."

1 JOHN 3:2-3

❖ ❖ ❖

True Christians long for the return of their King.

The words of the old hymn, "This world is not my home," express the attitude of every true child of God. True Christians have a hope in their heart, a hope focused on the return of the Lord Jesus Christ. Like the apostle Paul, we long to be set "free from the body of this death" (Rom. 7:24); we "groan within ourselves, waiting eagerly for our adoption as sons, the redemption of our body" (Rom. 8:23). We long for the day when "just as we have borne the image of the earthly, we shall also bear the image of the heavenly" (1 Cor. 15:49).

Our hope is a sanctifying one. John writes, "Every one who has this hope fixed on Him purifies himself, just as He is pure" (1 John 3:3), while Paul reminded Titus that "the grace of God has appeared, bringing salvation to all men, instructing us to deny ungodliness and worldly desires and to live sensibly, righteously and godly in the present age, looking for the blessed hope and the appearing of the glory of our great God and Savior, Christ Jesus" (Titus 2:11-13). Our hope is a sensible one, leading to godly, responsible living. It does not justify careless living (2 Thess. 3:6-15); there is no such thing as someone who is so heavenly minded that he is no earthly good.

Do you find yourself longing for Christ to return and "transform the body of [your] humble state into conformity with the body of His glory" (Phil. 3:21)? If so, take heart. That's another evidence that your salvation is genuine.

❖ ❖ ❖

Suggestions for Prayer: Pray with the apostle John, "Amen. Come, Lord Jesus" (Rev. 22:20).

For Further Study: In Philippians 3:20 Paul reminds us that "our citizenship is in heaven," while in Colossians 3:1-2 the apostle commands us to focus on heavenly things. Where is your focus? What do you spend your time on? Rearrange your priorities and schedule to give first place to eternal realities.

*"No one who is born of God practices sin, because His seed
abides in him; and he cannot sin, because he is born of God."*
1 JOHN 3:9

✧ ✧ ✧

*A decreasing pattern of sin in a believer's
life means his faith is genuine.*

A sinful life pattern is incompatible with salvation. If you could continue in the same sinful pattern after being saved from sin, that would mean salvation is ineffective. Therefore, 1 John 3 deals with the saving work of Christ and reveals just how effective it is.

Verse 5 says Christ "appeared in order to take away sins." If you say someone who has had the work of Christ applied to him is continuing in sin just as before, you are denying the purpose for which Christ came. He died to take away the pattern of sin as well as the penalty.

Therefore, if you are truly a believer you will relate to God in a totally new way, because the Christian "abides in Him" (v. 6). You are no longer a perpetual slave to sin, but you now have the option and ability to do good (see Rom. 6:14, 17-18). You will always be acutely sensitive to sin (Rom. 7; 1 John 1:8-9); yet, because of Christ's abiding in you, your struggle will decrease over the years, and sin will be less and less a pattern in your life.

That brings us to 1 John 3:9, which is a reminder that believers have been born anew by the Holy Spirit. Your new nature or new disposition of life is the "seed" verse 9 speaks of. Just as the seed of a plant, when placed in the soil, produces a distinct kind of life, the divine seed produces a righteous life in you that ends sin's dominance. And that seed will never die—1 Peter 1:23 says it is "imperishable."

What does all this mean to you if you're a genuine believer? It means you will see a decreasing pattern of sin in your life because you now have holy affections. It doesn't mean sin will be eliminated, because your unredeemed flesh is still present. It means the more you practice righteousness—with its right motives, right desires, right words, and right actions—the less you sin, and the more you can be assured you're a child of God.

✧ ✧ ✧

Suggestions for Prayer: If there is a frequent sin you struggle with, ask God to help you defeat it.

For Further Study: Record at least five truths contained in Romans 6:1-11. ✧ How do they help give victory over sin?

> *"The one who loves his brother abides in the light*
> *and there is no cause for stumbling in him."*
> 1 JOHN 2:10

✧ ✧ ✧

Loving other Christians gives
assurance to your own faith.

L oving fellow Christians is instinctive for genuine believers. Paul told the Thessalonians, "Now as to the love of the brethren . . . you yourselves are taught by God to love one another" (1 Thess. 4:9). He further encouraged them to "excel still more" in love (v. 10) because there is always room for believers to love one another more completely. Nevertheless, if we are truly saved we will show love, since love is inherent in our new nature (see Rom. 5:5).

Jesus said this about love among believers: "By this all men will know that you are My disciples, if you have love for one another" (John 13:35). If we are truly Christians, we will "fervently love one another from the heart" (1 Peter 1:22). Love is a test of our divine life and signifies that we have crossed over from darkness to light (1 John 3:14-15).

The apostle John goes on to define love as being sacrificial and practical: "We know love by this, that He laid down His life for us; and we ought to lay down our lives for the brethren. But whoever has the world's goods, and beholds his brother in need and closes his heart against him, how does the love of God abide in him? Little children, let us not love with word or with tongue, but in deed and truth" (vv. 16-18).

Therefore, you should ask yourself some basic questions: Do you care about other believers, or are you cold and indifferent? How do you respond to opportunities to give of yourself in various ministries? Do you look forward to having fellowship with other Christians—talking with them, discussing the things of God, studying the Word together, and praying with them? When you encounter a friend at church who has a need, are you willing to provide money, time, prayer, resources, service, or even a sympathetic ear?

If you can answer yes to those questions, you have great reason to be assured of your salvation. Like Peter, you can appeal to the love God sees in your heart (John 21:17). That love won't be perfect, but it's there and will manifest itself to others.

✧ ✧ ✧

Suggestions for Prayer: Pray that your love will grow stronger and be more consistent.

For Further Study: Read John 21:15-17. What should Peter's love result in? ✧ How does Galatians 6:10 support that?

"And whatever we ask we receive from Him, because we keep His commandments and do the things that are pleasing in His sight."

1 JOHN 3:22

✧ ✧ ✧

The answers to believers' prayers bring assurance of salvation.

A nother reliable way to know if you are a Christian is if God answers your prayers. The apostle John gives us the infallible reasoning for this statement. First, you can know your prayers will be answered if you keep His commandments (1 John 3:22). And second, John says the only way you can obey God's commandments is if you belong to Him (v. 24). Therefore, an obedient believer proves He is abiding in Christ and receives further assurance when his prayers are answered.

However, the only prayers God answers are the ones prayed according to His will. If you are an obedient believer, you will fashion your prayers in line with what Scripture says about His will. The answered prayer that follows will bring you confidence and assurance (see 1 John 5:13-15).

Some believers miss out on that assurance because of their skimpy prayer life, which obviously results in few answered prayers. How sad for them, and how disappointing for God, because He would do so much more for those Christians if they would only ask Him.

What about you? Has it been a pattern of your life to experience answered prayer? Ask yourself questions like the following: Have you prayed for someone's difficult situation and seen God turn it around to one of joy and blessing? Have you seen an unsaved person for whom you prayed come to Christ? Has God filled a void in your life after you prayed that He would? Have you ever prayed that God would help you in teaching His Word and then experienced much grace in presenting it with clarity? Have you prayed for boldness and power to proclaim the gospel and seen God work through you? Have you asked for contentment during a trial and received God's peace? Have you known forgiveness and a clear conscience after you prayed to that end?

If you can answer yes to those questions or ones like them, you have good reason to believe that you belong to the Lord and He belongs to you.

✧ ✧ ✧

Suggestions for Prayer: Thank the Lord for His power through prayer and for the answers He's granted you.

For Further Study: Read 1 Kings 17:1; 18:41-46. What does the second passage reveal about Elijah's prayer life? ✧ How does that support James 5:16b-18?

"By this we know that we abide in Him and He in us,
because He has given us of His Spirit."
1 JOHN 4:13

✧ ✧ ✧

Experiencing the ministry of the Holy Spirit
is evidence of genuine saving faith.

In John 14:26, Jesus described the Holy Spirit as "the Helper." One of the most important ways He helps us is by assuring us that we belong to God. Several works of the Holy Spirit, if present in our lives, give evidence of the genuineness of our salvation. In 1 Corinthians 12:3 Paul writes, "No one can say, 'Jesus is Lord,' except by the Holy Spirit." Apart from the convicting work of the Holy Spirit, you would not know who Christ was, nor would you confess Him as Savior and Lord. If you have experienced that work of the Holy Spirit, that is evidence you are a true child of God.

Another essential ministry of the Spirit is that of illuminating Scripture. First John 2:27 says, "The anointing which you received from Him abides in you . . . His anointing teaches you about all things." Do you understand the Bible when you read it? Does it convict you of sin? Does it lead you to rejoice and worship God? If so, that is evidence of the Spirit's illuminating work in your life.

Do you long for intimate fellowship with God? That, too, is the result of the Spirit's work in your life (Gal. 4:6). Do you feel compelled to praise God? The filling of the Spirit produces praise (Eph. 5:19). Does your life manifest the fruit of the Spirit (Gal. 5:22-23)? Are one or more of the gifts of the Spirit operating in your life (1 Cor. 12)? Those, too, are evidences of the Spirit's work in your life.

All of those ministries of the Holy Spirit are the way He "bears witness with our spirit that we are children of God" (Rom. 8:16). If they are manifest in your life, they provide evidence that you abide in God and He in you (1 John 4:13). Let the Holy Spirit's work in your life dispel the dark shadows of doubt.

✧ ✧ ✧

Suggestions for Prayer: Pray that God would help you examine your life for evidence of the Spirit's work.

For Further Study: Read 1 John 3:24. What is our part in obtaining assurance?
✧ Are there any commandments you are willfully violating? If so, confess them, repent of them, and begin to experience the blessedness of assurance.

"Beloved, do not believe every spirit, but test the spirits to see whether they are from God; because many false prophets have gone out into the world. By this you know the Spirit of God: every spirit that confesses that Jesus Christ has come in the flesh is from God; and every spirit that does not confess Jesus is not from God; and this is the spirit of the antichrist, of which you have heard that it is coming, and now it is already in the world."

1 JOHN 4:1-3

✧ ✧ ✧

God's children are able to discern false doctrine.

A sure mark of every false religious system is doctrinal error, particularly about the Person and work of Jesus Christ. Those systems deny that He is Savior and Lord, God in human flesh, the only way to the Father (John 14:6) because salvation comes only through Him (Acts 4:12).

A sure mark, then, of all true children of God is that they believe the truth about Jesus Christ and do not deviate into doctrinal error. Although they may be temporarily duped by false teaching, they will not be permanently deceived by it. The apostle John wrote, "[False teachers] are from the world; therefore they speak as from the world, and the world listens to them. We are from God; he who knows God listens to us; he who is not from God does not listen to us. By this we know the spirit of truth and the spirit of error" (1 John 4:5-6).

When you were saved, you were clear about who Christ was. "Whoever believes that Jesus is the Christ," writes John, "is born of God" (1 John 5:1). Had you not passed that doctrinal test, you wouldn't have been saved. God's children distinguish spiritual truth from doctrinal error because the Spirit of truth (John 14:16) indwells them.

"O Timothy," Paul exhorted his beloved son in the faith, "guard what has been entrusted to you, avoiding worldly and empty chatter and the opposing arguments of what is falsely called 'knowledge'" (1 Tim. 6:20). I pray that you will guard the precious treasure of truth entrusted to you in the Scriptures and so assure your heart that you belong to the God of truth.

✧ ✧ ✧

Suggestions for Prayer: Thank God for revealing His truth to us in the Bible.

For Further Study: Read John 1:1; Philippians 2:5-11; Colossians 2:9. What do they teach about the Person of Christ?

> *"Not as Cain, who was of the evil one, and slew his brother. And for what reason did he slay him? Because his deeds were evil, and his brother's were righteous. Do not marvel, brethren, if the world hates you."*
>
> 1 JOHN 3:12-13

✧ ✧ ✧

Christians are rejected by the world but accepted by God.

An ancient proverb states that you can judge a man's character by who his enemies are. That is also true in the spiritual realm. The world loves its own, but since Christ chose believers out of the world, the world hates them (John 15:19).

That this is true should come as no surprise to any student of God's Word. After all, the world hated Jesus so much that it killed Him. We, as His followers, can also expect hostility. "If the world hates you," Jesus said in John 15:18, "you know that it has hated Me before it hated you." "If they have called the head of the house Beelzebul," He added in Matthew 10:25, "how much more the members of his household!"

From the beginning of history, the unrighteous have hated the righteous. The apostle John noted the tragic story of unrighteous Cain, who murdered his righteous brother Abel in a fit of jealous rage (1 John 3:12; Gen. 4:1-8). In Acts 7:52 Stephen asked his accusers, "Which one of the prophets did your fathers not persecute? And they killed those who had previously announced the coming of the Righteous One, whose betrayers and murderers you have now become." Stephen's accusation aptly summarized the sad history of Israel, "who kill[ed] the prophets and ston[ed] those who [were] sent to her" (Matt. 23:37).

Peter noted the reason for the world's hostility to Christians when he wrote, "[Unbelievers] are surprised that you do not run with them into the same excess of dissipation, and they malign you" (1 Peter 4:4). Christians' lives are a threat because they rebuke unbelievers' sin and remind them of coming judgment.

Have you experienced the world's hostility, opposition, prejudice, rejection, or even persecution for your stand for Jesus Christ? If so, that's evidence that you belong to the One who also suffered rejection by the world.

✧ ✧ ✧

Suggestions for Prayer: Pray that God would enable you to rejoice in the face of persecution (Acts 5:41).

For Further Study: Read Philippians 1:28. What should your attitude be when you are rejected by the world?

*"Therefore, I shall always be ready to remind you of these
things, even though you already know them, and have been
established in the truth which is present with you."*

2 PETER 1:12

✧ ✧ ✧

***Remembering where you've been is the key
to getting where you want to go.***

The summer of 1980 was a turning point in my ministry. After nearly a dozen years as pastor of Grace Community Church, I took a three-month sabbatical. In my heart I wasn't sure if I would come back. I felt I had taught my congregation all I knew, and I feared boring them by reiterating the same old things.

But during that summer the Lord taught me a spiritual truth that revitalized my ministry. He showed me the importance of reminding believers of truth they already know. As I read and studied 2 Peter 1, I realized the Lord had called Peter to that same ministry. The more I thought about it, the more important I realized such a ministry is, for it is all too easy to forget spiritual truth. The tragic story of Israel, whose forgetfulness of spiritual truth led to disaster, is a sobering warning.

One of the primary purposes of Communion is to remember the glorious truths about our Lord and His sacrifice on our behalf. Remembrance is also an essential aspect of assurance of salvation.

What are we in danger of forgetting? As he begins his second epistle, Peter lists several key truths Christians must not forget. He reminds us of the realities of our salvation and of the saving faith God graciously granted us based on the righteousness of Jesus Christ (2 Peter 1:1), resulting in grace, peace, and knowledge of Him (v. 2). As a result, we have "everything pertaining to life and godliness, through the true knowledge of Him who called us by His own glory and excellence" (v. 3).

Having reminded us of the glorious truths of our salvation, Peter then calls us to remember several key virtues that need to be manifest in our lives. As we study them over the next several days, I pray that God will help you to remember what you know and thereby grow in your assurance of salvation.

✧ ✧ ✧

Suggestions for Prayer: Thank God for the unsearchable riches of His salvation.

For Further Study: Begin a program of Scripture memorization today to saturate your mind with the truths of God's Word.

"Now for this very reason also, applying all diligence,
in your faith supply moral excellence."
2 PETER 1:5

✧ ✧ ✧

God's provision does not preclude our responsibility.

There are some who believe that since God has provided everything needed for the Christian life, believers should expect Him to do everything for them. Their motto is, "Let go and let God!" If Peter had a motto for the Christian life, it would have been more along the lines of the popular World War II song, "Praise the Lord and Pass the Ammunition!" Peter knew the Christian life is a struggle in which believers need to expend the maximum effort to equip themselves with godly virtues—the virtues that, when present in our lives, produce assurance of salvation. He therefore prefaces the list of those virtues in verse 5 by saying, "Now for this very reason also," thus pointing us back to God's provision of salvation in verses 1-4. That provision is not meant to eliminate our efforts in living the Christian life but to enable and encourage them. We must, says Peter, live our Christian lives by "applying all diligence" to develop godly virtues.

Heading the list of virtues that should characterize our lives is "moral excellence." The Greek term *arete* can also be translated "virtue." In classical Greek literature, it often referred to the ability to perform heroic deeds. It refers to the quality that makes someone or something stand out as excellent. An *arete* knife was one that was sharp and cut well; an *arete* horse was one with speed and endurance; an *arete* singer was one who sang well.

"Moral excellence," it should be noted, is not an attitude but an action. In fact, some suggest the meaning "moral energy" for it—the moral energy that gives us the power to do excellent deeds. Our model for that kind of active excellence is Jesus Christ, who "went about doing good" (Acts 10:38).

Never waver in your pursuit of excellence. In the words of Paul to the Thessalonians, "Excel still more" (1 Thess. 4:1).

✧ ✧ ✧

Suggestions for Prayer: Thank God for supplying everything you need to live the Christian life. ✧ Ask Him to help you to be diligent to develop godly virtues in your life.

For Further Study: Read Proverbs 4:23; 8:17; 12:27; 13:4; 21:5. What do those passages teach about the importance of diligence?

". . . in your moral excellence, knowledge."

2 PETER 1:5

❖ ❖ ❖

Moral excellence cannot develop in an intellectual vacuum.

It's a frightening thing to realize the extent to which our culture downplays knowledge in favor of emotions. These days people are more likely to ask, "How will it make me feel?" instead of, "Is it true?" Sadly, the church has bought into the spirit of the age. Many people go to church, not to learn the truths of God's Word, but to get an emotional high. The focus of theological discussion also reflects the contemporary hostility to knowledge. To a shocking extent, truth is no longer the issue; the questions being asked today are, "Will it divide?" or "Will it offend?" To ask if a theological position is biblically correct is considered unloving, and those who take a stand for historic Christian truth are labeled as divisive.

But knowledge is inseparable from moral excellence and Christian growth. It should be obvious that people can't put into practice truths they don't know; we must first understand the principles of God's Word before we can live them out.

Peter knew well the importance of knowledge in developing a stable Christian walk and the assurance of salvation that accompanies it. Therefore, he urged his readers to add knowledge to their moral excellence. *Gnosis* ("knowledge") refers to insight, discernment, and proper understanding of truth. Lacking such knowledge, believers become "children, tossed here and there by waves, and carried about by every wind of doctrine" (Eph. 4:14). The resulting turmoil is not conducive to spiritual growth or the development of a settled assurance of salvation.

The Bible commends child-like (i.e., trusting, humble) faith, but not childish faith. Paul exhorted the Corinthians, "Brethren, do not be children in your thinking . . . in your thinking be mature" (1 Cor. 14:20). "So let us know, let us press on to know the Lord," urged Hosea. When we do so, "He will come to us like the rain, like the spring rain watering the earth" (Hos. 6:3).

I pray with the apostle Paul, "that your love may abound still more and more in real knowledge and all discernment" (Phil. 1:9).

❖ ❖ ❖

Suggestions for Prayer: Pray that God would enable you to "grow in the grace and knowledge of our Lord and Savior Jesus Christ" (2 Peter 3:18).

For Further Study: Read Proverbs 23:7 and Philippians 4:8. What do those verses teach about the importance of godly thinking?

> *"And in your knowledge, self-control,*
> *and in your self-control, perseverance . . ."*
> **2 PETER 1:6**

✧ ✧ ✧

Personal self-control demonstrates the certainty of your salvation.

In Peter's day, the word translated "self-control" was used to describe athletes. The successful ones abstained from sexual activity and an unhealthy diet for the sake of disciplined training exercises. You practice personal self-control when you control your desires and don't allow them to control you.

Let me share some practical tips that have helped me with self-control.

1. *Start small.* For example, begin by cleaning your bedroom or office, then extend that discipline to the rest of your home.

2. *Be on time.* This is more than good advice; it's based on Scripture (see Eccles. 8:6; Eph. 5:15-16). Learn to budget your time, and discipline your desires so you can arrive at places on time.

3. *Organize your life.* Use a schedule book, or make a daily list of things you need to do. Don't let circumstances control your time.

4. *Practice self-denial.* Periodically refrain from something that is all right just to remind yourself who's in charge. Sometime when you want a hot fudge sundae, have a glass of iced tea instead.

5. *Do the hardest job first.* Doing this will keep you from letting the difficult tasks slide by undone.

6. *Accept correction.* Constructive criticism helps you become more disciplined because it shows you what to avoid. Acknowledge the courage of the one who corrects you. It's almost always easier to keep silent, but that person, especially if he or she is a believer, spoke up because he or she likely had your best interest at heart.

7. *Welcome responsibility.* If you're qualified for a task or assignment that arises, such as opportunities at church, volunteer occasionally. That will prompt you to be disciplined and organized.

Some of the items on my list may not seem very spiritual and may even sound silly. However, I've found that pursuing discipline in the secular realm often carries over to the spiritual. Any theology that separates faith from practical conduct is heresy. Self-control is a great Christian virtue and solid proof that one's salvation is genuine.

✧ ✧ ✧

Suggestions for Prayer: Ask God to help you get better control of an area in which you lack discipline.

For Further Study: Read 1 Corinthians 9:25; 1 Timothy 3:2; Titus 1:8; 2:2. How do those verses underscore the importance of self-control? Explain.

*". . . And in your self-control, perseverance,
and in your perseverance, godliness."*

2 PETER 1:6

❖ ❖ ❖

Godly perseverance is a sure evidence of true salvation.

Commentator Michael Green has this to say about the believer who displays biblical perseverance: "The mature Christian does not give up. His Christianity is like the steady burning of a star rather than the ephemeral brilliance (and speedy eclipse) of a meteor." The Greek word translated "perseverance" in today's verse (*hupomone*) refers to consistent endurance in righteousness and faithfulness in resisting temptation.

The precise meaning for *hupomone* is hard to pinpoint. There is no exact English equivalent, and it's not common in classical Greek; but the Bible often uses it in reference to the toils and troubles that are unwelcome in life and produce inconvenience and harm. This word even includes the idea of death, as in the Jewish writings in which *hupomone* speaks of spiritual stamina that empowers people to die for their faith in God.

Despite its scriptural associations with painful difficulties and death, *hupomone* has a positive meaning. William Barclay notes, "*Hupomone* does not simply accept and endure; there is always a forward look in it. It is said of Jesus . . . that for the joy set before him, he endured the Cross, despising the shame (Hebrews 12:2). That is *hupomone*, Christian steadfastness. It is the courageous acceptance of everything that life can do to us and the transmuting of even the worst event into another step on the upward way."

Godliness is at the heart of scriptural perseverance. The Greek for "godliness" (*eusebeia*) denotes a practical awareness of God in every area of life—a God-consciousness. The word could also be translated "true religion" or "true worship." It gives God His rightful place by worshiping Him properly, something that is not often done in the contemporary church. Genuine public worship is more than "relevant" programs, new rituals, or catchy music—it contains much reverence for God.

If you are truly a Christian, you will also revere God in your devotional life and obediently persevere in His will daily. You will rejoice and be aware of God in every detail of life.

❖ ❖ ❖

Suggestions for Prayer: Ask the Lord to increase both your perseverance and godly worship.

For Further Study: Read Revelation 2:8-11; 3:7-13. What are the results and benefits of faithful perseverance?

"And in your godliness, brotherly kindness . . ."
2 PETER 1:7

✧ ✧ ✧

Real Christian discipleship will include
practical brotherly love.

A genuine love for God will invariably lead to a love for others. That's
what Jesus said of the two great commandments (Matt. 22:36-40) that
summarize the Ten Commandments. The apostle John also related love for
God and love for others: "If someone says, 'I love God,' and hates his brother,
he is a liar; for the one who does not love his brother whom he has seen, cannot love God whom he has not seen" (1 John 4:20).

The kind of love that's called "brotherly kindness" in today's verse is very
practical. It's a translation of the Greek *philadelphia*, which might best be rendered "friendship." We are to be affectionate toward one another. But that does
not always happen, especially for those attending big churches. There I fear many
people sit on the periphery without developing any relationships. They come to
the morning service and then go their way. But that's not Christian discipleship;
we're to add friendships to our faith and be involved in others' lives.

People in many different churches want to know more about discipleship,
as if it were some complex program surrounded in mystery. But discipleship
is simply friendship with a spiritual perspective. Disciples will talk about
God, the Scripture, ministry opportunities, and prayer requests—not merely
sports, the weather, gardening, or home remodeling. Each is concerned how
the other handles the daily affairs and important matters of life. I would
encourage you to build friendships and be a part of a Bible study and fellowship group—but make sure your small group does not become exclusive and
keep out newcomers.

I once talked to a pastor who had attended one of the annual pastors' con-
ferences at my church. I asked him what impressed him most about the con-
ference, and he said, "The love of the people for each other. I was drawn to
tears when I sensed them worshiping God in the midst of genuine love." He
had seen an application of Jesus' words, "By this all men will know that you
are My disciples, if you have love for one another" (John 13:35). You can't
get more practical about Christian love than that!

✧ ✧ ✧

Suggestions for Prayer: Pray for other members of your small group. If you're
not in one, ask God to lead you to a group.

For Further Study: Read 1 John 4:7-19. With whom does love originate? ✧
What are the results of that love?

> "*. . . And in your brotherly kindness, Christian love.*"
>
> 2 PETER 1:7

❖ ❖ ❖

Sacrificial love proves genuine faith.

C lassical Greek had three common terms for love. As we saw yesterday, *phileo* (*philadelphia*) is the love of give and take, best expressed in friendship. *Eros* is the love that takes—one loves another strictly for what he or she can get out of that person. It is typical of the world's sexual and lustful desires, which are always bent toward self-gratification. *Agape* is the love that gives. It is completely unselfish, with no taking involved. This is the highest form of love, which all the other virtues in 2 Peter 1 ultimately lead to. It seeks another's supreme good, no matter what the cost. *Agape* was exemplified perfectly by Jesus' sacrifice on our behalf.

But what does this highest type of love look like? A brief survey of the *one anothers* in the New Testament gives an excellent picture. We are commanded to:

> *Edify one another (Rom. 14:19).*
> *"Serve one another" (Gal. 5:13).*
> *"Bear one another's burdens" (Gal. 6:2).*
> *Submit to one another (Eph. 5:21).*
> *Forgive one another (Col. 3:13).*
> *Instruct one another (Col. 3:16).*
> *"Comfort one another" (1 Thess. 4:18).*
> *Rebuke one another (Titus 1:13).*
> *Encourage one another to do good (Heb. 10:24-25).*
> *Confess our sins to one another (James 5:16).*
> *"Pray for one another" (James 5:16).*
> *"Be hospitable to one another" (1 Peter 4:9-10).*

The Lord Jesus Christ was involved with individuals. He was a true friend who caringly, lovingly, and sensitively interacted with feeble, needy, and unimportant people and made them eternally important.

Nevertheless we still find people spiritualizing love into a meaningless term. "I love so-and-so in the Lord" really means, "He irks me, but I guess I have to love him if he's a believer." Don't let yourself say that. Instead, display genuine love.

❖ ❖ ❖

Suggestions for Prayer: Thank God that Christ showed *agape* love toward you on the cross.

For Further Study: Memorize one of the verses in the list of *one anothers*, and apply it at every appropriate opportunity.

> *"For if these qualities are yours and are increasing,*
> *they render you neither useless nor unfruitful in the*
> *true knowledge of our Lord Jesus Christ."*
> 2 PETER 1:8

❖ ❖ ❖

If you are a Christian, your life will produce spiritual fruit.

If you want to enjoy assurance of salvation in all its richness, you need to faithfully pursue all the virtues we have been studying this past week. The reason is simple—they produce fruit in the Christian life, and nothing is a better indicator of true salvation than that. It was the criterion Christ used to distinguish between the true and false believer (Matt. 7:15-20).

The reasonable question that ought to arise next is, what is fruit? The New Testament says it encompasses many righteous activities. Paul says winning souls to Christ is fruit (Rom. 1:13). The apostle calls the house of Stephanas "the first fruits of Achaia" (1 Cor. 16:15). In Philippians 4:17 Paul refers to money given in the support of ministry as fruit. The writer of Hebrews says praise is the fruit of our lips (Heb. 13:15). The act of praying is also a spiritual fruit.

Behind every one of those righteous actions is the right attitude, because "the fruit of the Spirit is love, joy, peace, patience, kindness, goodness, faithfulness, gentleness, self-control" (Gal. 5:22-23). If you act without a godly attitude, it is only legalism, not genuine spiritual fruit.

All the Spirit-endowed virtues, actions, and attitudes we have discussed, if they are in your life, will assure you that you'll be "neither useless nor unfruitful." "Useless" is also used in James 2:20 in relation to dead faith. If you incorporate into your life the virtues of 2 Peter 1:5-7, your faith will not be dead or ineffective.

"Unfruitful" is also used in Matthew 13:22 of the person with a weedy heart and of false, apostate teachers in Jude 12. When you don't live a virtuous life, you are the same as an apostate or a worldly hanger-on in the church.

"In the true knowledge of our Lord Jesus Christ" refers to true believers, those who possess truth as opposed to error. Because you know Christ, you have the ability to live a virtuous life (see Eph. 1:3; 2 Peter 1:3). When you do, God will give you true assurance.

❖ ❖ ❖

Suggestions for Prayer: Pray that God would strengthen any of the virtues that are weak in your life.

For Further Study: Read Matthew 7:13-23. What is the first essential for fruitfulness (vv. 13-14)? ❖ What will happen to many who do good works (vv. 22-23)?

*"For he who lacks these qualities is blind or short-sighted,
having forgotten his purification from his former sins."*
2 PETER 1:9

✧ ✧ ✧

*If you don't practice spiritual virtues now,
you'll forget their significance later.*

Physical nearsightedness and mental amnesia both are unwanted conditions. Nearsightedness (*myopia*) causes people's eyes to focus the parallel rays of light in front of the retina. They can clearly see things right in front of them, but the farther out they look, the more out of focus objects become.

Amnesia, of course, is memory loss. Sometimes it's selective, but usually it's total—everything prior to a certain time or incident. It often causes people to forget their name, their family, and everything about their identity and background.

Those two impairments should be even less welcome on the spiritual level. Professed believers who are unfruitful become spiritually nearsighted. They focus on temporal fads and passing earthly fashions. By the time they try to look ahead to eternity, it is so out of focus for them that they can't see it.

Those with spiritual amnesia, because they see no increase of spiritual virtue in their lives, forget they were supposed to be saved from their sinful lifestyles. They don't remember the spiritual "purification" (*catharsis*) that should have occurred in their lives—a reference to a deep internal purging or cleansing.

If you are not diligently pursuing spiritual virtue and moral excellence, you will have a very fuzzy view of your true condition. You may connect an outward action or emotional experience with the time you professed Christ, but you will not have a sense of assurance. Commentator Richard Bauckham explained it this way: "The 'knowledge of Jesus Christ' [v. 8], received at conversion, came as illumination to those who were blind in their pagan ignorance (2 Cor. 4:4), but Christians who do not carry through the moral implications of this knowledge have effectively become blind to it again."

Regarding 1 Peter 1:5-9, it all comes down to this: if you are seeing your life grow in moral virtue, you have proof of salvation and a reason for assurance. If you are not seeing your life grow in virtue, you have no proof of salvation and no reason for assurance. Be diligent to avoid spiritual myopia and amnesia in your life.

✧ ✧ ✧

Suggestions for Prayer: Pray that you would have clear spiritual vision at all times.

For Further Study: Read Hebrews 6:1-12. How can this passage help you avoid spiritual amnesia?

*"Therefore, brethren, be all the more diligent to make certain
about His calling and choosing you; for as long as you
practice these things, you will never stumble; for in this way
the entrance into the eternal kingdom of our Lord and
Savior Jesus Christ will be abundantly supplied to you."*

2 PETER 1:10-11

✧ ✧ ✧

*The pursuit of virtue results in assurance
now and eternal reward later.*

Assurance is a great blessing, as Peter tells us in verse 10 of today's passage. However, it is not the only thing you will enjoy if you are pursuing godly virtues. Years ago a Jewish teenager named Marvin learned about
the additional blessing of rewards from the lady who led him to Christ. Before
he left home to join the Marines as a struggling, often persecuted believer, she
told him: "You're a true Christian, Marvin. . . . One day when your earthly
life ends you will go to Heaven because of what the Messiah has done for you.
But if, when you get to Heaven, there is a great big parade and if in the front
of the parade there is a great big band—if you don't change your way of living, you'll be so far back in the line that you won't even hear the music."
Marvin got the message and eventually became a dedicated Christian teacher
and evangelist.

You and I also must be living our lives in light of eternity—laying up treasures in Heaven, pursuing the virtues symbolized by gold, silver, and precious
stones, not giving attention to those lesser things represented by wood, hay,
and straw (see 1 Cor. 3:10-15). Those of us who earnestly pursue the virtues
of 2 Peter 1 will receive a superabundant reward. And that's not a crass motive
for good works, because all believers will one day place their crowns
(rewards) before God's throne as an act of homage (see 2 Tim. 4:7-8; Rev.
4:10).

Examine yourself to see if there's any moral virtue in your life. If you see
none, you can't assume you're saved. If you see some and it's growing, though
not perfectly, you can be "certain about His calling and choosing you" (2 Peter
1:10). And you can be confident His reward "will be abundantly supplied to
you" (v. 11).

✧ ✧ ✧

Suggestions for Prayer: Thank the Lord for the eternal rewards that await
those believers who have been faithful.

For Further Study: Read Ephesians 1:18; 2:7; and 1 Timothy 6:17. What do
those verses say about God's blessings and rewards?

"For as long as you practice these things,
you will never stumble."
2 PETER 1:10

❖ ❖ ❖

Assurance of salvation lets us enjoy earthly blessings.

It is encouraging that scriptural assurance results in specific, practical blessings in the Christian life. Here are six I'd like to share with you today.

Assurance makes you praise God. There is no way you can be filled with praise and gratitude to God if you're not sure you're saved.

Assurance adds joy to your earthly duties and trials. No matter what happens to you, you can be certain that all will work out well in the end. Difficulties are easier to handle when you know they're temporary.

Assurance makes you zealous in obedience and service. If you're doubtful about your salvation, you will be apathetic and discouraged. But if you're sure, you will be hard-working and encouraged in serving the Lord.

Assurance gives you victory in temptation. When you are confident about your salvation, you can overcome the strongest temptation (see 1 Cor. 10:13). Even if you stumble occasionally, you will know that those events have not changed your standing before God. But you will be depressed and discouraged by temptation if you have no assurance. You'll doubt your ability to cope with temptations and will wonder if falling victim to one or two will send you to Hell.

Assurance gives contentment in this life. You'll rest secure in the promise that you have a glorious heavenly inheritance to look forward to. At the same time, you will be happy and satisfied that God "shall supply all your needs according to His riches in glory in Christ Jesus" (Phil. 4:9). But if you lack assurance of salvation, you'll scramble and reach for all the world's material goods and feel cheated when you don't obtain them.

Assurance removes the fear of death. If you know you're a child of God, you can be sure that the moment you die you will enter Heaven. If you don't have that assurance, however, you'll be even more afraid to die than one who has never heard of Christ.

If you are growing spiritually, you will have assurance, and that will let you enjoy these and other blessings as you look forward to being with the Lord for all eternity.

❖ ❖ ❖

Suggestions for Prayer: Pray that God would help you share the blessings of assurance with someone else.

For Further Study: Read Psalm 138. What was David thankful for? ❖ What reassurances are there for every believer?

"For where your treasure is,
there will your heart be also."
MATTHEW 6:21

✧ ✧ ✧

In wealthy countries, where the focus is on material things,
believers must strive for the right perspective on possessions.

Today's text answers the simple but age-old question, Where is your heart? When our Lord answers the question, it is clear He is referring to all of life's major preoccupations and investments—anything that receives most of our thinking, planning, and expenditure of energy.

The religious leaders of Jesus' day had their hearts in the wrong places. Among their many other sins, the Pharisees were thing-oriented—covetous, greedy, avaricious, and manipulative. Matthew 6:21 is right in the middle of a portion of the Sermon on the Mount that deals with the Pharisees' misplaced priorities regarding material possessions. The verse fits with Christ's overall purpose in the Sermon, which was to affirm His standard of righteous living in contrast to the Pharisees' inferior, hypocritical standard (Matt. 5:20).

Matthew 6:19-24 tells us how believers should view their luxuries and wealth. Most of us live in cultures that constantly challenge us with their emphases on materialism. We all spend some time thinking about those things, whether it be a house, a car, furniture, investment portfolios, computers, our wardrobes, or whatever. And many people become slaves to consumerism and greed. Therefore we need to deal with these issues and have a biblical viewpoint concerning the many material comforts we have.

Above all, if we want the same perspective on wealth that Jesus had, our view must far exceed that of the Pharisees with their proud, earthbound viewpoint. They were focusing all of their time and devotion on selfishly laying up worldly treasures. Theirs is not the godly standard of those who want to exemplify Christ in the midst of a materialistic society.

✧ ✧ ✧

Suggestions for Prayer: What thoughts and activities occupy most of your extra time? Pray that they would not be merely about things, but about the things of God.

For Further Study: You need to have a right view of yourself before any other area of life is properly understood. Read again the familiar opening passage of the Sermon on the Mount, Matthew 5:1-12. ✧ Memorize or meditate on one verse or more that ministers to a need you have.

> *"But godliness actually is a means of great gain,*
> *when accompanied by contentment. For we have brought*
> *nothing into the world, so we cannot take anything*
> *out of it either. And if we have food and covering,*
> *with these we shall be content."*
>
> 1 TIMOTHY 6:6-8

✧ ✧ ✧

Believers should not have a self-centered
preoccupation with money.

With all the attention modern society gives to money, what it can buy, and the dividends it can earn, Christians are continually challenged to view it properly. But Scripture provides us with much help and guidance in this area. It is replete with warnings and admonitions about how we are to act and think concerning money and wealth.

There are at least eight basic, biblical guidelines that when believed and followed will give us a God-centered view of money. First, having money in itself is not wrong (1 Sam. 2:7). Second, we ought to recognize that money is a gift from God and comes to us through His providence (Deut. 8:11-18). Third, we must be willing to lose our money, if that's God's will for us. Job said, "The Lord gave and the Lord has taken away. Blessed be the name of the Lord" (1:21). Fourth, we must not be partial toward those who have lots of money (James 2:1-10). Fifth, we must not arrogantly seek security from money (Prov. 11:28; 1 Tim. 6:17). Sixth, money-making pursuits should never be our highest priorities in life (Matt. 6:33). Seventh, we ought to use money for eternal purposes, namely, leading others to the Lord (Luke 16:9). Finally, we must not selfishly hoard or foolishly spend money. On the contrary, true generosity should characterize every believer (Prov. 11:24-25; Luke 6:38).

Just like a firearm, money can be used for good purposes and evil purposes, which means there is nothing inherently wrong with it. Therefore, the real issue does not concern money itself, but what our attitude is toward it. The Lord wants us to view money as He did and be content with what we have.

✧ ✧ ✧

Suggestions for Prayer: Confess your sinful attitude in one or more of the eight areas mentioned today. Pray that God would replace those sinful attitudes toward money with His righteous attitudes.

For Further Study: Read Deuteronomy 8:11-18. What divine favors does God remind the Israelites of? ✧ What sin is sure to befall any believer who forgets that God is the One who makes wealth possible?

"For the love of money is a root of all sorts of evil."
1 TIMOTHY 6:10

❖ ❖ ❖

There are specific indicators that warn us if we are loving money.

Today's verse is a classic reference and contains the overarching scriptural principle concerning our attitude toward money. In referring to the love of money, Paul is essentially talking about the sin of greed. That sin is a serious offense in God's eyes, which means we ought to desire with all our hearts to have victory over it. And we can begin to achieve such victory by recognizing the major warning signs of greed or money-love.

There are at least five major behavior and attitude symptoms that reveal the presence of greed in one's life. First, if you are truly a lover of money, you will be more concerned with acquiring it than with giving an honest, quality effort in everything you do. Believers are to pursue truth and excellence first of all, and God will see to it that we receive the proper monetary rewards.

Second, if you are greedy, you will feel that you never have enough money. Your attitude will be like the leech's daughters who constantly say, "Give," "Give" (Prov. 30:15).

Third, if you love money, you will tend to flaunt what it can buy. You will be unduly eager to show off clothing, your new car or truck, or the new property you just purchased.

Fourth, if you are a slave to greed, you will resent giving your money to support worthwhile causes or help other people. You will want to keep everything to spend on your own selfish desires.

Finally, if you are in love with money, it is likely you will sin to obtain more. That could include cheating on your income tax return or expense account report or shortchanging customers.

If you love God with all your heart, soul, mind, and strength (Deut. 6:4-5; Matt. 22:35-38), none of those symptoms will be in your life to hinder your pursuit of Him. That's what Jesus meant when He said we can't love and serve both God and money (Matt. 6:24).

❖ ❖ ❖

Suggestions for Prayer: Pray that God would make the allure of money so faint for you that you would never be a slave to greed.

For Further Study: Write out and memorize Philippians 4:11. Carry it with you, and quote it to counteract the greedy thoughts of dissatisfaction that arise periodically.

"But godliness actually is a means of great gain,
when accompanied by contentment."
1 TIMOTHY 6:6

❖ ❖ ❖

True wealth is found in contentment, not in monetary gain.

L ove of money and contentment are mutually exclusive. An ancient Roman proverb says, "Money is like seawater; the more you drink, the thirstier you get." Ecclesiastes 5:10 summarizes the point this way: "He who loves money will not be satisfied with money."

History has also demonstrated that no amount of riches can compensate for a lack of contentment. Millionaire financier John D. Rockefeller said, "I have made many millions, but they have brought me no happiness." That wealthiest of industrialists, Henry Ford, was quoted as saying, "I was happier doing mechanic's work."

The Cynic and Stoic philosophers of Paul's day were probably more content than any of the modern corporate tycoons. Those philosophers viewed the contented person as one who was self-sufficient, unflappable, and unmoved by outside circumstances. But true Christians have the best understanding of contentment because they know it comes from God. Paul told the Corinthian church, "Not that we are adequate in ourselves to consider anything as coming from ourselves, but our adequacy is from God" (2 Cor. 3:5; see also 9:8).

The genuine believer, therefore, sees contentment as more than merely a noble human virtue. For him, it derives from the sufficiency God the Father and Christ the Son provide (Phil. 4:19). Thus a godly person is not motivated by the love of money but by the love of God (see Ps. 63:1-5).

The richest person is the one who needs nothing else because he is content with what he has. He adheres to the philosophy of Proverbs 30:8-9, "Give me neither poverty nor riches; feed me with the food that is my portion, lest I be full and deny Thee and say, 'Who is the Lord?' Or lest I be in want and steal, and profane the name of my God."

Loving money deprives us of the contentment the writer of Proverbs alluded to and Paul wrote about. Such greed also leaves us spiritually impoverished and ignores the great gain that comes from true godliness—hardly the end result any of us should settle for simply because the love of money dominates our life.

❖ ❖ ❖

Suggestions for Prayer: Thank God that His daily and weekly provision has been and always will be sufficient for your needs.

For Further Study: Read Psalm 63:1-5. What attitudes result from the psalmist's efforts? ❖ What additional insights does the prophet add in Isaiah 55:2 and 58:11?

"For we have brought nothing into the world,
so we cannot take anything out of it either."
1 TIMOTHY 6:7

❖ ❖ ❖

Temporal concerns must not crowd out
the believer's focus on eternal things.

In Charles Dickens's memorable story *A Christmas Carol*, Ebenezer Scrooge learns through a series of dreams that life consists of far more important values than his selfish preoccupation with business and finance. In essence, Scrooge learns a lesson that reminds us of Jesus' sobering question, "For what does it profit a man to gain the whole world, and forfeit his soul?" (Mark 8:36). Dickens's story also dovetails well with today's verse, which reminds us how a temporal focus on greed robs us of an eternal perspective.

People who are enslaved to money-love spend all their time dealing with what is locked into time and space. They overlook and ignore that which has eternal value. Also, such people seem oblivious to the warning that "riches are not forever" (Prov. 27:24) and to the old expression that hearses do not pull trailers.

The Old Testament further instructs us of the fleeting nature of money and material possessions. Job said, "Naked I came from my mother's womb, and naked I shall return there" (1:21; see also Eccles. 5:15).

Jesus taught the disciples much about how foolish it is to focus on temporal wealth (see Matt. 6:19-21). Perhaps His sternest warning is in the parable of the rich fool (Luke 12:15-21). In it God condemns the smug self-confidence the man placed in his abundant crops: "But God said to him, 'You fool! This very night your soul is required of you; and now who will own what you have prepared?' So is the man who lays up treasure for himself, and is not rich toward God" (vv. 20-21).

A scenario like the rich man's is much more probable in today's materialistic societies. Perhaps that's why Jesus' parable is still so relevant and a potent reminder that any obsession with temporal riches, which causes us to miss God's eternal riches, is the height of folly.

❖ ❖ ❖

Suggestions for Prayer: Pray that today, in the midst of your normal responsibilities, God would keep your primary focus an eternal one.

For Further Study: Read Acts 19:18-41. How did many of the new converts demonstrate their commitment to the eternal over the temporal? ❖ In contrast, what did the anxiety of some of the unbelieving Ephesians lead to? Why? ❖ How was the disturbance finally brought to an end?

"And if we have food and covering, with these we shall be content."
1 TIMOTHY 6:8

✧ ✧ ✧

**God wants believers' lives to be simplified,
free from the burdens of material cares.**

Today's verse declares how Christians ought to be free from material distractions. The apostle Paul asserts that life's basic needs should be adequate to satisfy believers. He does not say it is wrong to own nice things, especially if God providentially allows you to have them. What is wrong is to have a selfish craving for money because you are discontent. The highest goal of the Christian life is to love God and glorify Him forever, not to pile up material goods. Even if you have wealth, the Lord wants you to use and manage it from a motivation that puts God first.

The problem you and I continually face is that our fast-paced, complex, technological societies place materialism first. Objects and things come before people; entertainment options replace conversations with members of our family. All this has so often caused us to lose the simple joys of life's relationships, which are the essence of Christian fellowship.

To keep those simple but essential joys primary, I'd invite you to apply the following principles. I've found them helpful in keeping my own life simplified and free from materialism.

First, evaluate every purchase as to how it would make your ministry more effective.

Second, since God owes you nothing, everything you receive from Him should make you thankful.

Third, learn to distinguish wants from needs, and thereby increase the amount of money you have available for the Lord.

Fourth, discipline yourself to spend less than you earn and save the rest for worthwhile causes and needs that arise. Do not amass credit card debt.

Lastly, learn to give sacrificially to God's kingdom.

If you implement these and other sound principles of Christian stewardship, you'll experience much joy and realize anew that the simple life means accepting what God provides and avoiding covetousness.

✧ ✧ ✧

Suggestions for Prayer: Pray that God would motivate you to be faithful in the five principles of good stewardship listed in the lesson. If you have not been following any of them, ask the Lord to help you start today.

For Further Study: Matthew 6:24-33 is one of Jesus' clearest statements on living the simple life. Is His discussion comprehensive? How so? ✧ Write down two or three ways in which you can seek His kingdom first.

*"But those who want to get rich fall into temptation
and a snare and many foolish and harmful desires
which plunge men into ruin and destruction."*
1 TIMOTHY 6:9

❖ ❖ ❖

The sin of loving money is also dangerous because of its harmful effects.

The sanctioning of new state lotteries over the past twenty years, officially done to "enhance revenues" and create new jobs, not only sustains many persons' addiction to gambling but also draws many others into a willingness to spend money they don't have. It illustrates how greed results in sinful entrapment for many people.

Scripture warns against becoming entrapped by material things: "The graven images of their gods you are to burn with fire; you shall not covet the silver or the gold that is on them, nor take it for yourselves, lest you be snared by it, for it is an abomination to the Lord your God" (Deut. 7:25).

In the first part of 1 Timothy 6:9, Paul's wording indicates a premeditated, settled desire for money. By their consuming drive and passion for more, the greedy are continually caught like animals in a trap. Their sinful love of money ends up controlling their lives and making them the unhappy victims of their own evil lusts.

The all-consuming pursuit of riches will ultimately ruin someone's spiritual life. In the conclusion of today's verse, Paul presents the image of one's entire person (body and soul) being destroyed. That's what, if left unchecked, a preoccupation with acquiring more and more money will do to us.

God's Word contains vivid examples of those devastated by money-love. Because Achan disobediently hid some wealth, Israel lost a battle, and Achan and his family were killed (Josh. 7:1-26). Judas betrayed Jesus for thirty pieces of silver and ended up committing suicide (Matt. 27:3-5). Ananias and Sapphira did not give the Lord the entire proceeds from the sale of their property and were struck dead for lying (Acts 5:1-11).

If you are at all tempted to discount greed's harmful effects or to rely on money for security, consider the prophet's sobering assertion: "Neither their silver nor their gold will be able to deliver them on the day of the Lord's wrath" (Zeph. 1:18).

❖ ❖ ❖

Suggestions for Prayer: Pray that all your friends and family, believers and unbelievers, would understand and avoid the bad effects of loving money.

For Further Study: Read James 5:1-5. When will the full consequences of greed become evident? ❖ How do James's words compare to the rebukes Jesus issued against the Pharisees?

> *"For the love of money is a root of all sorts of evil,*
> *and some by longing for it have wandered away from the faith,*
> *and pierced themselves with many a pang."*
> 1 TIMOTHY 6:10

✧ ✧ ✧

There's no doubt that the sinful effects of loving money
actually occur in some people.

It is hard to imagine a sin that has not been committed for the sake of greed. It can lead to self-indulgence, flaunting of possessions, lying, stealing, murder, distortion of justice, and abusing the poor.

Today we return to 1 Timothy 6:10 to note how the apostle Paul proves that loving money is indeed dangerous. He knew that some were actually "longing for it [money]" or reaching after it as far as they could figuratively stretch their arms and hands. That means such people would have been passionately pursuing money. Paul does not give any names, but it is reasonable to think he was referring to ones such as Demas, who was perhaps beginning to pursue worldly things even as Paul wrote this letter (see 2 Tim. 4:10).

Such people "wandered away from the faith" or departed from the body of Christian truth (see Jude 3). Like Demas, they were exposed to truth, but they eventually chose material goods and comforts in preference to God. Those apostates were in effect proving what we noted earlier this month: you can't serve both God and money (Matt. 6:24).

Such lovers of the temporal and the material also "pierced themselves with many a pang." The word "pierced" originally referred to running a skewer through an animal as it was placed on a spit. Those who love money more than God impale their own souls and end up experiencing much grief—a condemning conscience, an unfulfilled heart, and complete disillusionment with life (see Ps. 32:10).

So, what does all this teaching about the love of money mean for us? Simply that we must live our Christian lives pursuing God, not money and material possessions. Like David, we should desire to say, "As for me, I shall behold Thy face in righteousness; I will be satisfied with Thy likeness when I awake" (Ps. 17:15).

✧ ✧ ✧

Suggestions for Prayer: Thank God for all the resources He has blessed you with, and recommit them to His service.

For Further Study: Read Matthew 27:3-10 for more about the tragic consequences of Judas' love for money. How sympathetic were the Jewish leaders to his plight? ✧ What positive things can we learn from the aftermath of this episode (see Acts 1:15-26)?

*"Do not lay up for yourselves
treasures upon earth."*
MATTHEW 6:19

✧ ✧ ✧

A true believer is not to hoard earthly possessions.

You may remember this old adage: "The miser says coins are flat that they may rest in stacks; the spendthrift says they are round that they may roll." In Matthew 6:9 Jesus is specifically talking about the miser. The Greek verb translated "lay up" is *thesaurizete*, from which we get the word *thesaurus*—a treasury of words. Jesus is using a play on words by saying, "Do not treasure up treasures for yourselves." The context of the passage shows that He is referring to stockpiling or hoarding.

The Greek also conveys the idea of stacking or placing something horizontally, as one stacks coins. When something is stacked, it is not being used—it is in a passive condition. Conversely, whenever the Greek has the idea of a vertical sense, it speaks of an active use—being invested for some worthwhile purpose or goal. Jesus is here referring to wealth that is being placed in stacks—simply being stored for safekeeping; it is stored that way to make a show of wealth or to create an environment of lazy indulgence (cf. Luke 12:16-21).

It's clear from this passage, as well as from many others in Scripture, that Jesus is not advocating poverty as a means to spirituality. He only once told a person to "sell your possessions and give to the poor" (Matt. 19:21). In that particular case, the young man's wealth was a barrier between him and the lordship of Christ. It was a test to see if he was fully committed to turning over the control of his life to Christ. His response proved he was not (v. 22).

Unlike the rich young man, you are a follower of Christ and are to be fully committed to Him, no matter what it may cost you. If you have that kind of commitment, you will seek God's kingdom first instead of hoarding earthly possessions (cf. Matt. 6:33).

✧ ✧ ✧

Suggestions for Prayer: Ask the Lord to help you live unselfishly, not hoarding earthly possessions.

For Further Study: Read Proverbs 3:9, 13-15; 8:10, 19; 16:16. What virtues are better than temporal riches?

"Do not lay up for yourselves
treasures upon earth."
MATTHEW 6:19

❖ ❖ ❖

Wealth comes from God,
and we are to manage it wisely for Him.

John Wesley was a godly man who devoted his life to serving the Lord. What is not as well known perhaps is that he was rich, gaining most of his wealth from his published hymns and other works. At one point in his life he gave away 40,000 pounds sterling—a fortune in those days. When he died, his estate was worth only twenty-eight pounds, for he had given nearly everything to the Lord's work.

It is not wrong for Wesley, or any other believer, to own possessions or be wealthy. Both the Old and New Testaments recognize the right to material possessions, including money, land, animals, houses, clothing, and every other thing that is honestly acquired. Deuteronomy 8:18 says, "It is [God] who is giving you power to make wealth." God gives us the abilities and resources to obtain wealth. Job, known mostly for his suffering, was a wealthy man. Theologian Gleason Archer wrote, "Job was reputed to be the richest man of his time in all the region. . . . He was the largest stockholder on Wall Street, so to speak. Thus it could be said that this godly man had proved to be a good businessman, a fine citizen, and a father of a large family. As such he enjoyed the highest standing of any man in his community." In 1 Corinthians 4:7 the apostle Paul asks, "What do you have that you did not receive?" The implication is that we receive everything, including our material possessions, from God.

You are right to provide for your family, make reasonable plans for the future, make sound investments, have money to carry on a business, give to the poor, and support the Lord's work. But you are wrong if you are dishonest, greedy, covetous, stingy, and miserly about possessions. To honestly earn, save, and give is wise; to hoard and spend only on yourself is unwise and sinful.

❖ ❖ ❖

Suggestions for Prayer: Thank the Lord for providing for your temporal needs.

For Further Study: Read 1 Timothy 6:17. What are the rich instructed not to do? ❖ What does God richly supply you with? Why?

> *"Do not lay up for yourselves*
> *treasures upon earth."*
> MATTHEW 6:19

✧ ✧ ✧

The believer is to use his possessions unselfishly.

Some years ago I happened to have contact with two quite wealthy men during the same week. One was a former professor at a major university who through a series of investments made possibly a hundred million dollars. In the process, however, he lost his family, his happiness, and his peace of mind and had aged far beyond his years. The other man, a pastor, also made some investments and acquired great wealth but was not preoccupied with his investments. Because of his financial independence, he gave to his church over the years more than it paid him for being its pastor. He is one of the happiest, most contented, and most godly persons I have ever met. The difference between the two men was not their wealth, but their contrasting views about wealth.

In Matthew 6:19 Jesus taught the right way to view wealth by saying you are not to lay up treasure for yourselves. When you accumulate possessions simply for yourself—whether to hoard or to spend selfishly and extravagantly—those possessions become idols. Jesus is saying, "People in my kingdom shouldn't amass fortunes or stockpile things for themselves." Colossians 3:5 says, "Consider the members of your earthly body as dead to . . . greed, which amounts to idolatry." Covetousness is idolatry.

What about you? Are you consumed with extending God's kingdom instead of accumulating possessions for yourself? Do you desire to invest in eternity and God's causes, or are you being greedy and miserly? First Corinthians 10:31 says, "Whether, then, you eat or drink or whatever you do, do all to the glory of God." Glorify Him by investing in His kingdom and living unselfishly.

✧ ✧ ✧

Suggestions for Prayer: Ask God to help you use your possessions unselfishly for His glory.

For Further Study: What warning does Jesus give in Luke 12:15?

> *"Do not lay up for yourselves treasures upon earth, where*
> *moth and rust destroy, and where thieves break in and steal."*
> MATTHEW 6:19

❖ ❖ ❖

Heaven is the only safe place for treasure.

I n the Orient during biblical times, wealth was basically preserved in three ways. There was no paper, there were no bank books, there was nothing to match the kind of system we have. Wealth was identified in literal commodities: garments, grain, and gold or precious metals.

Garments in the Bible were always an expression of wealth. In Judges 14:12 Samson told the Philistines that if they could answer his riddle, he would give them "thirty linen wraps and thirty changes of clothes." But there is one problem with garments—moths eat them. Have you ever noticed that moths don't eat what you wear, only what you store? We tend to hoard, and a lot of our treasure is invested in our garments, waiting for moths to destroy them.

Grain was another source of wealth. The rich fool said he would tear down his barns and build larger ones to store all his grain and goods (Luke 12:18). In Matthew 6:19 the Greek word translated "rust" literally means "eating." The problem with grain is that mice, rats, worms, and vermin like to eat it.

The third commodity was gold or precious metal. The problem with this one is, where can a person hide it? He might keep it in his house, but a thief could break in and steal it. Therefore, it was common to find a secret place in a field and in the dark of night dig a hole and bury it. But thieves would lurk around at night and watch where men would bury their treasure, then later dig it up.

Nothing you own is completely safe from destruction or theft. And even if you keep your possessions perfectly secure during your entire life, you are certainly separated from them at death. That's why Jesus said you should lay up treasures in Heaven "where neither moth nor rust destroys, and where thieves do not break in or steal" (v. 20). What about you? Are you putting your treasure in a safe place?

❖ ❖ ❖

Suggestions for Prayer: Thank the Lord for providing a secure and eternal place where you can invest for His glory.

For Further Study: Read James 5:1-3. What happened to the commodities there?

*"Lay up for yourselves
treasures in heaven."*
MATTHEW 6:20

❖ ❖ ❖

The believer is to be generous in his giving.

The early church was not interested in accumulating great wealth for itself. In Acts 2, for example, thousands of pilgrims gathered in Jerusalem on the Day of Pentecost. When Peter preached the gospel on that day, 3,000 persons became believers, and soon afterward thousands more were added to the church. The pilgrims who became believers didn't want to return to their former homes since they were now part of the church. So the believers in Jerusalem had to absorb them. Since many of the inhabitants were undoubtedly poor, the early church had to give to meet their needs. As a result, believers "began selling their property and possessions, and were sharing them with all, as anyone might have need" (Acts 2:45). The early church illustrates what it means to lay up treasure in Heaven.

Like the early church, we are to lay up for ourselves treasure in Heaven (Matt. 6:20). What is our treasure in Heaven? In a broad sense it is "an inheritance which is imperishable and undefiled and will not fade away, reserved in heaven for you" (1 Peter 1:4). We could say that, above all, our treasure in Heaven is Christ.

In a specific sense, Jesus is referring in Matthew 6:20 to money, luxury, and wealth. He is saying that to lay up treasure in Heaven is to be generous and ready to share the riches God has given to us, instead of hoarding and stockpiling them. By being generous, you expose yourself to the full potential of all that eternal life can mean. First Timothy 6:18-19 says you are "to do good, to be rich in good works, to be generous and ready to share, storing up for [yourself] the treasure of a good foundation for the future." The more you send into Heaven, the greater the glory when you arrive. The greater the investment, the greater the reward. Make it your aim to invest for eternity, where you will never lose your reward.

❖ ❖ ❖

Suggestions for Prayer: Ask the Lord to help you be generous toward others who are in need.

For Further Study: According to Galatians 6:10, to whom are we to do good?

*"Where your treasure is,
there will your heart be also."*
MATTHEW 6:21

✧ ✧ ✧

The believer is to have a single-minded devotion to God.

British pastor Martyn Lloyd-Jones told the story of a farmer who one day went happily to his wife and family to report that their best cow had given birth to twin calves, one brown and one white. The farmer said, "I suddenly had an impulse that we must dedicate one of these calves to the Lord. We will sell one and keep the proceeds; the other we will also sell, but give the proceeds to the Lord's work." His wife asked him which one he was going to dedicate to the Lord. He replied, "There is no need to bother about that now. We will treat them both the same way, and when the time comes, we will do as I say." And off he went. A few months later the farmer entered his kitchen looking unhappy. When his wife asked him what was troubling him, he answered, "I have bad news to give you. The Lord's calf is dead."

We laugh at the story because we all tend to lay up treasure on earth. We want to be rich toward self but poor toward God. Jesus speaks directly to that wrong thinking by saying "Where your treasure is, there will your heart be also" (Matt. 6:21). Your heart and your treasure go together—they both need to be in Heaven. Our Lord is speaking of a single-minded devotion to God and His cause that is undistracted by the world.

Jesus is not saying that if you put your treasure in the right place, your heart will then be in the right place, but that the location of your treasure indicates where your heart already is. Spiritual problems are always heart problems. God's principle for His people has always been, "Honor the Lord from your wealth, and from the first of all your produce; so your barns will be filled with plenty, and your vats will overflow with new wine" (Prov. 3:9-10). What about you? Is that the principle by which you live?

✧ ✧ ✧

Suggestions for Prayer: Ask the Lord to help you have a single-minded devotion to His kingdom.

For Further Study: Read Luke 6:38 and 2 Corinthians 9:6. What is the common principle in both verses?

> *"The lamp of the body is the eye; if therefore your eye is clear,*
> *your whole body will be full of light. But if your eye is bad,*
> *your whole body will be full of darkness. If therefore the light*
> *that is in you is darkness, how great is the darkness!"*
> MATTHEW 6:22-23

❖ ❖ ❖

Generous giving brings spiritual understanding.

When people see, their body is filled with the light that comes in from the world their eyes perceive. But if their eye is dark (blind), there is no light and they perceive nothing. The eye is like a window—if a window is clean and clear, light floods the building; if a window is blacked out, no light enters. In Matthew 6:22-23 Jesus is saying the heart is like the eye. If your heart is toward God, your entire spiritual being is enlightened; but if your heart is toward material things and treasures of the world, you do not see spiritually as you should.

In verse 22 the Greek word translated "clear" is from a root word that means "generous." If your heart is generous, your whole spiritual life will be flooded with understanding. In contrast to the clear eye is the "bad" eye (v. 23). A bad or evil eye is a Jewish colloquialism used regularly in the Greek Old Testament and the New Testament to mean "grudgingly." Proverbs 28:22 says, for example, "A man with an evil eye hastens after wealth." If you hurry to be rich, you will be ungenerous, grudging, and selfish.

Let me simplify Matthew 6:22-23 to one statement: How you handle your money is the key to your spiritual perception. If your heart is in Heaven, you will have a generous spirit. If your treasure is on earth, you will be blind because of your greed. How total is the darkness of one who should see spiritually but is blind because of his own covetousness (v. 23)! Jesus' call to you and me is to see clearly by devoting ourselves to Him and laying up treasure in Heaven.

❖ ❖ ❖

Suggestions for Prayer: Ask the Lord to help you see opportunities where you can give generously to help extend His kingdom.

For Further Study: According to 2 Corinthians 9:6-12, what are some rewards for generosity?

> *"No one can serve two masters; for either he will hate the one and love the other, or he will hold to one and despise the other. You cannot serve God and mammon."*
>
> MATTHEW 6:24

❖ ❖ ❖

The believer is to serve God, not riches.

When reading Matthew 6:24, many people say, "I believe that you can serve two masters. I work two jobs." The reason they say that is they don't understand the Greek word translated "serve." It refers not to an employee in an 8-to-5 job but to a slave. A slave is one who is constantly and entirely devoted to his master. Romans 6:17-18 says that though you were once a slave of sin, God has freed you to become a slave of righteousness. You can serve God only with entire and exclusive devotion, with single-mindedness. In Matthew 6:24 Jesus is saying that if you try to serve two masters, God and riches, you will love one but hate the other.

The orders of these two masters are diametrically opposed. One commands to walk by faith, the other by sight; one commands to be humble, the other to be proud; one commands to set your affection on things above, the other on things of the earth; one commands to look at things unseen and eternal, the other at things seen and temporal; one commands to be anxious for nothing, the other to be anxious about everything. You can't obey both orders, and you can't serve two masters.

In 1905 Mary Byrne translated an Irish poem into prose, which was then set to music by Eleanor Hull. Today we know the poem as the hymn "Be Thou My Vision." One stanza of this hymn tells us how to view riches correctly.

> *Riches I heed not, nor man's empty praise—*
> *Thou mine inheritance, now and always;*
> *Thou and Thou only, first in my heart—*
> *High King of Heaven, my Treasure Thou art.*

May the words of the hymn be the song of your heart and the conviction of your life.

❖ ❖ ❖

Suggestions for Prayer: Thank Christ for being your Master who loves you perfectly and provides for your every need.

For Further Study: Read Exodus 5. How does this picture the conflict between serving God's interests and man's? Explain.

"To me, to live is Christ, and to die is gain."

PHILIPPIANS 1:21

✧ ✧ ✧

True contentment
is found only in Christ.

There has never been a society in the history of the world that has had as many commodities as Americans have. We are living in affluence that is unheard of in the world's history. The key philosophy behind it all is this: only as you accumulate enough assets to satisfy your particular lifestyle can you really be happy.

Sad to say, Christians have bought into that philosophy. Now, there's nothing intrinsically wrong with commodities, but it *is* wrong to think you'll find true happiness in them. If God chooses to give you material possessions, it's because of His good pleasure. But if you make those possessions the love of your life, you're being deceived about true contentment.

In Philippians 4:11-12 the apostle Paul says, "Not that I speak from want; for I have learned to be content in whatever circumstances I am. I know how to get along with humble means, and I also know how to live in prosperity; in any and every circumstance I have learned the secret of being filled and going hungry, both of having abundance and suffering need." He was saying, "I have contentment that is absolutely and totally unrelated to possessions."

Where did Paul find his contentment? In Philippians 1:21 he says, "To me, to live is Christ, and to die is gain." He found it in Christ, not in material possessions. Professor Howard Vos said of Paul, "Christ is all to him, he lives only to serve Christ, he has no conception of life apart from Christ. . . . Christ's goals, Christ's orientation to life and society and mission, are his." If you want to be like Paul and have true contentment, make Christ the love of your life, not material possessions.

✧ ✧ ✧

Suggestions for Prayer: If you are seeking happiness apart from the Lord, confess your sin and forsake it. Acknowledge that contentment is found only in Him

For Further Study: Read Ecclesiastes 2:18-26. What conclusions did the Preacher reach about daily contentment?

"The earth is the Lord's, and all it contains,
the world, and those who dwell in it."
PSALM 24:1

❖ ❖ ❖

God owns everyone and everything.

One day when John Wesley was away from home, someone came running to him, saying, "Your house has burned down! Your house has burned down!" Wesley replied, "No, it hasn't, because I don't own a house. The one I have been living in belongs to the Lord, and if it has burned down, that is one less responsibility for me to worry about."

John Wesley viewed his material possessions from a biblical perspective, for Scripture makes clear that God owns everything. In 1 Chronicles 29:11 David prayed, "All that is in heaven and in earth is Yours" (NKJV). God is the sole owner of everything, including you, your family, your house, and your car. Therefore, if you lose a possession, you don't really lose it because you never owned it.

Although God does own everything, He entrusts us to be wise stewards of all that He gives to us. Theologian Walter Kaiser wrote, "Material things, goods, and natural resources are in and of themselves 'good,' for they are all made by God: that is the constant refrain in the creation narrative of Genesis 1—'and God saw that it was good.' . . . The misuse of goods comes from unholy people. Forgetting that: (1) these are creations by God, (2) God gave men and women the ability to earn these possessions, and (3) goods must not be exalted to the level of ultimate or absolute concern and worth, people begin to worship the created realm rather than the Creator himself. Such idolizing of the things of this world violates the first commandment and leads to an inversion of values in life." We should worship God as the owner of all things, thank Him for whatever He entrusts to us, and never allow our possessions to be a cause to forget Him.

❖ ❖ ❖

Suggestions for Prayer: Ask God to help you be always mindful that He owns everything and to view the possessions He gives you in a way that honors Him.

For Further Study: Read the following verses, which show that God owns everything: Exodus 19:5; Leviticus 25:23; Psalm 50:10-11; 89:11; Haggai 2:8.

*"Thine is the dominion, O Lord, and Thou dost exalt
Thyself as head over all. Both riches and honor come
from Thee, and Thou dost rule over all."*

1 CHRONICLES 29:11-12

✧ ✧ ✧

*Trust God, who controls
everyone and everything.*

In Daniel 6, King Darius chose 120 princes to help him govern his kingdom. Over the princes he appointed three presidents, with Daniel being the
first president. The princes and other two presidents were jealous of Daniel,
so they devised a scheme against him. They told the king that he should make
a law requiring every person to make his requests only to the king for the next
thirty days. They said, "Anyone who makes a petition to any god or man
besides you . . . shall be cast into the lions' den" (v. 7). The king approved the
idea and signed it into law. The princes and two presidents were glad because
they knew Daniel prayed daily to his God (cf. v. 10).

As soon as Daniel's opponents found him praying, they reported the matter to the king. Although Darius did not want harm to come to Daniel, the king
could not reverse his law. As a result, Daniel was thrown into the lions' den.
When the king went to the den early the next morning, Daniel said to Darius,
"My God sent His angel and shut the lions' mouths, and they have not harmed
me" (v. 22). "So Daniel was taken up out of the den, and no injury whatever
was found on him, because he had trusted in his God" (v. 23). Daniel trusted
God because he knew that He was in control of everything.

Since God both owns and controls everyone and everything, don't put your
hope in riches or fear for your needs. God will take care of you. In his book
Trusting God, Jerry Bridges wrote, "God . . . so directs and controls all events
and all actions of His creatures that they never act outside of His sovereign
will. We must believe this and cling to this . . . if we are to glorify God by
trusting Him." Dare to be a Daniel: trust God, who controls all and promises
to care for you.

✧ ✧ ✧

Suggestions for Prayer: Thank the Lord for being in sovereign control of your
life.

For Further Study: What does Lamentations 3:37-38 say about God's control?

"Abraham raised his eyes and looked, and behold, behind him a ram caught in the thicket by his horns; and Abraham went and took the ram, and offered him up for a burnt offering in the place of his son. And Abraham called the name of that place The Lord Will Provide, as it is said to this day, 'In the mount of the Lord it will be provided.'"

GENESIS 22:13-14

❖ ❖ ❖

*When God provides for a believer,
He's being true to His name.*

The Old Testament gives God many names, but one of the most lovely is *Jehovah-Jireh*, translated in verse 14 of today's passage as "The Lord Will Provide." It is so much a characteristic of God that it's His name. We would never question that God is love and great and mighty and holy and just and good. But some question whether God provides. They doubt and are afraid that God isn't going to meet their needs. That is exactly what the Lord speaks to in Matthew 6:25-34 when He says, in summary, "Don't worry about what to eat, drink, or wear." The Lord is still *Jehovah-Jireh*. That is His name, and it is synonymous with one of His attributes.

God is a God who provides, and that is why David said, "I have been young, and now I am old; yet I have not seen the righteous forsaken, or his descendants begging bread" (Ps. 37:25). The world digs and scratches and claws to make sure it has enough. Unlike the world, your Father knows your needs, and He will always give you what you need.

You don't have to own everything, and you don't have to control everything to meet your needs. You can receive what God gives you to invest in His eternal kingdom and put away all anxiety about your needs. Worship God with your life, and rest assured in His promise to provide for you.

❖ ❖ ❖

Suggestions for Prayer: First Timothy 6:8 says, "If [you] have food and covering, with these [you] shall be content." Does contentment characterize your life? If not, confess that to the Lord, and thank Him for the many ways He so faithfully provides for you every day.

For Further Study: Read the following passages, which show God's faithfulness to provide: Deuteronomy 2:7; 1 Kings 17:1-16; 2 Kings 4:1-7. In what different ways does He give that provision?

> *"Let your character be free from the love of money,*
> *being content with what you have; for [the Lord] Himself has*
> *said, 'I will never desert you, nor will I ever forsake you.'"*
>
> HEBREWS 13:5

✧ ✧ ✧

God promises to provide for all your needs.

In World War II the death of many adults left many orphans. At the close of the war, the Allies provided some camps to feed the orphans and to try and find a place to relocate them. The children began to develop and grow, receiving the finest food and care. But in one of the camps, the officials became perplexed because the children couldn't sleep. They would eat three good meals, but at night they would lie awake. The camp authorities brought in some doctors to do a study of these orphans to find out why they couldn't sleep.

The doctors came up with a solution. Every night when the little children were put to bed, someone would come down the row of beds and place in each little hand a piece of bread. So the last thing the children experienced at night was grasping a piece of bread. In a matter of days they were all sleeping through the night. Why? Even though they were fed to the full during the day, experience had taught them that there was no hope for tomorrow. When they had that bread tucked in their hands, they knew that at least they would have breakfast the next day.

Similarly, God has given you a piece of bread for your hand. That bread is this promise: "My God shall supply all your needs according to His riches in glory in Christ Jesus" (Phil. 4:19). If you have that piece of bread in your hand, you can sleep.

You don't need to stockpile for the future. God is the owner of everything in the world, and He controls all the assets to provide for you because you are His child. Life for the Christian consists not in the abundance of things he possesses (Luke 12:15), but in being content with the things that he has (Heb. 13:5).

✧ ✧ ✧

Suggestions for Prayer: Thank God for His promise to provide for all your needs.

For Further Study: In Psalm 37:25, what was David's testimony about the Lord?

> *"Do not lay up for yourselves*
> *treasures upon earth."*
> MATTHEW 6:19

❖ ❖ ❖

You cannot pursue both God and riches.

Ours is a society consumed with material things. Status, success, and importance are all too often measured by a person's financial worth. Those with wealth flaunt it; those without wealth fake it. People often rack up huge debts in their desperate and futile pursuit of happiness through accumulating material things.

Sadly, that same materialistic mind-set permeates the church. Instead of offering an alternative, that of being distinct from the world, the church joins the world in its pursuit of riches. Most tragically of all, the saving message of the gospel of Jesus Christ is lost in the process.

It is not wrong to have possessions. Job, Abraham, and Solomon were among the wealthiest men of their day. But it is wrong to covet, to make the pursuit of material things the main goal of your life, to serve mammon instead of God. "Do not love the world," wrote the apostle John, "nor the things in the world. If anyone loves the world, the love of the Father is not in him" (1 John 2:15). James addressed these scathing words to those whose focus is on material things: "You adulteresses, do you not know that friendship with the world is hostility toward God? Therefore whoever wishes to be a friend of the world makes himself an enemy of God" (James 4:4). Behind much of the pursuit of riches in the church is a lack of trust in God's provision. Instead of finding security in His promise to supply all our needs (Phil. 4:19), we seek it in a house, a bank account, or a stock portfolio. God did not give us our money and possessions so we wouldn't have to trust Him. He gave them to us to enjoy (1 Tim. 6:17) and to test the legitimacy of our spirituality (Luke 16:11).

Whether you are rich or poor, your attitude toward your possessions and how you handle them is a test of your spirituality. How are you doing?

❖ ❖ ❖

Suggestions for Prayer: Pray with Agur, "Give me neither poverty nor riches; feed me with the food that is my portion, lest I be full and deny Thee and say, 'Who is the Lord?' Or lest I be in want and steal, and profane the name of my God" (Prov. 30:8-9).

For Further Study: What do the following verses teach about our attitude toward wealth: Psalms 49:5-9; 52:7; 62:10?

> *"Do not be anxious for your life, as to what you shall eat,*
> *or what you shall drink; nor for your body,*
> *as to what you shall put on."*
> MATTHEW 6:25

✧ ✧ ✧

God's Word commands us not to worry.

A story I once read reminded me that worry is like fog. According to the article, dense fog covering seven city blocks a hundred feet deep is composed of less than one glass of water—divided into sixty billion droplets. In the right form, a few gallons of water can cripple a large city. Similarly, the object of a person's worry is usually quite small compared to the way it can cripple his thinking or harm his life. Someone has said, "Worry is a thin stream of fear that trickles through the mind, which, if encouraged, will cut a channel so wide that all other thoughts will be drained out."

All of us have to admit that worry is a part of life. The Bible commands us, however, not to worry. To break that command is sin. Worry is the equivalent of saying, "God, I know You mean well by what You say, but I'm just not sure you can pull it off." Worry is the sin of distrusting the promises and providence of God; yet we do it all the time.

We don't worry about anything as much as we worry about the basics of life. In that regard we are similar to the people whom Jesus addressed in Matthew 6:25-34. They were worried about having sufficient food and clothing. I suppose if they were to try and legitimize their worry, they would say, "After all, we're not worrying about extravagant things. We're just worrying about our next meal, a glass of water, and something to wear." But there is no reason for a believer to worry about the basics of life since Jesus says He will provide for him. You are neither to hoard material possessions as a hedge against the future (vv. 19-24) nor be anxious about your basic needs (vv. 25-34). Instead of letting the fog of worry roll in, it's time to let it lift.

✧ ✧ ✧

Suggestions for Prayer: "Rejoice in the Lord always. . . . Be anxious for nothing, but in everything by prayer and supplication with thanksgiving let your requests be made known to God" (Phil. 4:4, 6).

For Further Study: What counsel does 1 Peter 5:7 give?

*"Do not be anxious for your life, as to what you shall eat,
or what you shall drink; nor for your body,
as to what you shall put on."*
MATTHEW 6:25

❖ ❖ ❖

*To worry about the future
is to sin against God.*

Someone has said, "You can't change the past, but you can ruin a perfectly good present by worrying about the future." Worry does ruin the present, but even more important for the believer is to recognize that worry is sin. Let's look at why that is so.

Worry means you are striking out at God. Someone might say, "Worry is a small, trivial sin." But that's not true. More important than what worry does to you is what it does to God. When you worry, you are saying in effect, "God, I just don't think I can trust You." Worry strikes a blow at God's integrity and love for you.

Worry means you are disbelieving Scripture. You can say, "I believe in the inerrancy of Scripture. I believe in the verbal, plenary inspiration of every word," and then just live your life worrying. You are saying you believe the Bible, but then worry about God fulfilling what He says in it.

Worry means you are being mastered by circumstances. Let the truths of God's Word, not your circumstances, control your thinking. By worrying, you make the circumstances and trials of life a bigger issue than your salvation. If you believe God can save you from eternal Hell, also believe He can help you in this world as He has promised.

Worry means you are distrusting God. If you worry, you're not trusting your Heavenly Father. And if you're not trusting Him, perhaps it's because you don't know Him well enough. Study God's Word to find out who He really is and how He has been faithful to supply the needs of His people in the past. Doing so will help give you confidence for the future. Allow His Word to indwell you richly so that you aren't making yourself vulnerable to Satan's temptations to worry.

❖ ❖ ❖

Suggestions for Prayer: Review the four points given above, and confess any sin to God.

For Further Study: Read Psalm 55:22; 1 Peter 5:7. What antidote to worry do both verses give?

"Do not be anxious for your life, as to what you shall eat,
or what you shall drink; nor for your body,
as to what you shall put on."
MATTHEW 6:25

✧ ✧ ✧

God gives you life and sustains your life.

I f you were living in Palestine during the time of Jesus, you might have been concerned about having the basics of life. That's because there were times when the snows didn't come to the mountains, and as a result the streams didn't run. When the streams dried up, there was no water. Crops didn't always produce either. They were subject to the onslaught of insects, disease, and weather. When the crops didn't produce, there was famine in the land. And when there was famine, there was also no income. When there was no income, there was no purchase of clothing.

When Jesus spoke the words of Matthew 6:25 to those people on the edge of a parched desert who were totally dependent upon natural resources, it must have been a shocking statement. Our Lord recognized that man, in whatever time he lives, becomes obsessed with the externals.

The externals that Jesus mentioned—food, drink, and clothing—all pertain to the body. The world believes that man lives because of his body, and man therefore lives for his body. But Jesus asked, "Is not life more than food, and the body than clothing?" (v. 25). In other words, your body does not give you life but is given life by God, who is the source of all life. Jesus is arguing from the greater to the lesser. If God gives you life (the greater), will He not also provide what you need for life (the lesser)? God gives you life and also sustains your life by providing food, drink, and clothing. Therefore, there's no reason for you to worry.

✧ ✧ ✧

Suggestions for Prayer: Thank God for giving you life and sustaining your life.

For Further Study: Read 1 Kings 19:1-8. How did the Lord provide for the prophet Elijah?

*"Look at the birds of the air, that they do not sow, neither do
they reap, nor gather into barns, and yet your heavenly Father
feeds them. Are you not worth much more than they?"*
MATTHEW 6:26

✧ ✧ ✧

*If God provides for the birds,
how much more will He provide for you.*

I can imagine our Lord standing on a hillside in Galilee, looking down over
the beautiful north end of the sea, the breeze rippling across the water, the
sun bright in the sky. The people were all gathered at His feet. As He was
speaking to them, some birds might have flown across the sky.

Our Lord gives life to every bird of the sky and also sustains each one. He
doesn't say to the birds, "I have given you life; now you figure out how to keep
it." And birds don't get together and say, "We have to come up with a strategy
to keep ourselves alive." Birds have no self-consciousness, no cognitive
processes, no ability to reason. But God has given them an instinct so that they
have a divine capacity to find what is necessary to live. God doesn't just create life—He also sustains it.

In Matthew 6:26 Jesus asked the people, "Are you not worth much more
than [the birds]?" He was arguing from the lesser to the greater. No bird was
ever created in the image of God or designed to be a joint-heir with Christ
throughout eternity. Jesus was saying, "If God sustains the life of a bird (the
lesser), don't you think He will take care of you (the greater)?" God's provision, of course, is no excuse for man's laziness. A bird has to work for its food,
and you have to work for yours. That's because God has designed that man
should eat bread by the sweat of his face (cf. Gen. 3:19). If you don't work,
you don't eat (cf. 2 Thess. 3:10). Just as God provides for the bird through its
instinct, so God will provide for you through your effort.

✧ ✧ ✧

Suggestions for Prayer: When you see the birds of the air, remind yourself of
the Lord's teaching, and thank Him for His faithfulness to you.

For Further Study: Read Psalm 104, which tells of God's care over all His
creation.

*"Which of you by being anxious
can add a single cubit to his life's span?"*
MATTHEW 6:27

✧ ✧ ✧

You can worry yourself to death, but not to life.

D r. Charles Mayo of the renowned Mayo Clinic wrote, "Worry affects the circulation, the heart, the glands and the whole nervous system. I have never met a man or known a man to die of overwork, but I have known a lot who died of worry." We live in a day when people worry about how long they will live. That's a harmful practice because you can worry yourself to death, but not to life.

In Matthew 6:27 Jesus said that worry cannot "add a single cubit" to a person's life span. A cubit was the distance from the elbow to the tips of the fingers—about eighteen inches. He was saying, "Which of you by worrying can lengthen your life?" Exercise and good health can help you function better while you're living your span, but you can't worry yourself into a longer life.

The quest for living longer is not new. In the early sixteenth century, Spanish explorer Juan Ponce de Leon set out to find the fountain of youth, a spring whose waters had the power to restore youth. Although no such fountain exists, there is something far better: a fountain of life. Proverbs 14:27 says, "The fear of the Lord is a fountain of life, that one may avoid the snares of death." By fearing the Lord you will experience life to the fullest and not worry. Proverbs 9:10-11 says, "The fear of the Lord is the beginning of wisdom, and the knowledge of the Holy One is understanding. For by me your days will be multiplied, and years of life will be added to you." I believe the Lord has sovereignly determined each person's life span—He has designed how long you will live. And He gives you the gift of life because He wants you to enjoy it to the fullest by fearing and obeying Him.

✧ ✧ ✧

Suggestions for Prayer: Praise the Lord that you may enjoy life fully by fearing Him.

For Further Study: According to John 10:10, why did Jesus come?

"And why are you anxious about clothing? Observe how the lilies of the field grow; they do not toil nor do they spin, yet I say to you that even Solomon in all his glory did not clothe himself like one of these. But if God so arrays the grass of the field, which is alive today and tomorrow is thrown into the furnace, will He not much more do so for you, O men of little faith?"

MATTHEW 6:28-30

✧ ✧ ✧

Observing the flowers is a way to remember that God cares for you.

In Matthew 6, some of the people to whom Jesus spoke perhaps had little clothing, no more than one set of coverings for their bodies. To assure them that God would provide for their basic needs, Jesus asked them to observe "the lilies of the field" (v. 28). That is a general term for all the wild flowers that graced the rolling hills of Galilee. There were many, including the anemones, gladioli, irises, narcissus, lilies, and poppies.

The people were also to observe how the flowers grow. They grow easily, freely, gorgeously; they flourish effortlessly. And flowers don't toil or spin. They don't make fancy thread to adorn themselves but have a texture and form and design and substance and color that man with all his ingenuity cannot even touch. Even King Solomon could not make a garment as fine as the petal of a flower. It has a beauty that only God can give.

Despite their beauty, however, flowers do not last long. They are alive today but tomorrow are cast into an oven (v. 30). A woman in that part of the world used a clay oven primarily for baking. If she wanted to hurry the baking process, she would build a fire inside the oven as well as under it. Fuel for the inside fire was usually dried grass and flowers, which she would gather from nearby fields. Jesus' point was this: If God lavishes such beauty on a flower that is here today and gone tomorrow, how much more will He clothe and care for you, one of His own children who will live forever.

✧ ✧ ✧

Suggestions for Prayer: To attack anxiety, ask the Lord to help you "set your mind on the things above, not on the things that are on earth" (Col. 3:2).

For Further Study: According to 1 Peter 5:5, how should you clothe yourself?

> *"Do not be anxious then, saying, 'What shall we eat?' or '*
> *What shall we drink?' or 'With what shall we clothe ourselves?'*
> *For all these things the Gentiles eagerly seek; for your*
> *heavenly Father knows that you need all these things."*
>
> MATTHEW 6:31-32

❖ ❖ ❖

To worry is to be like an unbeliever.

For us as believers, worry is needless because of God's bounty, senseless because of God's promise to provide, useless because of our inability to do anything, and faithless because by doing so we put ourselves in the same category as an unbeliever. In Matthew 6:32 the Greek term translated "Gentiles" can also be translated "pagans" or "heathen" and speaks of people without God and Christ. The Gentiles are consumed with seeking material gratification because they are ignorant of God's supply and can't claim His promise to provide. Instead of looking to God, they anxiously try to meet their needs on their own. But for a Christian to be preoccupied with material possessions and worry about the basics of life is a serious sin and uncharacteristic of his Christian faith.

The Christian faith says that God will supply all your needs and that you can trust Him (cf. Phil. 4:19). To worry about your food or your physical welfare or your clothing is to have a worldly mind. What about you? Do you face life like a Christian or an unbeliever? When things are difficult or the future is insecure, how do you react? Does your Christian faith affect your view of life? You should place everything in your life in the context of your faith—every trial, every anticipation of the future, and every present reality.

The Christian faith also says that "your heavenly Father knows" your needs (Matt. 6:32). If He knows your life and your needs, all you need to know is that He cares. And if He knows and cares, there's no need for you to worry about anything. Your Heavenly Father has all the resources and love to provide for you.

❖ ❖ ❖

Suggestions for Prayer: Praise your Father for knowing, caring, and providing for you.

For Further Study: Read and meditate on Psalm 145. Notice especially what God does in verses 14-16.

"Do not be anxious for tomorrow; for tomorrow will care for itself. Each day has enough trouble of its own."
MATTHEW 6:34

✦ ✦ ✦

The believer is not to worry about his future.

British pastor Martyn Lloyd-Jones said, "Although it is very right to think about the future, it is very wrong to be controlled by it." He was right, because worry is a tremendous force that will endeavor to defeat you. It will try to destroy you today by making you upset and anxious. But if it loses today, it will take you into the future until it finds something to make you worry about. In Matthew 6:34 Jesus says that you have enough to deal with today. Take the resources of today for the needs of today, or you will lose the joy of today.

Lack of joy is a sin too. Many people lose their joy because of worry about tomorrow, and they miss the victory God gives them today. That is not fair to Him. God gives you a glorious and blissful day today; live in the light and fullness of the joy of that day, and use the resources God supplies. Don't push yourself into the future and forfeit the joy of today over some tomorrow that may never happen. Learn this one little statement: fear is a liar. It will cause you to lose the joy of today. What's more, God gives strength for only one day at a time. He doesn't give you grace for tomorrow until tomorrow.

When the Bible says, "Jesus Christ is the same yesterday and today, yes and forever" (Heb. 13:8), it means He will be doing the same thing tomorrow that He was doing yesterday. If you have any questions about the future, look at the past. Did He sustain you then? He will sustain you in the future. Since there is no past, present, or future with Him, there is no need for you to worry.

✦ ✦ ✦

Suggestions for Prayer: Praise God for being the same yesterday, today, and forever.

For Further Study: Read Lamentations 3:21-24. What never ceases and never fails (v. 22)? ✦ What does that say about God (v. 23)? ✦ What does that give you (v. 21)?

". . . All these things shall be added to you"
MATTHEW 6:33

✧ ✧ ✧

*God will provide for those
who seek what is eternal.*

What did Jesus mean when He said we are to seek God's kingdom first? It means our top priority in life should be to seek what is eternal. That was the priority for the apostle Paul. In Acts 20 he was ready to leave for Jerusalem to defend the faith, not knowing if he might be put in prison or lose his life. The prospect of persecution did not deter him, for he said, "I do not consider my life of any account as dear to myself" (v. 24). He was not concerned about how long he would live or worried about what he would eat or wear. Instead, he wanted to "finish [his] course, and the ministry which [he] received from the Lord Jesus" (v. 24).

Seeking the kingdom means you want Christ's rule to be manifest in your life as righteousness, peace, and joy in the Holy Spirit (Rom. 14:17). So, when the lost see those spiritual qualities in your life instead of worry, they know the kingdom of God is there. That is an attractive testimony that the Lord can use to bring the lost to Himself. Seeking God's kingdom means desiring to extend His kingdom.

Seeking the kingdom also means you long for Jesus to return in His millennial glory. We will be joint-heirs with Christ (Rom. 8:1-7), reign with Him forever (Rev. 22:5), live in a new heaven and earth throughout all eternity (21:1), and have all the majesty and riches of eternal Heaven (21:1—22:5). There's no need to be preoccupied or worried about material things since the whole earth is going to be destroyed and the Lord is going to make a new one.

Instead of seeking riches, "seek . . . His righteousness" (Matt. 6:33). Pursue godliness and holiness, and "all these things shall be added to you" (v. 33). God will provide for those who live a righteous life.

✧ ✧ ✧

Suggestions for Prayer: According to Matthew 6:33, are the priorities of your life in the right order? ✧ Confess and forsake any sin, and thank the Lord for the privilege of serving Him.

For Further Study: Read Psalm 34:9-10. What is the promise to those who fear and seek the Lord?

*"The one who keeps His commandments abides in Him,
and He in him. And we know by this that He abides in us,
by the Spirit which He has given us."*

1 JOHN 3:24

✧ ✧ ✧

*Because the Holy Spirit affects every area of the Christian life, it is
vital that we have a balanced and correct view of His role.*

The church's understanding of the Spirit's Person and ministry has been
seriously distorted over the past few decades. Charismatics have given
an undue emphasis to certain pentecostal gifts so that subjective experience
is often elevated over objective scriptural truth.

At the same time, many non-charismatics have overreacted to charismatic
excesses by almost ignoring the Holy Spirit. For most, an in-depth study of
the Spirit does not fit with the pragmatic, psychological approach to solving
spiritual problems.

But we can't afford to go to either extreme; otherwise we'll miss out on
what it really means to know the Spirit and to minister by His power. He is
indispensable in saving us, enabling us to obey Jesus Christ, and ultimately
perfecting us in glory. Paul urged the Galatian believers not to abandon the
Holy Spirit but to lean completely on Him. "Are you so foolish? Having begun
by the Spirit, are you now being perfected by the flesh?" (Gal. 3:3).

Too many Christians are wasting time looking to seminars, gimmicks,
counselors, and novel interpretations of old truths to uncover "the secret" to
the abundant Christian life. But the key to such living is not a mystery or a
secret. The sufficiency of the Holy Spirit's ministry, as revealed through the
pages of God's fully reliable Word, is all the information and resources we'll
ever need to live fruitful and prosperous spiritual lives.

In today's verse, the apostle John is speaking of Christ's indwelling presence in the believer's life, which the Holy Spirit reveals to us. Therefore the
Spirit is working with the Lord Jesus in encouraging you, guiding you,
enlightening you, and empowering you for every good work (see John 14:16-
20; 16:13). By understanding the Spirit's role and allowing Him to work in
you daily, you'll begin to see your life becoming more like Christ each day.

✧ ✧ ✧

Suggestions for Prayer: Pray that God would grant you and everyone in your
church a proper and balanced understanding of the Spirit's role.

For Further Study: Jesus is portrayed as the Good Shepherd in John 10. Read
that chapter, and list the major characteristics He has as our Shepherd.

*"There is one body and one Spirit
just as also you were called in one hope of your calling."*
EPHESIANS 4:4

❖ ❖ ❖

*Although there were distinctions of ministry, one and the same Holy
Spirit has been at work in both the Old and New Covenants.*

The famous radio broadcast of October 30, 1938, in which Orson Welles
and his fellow actors fooled many of the American people into thinking
an actual invasion from Mars was occurring, is a classic example of how mis-
communication can drastically distort people's understanding of the facts.
Because many listeners failed to hear the disclaimer about the fictional nature
of the *War of the Worlds* dramatization, thousands were panicked into believing that Martians were beginning to invade New York City and the rest of the
East Coast. Not many hours after the program ended, most people realized it
was not a broadcast of actual events. Nevertheless, apologies and clarifica-
tions were necessary in subsequent days.

Scriptural truth is seldom miscommunicated with that same kind of sen-
sational result. But that doesn't mean we never need to correct previous thinking about certain doctrines. One of these concerns the Holy Spirit. Due to
popular teaching on the dissimilarities between the Old and New Covenants,
many Christians have understood the Spirit's Person and role as being sharply
different between the Testaments.

But the apostle Paul makes it clear in Ephesians 4:4 that there is but one Spirit
(also see 1 Cor. 12:11, 13). Paul also knew that since the Holy Spirit is God, He
is therefore unchanging; the same Spirit has been at work throughout redemptive history. We can believe with certainty that the Holy Spirit will always be the
saving agent who draws people to the Lord. That's what Jesus taught when He
instructed the Jewish teacher Nicodemus about the new birth (John 3:5-10).

There are important distinctives between the Holy Spirit's Old Covenant and
New Covenant roles (see Acts 1:5). His New Covenant work is more intimate
and personal for believers, but His essential character has always been the same.

We should rejoice that there is no confusion between two Spirits, but that
there is one Holy Spirit who has been active in God's plan, from Genesis 1:1
right to the present and for all eternity.

❖ ❖ ❖

Suggestions for Prayer: Thank the Lord for giving you a clear understanding
of the Holy Spirit's oneness.

For Further Study: Read John 3:1-15. What should Nicodemus already have
understood about the new birth? ❖ How far back does Jesus reach to make an
analogy about God's method of salvation?

*"But we all, with unveiled face beholding as in a mirror the
glory of the Lord, are being transformed into the same image
from glory to glory, just as from the Lord, the Spirit."*
2 CORINTHIANS 3:18

✧ ✧ ✧

*The Holy Spirit's transforming work is a central part of
the believer's sanctification.*

The children's fable *The Ugly Duckling* wonderfully illustrates the Holy
Spirit's transforming work in believers. The story is about an ugly young
bird who can't fit in with any of the other animals. It's not until he encounters the beautiful swans that his life starts changing. The swans are an irre-
sistible attraction for the duckling, something he can't forget after they leave
for the winter. Finally he makes the amazing discovery the following spring
that in spite of his feelings of inferiority, he is not a duck but a swan, just like
those creatures he has admired.

The days immediately following our conversion to Christ are often similar
to the ugly duckling's final experiences. We have a great sense of sinful
unworthiness and yet a powerful attraction to Jesus Christ. We respond that
way because we now know that character-wise He represents all we were created to be. And we soon come to realize that it's both a humbling and exciting process to be transformed into Christ's image.

Today's Scripture, my favorite verse, is an excellent short description of the
Spirit's transforming work. We won't see the glory of the Lord perfectly right
away, but we begin to see it with greater clarity once we know Jesus Christ
by faith.

Paul is referring to our basic sanctification, which is a progressive process
by which the Spirit changes us from one level of Christlikeness to another.
The end result will be our glorified position in Heaven, which is the Holy
Spirit's goal for us and the reason for our hope. The Spirit reveals what we
will be in Christ: "Beloved, now we are children of God, and it has not
appeared as yet what we shall be. We know that, when He appears, we shall
be like Him, because we shall see Him just as He is" (1 John 3:2).

✧ ✧ ✧

Suggestions for Prayer: Pray that you would focus more on Christ and less
on yourself as the Spirit transforms your life.

For Further Study: Read Psalm 40:1-10. What general attitude does David
have in that passage? ✧ How many times does he mention God there?

*"I will ask the Father, and He will give you another Helper,
that He may be with you forever; that is the Spirit of truth."*
JOHN 14:16-17

❖ ❖ ❖

*Jesus ministered by the power of the Holy Spirit,
and He has promised the same Spirit to all believers.*

The fluctuating economy of the 1990s and its changing workplace have left many workers with the sense that they'll probably have to change jobs several times during their careers.

Even though economies may enter new phases and leave people with uncertainties, God's promises remain completely reliable. His promise, made through His Son, our Lord and Savior, to send the Holy Spirit is one such pledge. This very important scriptural promise was first given in today's text, which Jesus gave to the disciples during the first part of His Upper Room discourse. His words, coming on the eve of His death, gave much comfort to the disciples; but the promise is also part of Christ's rich legacy to Christians today.

This promise consists of four elements. First, Jesus promises a *supernatural Helper*. He called Him "another" Helper, which means "another who is identical." He is sending us exactly the sort of Helper He was, except the Spirit lives in us (John 14:17).

Second, the promise means *supernatural life* for us. When we are saved and have the Holy Spirit, we become sensitive to Christ's working in the world, and we begin to see things from a divine perspective (John 14:19).

Third, the Spirit comes as a *supernatural Teacher* (John 14:26). This is one of the most vital aspects of the Spirit's ministry because it reminds us of our complete dependence on Christ.

Finally, Christ's promise of the Holy Spirit brings a *supernatural peace* (John 14:27). This is a peace that aggressively and positively deals with our daily troubles and turns them into joy (Phil. 4:7).

If you know and love the Lord Jesus and are obeying Him, the promise of the Spirit, with all its implications, is available for you to apply and enjoy (John 14:21; 15:5).

❖ ❖ ❖

Suggestions for Prayer: Thank God for the promise of the Spirit, and pray that you would fully realize every aspect of that promise.

For Further Study: Read 1 John 5:1-7. What does this passage say about the interrelationship of love for God and obedience to His commands? ❖ What are the basic characteristics of love and obedience?

"But when He, the Spirit of truth, comes,
He will guide you into all the truth."
JOHN 16:13

✧ ✧ ✧

The Holy Spirit has to come alongside believers
because they can't minister by their own strength.

As a Christian, you can be orthodox and correct about every detail of theology. You might even show a certain willingness and ability to minister. But unless and until you rely on the Holy Spirit for all you do, your efforts will be ineffective. Think of a new car that has the most polished exterior and the finest of accessories but no engine. It will look great, but it certainly won't run.

Unfortunately, that illustration applies all too often to contemporary believers. They tend to overlook or minimize the Holy Spirit's role—either by overreacting to charismatic extravagances or by focusing most of their attention on man-centered ministry techniques and "innovative" approaches. But the Lord impressed upon the disciples' hearts and minds on more than one occasion their need for the Holy Spirit's power and resources—from routine daily tasks like fishing (Luke 5:4-9) to more imposing ministry challenges like casting an evil spirit out of a man's son (Mark 9:14-29).

Because God has purposefully promised and sent the Spirit within the larger panorama of His sovereignty, we should have the same conviction about the need for the promised Helper as the disciples did shortly after Christ ascended. In conclusion, notice Peter's confidence in God's plan, as set forth in his sermon on the Day of Pentecost: "This Man [Jesus Christ], delivered up by the predetermined plan and foreknowledge of God, you nailed to a cross by the hands of godless men and put Him to death. And God raised Him up again. . . . Therefore having been exalted to the right hand of God, and having received from the Father the promise of the Holy Spirit, He has poured forth this which you both see and hear" (Acts 2:23, 33).

✧ ✧ ✧

Suggestions for Prayer: Confess any attitudes and actions that may have kept you from seeing the need to rely on the Holy Spirit. ✧ Pray that you would walk in greater dependence on Him this week.

For Further Study: Acts 1 marked a time of preparation for the coming of the promised Spirit. Read the chapter, and jot down ways in which the disciples prepared and previewed their faith in the promise.

*"For by one Spirit we were all baptized into one body,
whether Jews or Greeks, whether slaves or free, and we were
all made to drink of one Spirit."*

1 CORINTHIANS 12:13

✧ ✧ ✧

*The unity of the church is the best proof
that the Holy Spirit has come.*

Many people today look for some kind of evidence of reality—science and technology, New Age thought, Eastern religions, various brands of experience-oriented Christianity, or "seeker friendly" mega-church enterprises. But as I have said and written countless times before, Scripture alone points us toward a genuine, secure spiritual reality.

The fulfilled promise of the Holy Spirit's outpouring is one of the truest indicators of authentic spiritual activity. And 1 Corinthians 12:13 tells us how to recognize that He is truly ministering in our midst. In this verse Paul gives us a near perfect commentary on what occurred so spectacularly at Pentecost and has gone on less visibly ever since—the Spirit placed all believers into the Body of Christ, and all believers now have the same Holy Spirit.

The process of gathering believers into the church is a combined ministry of the Lord Jesus and the Spirit. In using the phrase "by one Spirit" in 1 Corinthians 12:13, Paul is saying that the Holy Spirit was Christ's agent in making us children of God. That means we don't need to look to other mystical signs and experiences to verify the Spirit's activity in ourselves or others. Jesus wants us simply to understand His words in John 7:37-39, "'If any man is thirsty, let him come to Me and drink. He who believes in Me, as the Scripture said, "From his innermost being shall flow rivers of living water."' But this He spoke of the Spirit, whom those who believed in Him were to receive."

Whenever we see people being saved and then maturing in Christ, we can be certain that the promised Spirit is at work. The reality of the promise is thus a constant reminder of the faithfulness and consistency of a sovereign God who is working to provide us with life's greatest sense of comfort, joy, and spiritual assurance.

✧ ✧ ✧

Suggestions for Prayer: Pray that your local church would maintain the unity of the Spirit and thereby testify to outsiders of His working.

For Further Study: Make a list from Ephesians 3:14-21 of the privileges and benefits believers should know if they are experiencing Christian unity.

*"For the law of the Spirit of life in Christ Jesus
has set you free from the law of sin and of death."*

ROMANS 8:2

✧ ✧ ✧

*The moment the Holy Spirit places us in Christ, He also
frees us from the power of sin and death.*

The third stanza of Charles Wesley's great hymn "And Can It Be?" describes the composer's thoughts regarding the Holy Spirit's saving work in his life:

*Long my imprisoned spirit lay
Fast bound in sin and nature's night.
Thine eye diffused a quick'ning ray:
I woke—the dungeon flamed with light!
My chains fell off, my heart was free,
I rose, went forth, and followed Thee.*

Romans 8:2 makes it clear that every Christian can and should share Wesley's exhilaration. The instant we by faith embrace Jesus Christ, the Spirit frees us from spiritual condemnation. Essentially, we become free to start a new life, different from anything we have known.

The Lord Jesus was certain that saving faith would work such a complete transformation (John 5:24). And the apostle Paul leaves no doubt that every person whom the Holy Spirit has sovereignly drawn into the Body of Christ has also been freed from the power of sin and death: "Now if we have died with Christ, we believe that we shall also live with Him, knowing that Christ, having been raised from the dead, is never to die again; death no longer is master over Him. For the death that He died, He died to sin, once for all; but the life that He lives, He lives to God. Even so consider yourselves to be dead to sin, but alive to God in Christ Jesus" (Rom. 6:8-11).

As you actively apply this freedom you have in Christ (see Col. 3:3-10), you will have the joyous reassurance that the Holy Spirit—"the Spirit of life in Christ Jesus"—will always be there to enable you to defeat sin and obey God.

✧ ✧ ✧

Suggestions for Prayer: Thank God for His grace that has enabled you to achieve what you could not on your own—victory over spiritual death.

For Further Study: Read Colossians 3:3-17. What sins are we to put off? ✧ What new traits are we to put on? ✧ What resources does the Lord provide for us (vv. 15-16)?

*"When the Helper comes, whom I will send to you
from the Father, that is the Spirit of truth, who proceeds
from the Father, He will bear witness of Me."*
JOHN 15:26

✧ ✧ ✧

*After He has drawn us to Christ,
the Holy Spirit helps us give Christ the preeminence.*

I n the spiritual realm it is important that our attention be kept focused in the right direction—toward the object of our faith, the Lord Jesus Christ. The Holy Spirit, through the writer of the Epistle to the Hebrews, helps us understand what such focus is all about: "Let us run with endurance the race that is set before us, fixing our eyes on Jesus, the author and perfecter of faith" (12:1-2).

John 15:26 is one of two references in the Gospel of John in which the Holy Spirit bears witness to Christ (see also John 16:14-15). Commentator Leon Morris tells us, "This bearing of witness was not an end in itself. Behind it was the purpose 'that all might believe through him.'" It has always been the Spirit's desire that people recognize Christ's authority and submit to His will (Phil. 2:9-13). Thus Paul further reminds us that "No one can say, 'Jesus is Lord,' except by the Holy Spirit" (1 Cor. 12:3).

We saw yesterday that the power and wisdom of the Spirit are crucial if any individual is to be transformed from spiritual condemnation to spiritual life. After that, it is just as necessary that we rely on the Holy Spirit to keep us focused on Jesus Christ and our ongoing responsibilities of obedience and service to Him. How foolish it is for any of us who profess Christ to then follow Him by looking to our own strength rather than His glory. We forget that the Spirit has given us a clear view of the freedom involved in following Jesus as Lord: "But whenever a man turns to the Lord, the veil is taken away. Now the Lord is the Spirit; and where the Spirit of the Lord is, there is liberty" (2 Cor. 3:16-17).

✧ ✧ ✧

Suggestions for Prayer: If you have tended to focus more on yourself than on Christ, confess that sin and ask that God would renew your focus on His Son.

For Further Study: Read the following passages from John's Gospel, and identify the witness to Christ in each one: 1:6-8; 5:31-37; 8:18; 10:25; 12:17.

*"To each one is given the manifestation of
the Spirit for the common good."*
1 CORINTHIANS 12:7

❖ ❖ ❖

*The Holy Spirit uses believers
to minister to other believers.*

Right in line with modern culture's emphasis on personal independence, it's often easy for one to say, "If I have the all-sufficient Holy Spirit living within me, that's all I need to live my Christian life." That is true, but because you are not completely sanctified, you do not always allow the Spirit to fully do His work. Therefore, God needs to use other believers to minister the Spirit's correction, exhortation, or encouragement.

The Bible is very clear about this. The Epistle to the Hebrews says God wants followers who do not waver in their profession of faith. And a primary way Christians will fulfill that is by regularly meeting together and seriously stimulating one another to love and good works (Heb. 10:23-25).

We don't have to look far for the proper setting in which to meet regularly and encourage one another. It's any Bible-believing local church that is exercising its spiritual gifts. These special gifts are simply the loving channels through which the Holy Spirit ministers to those within the fellowship of believers. Today's verse suggests that each of us has a gift, and this truth is explained a little more in verse 11: "One and the same Spirit works all these things, distributing to each one individually just as He wills." Here the apostle Paul reveals yet one more way in which the Holy Spirit sovereignly helps us and others to become more mature.

What's remarkable about the Spirit's working through us is that we become extensions of His voice. Perhaps you've thought of that comparison at times when you've shared the gospel with the lost. But the analogy fits equally well when you reach out and minister to someone within your church. The idea of being an extension of the Holy Spirit's ministry ought to encourage you toward greater faithfulness in using your spiritual gifts to help other believers. Likewise, it should make you more sensitive to the Spirit's correcting and edifying work in your life as others come alongside and minister to you (Col. 3:12-13).

❖ ❖ ❖

Suggestions for Prayer: Ask the Lord to keep you always faithful to the commands of Hebrews 10:23-25.

For Further Study: Read 2 Corinthians 8:1-7. What kind of example did the Macedonians set regarding aid to other believers? ❖ How should that motivate us (v. 7)?

"Now to Him who is able to do exceeding abundantly
beyond all that we ask or think, according to
the power that works within us . . ."
EPHESIANS 3:20

❖ ❖ ❖

Through the Holy Spirit, God gives His children
all the spiritual power they will ever need to live the Christian life.

I t's a joy to know that spiritual gifts are not like toys whose packages say "batteries required." What the Spirit provides is not dependent on perishable batteries for power. Instead, when the Spirit secures our new life in Christ, He also empowers and strengthens us with every spiritual resource we'll ever need to serve Christ and minister to others.

The Holy Spirit draws from an infinite supply of strength and power, as Paul indicates in Ephesians 3:20. In verse 16 he had just prayed that the Ephesians would "be strengthened with power through His Spirit in the inner man." Paul was certain that God's Spirit can do far more in the lives of believers than most of us ever imagine. So many of us don't get past the phrase "to Him who is able," and with that failure we limit how much the Holy Spirit can do in and through us.

Paul had much more than a theoretical understanding of the Spirit's infinite power supply—he experienced it firsthand. Even when he was stretched to the limit physically and spiritually, he said, "We are afflicted in every way, but not crushed; perplexed, but not despairing; persecuted, but not forsaken; struck down, but not destroyed" (2 Cor. 4:8-9). We can't attribute his inner perseverance to any other source than the Holy Spirit.

No matter how difficult or discouraging our own circumstances become, we have the very same Spirit. If we're hindered, we don't have to be frustrated. If we're puzzled, we don't have to be in despair. If we're persecuted, we don't have to face it alone. If we're dying from a physical disease, we can be alive in heart and spirit. Our outer person might be exhausted and hard-pressed, but we have the assurance that our inner self is being renewed with fresh strength daily from the Holy Spirit (2 Cor. 4:16).

❖ ❖ ❖

Suggestions for Prayer: Thank God today that even before your life encounters a crisis, you have the Holy Spirit as a source of strength and power to help meet that challenge.

For Further Study: Moses was uncertain that he could or would be empowered for God's ministry. Read Exodus 3:1—4:17. What excuses did Moses raise? ❖ How did God deal with each one?

> *"I will put My Spirit within you and cause you*
> *to walk in My statutes, and you will be*
> *careful to observe My ordinances."*
>
> EZEKIEL 36:27

✧ ✧ ✧

The Holy Spirit has always led
and will continue to lead believers to know God's will.

One of the Spirit's most practical ministries is to help believers know and follow God's will.

Ezekiel 36:27 plainly indicates that the Spirit has always been available to lead God's people. And Isaiah reminds us, centuries before Ezekiel's time, that the Lord "is He who put His Holy Spirit in the midst of them, who caused His glorious arm to go at the right hand of Moses" (Isa. 63:11-12).

The proceedings at the Jerusalem Council in Acts 15 wonderfully illustrate how the Spirit gave guidance to the New Testament church. The Council convened to determine what principles of conduct the Jewish-led early church should place on the many new Gentile converts who were now in the fellowship. After much prayerful discussion, the Council made the all-important decision that it was not necessary to adhere to Moses' law as a means of salvation.

The Council set down its concise recommendations in a letter that was the result of a Spirit-led consensus among the apostles and elders: "For it seemed good to the Holy Spirit and to us to lay upon you [Gentiles] no greater burden than these essentials" (Acts 15:28). The leaders were confident that their decision was from the mind of the Holy Spirit as reflected in Scripture; therefore they knew it was correct and in accord with God's will.

Romans 8:14, which says, "For all who are being led by the Spirit of God, these are sons of God," encourages us that we also can be certain of the Spirit's guidance. If we are faithful to hear, read, and study the Word, if we strive to obey it, and if we are sensitive to the Holy Spirit, then He will guide us into God's perfect will for our lives (see Ps. 119:105).

✧ ✧ ✧

Suggestions for Prayer: If you have an important decision to make, pray that you would have the discernment to know and follow God's will. ✧ If no major decision faces you now, thank God that the Spirit is always present to provide guidance.

For Further Study: Read Proverbs 3:1-6. What does this say about the importance of God and His Word in knowing His will? ✧ Memorize verses 5-6.

*"Walk by the Spirit, and you will not
carry out the desire of the flesh."*
GALATIANS 5:16

❖ ❖ ❖

*We must focus on God and His Word
as we begin to walk by the Spirit.*

Paul's directive to the Galatians in today's verse may sound like an imprac-
tical platitude. But to the apostle this command was a foundational truth
for how all Christians should live their daily lives. The Greek for "walk" could
be translated, "keep on continually walking." Life transpires one day at a time,
and believers should routinely take each day one step at a time.

In walking by the Holy Spirit, our chief opposition is our own flesh (Gal.
5:17). Therefore, it is crucial that we possess the scriptural strategy for our
spiritual walk and that we know how to practically and effectively carry it out.

The first part of our strategy has to be a daily intake of God's Word. Psalm
1:2 says that the man who walks on a godly path will "delight . . . in the law
of the Lord, and in His law he meditates day and night." Meditation (patiently
and thoroughly reflecting on a passage of Scripture) helps us effectively seal
the Word in our hearts so we can obediently apply it and minister it in accordance with God's Spirit.

Secondly, if we want to walk by the Spirit, we must focus on God and allow
Him to renew our minds. The key is found in Paul's familiar command: "Do
not be conformed to this world, but be transformed by the renewing of your
mind, that you may prove what the will of God is, that which is good and
acceptable and perfect" (Rom. 12:2). The believer who lives that way will
undoubtedly walk by the Spirit because he will also be one who worships God
"in spirit and truth" (John 4:24). As one Bible teacher so aptly phrased it,
"Find me a worshiper of God, and I will show you a stable man with his mind
in control, ready to meet the present hour with refreshment from above."

❖ ❖ ❖

Suggestions for Prayer: Pray today that the Lord would help you to begin
removing everything from your life that is preventing you from worshiping
Him wholeheartedly.

For Further Study: Joshua 1:8; Psalm 19:7-8; John 8:31-32; Romans 15:4;
2 Timothy 2:15; and Hebrews 4:12 all refer to God's Word. Read them and
write down all the different things they say about the importance of Scripture.
❖ What should motivate you to have a better intake of the Word?

*"Be of sound judgment and sober spirit
for the purpose of prayer."*
1 PETER 4:7

✧ ✧ ✧

*Spending time with God in prayer is another
crucial element in walking by the Spirit.*

During my regular times in the Word, I often don't know where Bible study ends and meditation begins, or where meditation turns into prayer. My devotions are definitely a seamless process in which I read Scripture, meditate on it, and pray that God would help me understand it. I'm sure that many of you have had the same experience. It ought to be like that for any believer who is faithful in spending time with the Lord daily.

Along with meditating on Scripture and focusing on God, prayer is an essential component of our strategy to walk by the Holy Spirit. An attitude of moment-by-moment prayer, patterned after 1 Thessalonians 5:17 ("Pray without ceasing"), will greatly help us walk in step with the Spirit.

"Pray without ceasing" obviously does not mean believers are to spend every waking moment in formal prayer. Paul's command to the Thessalonians refers to recurring prayer, not a ceaseless uttering of words from a certain posture.

To pray as part of our spiritual walk means we bring every temptation before God and ask for His help. It means we thank Him for every good and beautiful experience. It means we ask the Lord to allow us to join the fight against evil. It means when we have an opportunity to witness, we pray that God would help us be faithful and that He would draw the person to Himself. And finally, this kind of prayer means we'll turn to God as our Deliverer whenever we have trials.

Thus, walking by the Spirit is a lifestyle of continual prayer. All of our thoughts, actions, and circumstances become opportunities to commune with God. And if that is true, we obey Paul's exhortation to the Ephesians, "With all prayer and petition pray at all times in the Spirit, and with this in view, be on the alert with all perseverance and petition for all the saints" (Eph. 6:18).

✧ ✧ ✧

Suggestions for Prayer: Take a brief prayer list with you (on an index card) today, and try to pray through it several times during the day.

For Further Study: Matthew 6:1-8 leads into Jesus' presentation of the Lord's Prayer. What general attitude has no place in prayer? ✧ List the specific things Christ warns against, along with those He commends in this passage.

> *"Brethren, even if a man is caught in any trespass, you who*
> *are spiritual, restore such a one in a spirit of gentleness."*
> GALATIANS 6:1

✧ ✧ ✧

Those walking by the Spirit
are to restore sinning fellow believers.

God never intended that the spiritual walk be an end in itself. Instead, He wants believers to have a positive influence on fellow believers so that the church will be purified and built up. Galatians 6:1 reveals how those who walk by the Spirit ought to minister to others within the Body of Christ. Paul says they are to restore other brothers and sisters who might have fallen into sin.

"Caught in any trespass" denotes falling into a sin and becoming bound by it, just as an animal might become caught in a trap. Whenever another believer we know gets ensnared by any sin—no exception—the Holy Spirit wants "you who are spiritual" to seek his or her restoration. The "spiritual" designation does not refer to some elite class of Christians but simply includes anyone who is walking by the Spirit.

The one who is spiritual and is relying on the Spirit's wisdom and guidance will restore the sinning believer with patience. The Greek verb in Galatians 6:1 translated "restore" strongly implies that spiritual restoration will need to be a methodical, persevering process. (The Greek originally referred to the mending of fishing nets or the realigning of a frame or joint.)

The verse further indicates that we must approach the entire restoration process with "gentleness." As believers who have this fruit of the Spirit (Gal. 5:23), such an approach should be almost automatic for us. But since we are merely sinners saved by grace, we need Galatians 6:1 and other reminders of the right way to restore a sinning brother or sister: "And yet do not regard him as an enemy, but admonish him as a brother" (2 Thess. 3:15).

✧ ✧ ✧

Suggestions for Prayer: Pray that your church leaders would be faithful in confronting and seeking to restore those members who fall into sin.

For Further Study: Read Galatians 5:16-26. What two things within the believer are at odds early in the passage? ✧ Record two or three observations that are most striking to you about the contrasts between the individual good and evil character traits listed here.

> *"Bear one another's burdens,*
> *and thus fulfill the law of Christ."*
> GALATIANS 6:2

❖ ❖ ❖

Those who walk by the Spirit
will lovingly bear one another's burdens.

The Lord Jesus presents love for God and love for our neighbor as the great summary of the entire Law (Matt. 22:37-40).

It only makes sense, then, that love will characterize the life of any Christian who is walking by the Spirit. Love will also be an integral part of any Spirit-assisted ministry to others. Paul tells us in today's verse that when we help other believers hold up their particular burdens, we are obeying "the law of Christ" or the law of love, which James calls "the royal law" (James 2:8).

But what exactly does Galatians 6:2 mean when it commands us to "bear one another's burdens"? Commentator William Hendriksen gives us this general but helpful observation: "This does not merely mean 'Tolerate each other,' or 'Put up with each other.' It means: 'Jointly shoulder each member's burdens.'"

The actual word *burden* calls to mind a variety of possible sins, difficulties, and responsibilities; but Paul was using the Greek term that refers to an extremely heavy and unbearable load. It's a load that one person alone can't carry, which underscores again that Christians need each other. The Holy Spirit wants each member of the church involved in a ministry of mutual support.

The essence of burden-bearing is spiritual accountability and responsibility. One of the most practical ways we can bear someone else's burden is to talk and pray regularly with him or her about spiritual issues and measure that person's progress in overcoming a certain sin or temptation.

Bearing the burdens of another believer is a wonderful, reciprocal learning process in which both individuals can benefit from God's truth and understand more about His will for their lives (see Gal. 6:6). As we become more sensitive and obedient to Him, the Holy Spirit orchestrates this ministry and gives us the privilege of instructing and upholding others as we continue to walk in Him day by day.

❖ ❖ ❖

Suggestions for Prayer: Thank God that His Spirit is powerful enough to help us bear the heaviest burdens of fellow believers.

For Further Study: Read the Epistle to Philemon. What things did Paul probably do to bear Onesimus's burdens? ❖ How was the entire letter a form of burden-bearing by Paul for Philemon?

"Be filled with the Spirit."
EPHESIANS 5:18

❖ ❖ ❖

God wants every aspect of the believer's being
to be under the complete control of the Holy Spirit.

Pleroo, the basic Greek word for "be filled," offers three shades of meaning that illustrate what Paul's command to be Spirit-filled means. First,
the word describes the *pressure of wind* filling a ship's sails and moving the
vessel across the water. That parallels the Holy Spirit's leading us down the
pathway of spiritual obedience. We aren't primarily motivated by our own
plans and desires, but we allow the Spirit's gracious pressure to move us in
the right direction.

The well-known pain reliever Alka-Seltzer effectively illustrates the second meaning, *permeation*. If you drop two Alka-Seltzers into a glass of water,
they immediately fizzle and soon transform themselves into clear bubbles
throughout the water and permeate it with a distinct flavor. That's how God
wants the Holy Spirit to fill our lives, so that there will be no doubt in others'
minds that we possess the distinct and pervasive savor of the Spirit.

Pleroo's third and primary shade of meaning is that of *domination* or *total
control*. In Luke 6:11 the scribes and Pharisees "were filled with rage" when
Jesus healed a man on the Sabbath. Jesus said, "Sorrow has filled your heart"
(John 16:6) when He described the disciples' reaction to the news that He was
soon departing. In those two examples, *pleroo* denotes an emotion that thoroughly dominated the people's thoughts and excluded everything else.

In regard to earthly concerns, such overwhelming feelings can be waste-
ful, foolish, and even harmful. But it is beneficial and completely in agreement with the Lord's will when we yield every thought, feeling, and action to
the absolute domination of the Holy Spirit. This yielding will occur in our
Christian lives only when we obey another of Paul's commands, "Let the
word of Christ richly dwell within you" (Col. 3:16). In practice, the Spirit-
filled walk is a matter of knowing God's Word and obeying it.

❖ ❖ ❖

Suggestions for Prayer: Ask God to forgive you for the times when you have
not allowed His Spirit to completely fill and control your life.

For Further Study: Read and compare Isaiah 6 and Revelation 1:9-18. What
reactions did the prophet Isaiah and the apostle John both have to the notion
of God's overwhelming power and control? ❖ What other general similarities
are present in their visions?

> *"Speaking to one another in psalms and hymns and*
> *spiritual songs, singing and making melody with*
> *your heart to the Lord."*
> EPHESIANS 5:19

✧ ✧ ✧

If we are Spirit-filled, we will have
songs of praise in our hearts and on our lips.

O nce a Christian knows about being Spirit-filled and walking by the Spirit, it is still fair for him or her to ask, "But how can I know if the Holy Spirit is really at work in my life?" Ephesians 5:19 answers this question by declaring one of the unmistakable evidences of the Spirit's full operation in our lives—we will have a song in our hearts.

The Bible does not give us much detail about the practical use of music and song, but there are enough references so that its significance to God and His people is clear. The Israelites praised God after He rescued them from the Egyptians (Ex. 15). The Psalms are filled with songs and praise, epitomized by the final verse, "Let everything that has breath praise the Lord. Praise the Lord!" (150:6).

In the New Testament, Jesus and the disciples closed the Last Supper by singing a hymn (Matt. 26:30). Paul and Silas sang while they were imprisoned at Philippi (Acts 16:25). During his vision in Revelation 5, the apostle John sees this: "When He [Christ, the Lamb] had taken the book, the four living creatures and the twenty-four elders fell down before the Lamb, having each one a harp, and golden bowls full of incense, which are the prayers of the saints. And they sang a new song" (vv. 8-9).

That "new song" John was about to hear sung before God's throne was not just new chronologically—it was new qualitatively. Here as elsewhere in the New Testament, "new" is used in relation to God's salvation, which means it makes perfect sense for us to sing a new song—one that is far better than the world's songs—if we are saved and filled with the Holy Spirit. Words of genuine praise should well up in our hearts often and at the appropriate times break forth from our lips as we reflect the joy of the Spirit-filled life.

✧ ✧ ✧

Suggestions for Prayer: Thank God specifically for some of your favorite hymns.

For Further Study: Read Revelation 5:1-14 for the complete context of John's new song. What is the song's theme? ✧ How many eventually join in the praises?

> *"Always giving thanks for all things in the name of*
> *our Lord Jesus Christ to God, even the Father."*
> EPHESIANS 5:20

✧ ✧ ✧

Sincere thanks to God will result at all times
if we are truly filled with the Spirit.

I'm convinced that gratitude is the single greatest act of personal worship we can render to God. And today's verse plainly asserts that thankfulness should be a well-rounded, consistent response to whatever God allows to happen in our lives (see 1 Thess. 5:18). Such a thankful attitude is impossible in our own strength, but as the Holy Spirit indwells us, He graciously and mercifully enables us to be thankful at all times, without exception.

It follows that if a Spirit-filled believer is enabled to give thanks *at all times*, he will also be strengthened to give thanks *"for all things."* Implicit in Paul's words are the hard things (see also James 1:2-5; 1 Peter 2:20-21); but there are also dozens of blessings that we must not neglect to be grateful for. Here are some primary examples: God's goodness and mercy (Ps. 106:1), the gift of Jesus Christ (2 Cor. 9:15), the gospel's triumph (2 Cor. 2:14), and victory over death (1 Cor. 15:56-57).

The Spirit-filled Christian will always display his gratefulness *in the name of Christ to God the Father*. We could not be thankful at all if it were not for the Person and work of Jesus Christ. So to be thankful in His name simply means it will be consistent with His character and deeds (see Eph. 1:5-8, 11-12).

God is the ultimate object of all our thanksgivings, and *Father* is the name that highlights His loving benevolence and the constant flow of His gracious gifts that come to those who know Him (see James 1:17). We just can't escape the importance of our continually offering thanks to God on every occasion, for everything. Hebrews 13:15 presents us with this excellent summary: "Through Him then, let us continually offer up a sacrifice of praise to God, that is, the fruit of lips that give thanks to His name."

✧ ✧ ✧

Suggestions for Prayer: Think of something you have not thanked God for in the past. Confess that neglect, and begin thanking Him for it regularly from now on.

For Further Study: Read 2 Chronicles 20:1-23. How was that opportunity for gratitude different from those mentioned in the lesson? ✧ How did Jehoshaphat demonstrate His trust in God?

"Be subject to one another in the fear of Christ."
EPHESIANS 5:21

✧ ✧ ✧

Spirit-filled believers will submit to one another.

To the world, *submission* implies personal weakness or the coercive dominance of one person by another stronger, more intimidating individual. Such perspectives, however, are unbiblical. The noted expositor Martyn Lloyd-Jones describes *submission*'s original meaning in a military context, which helps us understand its scriptural definition:

> It is the picture of soldiers in a regiment, soldiers in a line under an officer . . . and if he [the soldier] begins to act on his own, and independently of the others, he is guilty of insubordination and will be punished accordingly. Such is the word the Apostle uses; so what he is saying amounts to this—that we who are filled with the Spirit are to behave voluntarily in that way with respect to one another. We are members of the same regiment, we are units in this same great army. We are to do that voluntarily which the soldier is "forced" to do.

In addition to Ephesians 5:21, the New Testament repeatedly expresses the importance of submitting to one another. Philippians 2:3-4 tell us how mutual submission ought to operate: "Do nothing from selfishness or empty conceit, but with humility of mind let each of you regard one another as more important than himself; do not merely look out for your own personal interests, but also for the interests of others." And Hebrews 13:17 commands us to submit to our spiritual leaders: "Obey your leaders, and submit to them; for they keep watch over your souls, as those who will give an account. Let them do this with joy and not with grief, for this would be unprofitable for you."

The only way we can possess any of those traits or exhibit any of that behavior is to be continuously filled with the Holy Spirit. Then we will be able to voluntarily and joyfully submit to the Lord and one another in love, just as the apostle John urges: "Beloved, let us love one another, for love is from God; and every one who loves is born of God and knows God" (1 John 4:7).

✧ ✧ ✧

Suggestions for Prayer: Examine your heart and see if your attitude has been a biblically submissive one. ✧ Ask God's Spirit to reveal and correct any sinful shortcomings you've had in that regard.

For Further Study: Read Romans 12:10; 1 Corinthians 4:7; 1 Timothy 5:21; James 2:1. List comparisons and contrasts between these verses and what Philippians 2:3-4 says about mutual submission.

> *"In order that the requirement of the Law*
> *might be fulfilled in us, who do not walk according*
> *to the flesh, but according to the Spirit."*
>
> ROMANS 8:4

✧ ✧ ✧

> *If the Holy Spirit resides within us,*
> *we will be able to fulfill the demands of God's law.*

Augustine once said, "Grace was given, in order that the law might be fulfilled." When God saves us He, by His Spirit, creates within us the ability to obey His perfect law. Because we now live "according to the Spirit"—walking by the Spirit and being filled with the Spirit—we are able to do the righteous things God's law requires.

Isn't it wonderful that the Lord no longer expects His law to be lived out only by means of an external code of ethics? Now holiness, righteousness, and obedience to the law are internal, the products of the indwelling Holy Spirit (see Ezek. 11:19-20).

God's salvation is more than a spiritual transaction by which He imputed Christ's righteousness to us. It is more than a forensic action by which He judicially declared us righteous. As great and vital as those doctrines are, they were not applied to us apart from God's planting His Spirit within our hearts and enabling our lives to manifest the Spirit's fruit: "love, joy, peace, patience, kindness, goodness, faithfulness, gentleness, self-control" (Gal. 5:22-23).

We need to remind ourselves regularly that God's purpose for us after He redeemed us was that we might live a holy life filled with good works (Eph. 2:10; Titus 2:14). Whenever you are disobedient to God's will and purpose, you are quenching the Holy Spirit and fighting against yourself and what you know is right. Such disobedience makes about as much sense as the person who holds his breath for no reason and therefore makes his lungs resist their natural function. The believer who disobeys, especially one who persists in a sin, prevents the Spirit from naturally leading him along the path of holiness.

We are not perfect after our salvation—that won't happen until glorification (1 John 3:2-3)—but the Holy Spirit will empower us to live in ways pleasing to God, which is the kind of righteousness that fulfills His law.

✧ ✧ ✧

Suggestions for Prayer: Thank the Lord that you don't have to meet the demands of the law solely by your own strength.

For Further Study: Read Romans 6. What happened to your old self at the time of your conversion? ✧ How must that affect the way you live?

> *"You are not in the flesh but in the Spirit, if indeed*
> *the Spirit of God dwells in you. But if anyone does not have*
> *the Spirit of Christ, he does not belong to Him."*
>
> ROMANS 8:9

✧ ✧ ✧

The indwelling Holy Spirit gives us
an assurance of salvation.

Assurance of salvation is essential to our Christian lives, and I can't imagine living without it. And we must have clarity about it from a truly *biblical* standpoint. This begins with realizing that a genuine believer is in the Spirit and has been given a new nature (see John 3:6). If the Holy Spirit lives in you, you are no longer controlled by the sinful tendencies of the flesh, as Paul suggests in Romans 8:9. The Greek term for "dwells" indicates that the Holy Spirit makes His home in you and in every believer.

But today's verse also points out that if someone does not have the Holy Spirit within him, he doesn't belong to Christ. From time to time—perhaps for you it's the first time—we need to be warned about that. Being in the Spirit is not merely professing Jesus, having a pious appearance, or attending church. No matter what we claim, if we aren't fulfilling God's law, desiring to walk by the Spirit, and wholeheartedly seeking the things of the Spirit, He is not in us.

Second Corinthians 13:5 exhorts, "Test yourselves to see if you are in the faith; examine yourselves!" You can do this by looking for evidences of the Holy Spirit in your life. Have you sensed the presence of the Spirit's fruit in your life (Gal. 5:22-23)? Do you struggle with sin and have a desire to be free from all its influences (Rom. 7:14-25; Gal. 5:16-17)? Have you experienced the actions and attitudes the Holy Spirit brings to your daily life, as we studied earlier this month? Do you yearn for a closer communion with God and a deeper fellowship with other believers? If you can answer yes to these questions, you have solid reasons to be sure the Spirit lives in you and to know for certain that you belong to Jesus Christ.

✧ ✧ ✧

Suggestions for Prayer: Thank God for the reminders His Spirit gives you that you belong to Christ.

For Further Study: Read 1 John 5:1-12. What indicators does John give us that would also provide us with an assurance of salvation? ✧ What role does the Holy Spirit have in this passage?

> *"For all who are being led by the Spirit of God, these are sons*
> *of God. For you have not received a spirit of slavery leading to*
> *fear again, but you have received a spirit of adoption as sons*
> *by which we cry out, 'Abba! Father!' The Spirit Himself bears*
> *witness with our spirit that we are children of God."*
>
> ROMANS 8:14-16

❖ ❖ ❖

The Holy Spirit confirms in our hearts
the reality of adoption into God's family.

In first-century Rome, people did not practice adoption exactly the same as they do today. A father sometimes adopted a young man outside the family to be the primary heir of the father's name and estate. If the father considered his natural sons unworthy, he would find someone else with the qualities he wanted in a son. The adopted son would then take precedence over any of the real sons in the inheritance process. Thus the new son received many rights and privileges he would not have had otherwise; he was not merely a second-class citizen rescued from homelessness.

Likewise, it requires more than a natural birth process for us to become members of God's family. We become God's children because He sovereignly chose to grant us spiritual rebirth (John 1:12-13). That's the substance of biblical adoption.

Therefore, adoption and regeneration are both terms that describe how God brought us to Himself (see 2 Cor. 5:17). Regeneration makes us sons and daughters and prepares us for our eternal inheritance. Adoption names us "sons of God" and actually gives us the title to our inheritance. Once this occurs, all our former debts (sins) are canceled, and we have a right to be in God's presence without condemnation.

The entire process of adoption is superintended by the Holy Spirit, who repeatedly confirms its reality in our hearts. He transfers us from an alien family into God's family and thus "bears witness with our spirit that we are children of God" (Rom. 8:16). If you are a Christian, you can, by the indwelling Spirit, know that you are legally and eternally God's child.

❖ ❖ ❖

Suggestions for Prayer: Ask the Lord to give you a renewed sense of joy and thanksgiving throughout this day as you remember the blessings of being his adopted child.

For Further Study: Read Genesis 12:1-8. What commands and promises did God make? ❖ Had Abraham known God in the same way prior to this passage? ❖ Does God's promise in any sense parallel the concept of adoption? Explain.

"And if children, heirs also, heirs of God and fellow-heirs
with Christ, if indeed we suffer with Him in order
that we may also be glorified with Him."
ROMANS 8:17

✧ ✧ ✧

The Holy Spirit confirms within
our hearts the hope of eternal glory.

I believe people today instinctively know they are devoid of glory (see Rom. 1:18-21), but they explore all the wrong avenues in seeking to regain it. They look for personal glory by building successful careers, spending many hours in community service, being generous to charities, and so forth. But such efforts only lead to jealousy and pride. Unregenerate men and women simply cannot know the glory that was present before the Fall.

However, there is coming a day when believers will be transformed fully into Christ's likeness, having a complete reflection of God's glory. We will receive a perfect, radiant glory that is far better than the glory Adam and Eve knew in the Garden of Eden before they sinned.

Glorification completes the reality of salvation. From before the foundation of the world, the Lord planned to save those who believe and conform them to the image of Christ (Rom. 8:29-30). Therefore, every believer lives in the hope of future glory, a hope best summarized by the following two verses: "As for me, I shall behold Thy face in righteousness; I will be satisfied with Thy likeness when I awake" (Ps. 17:15). "Beloved, now we are children of God, and it has not appeared as yet what we shall be. We know that, when He appears, we shall be like Him, because we shall see Him just as He is" (1 John 3:2).

The Holy Spirit guides us through different levels of glory while we are still on earth. As we consider the glory of the Lord, the Spirit gradually restores the honor we lost in the Fall. He encourages us by restoring our dignity. Salvation is the path to glory, and once we start down that path we will come to its final goal, which is being fully conformed to the image and glory of Jesus Christ (2 Cor. 3:18).

✧ ✧ ✧

Suggestions for Prayer: Pray that you would be content in allowing the Spirit to help you realize God's glory.

For Further Study: Mark 9:1-8 contains an account of Christ's transfiguration. How was this event a preview of future glory? ✧ How was it unlike anything the disciples had seen (v. 3)? ✧ How did Peter reflect the other disciples' amazement (vv. 5-6)?

> *"But the Spirit Himself intercedes for us with*
> *groanings too deep for words."*
> ROMANS 8:26

✧ ✧ ✧

Because He understands our struggles in this life, the Holy Spirit
continually prays for us before the Father's throne.

I n the midst of life's many difficulties and stressful times, there is hardly anything more comforting than knowing you have a friend—someone on your side. In the legal realm, an attorney formally argues your case when you need to settle a judicial or financial dispute. This concept of friend and advocate is right at the heart of the Holy Spirit's role as our *Paraclete*, one called alongside to help (John 14:16).

Paul's words in today's passage comfort us with the knowledge that the Spirit is fulfilling the promise of John 14 by being on our side and shepherding us toward Heaven. In the process He is continuously ensuring the security of our salvation and interceding for us and all believers, just as Christ does (see Luke 22:31-32; Heb. 7:25).

We would be at an eternal loss if the Holy Spirit did not intercede for us. He understands our sinful frailties and knows that, by our own wisdom, we don't know how to pray properly for ourselves or how to consistently maintain our walk with the Lord. This intercession is done "with groanings too deep for words" (Rom. 8:26).

Those "groanings" refer to divine communications between the Father and the Spirit that transcend any human language. They are more like sighs that can't be put into words. That means we can't know precisely what the Holy Spirit says when he intercedes on our behalf, but we can be certain that He is praying for us.

The Spirit's lofty ministry of intercession reminds us again of how utterly dependent we are on Him to support us and help us with our daily discipleship. As the Christian writer A.W. Pink once said, "Only by His [the Spirit's] strengthening of the heart are we delivered from being engrossed in the things around us, and our earthbound affections are drawn to things above."

✧ ✧ ✧

Suggestions for Prayer: Thank God that when you are perplexed or confused and unsure how to pray, the Spirit will already be interceding for you.

For Further Study: Jesus' most notable time of intercession for His disciples came in John 17. Read this chapter, and record the items that compose His intercessory list. How do these apply to us?

"These things I have spoken to you in figurative language;
an hour is coming when I will speak no more to you in figurative
language, but will tell you plainly of the Father."
JOHN 16:25

✧ ✧ ✧

Jesus' teaching in figurative language revealed the need
for further enlightenment by the Holy Spirit.

Jesus left His disciples a storehouse of valuable information that would require additional teaching from the Holy Spirit to make it understandable. The "figurative language" our Lord sovereignly used was made up of many veiled but pointed statements, filled with rich meaning. Even Christ's closest followers, when they first heard Him, often understood only the basics of His teachings.

Jesus used various veiled statements whose deeper meanings were not revealed until the Holy Spirit gave believers special insight. One such statement is John 2:19, "Destroy this temple, and in three days I will raise it up." The truth that Jesus was teaching—His death and resurrection—became clearer later on. John 6:53-58 speaks of eating Jesus' flesh and drinking His blood. Many of the Jews took this teaching literally and did not understand that Jesus was referring to believers' intimate, spiritual communion with Himself.

In addition to those and other figurative expressions (see John 6:35; 8:12), the Lord knew His disciples would not understand certain truths right away (John 16:12). They were spiritually ignorant and unable to grasp every teaching prior to Christ's death. But once He died and rose again and the Holy Spirit came, they would understand Jesus' teaching about His relationship to the Father, as the end of today's verse indicates.

Whenever Christ used figurative language, it was clear enough to make it meaningful, but veiled just enough so the Spirit could reveal more profound truth later on. Having access to that unveiled truth is the blessed privilege we have today, thanks to the indwelling Holy Spirit who has come as our teacher, just as Jesus promised in John 14:26 and 16:13. We need to take full advantage of the Spirit's teaching ministry every time we hear the Word expounded or read or study it for ourselves.

✧ ✧ ✧

Suggestions for Prayer: When you study the Word, ask the Lord and His Spirit to help you see beneath the surface and understand as much biblical truth as possible.

For Further Study: Read John 6:32-58. What does the Bread of Life provide? ✧ How is it better than manna? ✧ What made some of the Jews stumble at Jesus' words?

> *"These things I have spoken to you in figurative language; an hour is coming when I will speak no more to you in figurative language, but will tell you plainly of the Father."*
>
> JOHN 16:25

✧ ✧ ✧

We understand truth thanks to the teaching ministry of the Holy Spirit.

Scripture makes it clear that the disciples and all subsequent believers would need additional divine assistance to understand all of God's teachings. Jesus Himself knew that, as we saw in yesterday's lesson. And the apostle Paul alludes to that fact in 1 Corinthians 2:9: "Just as it is written, 'Things which eye has not seen and ear has not heard, and which have not entered the heart of man, all that God has prepared for those who love Him.'" Our human minds and senses by themselves can't give us an understanding of God's truth. That's why we need the Holy Spirit.

In John 16:25 Jesus says, "An hour is coming when I . . . will tell you plainly." That reference is to the Day of Pentecost, when the Holy Spirit was poured forth to permanently indwell the disciples and all other believers. Therefore, Jesus is saying that the Spirit will help us understand God's truth, even the veiled mysteries and figurative statements in His Word.

We know and understand all that we do about God only because His Spirit is our teacher. The Holy Spirit is the one who knows the mind of God and teaches us the deep things of God from Scripture (1 Cor. 2:10-14). All the New Testament epistles were written to plainly explain Christ's teachings to us. At times the Spirit teaches us directly through the Word, and other times He uses people to teach us and unveil what was previously a mystery. But it's all His working, it's reliable, and we can thank Him every day for granting us spiritual understanding.

✧ ✧ ✧

Suggestions for Prayer: If there is a Scripture passage that has been unclear to you, pray that God would clarify it for you as you study it again, or that He would lead you to someone who can help you understand it. ✧ Pray for an unbeliever who has been struggling with accepting God's truth. Ask the Spirit to draw that person to the Lord and unlock Scripture's truths.

For Further Study: Read Acts 8:26-38. What does this passage teach about the importance of obeying the Spirit's direction? ✧ How did Philip and the Ethiopian exhibit different aspects of that obedience?

"Whenever Moses is read, a veil lies over their heart;
but whenever a man turns to the Lord, the veil is taken away."
2 CORINTHIANS 3:15-16

✧ ✧ ✧

One of the most important truths the Holy Spirit
unveils for us is the glory of the New Covenant.

The Old Testament contains many veiled statements, types, prophecies, and parables. The Israelites didn't understand most of those things because the Old Testament didn't have plainness of speech. Its glory was veiled and was even described as fading away (2 Cor. 3:13-14).

In contrast to the Old Covenant, the present New Covenant age is characterized by the clarity of all the key doctrinal and practical passages in the New Testament. This progress from the veiled glory of the previous era to the unveiled glory of the present era occurred when the Holy Spirit came in the Book of Acts. All that God wants us to know and do is clearly brought into focus now because of the teaching ministry of the indwelling Spirit.

The Spirit guides and enlightens New Covenant believers as they read and study God's Word. Therefore, there is no longer any need, for example, to unscramble the pictures and prophecies regarding Christ. Thus Paul can say, "We use great plainness of speech" (2 Cor. 3:12, KJV). He goes on to say in verses 17-18, "Now the Lord is the Spirit; and where the Spirit of the Lord is, there is liberty. But we all, with unveiled face beholding as in a mirror the glory of the Lord, are being transformed into the same image from glory to glory, just as from the Lord, the Spirit."

Those verses describe the essence of the Christian life: becoming like Jesus Christ. The only way to do that is to know well the unveiled glory of the New Covenant and allow the Holy Spirit to change you more and more into the Savior's image.

✧ ✧ ✧

Suggestions for Prayer: As you go through this day, ask the Lord to remind you often of the glory, clarity, and freedom you have under the New Covenant. ✧ Pray that all your actions would reflect this truth.

For Further Study: Hebrews 8 begins a discussion and outline of the superiority of the New Covenant. Read this chapter, and record what it says are differences and improvements from the Old to the New Covenant. ✧ Who mediates the New Covenant?

> *"And He gave some as apostles, and some as prophets,*
> *and some as evangelists, and some as pastors and teachers,*
> *for the equipping of the saints for the work of service,*
> *to the building up of the body of Christ."*
> EPHESIANS 4:11-12

❖ ❖ ❖

God has given every believer certain gifts and functions
to contribute to the health of the church and
enable it to communicate the gospel to the world.

God fervently desires to reach the whole world with the gospel's truth (Acts 1:8). Therefore, the Holy Spirit has specially energized members of Christ's Body, the church, to fulfill God's great desire for the world. In Old Testament times, Israel was God's agency to reach other peoples. During New Testament history, Christ and the apostles were the outreach vehicles God used. Today the church is the channel God uses to tell the world about His nature and His truth.

The Lord wants this collection of believers to be strong and functioning well. Besides providing the gifted church leaders mentioned in today's verses, it is God's plan to equip every member with a specific gift that will help the church grow and be a healthy witness to its community. Just as a human body has a variety of organs that must function and interact properly for the vitality of the entire body, any believer's consistent use of his gift helps to build up the church.

Spiritual gifts are not showered randomly, but God gives believers differing gifts so the church might display a composite reflection of Christ's character. Therefore, believers will never begin to reach their full spiritual maturity unless all the gifts are being ministered among members of the church.

For instance, if a pastor ministers by preaching, his people should communicate more effectively. If someone ministers the gift of mercy, another believer receives the direct benefit but also learns how to show mercy. As spiritual gifts are used, everyone is built up to be more like Christ and manifest His character traits. By this process, the Holy Spirit helps the church to reflect the total Person of Christ. How are you doing in contributing your gift to God's plan?

❖ ❖ ❖

Suggestions for Prayer: Pray that the leaders and all the members of your church would consistently display a unified, solidly biblical testimony to the community.

For Further Study: Read Acts 1:12-14; 2:1-4, 37-47. How did the early believers demonstrate their unity? ❖ What were the primary results of the Spirit's ministry on the Day of Pentecost?

> *"But to each one is given the manifestation*
> *of the Spirit for the common good."*
> 1 CORINTHIANS 12:7

❖ ❖ ❖

God wants every Christian to understand
spiritual gifts and use his or hers wisely.

A spiritual gift is a channel through which the Holy Spirit ministers to the Body of Christ (1 Cor. 12:11). The day we were born again into God's family, His Spirit distributed to us a spiritual gift. Therefore, having a spiritual gift does not mean a believer is "spiritual." What we really must ask is, "Is the channel clear?" Hypothetically, someone could have all the recorded spiritual gifts and not be using any of them. Or that believer could be greatly abusing some gifts. In either case, such a person would not be spiritual.

It is also incorrect to equate a natural ability with a spiritual gift. Someone might say, "My gift is baking pies"; another might say, "I'm good at playing the piano." Those are wonderful and useful abilities, but they are natural abilities, not spiritual gifts.

Paul illustrates the difference between abilities and gifts. He could have used his knowledge of philosophy and literature to write and deliver great orations. However, this is what he said to the Corinthians: "I did not come with superiority of speech or wisdom, proclaiming to you the testimony of God. For I determined to know nothing among you except Jesus Christ, and Him crucified" (1 Cor. 2:1-2). The Holy Spirit uses the abilities of people like Paul and speaks through them, but He expresses Himself in a supernatural way, which is not necessarily related to the person's natural skills.

If we rely on our own ability to produce spiritual fruit, we hinder what the Spirit wants to do in us. Instead, ponder what Peter says about using your gift: "As each one has received a special gift, employ it in serving one another, as good stewards of the manifold grace of God. Whoever speaks, let him speak, as it were, the utterances of God; whoever serves, let him do so as by the strength which God supplies; so that in all things God may be glorified through Jesus Christ" (1 Peter 4:10-11).

❖ ❖ ❖

Suggestions for Prayer: Thank the Lord for the special spiritual gift He has given you. Ask that He would help you use it faithfully, to its full potential.

For Further Study: Read Romans 12:4-8 and list the spiritual gifts mentioned there. What does 1 Corinthians 12, especially verses 12-31, emphasize regarding the use of the various gifts within the church?

> *"Now we have received, not the spirit of the world,*
> *but the Spirit who is from God, that we might know the*
> *things freely given to us by God."*
> 1 CORINTHIANS 2:12

❖ ❖ ❖

To be effective, spiritual gifts must be used in the power
of the Holy Spirit, not in the power of the flesh.

One of the constant battles all believers face is to avoid ministering their spiritual gifts in the power of the flesh. Even those of us who are called to be preachers (prophets) need to subject our spirits to other mature believers (1 Cor. 14:32). As a pastor, I am not spiritual just because I stand behind a pulpit and preach. Paul instructs us, "Let two or three prophets speak, and let others pass judgment" (1 Cor. 14:29). Those who teach God's Word are not infallible; therefore, they must allow other qualified believers to verify the truth of what they proclaim.

Whenever Christians rely on their own strength, wisdom, and desire to minister, whatever they accomplish is a mockery and a waste. But whenever they minister by the Spirit's power, the result is pleasing to God and has lasting value ("gold, silver, precious stones. . . . If any man's work which he has built upon it remains, he shall receive a reward," 1 Cor. 3:12, 14). Essentially, all a believer needs to pray is, "Spirit of God, use me," and divine energy will activate and flow through his or her ministry to fellow believers and unbelievers.

You can use your spiritual gift effectively by faithfully following three basic steps: *Pray*—continually confess and turn from your sins (1 John 1:9) and ask God to use you in the Holy Spirit's power. *Yield yourself*—always determine to live according to God's will, not the world's (Rom. 6:16; 12:1-2). *Be filled with the Spirit*—let the Spirit control all of your thoughts, decisions, words, and actions. Commit everything to Him, and He will minister through you.

❖ ❖ ❖

Suggestions for Prayer: Confess any and all times lately that you have counted on your human ability rather than on the Spirit's power to minister to others. ❖ Pray that this week God would give you a clear opportunity to exercise your spiritual gift for His glory.

For Further Study: Read 1 Samuel 15:1-23. In what way did King Saul use his own insight rather than follow God's command? ❖ What can be the consequence of such disobedience (vv. 22-23; see also 1 Sam. 13:8-14)?

*"For all have sinned
and fall short of the glory of God."*
ROMANS 3:23

✧ ✧ ✧

Sin is pervasive and deadly.

When the early church father Chrysostom remarked, "I fear nothing but sin," he correctly identified sin as the greatest threat any person faces. Sin mars all the relationships people are involved in: with other people, with themselves, and, most significantly, with God. Sin causes suffering, disease, and death in the physical realm and also causes spiritual death—eternal separation from God in Hell.

Because sin is so deadly, we need to carefully define it, so we can understand and avoid it. First John 3:4 sums up the essence of sin when it says, "Sin is lawlessness." Sin is refusing to obey God's law; it is rejecting God's standards; it is, in fact, living as if God did not exist.

In 1 John 5:17, the apostle John adds to his definition of sin, describing it as "unrighteousness." James defines sin as failing to do what is good (James 4:17). Paul defines it as lack of faith (Rom. 14:23). Sin is the ultimate act of ingratitude toward the God "who richly supplies us with all things to enjoy" (1 Tim. 6:17).

Sin pollutes the sinner, prompting Paul to refer to it as that "defilement of flesh and spirit" (2 Cor. 7:1) from which sinners are in desperate need of cleansing. No amount of human effort, however, can cleanse a person of sin. Such self-effort is as futile as attempting to change the color of one's skin (Jer. 13:23). Only through the death of Jesus Christ, the perfect sacrifice for sin (Heb. 10:12), is forgiveness and cleansing available (1 John 1:7).

Sin is the only thing that God hates (cf. Jer. 44:4), and so must believers (Ps. 97:10; Amos 5:15). The great Puritan writer Thomas Watson noted that a prerequisite for sanctification is such hatred for sin. Renew your commitment today to grow in your relationship with the Lord by hating evil (Prov. 8:13).

✧ ✧ ✧

Suggestions for Prayer: Pray for yourself and others that you would not be deceived by the subtleness of sin (Heb. 3:13).

For Further Study: Identify the sins you struggle with the most. ✧ Using a concordance and other study tools, find out what the Bible says about those sins. ✧ Form a biblical plan of attack to combat them.

"But I see a different law in the members of my body,
waging war against the law of my mind, and making me
a prisoner of the law of sin which is in my members."
ROMANS 7:23

❖ ❖ ❖

Sin is the deadliest plague ever to affect mankind.

Throughout history, deadly plagues have ravaged the human race. In just three years (1348-1350), the infamous "Black Death" (an outbreak of bubonic plague) killed half the population of Europe. In our own times, diseases such as AIDS have reached epidemic proportions.

But there is one plague that is far deadlier than all the others combined: sin. Sin has affected everyone who has ever lived (Rom. 3:19, 23). And unlike other plagues, sin kills everyone it infects (Rom. 5:12).

While sin invariably causes physical and (apart from faith in Christ) spiritual death, it has many other devastating consequences. Sin corrupts the mind (Jer. 17:9; Eph. 4:17-19), the will (cf. Jer. 44:16-17), and the affections (John 3:19; 1 John 2:15). Sin brings people under the control of Satan (John 8:44; Eph. 2:2) and makes them the objects of God's wrath (Eph. 2:3). Sin robs people of peace (Isa. 48:22) and replaces it with misery (Job 5:7; Rom. 8:20).

Although as Christians we experience God's gracious forgiveness, sin still has serious consequences in our lives. Sin grieves the Holy Spirit (Eph. 4:30), causes God not to answer our prayers (1 Peter 3:7), limits our ability to serve God (2 Tim. 2:20-21), or even disqualifies some from Christian service (1 Cor. 9:27). It also renders our worship hypocritical and unacceptable (Ps. 33:1; Isa. 1:14), causes God to withhold blessing (Jer. 5:25), robs us of joy (Ps. 51:12), subjects us to God's chastening (Heb. 12:5-11), hinders our spiritual growth (1 Cor. 3:1-3), and pollutes our fellowship with Him (1 Cor. 10:21). Most significantly, sin causes our lives to dishonor Him (1 Cor. 6:19-20).

Every true Christian despises sin and yearns to be free from it. Do you realize the deadly nature of sin? I pray that the cry of your heart would echo that of Paul's: "Wretched man that I am! Who will set me free from the body of this death?" (Rom. 7:24).

❖ ❖ ❖

Suggestions for Prayer: Thank God for delivering you from sin, and pray that He would give you a holy hatred for it.

For Further Study: Read Romans 7—8. How did Paul view his struggle with sin? ❖ What was the key to overcoming it?

> *"If we say that we have not sinned, we make*
> *Him a liar, and His word is not in us."*
> 1 JOHN 1:10

❖ ❖ ❖

Confession is the first step toward defeating sin.

I t is often true that the hardest part of dealing with a problem is admitting that you have one. Beginning with Adam and Eve (Gen. 3:11-13), people have denied responsibility for their sins, and our generation is no exception. To acknowledge that one is a sinner, guilty of breaking God's holy law, is not popular. People call sin by a myriad of other names, futilely hoping to define it out of existence. They do so, motivated by their innate awareness that there is a moral law and that there are consequences for violating it (Rom. 1:32).

But God's people have always recognized the necessity of confession. After committing the terrible sins of adultery and murder, David acknowledged to Nathan the prophet, "I have sinned against the Lord" (2 Sam. 12:13). Later he cried out to God, "For I know my transgressions, and my sin is ever before me. Against Thee, Thee only, I have sinned, and done what is evil in Thy sight" (Ps. 51:3-4). Faced with a vision of the awesome majesty and holiness of God, Isaiah declared, "Woe is me, for I am ruined! Because I am a man of unclean lips, and I live among a people of unclean lips" (Isa. 6:5). Daniel was a man of unparalleled integrity, yet part of his prayer life involved confessing his sin (Dan. 9:20). Peter, the acknowledged leader of the apostles, said to Jesus, "Depart from me, for I am a sinful man, O Lord!" (Luke 5:8). The apostle Paul, the godliest man who ever lived (except for Jesus Christ), wrote this about himself: "It is a trustworthy statement, deserving full acceptance, that Christ Jesus came into the world to save sinners, among whom I am foremost of all" (1 Tim. 1:15).

The examples of those godly men illustrate a fundamental biblical truth: constant confession of sin characterizes true Christians (1 John 1:9). Those who claim to be believers but refuse to confess their sins deceive themselves (1 John 1:8) and make God a liar (1 John 1:10).

❖ ❖ ❖

Suggestions for Prayer: Confess and forsake your sins today, and experience the blessedness of God's forgiveness (Prov. 28:13).

For Further Study: Read and meditate on Nehemiah's masterful prayer of confession in Nehemiah 1.

"God is light, and in Him is no darkness at all."
1 JOHN 1:5

✧ ✧ ✧

*God's truthfulness and holiness
are powerful motives not to sin.*

L ight and darkness are familiar metaphors in Scripture. Intellectually, light refers to truth, and darkness to error; morally, light refers to holiness, and darkness to evil.

Intellectually, the Bible reveals God as the God of truth. In Exodus 34:6 God described Himself to Moses as "The Lord, the Lord God, compassionate and gracious, slow to anger, and abounding in lovingkindness and truth." Both Psalm 31:5 and Isaiah 65:16 refer to Him as the "God of truth." In the New Testament, Jesus called Himself "the way, and the truth, and the life" (John 14:6).

Not only is God true, but so also is His Word. In 2 Samuel 7:28 David exclaimed, "O Lord God, Thou art God, and Thy words are truth." The Lord Jesus prayed to the Father, "Sanctify them in the truth; Thy word is truth" (John 17:17). The Bible, "the word of truth" (2 Tim. 2:15), imparts the light of knowledge. In the familiar words of the psalmist, "Thy word is a lamp to my feet, and a light to my path" (Ps. 119:105).

Morally, light describes God's absolute holiness and separation from evil. Psalm 5:4 says of Him, "No evil dwells with Thee." "Thine eyes are too pure to approve evil," said the prophet Habakkuk to God, "and Thou canst not look on wickedness with favor" (Hab. 1:13). Because God is light in the sense of truth, He cannot lie (Titus 1:2). When His Word promises that things will go well with the righteous (Isa. 3:10) and that sin brings consequences (Prov. 11:5), we can be certain that is exactly what will happen. Because God is moral light, we know that He is neither the cause of any evil we encounter, nor the source of our temptation (James 1:13).

Understanding the truth that God is light is foundational to dealing with sin in our lives.

✧ ✧ ✧

Suggestions for Prayer: Praise God that He has revealed His truth in the Bible. ✧ Ask God to give you a deeper understanding of His holiness as you study the Scriptures.

For Further Study: Read Proverbs 11:3; 19:3; James 1:13-15. Based on those passages, how would you answer someone who blames God for the bad things that happen to him or her?

*"If we say that we have fellowship with Him and yet walk in
the darkness, we lie and do not practice the truth."*

1 JOHN 1:6

❖ ❖ ❖

*Those who deny the reality of their sin affirm
the unreality of their salvation.*

Ours is a society that rejects the concept of individual responsibility. People blame society, their parents, their genes—anything but their own actions and choices—for their problems. The biblical teaching that all people are responsible for breaking God's holy law is scoffed at as primitive, unsophisticated, and harmful to a healthy self-esteem.

Even some who claim to be Christians refuse to acknowledge their sin. They say, "I make mistakes. But I'm a good person. Surely God won't reject me!" Such people are tragically deceived and will miss out on salvation; those who don't see themselves as lost will not seek God's gracious salvation. In the words of the Lord Jesus Christ, "It is not those who are healthy who need a physician, but those who are sick; I did not come to call the righteous, but sinners" (Mark 2:17).

The apostle John gives three characteristics of those who deny their sin.

First, they walk in darkness (1 John 1:6). That reveals that they are not saved, since only those who "walk in the light" are cleansed from their sins by the blood of Christ (1 John 1:7).

Second, they are self-deceived (1 John 1:8). The Bible makes it unmistakably clear that all people are sinners (2 Chron. 6:36; Rom. 3:23); there are no exceptions (Rom. 3:12).

Third, they defame God, making Him out to be a liar (1 John 1:10) by denying what His Word affirms—that they are sinners. That is a serious, blasphemous accusation to make against the God who cannot lie (Titus 1:2), whose word is truth (John 17:17).

In Luke 18, Jesus described two men praying in the temple. One, a proud, self-righteous Pharisee, denied his sin. The other, a despised tax-gatherer, cried out, "God, be merciful to me, the sinner!" Which of the two do you identify with?

❖ ❖ ❖

Suggestions for Prayer: Thank God, "who has called you out of darkness into His marvelous light" (1 Peter 2:9).

For Further Study: Read the following passages: John 8:12; Acts 26:18; Ephesians 5:1-2, 8; Colossians 1:12-13; 1 Thessalonians 5:4-5. Is it possible for a Christian to habitually walk in darkness (lead a life of continuous, unrepentant sin)? Explain.

"If we walk in the light as He Himself is in the light,
we have fellowship with one another, and the blood of
Jesus His Son cleanses us from all sin."
1 JOHN 1:7

❖ ❖ ❖

God is light, and His children share His nature.

First John 1:5 aptly describes God's nature as "light" (truth and holiness). Because they partake of His nature (2 Peter 1:4), His children also walk in the light. It must be understood that we don't *become* God's children by walking in the light, but rather we walk in the light because we *are* His children. The Greek verb describes continuous action and could be translated, "If we habitually or continuously walk in the light. . . ." It's an indicator of character; a definition of a true Christian, just as walking in the darkness characterizes unbelievers.

Two significant benefits come to believers because they walk in the light. These are privileges granted only to Christians; unbelievers who think they possess them deceive themselves.

First, believers experience fellowship with God. "One another" in 1 John 1:7 does not refer to other Christians. Although it is certainly true that believers enjoy fellowship with each other, that is not what this verse is teaching. The use of the pronoun "his" later in the verse makes it clear that the fellowship in view here is with God. That fellowship is mutual, "with one another." Believers share a common life with God, experience His presence through the indwelling Holy Spirit, and commune with Him through prayer and the reading of His Word.

Second, believers experience cleansing from sin. "The blood of Jesus His Son" is the agency of that cleansing. Christ's blood is symbolic of His sacrificial death on the cross, where full payment was made for believers' sins. Once again it must be noted that walking in the light does not earn forgiveness; rather, forgiveness is freely granted to those who walk in the light (who are Christians).

In view of those glorious truths, I would leave you today with the challenge of the apostle Paul: "Now you are light in the Lord; walk as children of light" (Eph. 5:8).

❖ ❖ ❖

Suggestions for Prayer: Ask God to help you "let your light shine before men in such a way that they may see your good works, and glorify your Father who is in heaven" (Matt. 5:16).

For Further Study: Look up the following passages, noting what each teaches about forgiveness of sin: Ephesians 1:7; Hebrews 9:14; 10:14; 1 Peter 1:18-19; Revelation 1:5-6.

"If we confess our sins, He is faithful and righteous to forgive us our sins and to cleanse us from all unrighteousness."
1 JOHN 1:9

✧ ✧ ✧

Continuous confession characterizes Christians.

Yesterday we learned that the only condition for receiving God's gracious forgiveness is to "walk in the light"—in other words, to be a true Christian (1 John 1:7). At first glance, today's verse appears to contradict that truth by adding a condition—namely, confession of sin. Such is not the case, however. First John 1:9 could be translated, "If we are the ones confessing our sins, He is forgiving us." This verse looks at salvation from man's perspective and defines Christians as those who are continually confessing their sins. Confession, like saving faith, is not a one-time act but a continuous pattern throughout our lives.

What is confession? The Greek word means "to say the same thing." Confession, then, is agreeing with God about our sin. Confession affirms that God is just when He chastens us for our sins. It also restores us to the place of His blessing—something He is always "faithful" to do. Proverbs 28:13 reinforces that truth, promising that "he who conceals his transgressions will not prosper, but he who confesses and forsakes them will find compassion."

Some may question how a holy God can be "righteous" and still forgive sins. John has already answered that by noting in verse 7 that forgiveness comes through the sacrificial death of the Lord Jesus Christ. Paul declares that "God displayed [Christ] publicly as a propitiation in His blood through faith . . . for the demonstration, I say, of His righteousness at the present time, that He might be just and the justifier of the one who has faith in Jesus" (Rom. 3:25-26).

True confession involves sorrow because sin has offended God (2 Cor. 7:10)—not mere remorse because of its negative consequences in one's life (as was the case with Saul [1 Sam. 15:24] and Judas [Matt. 27:3]). It also involves repentance—turning away from sin and no longer embracing it (cf. Acts 19:18-19; 1 Thess. 1:9).

Is there a sin you've been clinging to? If so, confess and forsake it today, and experience God's blessed forgiveness.

✧ ✧ ✧

Suggestions for Prayer: Praise God for being "good, and ready to forgive, and abundant in lovingkindness to all who call upon [Him]" (Ps. 86:5).

For Further Study: Memorize Psalm 139:23-24 to remind you of the need for God's help in confessing your sins.

> *"Wash me thoroughly from my iniquity,*
> *and cleanse me from my sin."*
> PSALM 51:2

❖ ❖ ❖

True confession involves a proper understanding of sin.

K ing David was a man after God's own heart (1 Sam. 13:14). He was far
from perfect, however. He was not an effective father (1 Kings 1:5-6), nor
did he always trust God (1 Sam. 21:10—22:1). But by far his greatest failings
were his horrible sins of adultery with Bathsheba and the subsequent murder
of her husband (2 Sam. 11—12). After Nathan the prophet confronted him with
his sin, David poured out his heart in confession to God. During the next three
days, we will learn from that prayer (Ps. 51) some key marks of true confession.

Confession, first of all, involves a right view of sin. In Psalm 51 David summarized the biblical view of sin.

First, sin deserves judgment. In verse 1 David pleaded, "Be gracious to me,
O God, according to Thy lovingkindness; according to the greatness of Thy
compassion blot out my transgressions." True confession must begin with an
admission of guilt.

Second, sin demands cleansing. In verse 2 David asked God to cleanse him
from the guilt of his sin. Since God's "eyes are too pure to approve evil" and
He cannot "look on wickedness with favor" (Hab. 1:13), only those cleansed
from their sins can enter His presence. True confession acknowledges the
defilement sin causes, and it pleads for God's cleansing (1 John 1:7, 9).

Third, sin is our responsibility. Unlike Adam (Gen. 3:12) and Eve (Gen. 3:13),
David accepted full responsibility for his sin. In verses 1 and 3 he referred to his
sins as "my transgressions." True confession does not blame others for sin.

Fourth, all sin is ultimately against God. David admitted that when he said
to God, "Against Thee, Thee only, I have sinned" (v. 4). True confession recognizes God as the supreme Lawgiver.

Fifth, sin is part of human nature. "Behold, I was brought forth in iniquity,"
David acknowledged in verse 5, "and in sin my mother conceived me." David
accepted the biblical teaching of total depravity—that all men inherit Adam's sin
(Rom. 5:12). True confession looks inward for the cause of sin, not to external
factors.

Does your confession reflect a right view of sin?

❖ ❖ ❖

Suggestions for Prayer: Praise God that He doesn't keep a record of your sins
(Ps. 130:3-4).

For Further Study: Why is acknowledging sin important (Josh. 7:19)?

> *"Against Thee, Thee only, I have sinned, and done what is evil
> in Thy sight, so that Thou art justified when Thou dost
> speak, and blameless when Thou dost judge."*
>
> PSALM 51:4

❖ ❖ ❖

True confession involves a proper understanding of God.

Today we will see a second element of true confession in David's prayer in Psalm 51: true confession requires not only a proper view of sin, but also a proper view of God. David gives us an understanding of four essential truths about God.

First, God is holy. Affirming God's omniscience, David declared, "Behold, Thou dost desire truth in the innermost being, and in the hidden part Thou wilt make me know wisdom" (v. 6). David knew that because God is holy, He is never satisfied with mere external behavior.

Second, God is powerful. David prayed, "Purify me with hyssop, and I shall be clean; wash me, and I shall be whiter than snow. Make me to hear joy and gladness" (vv. 7-8). David believed God had the power to change him—unlike some who think their sinful habits are too strong for Him to overcome.

Third, God will chastise believers for their sins. David pleaded with God, "Let the bones which Thou hast broken rejoice" (v. 8). He alluded to the way shepherds sometimes dealt with wayward sheep. They would take such troublesome sheep and break one of their legs. Then they would set the leg and carry the sheep while the leg healed. Afterwards the sheep would remain close to the shepherd. Through this picturesque metaphor, David described God's chastisement of him for his sin.

Fourth, God is a forgiving God. "Hide Thy face from my sins," pleaded David, "and blot out all my iniquities. . . . Deliver me from bloodguiltiness, O God, Thou God of my salvation" (vv. 9, 14). David obviously believed God would forgive his sin or he would never have asked Him for forgiveness. In Isaiah 43:25 God Himself affirmed that He is a forgiving God: "I, even I, am the one who wipes out your transgressions for My own sake; and I will not remember your sins."

Does your confession reflect a right view of God?

❖ ❖ ❖

Suggestions for Prayer: Praise God for His holiness, power, and forgiveness.

For Further Study: Read the prayers of the exiles (Neh. 9:5-38) and Daniel (Dan. 9:4-19). What do those prayers tell you about their views of God?

*"Behold, Thou dost desire truth in the innermost being, and in
the hidden part Thou wilt make me know wisdom."*
PSALM 51:6

❖ ❖ ❖

True confession involves a proper understanding of oneself.

The supreme goal pursued by many in our narcissistic culture is a "healthy" self-esteem. Even Christians have jumped on the self-esteem bandwagon, misconstruing Jesus' command to "love your neighbor as yourself" (Matt. 19:19) as a mandate for self-love. But the Bible nowhere commands us to pursue self-esteem; instead, it commands us to be holy (1 Peter 1:16). In Psalm 51, David gives three reasons why holiness is imperative in the life of every Christian.

First, because of unbelievers. David knew he could be a witness for God only if his life was holy. In verse 13 he noted that it was only after God forgave him that he could "teach transgressors [God's] ways" and see "sinners ... converted to [Him]." "You are a chosen race," Peter agrees, "a royal priesthood, a holy nation, a people for God's own possession, that you may proclaim the excellencies of Him who has called you out of darkness into His marvelous light" (1 Peter 2:9). Nothing shuts a Christian's mouth so tightly as guilt over unconfessed sin.

Second, because of God. In verse 14 David acknowledged that only when his life was pure could he praise God. He prayed, "Deliver me from bloodguiltiness, O God, Thou God of my salvation; then my tongue will joyfully sing of Thy righteousness." In verses 16-17 David attested that God desires holiness of life, not conformity to external ritual, in His children. When believers lead holy lives, God is pleased; when they sin, He is dishonored (2 Sam. 12:14).

Third, because of other Christians. Believers' sin always affects, directly or indirectly, other Christians. As king, David's sin affected both his family and the entire nation of Israel (2 Sam. 12:10-12). Thus he concluded his prayer of confession by praying for the nation: "By Thy favor do good to Zion; build the walls of Jerusalem. Then Thou wilt delight in righteous sacrifices, in burnt offering and whole burnt offering; then young bulls will be offered on Thine altar" (vv. 18-19).

Does your confession reflect a right view of yourself?

❖ ❖ ❖

Suggestions for Prayer: Pray that God would enable you to "cleanse [yourself] from all defilement of flesh and spirit, perfecting holiness in the fear of God" (2 Cor. 7:1).

For Further Study: What do Psalm 66:18 and 1 Peter 3:7 teach about the connection between holiness and prayer?

*"How shall we who died to sin
still live in it?"*
ROMANS 6:2

✧ ✧ ✧

In Christ, believers are dead to sin.

As a pastor, I frequently encounter people who profess to be believers, yet are living in all kinds of vile sins. The incongruity of people claiming to be believers while living in constant, unrepentant sin was not lost on the apostle Paul. In Romans 6:1 he asked the rhetorical question, "Are we to continue in sin that grace might increase?" In verse 2 he answered his own question by exclaiming "May it never be!"—the strongest, most emphatic negation in the Greek language. It expressed Paul's horror and outrage at the thought that a true Christian could remain in a constant state of sinfulness. For a person to claim to be a Christian while continuing in habitual sin is absurd and impossible.

Paul goes on in verse 2 to explain why believers cannot continue to live in sin, asking, "How shall we who died to sin still live in it?" His point is that believers, at salvation, died to sin. Therefore, they cannot live in a constant state of sinfulness, because it is impossible to be both dead and alive at the same time. Those who continue in unrepentant sin thereby give evidence that they are spiritually dead, no matter what they may claim.

Unbelievers are "dead in [their] trespasses and sins" (Eph. 2:1), walking "according to the course of this world, according to the prince of the power of the air, of the spirit that is now working in the sons of disobedience" (v. 2). Believers, on the other hand, have been "delivered . . . from the domain of darkness, and transferred . . . to the kingdom of His beloved Son" (Col. 1:13).

Christians no longer live in the realm of sin, though they still commit sins.

Having a proper understanding of the believer's relationship to sin is foundational to progressing in holiness. Take comfort today in the reality that sin, though still dangerous, is a defeated foe.

✧ ✧ ✧

Suggestions for Prayer: Praise God who, because of His mercy and love, made us alive together with Christ (Eph. 2:4-5). ✧ Ask Him to help you walk worthy of that high calling (Eph. 4:1).

For Further Study: Read the following passages: John 8:31; 2 Cor. 13:5; James 2:14-26. Is every profession of faith in Jesus Christ genuine? Explain.

*"Do you not know that all of us who have been baptized into
Christ Jesus have been baptized into His death?"*

ROMANS 6:3

❖ ❖ ❖

Believers are united with Christ.

A person who believes Christians are free to continue sinning betrays a
fundamental lack of understanding of what a Christian is. Christians are
not merely guilty sinners declared righteous by God because Christ has satisfied the demands of God's righteousness on their behalf. That truth, which
theologians call justification, is indeed an essential one. But there is much
more to salvation than justification. Believers are also placed into union with
Jesus Christ.

Paul introduces this momentous truth by means of the analogy of water baptism. Some wrongly interpret this passage to teach that baptism itself places us
into union with Christ. But Paul had just spent three chapters (Rom. 3—5) teaching that salvation is solely by faith in Christ. He would hardly then turn around
in chapter 6 and teach that it was by ritual. The apostle, as he did in 1 Corinthians
10:1-2, used baptism in a metaphorical sense. (The Greek word translated "baptism" simply means "to immerse," not necessarily in water.)

Paul also uses other metaphors to describe believers' union with Christ. In
Galatians 3:27 he says believers have put on Christ, while 1 Corinthians 6:17 says
Christians are joined to Him. But none is so graphic as that of baptism; the leaving of one environment (air) and entering another (water) symbolizes believers
leaving Satan's realm (Eph. 2:2) and entering that of the Lord Jesus Christ.

What does our union with Christ mean in our everyday lives? First, it provides the means of fellowship with both Jesus and the Father (1 John 1:3). It
also should motivate us to avoid sinning. In 1 Corinthians 6:15, Paul chided
the Corinthians for their lax view of sexual sin: "Do you not know that your
bodies are members of Christ? Shall I then take away the members of Christ
and make them members of a harlot? May it never be!" Finally, our union with
Christ provides hope of future glory (Rev. 3:21).

What a blessed privilege and awesome responsibility is ours, to have our
lives inextricably bound with the Son of God (Col. 3:3)!

❖ ❖ ❖

Suggestions for Prayer: Praise God for all the blessings resulting from your
union with Christ.

For Further Study: Read 2 Peter 1:3-4. In light of our union with Christ, do
we lack anything necessary for living the Christian life?

*"Therefore we have been buried with Him
through baptism into death, in order that as Christ
was raised from the dead through the glory of the Father,
so we too might walk in newness of life."*

ROMANS 6:4

❖ ❖ ❖

***Union with Christ means participation in
His death, burial, and resurrection.***

B elievers are united with Christ not only in His life, but also in His death.
When believers come to faith in Christ, they symbolically share in His
death, dying to sin in order to live to God (Rom. 6:10-11).

That reality has profound implications. Having died to the old life of sin
and been raised to share new life in Christ, believers *cannot* continue in the
same old patterns of sin. They now live in an entirely different realm. Those
who die in Christ live in Christ. In the words of the great nineteenth-century
theologian Charles Hodge, "There can be no participation in Christ's life
without a participation in his death, and we cannot enjoy the benefits of his
death unless we are partakers of the power of his life. We must be reconciled
to God in order to be holy, and we cannot be reconciled without thereby
becoming holy."

As a result, believers cannot help but "walk in newness of life." *Walk*
describes daily spiritual conduct. Believers have a new direction in life; they
no longer live like they did before they were saved (1 Peter 4:3-4).

In his classic hymn "And Can It Be?" Charles Wesley wrote:

*No condemnation now I dread:
Jesus, and all in Him, is mine!
Alive in Him, my living Head,
And clothed in righteousness divine,
Bold I approach the eternal throne,
And claim the crown, thru Christ my own.*

Is that the song of your heart today?

❖ ❖ ❖

Suggestions for Prayer: Praise God for rescuing you from sin and death and
making you alive with Christ.

For Further Study: Study the following passages: Galatians 5:16; Ephesians
5:2; Philippians 3:17-18; Colossians 1:10; 1 John 1:7. What do they tell you
about the Christian's walk?

> *"Knowing this, that our old self was crucified with Him, that our body of sin might be done away with, that we should no longer be slaves to sin; for he who has died is freed from sin."*
> ROMANS 6:6-7

✧ ✧ ✧

Having died with Christ, believers are no longer under sin's control.

Years ago a book with the amusing title "It Ain't Gonna Reign No More" appeared. Though humorous, that title aptly summarizes the believer's relationship to sin. Christians still commit sins but are no longer under sin's dominion.

When we were united with Christ in His death (Rom. 6:5), "our old self was crucified with Him" (verse 6). Our "old self" equals what we were before salvation—lost in sin and bound for Hell. It is the unregenerate nature we inherited from Adam (Rom. 5:12; 1 Cor. 15:22).

Some argue that believers now have both an old and new nature—a sort of spiritual split personality. The conflict between those two natures, they believe, is responsible for the struggles of the Christian life, as the believer strives to crucify his old self. But notice that Paul does not command us to crucify our old self; he tells us that has already happened (cf. Gal. 2:20; Col. 3:9-10).

The expression "that our body of sin might be done away with" approaches this same truth from a slightly different perspective. It notes the close connection between the body and sin (Rom. 8:10, 13) and describes the absolute domination of sin in the life of an unbeliever. That domination is broken at salvation.

Paul is not teaching, however, that believers' sin natures have been eradicated, and hence they no longer sin. The Greek word translated "done away with" does not mean "destroyed" but "rendered inoperative" or "deprived of its strength, influence, or power." Christians are no longer slaves to sin; its tyranny in our lives has been broken.

Be encouraged today in your battle with sin because though it is still a dangerous enemy, sin is no longer your master.

✧ ✧ ✧

Suggestions for Prayer: Praise God for delivering you from sin's power. ✧ Pray that He would deliver you from sin's presence in your life.

For Further Study: Read the following passages: Romans 6:19; 12:1-2; 1 Corinthians 6:19-20. What is your part in the battle against sin? ✧ What practical steps can you take to more effectively defeat sin in your life?

> *"Now if we have died with Christ, we believe that we shall*
> *also live with Him, knowing that Christ, having been raised*
> *from the dead, is never to die again; death no longer is master*
> *over Him. For the death that He died, He died to sin,*
> *once for all; but the life that He lives, He lives to God."*
>
> ROMANS 6:8-10

✧ ✧ ✧

God frees us from sin through the death of His Son.

As a good teacher, the apostle Paul understood that important truths bear repeating. Thus in today's passage he repeats and expands on the important truth he presented earlier in Romans 6: believers died with Christ. Through that death, sin's dominion over us was broken.

The rock-solid foundation of the believer's forgiveness from sin is Christ's victory over sin and death. When our Lord rose from the dead, He proved that He had shattered the power of sin and death (Rom. 4:25; 1 Cor. 15:54-57). And since believers are identified with Christ in His death and resurrection (Rom. 6:3-5), we, too, share in His victory.

That Christ was the perfect sacrifice for sin is an essential New Testament truth. The Book of Hebrews expresses that important reality repeatedly, nowhere more clearly and forcefully than in 10:10-14: "By this will we have been sanctified through the offering of the body of Jesus Christ once for all. And every priest stands daily ministering and offering time after time the same sacrifices, which can never take away sins; but He, having offered one sacrifice for sins for all time, sat down at the right hand of God, waiting from that time onward until His enemies be made a footstool for His feet. For by one offering He has perfected for all time those who are sanctified."

Christ "died to sin" not only to break its power but to pay its penalty—death (Rom. 6:23)—on our behalf. "He Himself bore our sins in His body on the cross," wrote Peter, "that we might die to sin and live to righteousness; for by His wounds you were healed" (1 Peter 2:24).

Believers are dead to sin's power and penalty. "Thanks be to God through Christ Jesus our Lord" (Rom. 7:25)!

✧ ✧ ✧

Suggestions for Prayer: Praise God for sending His Son to bear your sins (2 Cor. 5:21).

For Further Study: Memorize 1 Corinthians 6:20 to help motivate you to glorify God with your life.

"Even so consider yourselves to be dead to sin,
but alive to God in Christ Jesus."

ROMANS 6:11

❖ ❖ ❖

You must act on what you know to be true.

A foundational biblical principle is that people must understand the truth before they can live it out in their lives. Put another way, duty is always based on doctrine. The first ten verses of Romans 6 lay the solid foundation of truth upon which believers can build their lives. Several times so far (vv. 3, 5, 6, 8) Paul has exhorted Christians to understand the truth of their union with Christ in His death and resurrection. Now he exhorts us to act on it.

"Consider" translates a Greek word that means "to calculate," "to compute," "to take into account." Paul urges believers to come to a settled conviction about their death to sin through their union with Christ.

Why do some question the liberating truth that in Christ they are dead to sin? Some are victimized by an inadequate view of salvation, seeing it as a mere change in their legal standing before God. Salvation involves far more, however; it involves a transformation of life. Those who believe their Christian life to be a constant battle between their old and new selves will not be able to consider themselves dead to sin. The accusations of Satan (Rev. 12:10) and conscience also make it very difficult for some to count on their death to sin. But the biggest difficulty Christians face in believing sin is a defeated enemy is their constant battle with it. That struggle makes it hard to believe we're really dead to sin's power (Rom. 7:15-24). Nevertheless, the Bible teaches that Christ's holiness imputed to believers has released us from sin's dominion. Therefore, Christians can choose not to sin and are never forced to sin.

Consider yourself to be dead to sin, and experience the blessings of triumph over temptation (1 Cor. 10:13), sin (which can never cause you to lose your salvation, Heb. 7:25), and death (John 11:25-26).

❖ ❖ ❖

Suggestions for Prayer: Thank God for His gracious provision of salvation in Jesus Christ.

For Further Study: Read the following passages: Hosea 4:6; Isaiah 1:3; Colossians 3:8-10. What do they teach about the importance of doctrinal knowledge in the Christian life?

"Therefore do not let sin reign in your mortal body that you should obey its lusts, and do not go on presenting the members of your body to sin as instruments of unrighteousness; but present yourselves to God as those alive from the dead, and your members as instruments of righteousness to God. For sin shall not be master over you, for you are not under law, but under grace."

ROMANS 6:12-14

✧ ✧ ✧

Believers are to yield themselves
to God, not to sin.

Three key words in Romans 6 define the believer's relationship to sin: "know" (vv. 3, 6, 9), "consider" (v. 11), and "present" (v. 13). The first two speak of understanding and believing that we are dead to sin. The third demands of us active obedience in our lives based on that truth. Since we are truly dead to sin, we must not allow it to be the dominant force in our lives.

Sin is a dethroned monarch, but it is still present in this fallen world and desires to lure the believer back into its grasp. Knowing that, Paul exhorts Christians, "Do not let sin reign in your mortal body that you should obey its lusts." He says, "Sin has no right to rule; so don't let it!" Peter echoed that thought in 1 Peter 2:11: "Beloved, I urge you as aliens and strangers to abstain from fleshly lusts, which wage war against the soul."

How does a believer keep sin from reigning? Negatively, believers defeat sin by no longer "presenting the members of [their bodies] to sin as instruments of unrighteousness." We must make sure that our thoughts, speech, and actions are not used for unrighteous purposes. Positively, we must yield all of our faculties to God as "instruments of righteousness." To do both requires self-discipline—like that which Paul expressed in 1 Corinthians 9:27: "I buffet my body and make it my slave, lest possibly, after I have preached to others, I myself should be disqualified."

Yield to sin, and experience chastening and sorrow; yield to God, and experience joy and blessing. Which will you choose today?

✧ ✧ ✧

Suggestions for Prayer: Is there a part of your life (thoughts, speech, actions, habits) where sin still reigns? If so, confess it to God, and ask for His help in breaking sin's hold in that area.

For Further Study: Memorize Romans 12:1 to help you remember the importance of yielding your body to God.

> *"What then? Shall we sin because we are not under law but under grace? May it never be! Do you not know that when you present yourselves to someone as slaves for obedience, you are slaves of the one whom you obey, either of sin resulting in death, or of obedience resulting in righteousness?"*
> ROMANS 6:15-16

❖ ❖ ❖

Freedom from *sin does not mean freedom* to *sin.*

From Paul's day until now, the gospel of grace has been accused of providing license to sin. If salvation is the gift of God's grace, legalists argue, wholly apart from human works, what will motivate people to lead holy lives? In the face of such opposition, Paul never gave an inch on the vital issue of salvation by grace—and neither can we. The Bible teaches a salvation that is entirely by God's free grace through faith and in which human works play no part.

But there is a second way in which the doctrine of salvation by grace may be perverted. Fulfilling the legalists' fears, some believe that since God's grace covers all their sins, they can live as they choose. In today's passage Paul addresses that error.

The very thought of a Christian living in persistent, habitual sin horrified Paul. To the hypothetical question "Shall we sin because we are not under law but under grace?" Paul responded emphatically, "May it never be!" As in verse 2, the apostle used the strongest form of negation in the Greek language. In our English vernacular, Paul was saying "Ridiculous! Impossible! No way!" He went on to point out the self-evident truth that no one can serve two masters. Everyone is either a servant of sin or a servant of God; there is no third option. And the one to whom people habitually yield their obedience is their real master, no matter what they may claim.

Don't be deceived by those who claim that since Christians are forgiven, they can therefore sin at will. Such people know nothing of God's grace, which, far from giving us license to sin, "instruct[s] us to deny ungodliness and worldly desires and to live sensibly, righteously and godly in the present age" (Titus 2:12).

❖ ❖ ❖

Suggestions for Prayer: Praise God for His grace, which is always greater than your sin (Rom. 5:20).

For Further Study: Read Joshua 24:14-27; Matthew 4:8-11; and 1 Thessalonians 1:8-9. Spend some time in prayer, asking God to help you renew your commitment to serve Him.

> *"But thanks be to God that though you were slaves*
> *of sin, you became obedient from the heart to that form*
> *of teaching to which you were committed, and having been*
> *freed from sin, you became slaves of righteousness."*
>
> ROMANS 6:17-18

✧ ✧ ✧

True freedom comes from being a servant of Jesus Christ.

I once knew a man who, though intellectually convinced that the gospel was true, balked at committing his life to Jesus Christ. When I asked him why, he replied, "Because I don't want to give up my freedom." He understood clearly that genuine saving faith requires submission to Christ's lordship. But he was tragically deceived in thinking that non-Christians are free—they aren't. Unbelievers are slaves to sin (John 8:34). Only Christians have true freedom (John 8:31-32)—the freedom *not* to sin.

Paul reminded the Roman Christians that before they were saved, they "were slaves of sin." The apostle's use of the imperfect tense indicates that the Romans, like all unbelievers, had been in a continual state of slavery to sin. Every human ever born—since Adam and Eve plunged the human race into sin—has been born enslaved to sin—except of course, for Christ.

When a person comes to faith in Christ, he or she becomes "obedient from the heart" to the Lord Jesus Christ. A Christian's initial act of obedience, repenting and believing the gospel message (Mark 1:15), is the first step in a lifelong path of obedience. In the words of the apostle Peter, Christians are those who "have in obedience to the truth purified [their] souls" (1 Peter 1:22).

Paradoxically, it's only those who have made themselves servants of Jesus Christ who are truly free. They alone are free to do what is right; even unbelievers' "good deeds" are sinful, since they aren't done to glorify God. Christian liberty is not the freedom to choose to sin, but the freedom to choose not to.

Renew today your commitment to be an obedient servant of God, knowing that "you are not your own. For you have been bought with a price" (1 Cor. 6:19-20).

✧ ✧ ✧

Suggestions for Prayer: Praise God for freeing you from slavery to sin. ✧ Ask Him to show you those areas in your life that you have not yielded fully to Him.

For Further Study: Memorize Matthew 5:6; 1 Timothy 6:10-12; and Hebrews 12:14. ✧ Ask God to help you pattern your life after Jesus Christ.

> *"I am speaking in human terms because of the*
> *weakness of your flesh. For just as you presented your*
> *members as slaves to impurity and to lawlessness, resulting in*
> *further lawlessness, so now present your members as slaves*
> *to righteousness, resulting in sanctification."*
>
> ROMANS 6:19

❖ ❖ ❖

You must live consistent with your new nature.

It is a truism that in the spiritual realm, no one stands still. Sin leads to more sin, while holy living leads to further righteousness. All unbelievers are slaves of sin and have no choice but to sin; yielding to sin comes naturally to them. They are inwardly full of "impurity" and hence outwardly given to "lawlessness." They continually spiral downward; sin leads to more sin, which leads in turn to still more sin. Ultimately, sin will drag a person into the depths of Hell.

For Christians, however, the spiral is an upward one. Having become new creatures at salvation (2 Cor. 5:17), believers are no longer servants of sin. The Christian life is the process of bringing one's lifestyle into line with one's nature. As believers "present their members as slaves to righteousness," the inevitable result is further "sanctification." Decreasing frequency of sin, therefore, is a sure sign of a mature believer.

Paul knew all too well from his own experience that the believer's body is a battleground. In his spiritual autobiography he wrote, "I find then the principle that evil is present in me, the one who wishes to do good. For I joyfully concur with the law of God in the inner man, but I see a different law in the members of my body, waging war against the law of my mind, and making me a prisoner of the law of sin which is in my members. Wretched man that I am! Who will set me free from the body of this death?" (Rom. 7:21-24).

How are you faring in the daily battle with sin? If victories are few and far between, perhaps you have forgotten Paul's exhortation to "present your bodies a living and holy sacrifice, acceptable to God, which is your spiritual service of worship" (Rom. 12:1).

❖ ❖ ❖

Suggestions for Prayer: Pray with the psalmist, "Establish my footsteps in Thy word, and do not let any iniquity have dominion over me" (Ps. 119:133).

For Further Study: Identify one area in which you lack self-control. Use a concordance to see what Proverbs teaches about your problem.

> *"For the wages of sin is death, but the free gift of God*
> *is eternal life in Christ Jesus our Lord."*
> ROMANS 6:23

❖ ❖ ❖

Christ paid a debt He did not owe
to free us from a debt we could not pay.

In the scientific realm there are universal laws, such as the law of gravity. These laws are built into the creation by its all-wise Creator and keep it functioning normally.

Just as God has made inexorable laws to govern the physical dimension, so also has He decreed universal spiritual principles. The most significant of those spiritual laws is that sin demands death; death is the wages sin pays. The Greek word translated "wages" was commonly used to speak of giving compensation for service rendered. When God sentences sinners to Hell, He is merely giving them the compensation that they have earned and that His justice demands.

In sharp contrast to the inexorable law of sin and death is the gracious "free gift of God"—"eternal life in Christ Jesus our Lord." Eternal life is not a wage but a gift, and hence it can't be earned. Good works, church attendance, or religious rituals will not entitle anyone to it. After recounting his religious credentials—credentials unsurpassed in first-century Judaism (Gal. 1:14)—Paul dismissed them as "loss for the sake of Christ" (Phil. 3:7).

The free gift of eternal life comes only through "Christ Jesus our Lord." In Acts 4:12 Peter declared that "there is salvation in no one else; for there is no other name under heaven that has been given among men, by which we must be saved." And in John 14:6 Jesus said simply, "I am the way, and the truth, and the life; no one comes to the Father, but through Me."

"Thanks be to God for His indescribable gift" (2 Cor. 9:15)!

❖ ❖ ❖

Suggestions for Prayer: Have you lost touch with the reality that "the law of the Spirit of life in Christ Jesus has set you free from the law of sin and of death" (Rom. 8:2)? If so, spend some time in prayer today, thanking God for giving you eternal life.

For Further Study: What do the following passages teach about the possibility of earning eternal life: Romans 3:28; Galatians 2:16; 3:11; Philippians 3:9; Titus 3:5?

> *"Therefore, my brethren, you also were made*
> *to die to the Law through the body of Christ."*
> ROMANS 7:4

❖ ❖ ❖

The law can no longer punish
those who have died with Christ.

It's an axiomatic truth that laws don't apply to dead people. No policeman would issue a ticket to a drunk driver who was killed in an accident. Nor was Lee Harvey Oswald tried for killing President Kennedy, since he himself was killed by Jack Ruby. In Romans 7:2-3 Paul uses marriage to illustrate that truth: "For the married woman is bound by law to her husband while he is living; but if her husband dies, she is released from the law concerning the husband. So then if, while her husband is living, she is joined to another man, she shall be called an adulteress; but if her husband dies, she is free from the law, so that she is not an adulteress, though she is joined to another man." Paul's point is simple: death ends a marriage because the laws regarding marriage don't apply to the dead.

The same principle holds true in the spiritual realm. Since believers have died with Christ (Rom. 6:3-7), the law can no longer condemn them; it no longer has authority over them. Paul's use of a passive verb ("were made to die") indicates that believers don't make themselves dead to the law; they were made dead to the law through a divine act.

The only provision for paying the penalty the law demands is the Lord Jesus Christ's death on the cross. To the Corinthians Paul wrote, "He made Him who knew no sin to be sin on our behalf, that we might become the righteousness of God in Him" (2 Cor. 5:21). The apostle repeated that truth in Galatians 2:19-20: "For through the Law I died to the Law, that I might live to God. I have been crucified with Christ; and it is no longer I who live, but Christ lives in me; and the life which I now live in the flesh I live by faith in the Son of God, who loved me, and delivered Himself up for me."

❖ ❖ ❖

Suggestions for Prayer: Thank God that you are no longer under the law's condemnation (Rom. 8:1).

For Further Study: Read Romans 3:20; 7:12; Galatians 3:24-25. Since the law can't save anyone, what is its purpose?

". . . That you might be joined to another, to Him who was
raised from the dead, that we might bear fruit for God."
ROMANS 7:4

❖ ❖ ❖

No longer married to the law,
the believer is now married to Jesus Christ.

Of the many New Testament metaphors used to describe the church, the most intimate is that of the bride of Christ. Paul describes that relationship in Ephesians 5:24-27: "But as the church is subject to Christ, so also the wives ought to be to their husbands in everything. Husbands, love your wives, just as Christ also loved the church and gave Himself up for her; that He might sanctify her, having cleansed her by the washing of water with the word, that He might present to Himself the church in all her glory, having no spot or wrinkle or any such thing; but that she should be holy and blameless."

By describing Christ as "Him who was raised from the dead," Paul stresses the believer's union with Jesus not only in His death but also in His resurrection (Rom. 6:4-5). Thus, our marriage bond with the living Savior will last forever.

The result of our union with Christ is "that we might bear fruit for God." It is the goal of every believer's life to glorify God by bearing fruit. There is no such thing as a Christian who bears no fruit, because the inevitable result of salvation is a transformed life. Jesus continues that process of transformation throughout our lives, continually pruning us so that we may produce even more fruit to His glory (John 15:1-2).

Spiritual fruit may be defined as any righteous act that glorifies God. It may consist of godly, Spirit-produced attitudes (Gal. 5:22-23), praise to God (Heb. 13:15), others led to Christ (Rom. 1:13), giving to those in need (Rom. 15:26-28), and righteous living (Phil. 1:11).What a great privilege is ours, to be eternally "one spirit" (1 Cor. 6:17) with the Lord of Glory!

❖ ❖ ❖

Suggestions for Prayer: Pray that God would enable you to do all things for His glory (1 Cor. 10:31).

For Further Study: Read the list of the fruit of the Spirit Paul gives in Galatians 5:22-23. Using a concordance, Bible dictionary, or other reference tools, study each aspect of fruit listed. ❖ Look for ways to implement into your daily life what you learn.

*"For while we were in the flesh, the sinful passions, which were
aroused by the Law, were at work in the members
of our body to bear fruit for death."*

ROMANS 7:5

✧ ✧ ✧

Four key terms characterize those who are not in Christ.

In our fallen, cursed world, disasters are commonplace. Fires, floods, earthquakes, volcanic eruptions, hurricanes, tornadoes, and other natural disasters happen somewhere every day. Added to those natural disasters are the man-made ones, such as war, acts of terrorism, plane crashes, train wrecks, etc.

But far greater than any of those disasters, and the one from which they all stem, was the entrance of sin into the human race. Sin renders fallen men spiritually dead, cuts them off from fellowship with God, and consigns them to eternal punishment in Hell.

In today's verse Paul introduces four words that describe man's unregenerate state: *flesh*, *sin*, *law*, and *death*. Those four words are interconnected: the flesh produces sin, which is stimulated by the law, resulting in death. Let's consider each one individually.

The term *flesh* is used two ways in Scripture. It is sometimes used in a physical sense to speak of human existence. John used it to describe Christ's incarnation in John 1:14 and 1 John 4:2. But in its moral sense, "flesh" represents the believer's unredeemed body (Gal. 5:13; Eph. 2:3). While believers are no longer "in the flesh" (Rom. 8:9) as are unbelievers, the flesh is still in us. It is the seat of temptation, the beachhead from which Satan launches his attacks.

Sin (or "sinful passions") energizes the flesh, which in turn produces further sin. Those "sinful passions," Paul says, "were aroused by the Law"; they are exposed by *the law* because fallen man's rebellious nature makes him desire to do what is forbidden. The end result of this downward spiral is *"death"*—both physical and spiritual.

What a merciful God we serve, who "even when we were dead in our transgressions, made us alive together with Christ" (Eph. 2:5).

✧ ✧ ✧

Suggestions for Prayer: Pray for the unbelievers in your life, that God would open their hearts to respond to the gospel (Acts 16:14).

For Further Study: What do the following passages teach about the Christian's relationship to the law—Romans 8:2-4; 10:4; Galatians 3:13; 5:18; Philippians 3:9. ✧ Does that mean believers can live as they please? (See 1 Cor. 9:21.)

*"For we maintain that a man is justified by faith
apart from works of the Law."*
ROMANS 3:28

❖ ❖ ❖

Being dead in sin, man is unable to save himself.

A s we've seen this month, the most serious problem facing the human race is not the destruction of the environment, crime, or the threat of nuclear war; it is sin. The former threaten us with physical death, the latter with spiritual death. Thus it follows that the greatest news ever known is that "Christ Jesus came into the world to save sinners" (1 Tim. 1:15). Hell may be the destiny of man, but that is not the desire of God's heart. Peter notes that the Lord "is patient . . . not wishing for any to perish but for all to come to repentance" (2 Peter 3:9).

Because of His great love for sinners, God sent His Son "to be the propitiation for our sins" (1 John 4:10). Since God's gracious gift of salvation is appropriated by faith, it is not surprising that justification by faith is the theme of Romans (see Rom. 1:16-17). The apostle shows that all men are guilty before God and in need of justification (chaps. 1—2). He then describes justification in chapters 3—4. Then he presents the results of justification in chapters 5—6.

Two key words are associated with justification in Romans: *grace* and *faith*. In Romans 3:24 Paul declares that we are "justified as a gift by His grace through the redemption which is in Christ Jesus," while in verse 28 he says, "For we maintain that a man is justified by faith apart from works of the Law." The promise of justification to Abraham, Paul notes, was "by faith, that it might be in accordance with grace" (Rom. 4:16). Faith and grace are both linked to justification again in Romans 5:1-2: "Therefore having been justified by faith, we have peace with God through our Lord Jesus Christ, through whom also we have obtained our introduction by faith into this grace in which we stand."

In this day of doctrinal vacillation, I pray that you will stand firm in your commitment to the doctrine of justification by grace alone through faith alone.

❖ ❖ ❖

Suggestions for Prayer: Thank God for His mercy and love in saving you when you were dead in sin (Eph. 2:4-5). ❖ Ask Him to help you walk worthy of your salvation (Eph. 4:1).

For Further Study: Read Romans 1—6, noting what it teaches about man's lost state and God's gracious provision of salvation.

"What shall we say then? Is the Law sin? May it never be!
On the contrary, I would not have come to know sin except
through the Law; for I would not have known about coveting
if the Law had not said, 'You shall not covet.'"

ROMANS 7:7

✧ ✧ ✧

God's holy standard exposes man's rebellious heart.

So far in Romans, Paul has told us what the law can't do: it can't save us (3—5) or sanctify us (6). At this point the apostle anticipates and answers a question that naturally arises: What, then, was the purpose of the law? Was it evil? In the next few days we're going to consider three important purposes the law served.

First, the law reveals sin. Sin is a violation of God's righteous standard (1 John 3:4); if no such standard existed, there would be no sin. In Romans 3:20 Paul said that "through the Law comes the knowledge of sin." Romans 4:15 adds, "Where there is no law, neither is there violation," and Romans 5:13 reveals that "sin is not imputed when there is no law."

To the question "Is the Law sin?" Paul replies emphatically, "May it never be!" Such a question is as absurd as it is blasphemous; an evil law could never proceed from a holy God. Paul goes on to say, "I would not have come to know sin except through the Law." The law brought the proud Pharisee Saul of Tarsus face to face with his utter sinfulness, revealing his need for a Savior and preparing his heart for his life-changing encounter with the Lord Jesus Christ on the road to Damascus.

The specific commandment Paul cites, the injunction against coveting, is revealing. Coveting is an internal attitude, not an external act. It was the realization that God's law applied to his attitudes, not merely his external behavior, that devastated Paul. He was forced to realize that all his external self-righteousness was worthless because his heart wasn't right.

I pray that you too will be "obedient from the heart to that form of teaching to which you were committed" (Rom. 6:17).

✧ ✧ ✧

Suggestions for Prayer: Pray with the psalmist, "Search me, O God, and know my heart; try me and know my anxious thoughts; and see if there be any hurtful way in me, and lead me in the everlasting way" (Ps. 139:23-24).

For Further Study: Read Isaiah 1:14-20; Amos 5:21-27; Matthew 23:25-28. What does God think of mere outward conformity to His law?

*"But sin, taking opportunity through the
commandment, produced in me coveting of every kind;
for apart from the Law sin is dead."*

ROMANS 7:8

❖ ❖ ❖

*When confronted with God's holy law,
sinful men are motivated not to obey it, but to break it.*

It is a perverse fact of fallen human nature that the surest way to get people to do things is to tell them not to do them. When people see a sign reading "Keep off the grass!" or "Don't pick the flowers!" their first impulse is often to trample the grass and take some flowers.

The same is true in the spiritual realm. God's law reveals what is right and what is wrong—and sinful men choose to do what is wrong. In his classic allegory *Pilgrim's Progress*, John Bunyan vividly depicts the seemingly paradoxical truth that the law does not restrain sin but stirs it up. In the house of Interpreter, Christian was shown a large, dust-filled room. A man with a broom, representing the law, appeared and began to sweep. The resulting dust cloud nearly choked Christian. Bunyan's point was that just as sweeping a dusty room does not remove the dust but only stirs it up, so the law does not restrain sin but merely aggravates it.

Does that mean the law is evil? Certainly not. "The Law is holy" (Rom. 7:12) since it derives from a holy God. And it does sinners good by exposing their sin and revealing to them their need for a Savior. The law, then, is not the culprit—sin is.

Using himself as an illustration, Paul notes that "sin, taking opportunity through the commandment, produced in me coveting of every kind." "Opportunity" translates a Greek word used in military terms to speak of a base of operations from which attacks could be launched. Sin used the law—especially the knowledge of right and wrong it brought—to launch its attacks on Paul.

Don't be afraid in your evangelism to confront sinners with the demands of God's holy law. They must face their utter inability to meet its demands before they will recognize their need for a Savior.

❖ ❖ ❖

Suggestions for Prayer: Pray that God would help you discern the subtlety of sin's attacks against you.

For Further Study: Read 2 Kings 17:13-16. Did the Israelites' knowledge of God's law keep them from sinning?

"And I was once alive apart from the Law; but when the commandment came, sin became alive, and I died; and this commandment, which was to result in life, proved to result in death for me; for sin, taking opportunity through the commandment, deceived me, and through it killed me."

ROMANS 7:9-11

❖ ❖ ❖

The law shatters all of man's attempts at self-righteousness.

The old saying "ignorance is bliss" is rarely true, and in the spiritual realm it is deadly. As a Pharisee, one of the rising stars of first-century Judaism (Gal. 1:14), Paul thought himself very much "alive apart from the Law." When convicted of his utter sinfulness by the law, however, Paul "died"; that is, his false sense of security and self-satisfaction was shattered. The enormity of his guilt became evident to him, and he realized he could not save himself. He recognized he was "helpless" (Rom. 5:6) and desperately in need of the divine Physician (Matt. 9:12).

To his dismay, Paul found that the "commandment, which was to result in life, proved to result in death" for him. The law was given to provide blessing and joy (Prov. 3:1-2) by guiding men in the path of righteousness. That purpose, however, can't be accomplished in the unsaved, since they lack the ability to keep the law. Shut out from its blessings by their disobedience, they face its curses. Instead of providing Paul with a rich, meaningful life, the law devastated him.

Paul further realized that he had been deceived by sin. He had thought himself "blameless" (Phil. 3:6), doing God's work by persecuting Christians (cf. John 16:2). But instead of satisfaction, he found only misery, disillusionment, and disappointment.

Like Paul, millions today are tragically deceived. The deceitfulness of sin leads them to think they can please God and obtain His blessing by their good works or religious activity. Such trust in self-righteousness is the hallmark of all false religion. But those who trust in themselves will see no need for a Savior and will be eternally lost. What are you trusting in? Can you say with the hymn writer:

❖ ❖ ❖

Suggestions for Prayer: Ask God to help you obey His commandments.

For Further Study: Read Hebrews 3:13. Are believers also in danger of being deceived by sin?

"For we know that the Law is spiritual; but I am of flesh, sold into bondage to sin. For that which I am doing, I do not understand; for I am not practicing what I would like to do, but I am doing the very thing I hate. But if I do the very thing I do not wish to do, I agree with the Law, confessing that it is good. So now, no longer am I the one doing it, but sin which indwells me."

ROMANS 7:14-17

❖ ❖ ❖

Believers have been freed from sin's power,
but not from its presence.

Romans 7:14-25 is perhaps the most autobiographical passage in all of Scripture. In this poignant account Paul describes in vivid, striking language his battle with indwelling sin. So powerful is that language that some believe it refers to Paul's life before his conversion. But the apostle describes himself as one who seeks to obey God's law and who hates evil (vv. 15, 19, 21), who is humble and broken over his sin (v. 18), and who acknowledges Jesus Christ as Lord and serves Him with his mind (v. 25). None of those things characterize an unbeliever.

The word "for" indicates that Paul is not beginning a new subject but is continuing with the thought from the first part of Romans 7, that the law reveals our sin. The law is not the problem but reveals the problem—sin. The apostle then makes the startling statement that he is "of flesh, sold into bondage to sin." "Flesh" is our unredeemed humanness—that part of us that is still sinful and fights against our new natures. Paul's words do not mean that God had only partially saved him; rather, they emphasize that sin is still a powerful force in believers' lives and is not to be trifled with.

Christians are under attack from the outside, from Satan and the evil world system. But we also have a "fifth column"—the flesh inside us, aiding and abetting those attacks. Fight the flesh today by making "no provision for [it] in regard to its lusts" (Rom. 13:14).

❖ ❖ ❖

Suggestions for Prayer: "Keep watching and praying, that you may not enter into temptation; the spirit is willing, but the flesh is weak" (Matt. 26:41).

For Further Study: What do the following passages teach about the possibility of a believer's being "sold into bondage to sin"—Psalm 51:1-5; Isaiah 6:5; 1 John 1:8-10?

> *"Wretched man that I am! Who will set me*
> *free from the body of this death? Thanks be to God*
> *through Jesus Christ our Lord!"*
> ROMANS 7:24-25

✧ ✧ ✧

Christians have been delivered from sin's power
and will one day be delivered from its presence.

The godly Puritan writer Thomas Watson once said that a sure sign of sanctification is a hatred and loathing of sin. It was his hatred of sin that caused Paul to cry out as he wrapped up his spiritual autobiography, "Wretched man that I am! Who will set me free from the body of this death?" That cry expresses the distress and frustration the apostle experienced in his spiritual battle. David expressed that same frustration in Psalm 13:1-2: "How long, O Lord? Wilt Thou forget me forever? How long wilt Thou hide Thy face from me? How long shall I take counsel in my soul, having sorrow in my heart all the day?"

When he exclaimed, "Who will set me free from the body of this death?" Paul referred to his physical body that was subject to sin and death. It is there that the battle with sin is joined. The verb translated "set me free" was used to speak of a soldier rescuing a wounded comrade in the midst of battle. Paul longed to be rescued from his sinful, unredeemed flesh.

But the story doesn't end there, with Paul frustrated and in despair. Certain of his eventual triumph over sin, the apostle says, "Thanks be to God through Jesus Christ our Lord!" As he goes on to explain in Romans 8:18-19, 22-23 (and in 1 Cor. 15:53, 57), believers will one day receive their glorified bodies and enter Christ's presence, never to struggle again with sin. Paul elaborates on that glorious truth in Philippians 3:20-21: "For our citizenship is in heaven, from which also we eagerly wait for a Savior, the Lord Jesus Christ; who will transform the body of our humble state into conformity with the body of His glory, by the exertion of the power that He has even to subject all things to Himself."

What a triumphant hope is ours!

✧ ✧ ✧

Suggestions for Prayer: Thank God in advance for the glorified body that will one day be yours.

For Further Study: Read 1 John 3:2-3. Are you fixing your hope on your glorification when Christ returns? ✧ Is that hope having a purifying effect on your lifestyle now?

"For we do not have a high priest who cannot sympathize
with our weaknesses, but one who has been tempted
in all things as we are, yet without sin."
HEBREWS 4:15

✧ ✧ ✧

Jesus Christ provides us with the
perfect example of how to defeat temptation.

Perhaps you've heard the joke, "I can resist anything but temptation!" Unfortunately, that is all too often true in our lives. Learning how to successfully resist temptation is vitally important, for we sin only when we yield to temptation.

Christians throughout history have recognized the importance of resisting temptation. One early believer wrote, "Fly from all occasions of temptation, and if still tempted, fly further still. If there is no escape possible, then have done with running and show a bold face and take the two-edged sword of the Spirit." The desire to escape temptation has led many in the history of the church to attempt heroic but ultimately futile feats of ascetic self-denial. So desperate did one monk become that he threw himself into a thicket of thorn bushes! Unfortunately, that did not bring him the relief from temptation that he so desperately sought.

The way to successfully resist temptation was modeled by our Lord Jesus Christ when He was tempted. We must first understand our enemy's plan of attack and, secondly, make use of our spiritual resources.

Satan made a three-pronged assault on Jesus—the same three ways he tempts us. First, he tempted Jesus to doubt God's goodness by commanding the stones to become bread (Matt. 4:3). That implies that God didn't care enough about Jesus to provide for His physical needs. Second, he tempted Jesus to doubt God's love, suggesting that He test that love by leaping from the pinnacle of the temple (Matt. 4:5-6). Finally, he tempted Jesus to compromise God's truth, promising Him the kingdom without the cross if Jesus would worship him (Matt. 4:8-9).

To each of Satan's temptations, Jesus replied, "It is written" (Matt. 4:4, 7, 10). He thereby showed us the resource for defeating temptation: the Word of God (cf. Eph. 6:17). Do you find yourself overcome by temptation? Then follow our Lord's example and take up the sword of the Spirit today!

✧ ✧ ✧

Suggestions for Prayer: Pray that God would make you alert to Satan's attacks.

For Further Study: Make a list of specific verses you can use to combat the specific temptations you face.

*"Who among you is wise and understanding? Let him show by
his good behavior his deeds in the gentleness of wisdom."*

JAMES 3:13

✧ ✧ ✧

Wisdom is the art of living life skillfully.

Most philosophers throughout history have believed that if a person
could acquire anything, it should be wisdom, because wisdom would
allow him to obtain anything else. That philosophy matches Scripture.
Proverbs 4:7 says, "Acquire wisdom; and with all your acquiring, get understanding." Many people claim to be wise, but it's also true that no fool in our
world is a self-confessed fool—everyone believes he's an expert. The world
offers a sea of opinions, but the bottom line is that no one's opinion is worth
more than anyone else's.

The only trustworthy perspective on wisdom—on who is wise and who
isn't—is God's. In James 3:13 He gives His divine insight on the matter by
first asking, "Who among you is wise?" The Greek term translated "wise" is
sophos. The Greeks used it to refer to speculative knowledge, theory, and philosophy. But the Hebrews infused wisdom with a deeper meaning: skillfully
applying knowledge to the matter of practical living.

God also asked, "Who among you is . . . understanding?" The Greek word
translated "understanding" is used only here in the New Testament and refers
to a specialist or a professional who is highly skilled in applying his knowledge to practical situations. In other words, God is asking, "Who among you
has practical skill? Who among you is truly a professional and specialist in
the art of living?"

The only one who can live life skillfully is the one who lives according to
God's wisdom, and He gives His wisdom to all who receive His salvation and
obey His Word. What about you? Are you living life skillfully? If so, your life
will manifest good behavior and a meek spirit (James 3:13). Determine to live
your life according to God's wisdom, not the world's opinions.

✧ ✧ ✧

Suggestions for Prayer: Ask God to help you live life skillfully each day by
obeying His Word.

For Further Study: As a Christian, you are responsible to appropriate God's
wisdom in your life on a daily basis. To help you do so, begin a daily reading
program in Proverbs. Read one chapter a day, and let God's wisdom penetrate
every aspect of your life.

> *"Who among you is wise and understanding? Let him show by
> his good behavior his deeds in the gentleness of wisdom."*
> JAMES 3:13

✧ ✧ ✧

Divine wisdom produces a changed life.

The one who possesses godly wisdom will show it in his life. That's why James says, "Let him *show* by his good behavior his deeds" (3:13, emphasis added). The phrase "let him show" is a command to demonstrate one's wisdom and understanding. That is the thrust of James 2:14-26, summarized in verse 26: "Faith without works is dead." A person's claim to have faith will be validated by his works. Similarly, James is saying that if you claim to be wise, you need to demonstrate it. From God's perspective, wisdom is made manifest by the way a person conducts his life.

How will a person show he has true wisdom? By his "good behavior" (3:13). The Greek word translated "good" means "lovely," "beautiful," "attractive," "noble," or "excellent." The term translated "behavior" speaks of one's lifestyle or activity. If a person truly has divine wisdom and living faith, he will show it by his good conduct and excellent lifestyle.

James becomes specific when he says, "Let him show by his good behavior *his deeds*" (v. 13, emphasis added). He is focusing on the details. The wisdom of God alters not only your general conduct, but also what you do specifically. Every act within a person's life is consistent with how he conducts his entire life. If it's a life based on the wisdom of God, each aspect of his life will reveal that. The general pattern of his life and the specific things he does will reflect the work, the way, and the will of God. Take time to examine your life and see whether your conduct proves that you possess the true wisdom of God.

✧ ✧ ✧

Suggestions for Prayer: A wise person will manifest good behavior. Read Psalm 119:33-40, making the prayer of the psalmist your own.

For Further Study: Your conduct will reveal whether you're living wisely. What do the following verses say about how you should live: Philippians 1:27; 1 Timothy 4:12; 1 Peter 2:12; and 2 Peter 3:11?

> *"Who among you is wise and understanding? Let him show by*
> *his good behavior his deeds in the gentleness of wisdom."*
> JAMES 3:13

✧ ✧ ✧

A wise person is a gentle person.

A believer will demonstrate that he possesses the wisdom of God not only by his behavior, but also by his attitude. True wisdom is characterized by gentleness and is the opposite of self-promotion and arrogance. Gentleness is the trait that characterized our Lord. In Matthew 11:29 He says, "Take My yoke upon you, and learn from Me, for I am gentle and humble in heart." It is also a trait belonging to all the members of His kingdom. In Matthew 5:5 the Lord says, "Blessed are the gentle, for they shall inherit the earth." "Gentleness" is also a fruit of the Spirit (Gal. 5:23).

The word translated "gentleness" is from the Greek word *praus*, which can also be translated "meek" or "tender." *Praus* is often used of a gentle voice, a gentle breeze, or a gentle animal. It was also used of a horse that was broken. The Greeks characterized meekness as power under control; in the believer's case, that means being under the control of God. It's a freedom from malice, bitterness, or any desire for revenge. The only way to truly define meekness is in the context of relationships because it refers to how we treat others. It should characterize our relationship with both man and God.

How about your attitude? Is it characterized by meekness, humility, gentleness, and mildness, or do you tend to display an arrogant, selfish attitude toward others?

✧ ✧ ✧

Suggestions for Prayer: Christ is the perfect example of gentleness. Thank Him for this attribute, and ask Him to help you be like Him.

For Further Study: In 1 Thessalonians 2:7 what analogy does Paul use to characterize his ministry? ✧ Also read 2 Timothy 2:24 and Titus 3:2. To whom should we be gentle?

> *"Who among you is wise and understanding? Let him show by his good behavior his deeds in the gentleness of wisdom."*
>
> JAMES 3:13

❖ ❖ ❖

Wisdom teaches us how to handle adversity.

In his wonderful commentary on the book of James, Robert Johnstone wrote the following about meekness:

> *That "the meek" should "inherit the earth"—that they bear wrongs, and exemplify the love which "seeketh not her own"—to a world that believes in high-handedness and self-assertion, and pushing the weakest to the wall, a statement like this of the Lord from Heaven cannot but appear an utter paradox. The man of the world desires to be counted anything but "meek" or "poor in spirit," and would deem such a description of him equivalent to a charge of unmanliness.*
>
> *Ah, brethren, this is because we have taken in Satan's conception of manliness instead of God's. One man has been shown us by God, in whom His ideal of man was embodied; and He, when He was reviled, reviled not again; when He suffered, threatened not, but committed Himself to Him that judgeth righteously: He for those who nailed Him to the tree prayed, "Father, forgive them; for they know not what they do." The world's spirit of wrath, then, must be folly; whilst than a spirit of meekness like His, in the midst of controversy, oppositions, trials of whatever kind, there can be no surer evidence that "Jesus is made of God to His people wisdom"* (The Epistle of James *[Minneapolis: Klock & Klock, 1978], 272-273).*

Johnstone recognized more than a hundred years ago what we need to know today—that the wisdom of man is arrogant, conceited, and self-serving, whereas the wisdom of God is humble, meek, and non-retaliatory.

The contrast between false wisdom and true wisdom is crystal-clear. Be sure you handle adversity in a Christlike way, knowing that every detail of your life is under God's sovereign control.

❖ ❖ ❖

Suggestions for Prayer: Thank the Lord for His example of how to respond to adversity (cf. 1 Peter 2:21-24).

For Further Study: Read Philippians 2:1-11, applying Christ's example to your life (vv. 1-5).

"Fear God and keep His commandments."
ECCLESIASTES 12:13

❖ ❖ ❖

Living life apart from God is futile.

The Book of Ecclesiastes is greatly misunderstood. It is a difficult book to read simply because it is hard to understand. Everything in it appears wrong and as if it doesn't fit with the rest of Scripture. But it is part of the Old Testament wisdom literature because it is a statement of human wisdom. Ecclesiastes tells us how man perceives his world, God, and the realities of life.

Most scholars believe Ecclesiastes was penned by Solomon. They debate whether he wrote it before he was a true believer or after. He may have written it in retrospect, or he may have penned it sometime before he had a full understanding of the life-changing truth of God.

Ecclesiastes is a fascinating book because it reveals the folly, uselessness, senselessness, and frustration of human wisdom—that which James calls "earthly, natural, demonic" (James 3:15). In Ecclesiastes 1:16 Solomon says to himself, "Behold, I have magnified and increased wisdom more than all who were over Jerusalem before me." That verse shows me that when God initially gave Solomon wisdom, He gave it to him on a human level. He gave Solomon wisdom to make successful decisions and judgments as king. But although divine wisdom was available to him, I believe Solomon opted for human wisdom the greater portion of his life. And that wisdom was never able to answer his ultimate questions.

The sum of Solomon's perspective on human wisdom is in Ecclesiastes 4:2-3: "I congratulated the dead who are already dead more than the living who are still living. But better off than both of them is the one who has never existed." That's a death wish and is the logical end of worldly wisdom—futility.

Fortunately, Solomon did eventually embrace true wisdom. At the end of his book, he said, "The conclusion, when all has been heard, is: fear God and keep His commandments, because this applies to every person" (12:13). What then can satisfy your heart and make life worth living? The wisdom of God alone.

❖ ❖ ❖

Suggestions for Prayer: Ask God to help you follow His ways for a blessed and fulfilled life.

For Further Study: Read Proverbs 3:13-26, noting how the benefits of true wisdom are in contrast to what Solomon experienced.

"Where can wisdom be found?"

JOB 28:12

✧ ✧ ✧

Wisdom is found in a Person, not a place.

In ancient days men would drill a shaft deep into a mountain or the ground, suspend themselves with a rope, and hang in the shaft while they tried to find some metal or precious stone to mine. In the Old Testament Job described the process this way: "He [man] sinks a shaft far from habitation, forgotten by the foot; they hang and swing to and fro far from men" (Job 28:4). The miner searched far below the earth's surface for "anything precious" (v. 10).

Man goes to great efforts to search for precious metals. "But," Job says, "where can wisdom be found? And where is the place of understanding? Man does not know its value, nor is it found in the land of the living. . . . Pure gold cannot be given in exchange for it, nor can silver be weighed as its price" (vv. 12-13, 15). Nothing in the world can buy wisdom, and it can't be found in the things of the world.

So where does wisdom come from? Job says, "It is hidden from the eyes of all living. . . . Abaddon [Destruction] and Death say, 'With our ears we have heard a report of it.' God understands its way; and He knows its place" (vv. 21-23). If you are searching for wisdom, go to God. He knows where wisdom is because "He looks to the ends of the earth, and sees everything under the heavens. . . . And to man He said, 'Behold, the fear of the Lord, that is wisdom; and to depart from evil is understanding'" (vv. 24, 28).

What is true wisdom? To fear God and depart from evil. Wisdom isn't a question of how much you know, but of whether you love the Lord your God and depart from sin. Only when you pursue God will you know true wisdom.

✧ ✧ ✧

Suggestions for Prayer: Ask God to help you adorn your life with the ornaments of His true wisdom and have a winsome testimony that attracts others to Christ.

For Further Study: Read the following verses, noting how both the Old and New Testaments tell us that God is the source of true wisdom: Job 9:4; Psalm 104:24; Proverbs 3:19-20; Romans 11:33; Ephesians 3:10; 1 Timothy 1:17 (NKJV).

"The fear of the Lord, that is wisdom."
JOB 28:28

❖ ❖ ❖

Being wise begins with knowing God.

The fear of the Lord is the most basic idea related to wisdom and is the key to understanding it. The Book of Proverbs especially teaches us that the fear of the Lord is inextricably linked to wisdom: "The fear of the Lord is the beginning of knowledge; fools despise wisdom and instruction" (Prov. 1:7). *Knowledge, wisdom, instruction,* and *understanding* are often used as synonyms in Proverbs. The link between fear of the Lord and wisdom is also evident in Proverbs 9:10: "The fear of the Lord is the beginning of wisdom, and the knowledge of the Holy One is understanding." Since wisdom and understanding are parallel, so are the fear of the Lord and knowledge of the Holy One. To know God and to fear God are one and the same.

What does it mean to fear God? It's a reverential trust, or simply another way of describing saving faith. We begin to be wise when we revere God and trust in Him. When an Old Testament saint wanted to evangelize, he might have said, "Fear God!"

When you read in the Bible of people fearing God or that fearing God is linked to wisdom, that means a person can't even begin to be wise until he is first converted. Fearing God is the initiation of a life of faith. As long as a person has only human wisdom, he can't know God or true wisdom.

The fear of the Lord is your entrance to wisdom. It will prolong your life, fulfill your life, enrich your life—it *is* your life (cf. Prov. 10:27; 14:27). It will open the continual flow of God's wisdom to you. The significance of everything is tied to the wisdom of God, which alone will give you proper values, guidance, instruction, and perspective in life. Apply His wisdom to your life daily, and enjoy all the benefits that wisdom has to offer.

❖ ❖ ❖

Suggestions for Prayer: Praise God for His wisdom by which you are so abundantly blessed.

For Further Study: God's wisdom enriches our life and gives us proper values and instruction. Read Proverbs 10:1-12, and notice how that is so.

> *"The fear of the Lord is the beginning of wisdom; a good*
> *understanding have all those who do His commandments."*
> PSALM 111:10

❖ ❖ ❖

Saving faith is obedient faith.

The wisdom of God resulting from the fear of the Lord leads to obedience. When we fear the Lord, we submit to His wisdom and commit ourselves to keeping His commandments. In the New Testament Jesus said the same thing: "If you love Me, you will keep My commandments" (John 14:15). We aren't always as obedient as we ought to be, but the pattern of our lives turns from disobedience to a submissive heart of obedience. First John 2:3 says, "By this we know that we have come to know Him, if we keep His commandments." A person's claim to be a Christian is meaningless if he's not obedient.

From a positive perspective, fearing the Lord involves obeying His commandments; from a negative perspective, it involves turning away from evil. Job 28:28 says, "The fear of the Lord, that is wisdom; and to depart from evil is understanding." Equal to wisdom is understanding, and equal to fearing the Lord is departing from evil. Proverbs 8:13 says, "The fear of the Lord is to hate evil." Obeying the Lord's commandments and shunning evil are dynamics that work in the soul of one who truly fears God. The fear of the Lord is not some feeling you try to generate within yourself; it's the result of believing in the true God and living a life of love and obedience to Him. What about you? Does obedience to God's Word characterize your life?

❖ ❖ ❖

Suggestions for Prayer: Jesus Christ paid the price for your sin and ushered you into a relationship with God. Honor His work by obeying His Word, and ask Him to help you see evil from His perspective.

For Further Study: Read the following verses: Deuteronomy 6:1-2, 13-15, 24; 8:6; 10:12-13; 13:4; 17:19; 28:58-59; 31:12. What characterizes the life of a person who fears the Lord?

"Has not God madem foolish the wisdom of the world?"
1 CORINTHIANS 1:20

❖ ❖ ❖

Knowing Christ makes the believer
wiser than the world.

Lawrence Toombs, in his 1955 article "O.T. Theology and the Wisdom Literature," said, "Wisdom is to be found with God and nowhere else. And unless the quest for wisdom brings a man to his knees in awe and reverence, knowing his own helplessness to make himself wise, wisdom remains for him a closed book" (*The Journal of Bible and Religion*, 23:3 [July 1955], 195). It's wonderful to have the book of God's wisdom opened to us as believers.

Through God's book of wisdom it's easy for any believer to analyze the world. People who have no biblical background find it difficult to resolve controversial issues like capital punishment, abortion, or homosexuality. But the Bible has clear answers for those seemingly complex issues: If you take a life, you should die (Gen. 9:6); the life within the womb is a person made by God (Ps. 139:13); and homosexuality is not an alternate lifestyle but a damning sexual sin like adultery or fornication (1 Cor. 6:9-10; Rom. 1:26-27).

As a Bible-believing Christian you may not be considered "noble" or "mighty" by the world's standards (1 Cor. 1:26) and may be seen as the refuse of the world (1 Cor. 4:13); but you have the answers to the important questions. Because of God's sovereign, gracious work, you've been ushered into the wisdom of God through fear of the Lord. The apostle Paul said, "You are in Christ Jesus, who became to us wisdom from God" (1 Cor. 1:30). Once you fear God, His wisdom continually flows to you. Paul told the Colossians that in Christ dwells "all the treasures of wisdom and knowledge" (2:3). Since Christ dwells in you, you possess the very wisdom of God!

❖ ❖ ❖

Suggestions for Prayer: Praise the Lord for the privilege of knowing Him and His will through His Word and His Spirit. ❖ Pray that you might manifest the wisdom of the living God so that the world sees Christ in you.

For Further Study: Read 1 Corinthians 1:18-31. How does the apostle Paul contrast God's wisdom with the world's?

> *"If you have bitter jealousy and selfish ambition in your heart,*
> *do not be arrogant and so lie against the truth."*
>
> **JAMES 3:14**

❖ ❖ ❖

A wise person lives
for God and others, not for self.

Having characterized spiritual wisdom in the preceding verse, James begins to analyze worldly wisdom in verse 14. Worldly wisdom is not of God. It has no relationship to Him, is not obedient to Him, and has no knowledge of His truth.

What is the motive of someone who lives according to worldly wisdom? "Bitter jealousy and selfish ambition." The Greek word translated "bitter" also means "harsh" and is used of bitter, undrinkable water. "Bitter jealousy" carries the idea of a harsh, bitter self-centeredness that produces a resentful attitude toward others. People with bitter jealousy live in a world that focuses on themselves. They react in a jealous manner toward anyone who threatens their territory, accomplishments, or reputation. They resent anyone who threatens to crowd their slice of this world. They consider people who differ from them as implacable enemies. And they are bitterly jealous of anyone who is successful.

The Greek term translated "selfish ambition" refers to a personal ambition that creates rivalry, antagonism, or a party spirit. That's another way of pointing to self. The person who follows human wisdom begins with a "bitter jealousy" that creates an attitude of competition and conflict. Then "selfish ambition" generates a party spirit and bitterness toward others. James is saying that ungodly wisdom is self-centered, and its goal is personal gratification at any cost.

What about you? Are you motivated by jealousy and selfish ambition? Be honest in your evaluation. Take a serious inventory of your heart and ask yourself, *Am I serving others instead of fulfilling my own desires at the expense of others?*

❖ ❖ ❖

Suggestions for Prayer: Ask God to convict you when you put yourself before Him and others. ❖ Repent of any present situations in which you are doing that very thing.

For Further Study: Read the following verses: Genesis 37:4; 1 Samuel 18:8; Luke 15:25-30; 22:24. What was the sin in each example? ❖ Read and study 1 Corinthians 13:4-7 to learn how the qualities of love are opposite to human wisdom.

> *"If you have bitter jealousy and selfish ambition in your heart,*
> *do not be arrogant and so lie against the truth."*
> **JAMES 3:14**

✧ ✧ ✧

Humility is the hallmark
of a wise person.

James says that if a person has a self-centered motive for life, he should stop arrogantly boasting. He should stop claiming to possess true wisdom. Why? Because he is lying "against the truth." In verse 13 James indicates that if a person claims to have God's wisdom, he must show it. If I see you are motivated by self-centeredness and pride, you ought to stop your arrogant boasting about having the wisdom of God. The fact is, you're lying against what is obviously true. Stop claiming to have what you don't have.

"The truth" refers to the saving gospel. Both James 1:18 ("In the exercise of His will He brought us forth by the word of truth") and James 5:19 ("If any among you strays from the truth, and one turns him back . . .") link the truth with the gospel. Anyone who claims to have the wisdom of God but lives a life motivated by "bitter jealousy and selfish ambition" is obviously lying in the face of the gospel. No pretentious claims to a possession of divine wisdom are convincing when they come out of a heart totally motivated by human wisdom.

James is calling you to take an inventory of your heart. Take a look at yourself. What motivates you? Are you motivated by the things that honor God? Are you motivated by a love for others? Are you motivated by humility and unselfishness? There is no single characteristic of unredeemed man more obvious than his pride. And there is nothing more characteristically evident of a redeemed person than his humility.

✧ ✧ ✧

Suggestions for Prayer: Ask God to help you have a humble attitude and make you more aware of how you can serve Him and others every day.

For Further Study: The wise person seeks to be humble. To help you manifest humility in your life, meditate on the following verses: Proverbs 16:19; 22:4; Isaiah 57:15; Micah 6:8; Matthew 18:4; James 4:10; 1 Peter 5:5. ✧ Memorize at least one Old Testament verse and one New Testament verse from this list.

> *"This wisdom is not that which comes down*
> *from above, but is earthly, natural, demonic."*
> JAMES 3:15

❖ ❖ ❖

True wisdom is from God;
false wisdom is from the Devil.

Wisdom that is bitterly jealous and self-centered is not "from above." Such traits constitute a wisdom that doesn't come from God, the source of true wisdom (cf. 1:5, 17). Human wisdom, rather than being from above, is "earthly" (3:15). It is limited to the sphere of time and space and marked by the curse of man's own fallenness, which is characterized by pride and self-centeredness. Everything the world initiates in the way of supposed truth is self-centered. Unregenerate man's finite system demands an earthly wisdom and nothing more.

Man's wisdom is also "natural" (v. 15), which means "fleshly" and refers to man's humanness and frailty. First Corinthians 2:14 says, "A natural man does not accept the things of the Spirit of God." The natural man is sensual. All his feelings, impulses, and appetites are locked up in a fallen and corrupted system. All of man's wisdom comes from his unsanctified heart and unredeemed spirit.

Besides being earthly and natural, human wisdom is "demonic" (James 3:15). This is the only place in the New Testament where the Greek word translated "demon" appears in its adjectival form. Human wisdom is actually generated by demons, who have been made captive to the same evil system as man. Satan and his agents disguise themselves as ministers of light when in fact they are ministers of darkness (2 Cor. 11:14-15).

The wisdom of the world is spawned by demons, reflects man's humanness, and proceeds no further than the fallenness of mankind. Since that is so, be sure to "be strong in the Lord, and in the strength of His might" (Eph. 6:10). Don't let Satan and the world beguile you with their so-called wisdom.

❖ ❖ ❖

Suggestions for Prayer: Pray to be "filled with the knowledge of His will in all spiritual wisdom and understanding, so that you may walk in a manner worthy of the Lord" (Col. 1:9-10).

For Further Study: According to 2 Corinthians 10:3-5 and Colossians 2:8, how is the believer to fight against Satan and his demonic wisdom?

> *"Where jealousy and selfish ambition exist,*
> *there is disorder and every evil thing."*
> JAMES 3:16

✧ ✧ ✧

False wisdom ruins lives.

R enowned eighteenth-century theologian Jonathan Edwards said the following about the effect of the Fall on man:

> *Sin, like some powerful astringent, contracted his soul to the very small dimensions of selfishness; and God was forsaken, and fellow-creatures forsaken, and man retired within himself, and became totally governed by narrow and selfish principles and feelings. Self-love became absolute master of his soul, and the more noble and spiritual principles of his being took wings and flew away.*

Edwards's analysis certainly agrees with what James is saying: man is self-centered (cf. James 3:14, 16). Where self-centeredness exists, there will be negative results. One such result is "disorder" (v. 16). The term refers to disorder that comes out of instability and chaos. Earthly wisdom will never produce harmony or love because it's proud and self-indulgent. It destroys intimacy, love, unity, and fellowship, and in its place brings discord and chaos. You can see the result of earthly wisdom all over our world today. Anger, bitterness, lawsuits, and divorces are just part of the legacy.

"Every evil thing" also results from earthly wisdom (v. 16). The phrase speaks of something worthless or vile. Greek scholar R.C. Trench said it contemplates evil, "not so much that either of active or passive malignity, but rather of its good-for-nothingness, the impossibility of any true gain ever coming forth from it." The Greek word translated "thing" implies that false wisdom produces nothing of any practical value. At its best it produces worthless things; at its worst it produces vile things.

Which kind of life do you prefer? One that is characterized by love and unity, or by instability and chaos? A life with fulfillment and meaning, or with emptiness? If you want a life that satisfies and has eternal value, choose divine wisdom!

✧ ✧ ✧

Suggestions for Prayer: Thank God for giving you His Word so you can know how to live wisely and avoid the negative results of man's wisdom.

For Further Study: Following human wisdom leads only to evil. Memorize Proverbs 4:27 to help you stay on the path of true wisdom.

"The wisdom from above is first pure."

JAMES 3:17

✧ ✧ ✧

A pure life is necessary for a wise life.

A person whose life is characterized by true wisdom will seek to be pure. The Greek word translated "pure" in James 3:17 refers to spiritual integrity and moral sincerity. It is freedom from bitter jealousy, selfish ambition, and arrogant self-promotion. Christ is the perfect example of purity (1 John 3:3).

A true believer will have pure desires. The deepest part of him desires to do God's will, serve God, and love God. In Romans 7:15-21 the apostle Paul testifies that when he sinned, he was doing what he didn't want to do. In Psalm 51:7 David cries out, "Purify me with hyssop, and I shall be clean; wash me, and I shall be whiter than snow." The true believer hates his sin. Rising out of his innermost being is a longing for what is clean, pure, holy, and honest.

Purity of heart is the motive of someone who seeks to live a life of godly wisdom (cf. Ps. 24:3-4). God says he will "take the heart of stone out of their flesh and give them a heart of flesh" (Ezekiel 11:19); that new heart will be consumed with purity rather than self. You do still sin because your new heart is incarcerated in your old flesh. But your new heart fights against your flesh. That's why Paul said, "I joyfully concur with the law of God in the inner man, but I see a different law in the members of my body, waging war against the law of my mind, and making me a prisoner of the law of sin which is in my members" (Rom. 7:22-23).

In the Sermon on the Mount Jesus said, "Blessed are the pure in heart, for they shall see God" (Matthew 5:8). As you persevere in battle against the world, the flesh, and the Devil, be encouraged by reminding yourself that one day the fight will be finished. The apostle John said it this way: "We know that, when He appears, we shall be like Him, because we shall see Him just as He is" (1 John 3:2).

✧ ✧ ✧

Suggestions for Prayer: Read Psalm 51:1-17, making David's prayer your own.

For Further Study: According to Matthew 5:48 and 1 Peter 1:15-16, what is God's standard of purity?

> *"The wisdom from above is first pure, then peaceable,*
> *gentle, reasonable, full of mercy and good fruits,*
> *unwavering, without hypocrisy."*
> JAMES 3:17

✧ ✧ ✧

True wisdom is evident in a person's behavior.

What is true wisdom? James answers that question in verse 17 by pointing out the characteristics or qualities of true wisdom. After purity, the next quality is "peaceable," which means "peace loving" or "peace promoting." It refers to someone who doesn't create confusion or disorder. He doesn't promote himself or compromise truth but makes peace.

True wisdom is also "gentle." A gentle person will submit to dishonor, disgrace, mistreatment, and persecution with an attitude of humility, courteousness, kindness, patience, and consideration. He will not display hatred, malice, or revenge.

True wisdom is also characterized as "reasonable." It refers to someone who is willing to yield, who is easily persuaded, teachable, and compliant. It was used of a person who willingly submitted to military discipline or who observed legal and moral standards in life and willingly submitted to them. A wise person manifests such "reasonable" traits concerning God's standards for life.

"Full of mercy" refers to someone who shows concern for people who suffer and is quick to forgive. He demonstrates kindness and compassion toward others.

"Good fruits" refer to all good works in general or a wide variety of spiritual deeds. The Christian demonstrates the genuineness of his salvation through his good deeds—works that are produced by faith (James 2:14-20) and are called "the fruit of the Spirit" (Gal. 5:22-23) or "the fruit of righteousness" (Phil. 1:11).

"Unwavering" refers to someone who is consistent and doesn't vacillate. He is undivided in his commitment, doesn't make unfair distinctions, and is sincere in his faithfulness to God.

"Without hypocrisy" is the climax of true wisdom and speaks of someone who is utterly genuine. He isn't a phony or fake. A truly wise person manifests sincere behavior.

If true wisdom is part of your life, it will be evident in your behavior. Make it your aim to reflect the qualities of true wisdom so that others may see Christ in you.

✧ ✧ ✧

Suggestions for Prayer: Ask God to help you develop the qualities of true wisdom in your life. But before you do, make sure you're being motivated by a pure heart.

For Further Study: Read Matthew 5:1-16, noting how the words of Christ parallel James 3:17.

> *"The seed whose fruit is righteousness*
> *is sown in peace by those who make peace."*
> JAMES 3:18

❖ ❖ ❖

A wise life is a righteous life.

Puritan minister Richard Baxter said, "Wisdom is honorable because it is the skill of doing good." Like Baxter, James also sees a connection between wisdom and doing good. James 3:18 is in the present tense and literally reads, "The fruit of righteousness is being sown in peace by them that make peace." At first glance it seems strange that James would say the "fruit of righteousness is being sown" because usually seed is sown. But harvested fruit also becomes seed for the next crop. The fruit of righteousness is sown again in peace by those who make peace.

Where true wisdom exists, true righteousness follows. And that becomes seed and generates more righteousness. That's the law of sowing and reaping. It is a continual cycle: one righteous act harvested from the field of true wisdom becomes the seed to grow another righteous act. Those who make peace receive the benefit from it, and righteousness flourishes in a climate of peace. The bottom line is that peacemakers aren't preoccupied with themselves.

The life of a farmer illustrates what James is saying. The seeds that a farmer plants in the spring are what he eventually harvests in the fall. Similarly, by sowing righteous deeds each day of your life, you can be assured of what you'll reap: a life that reflects true wisdom. Make it your aim to live righteously!

❖ ❖ ❖

Suggestions for Prayer: Worship the Lord for being righteous, and ask Him to help you obey His Word and live a righteous life.

For Further Study: James follows a clear line of thought: if one professes to be a Christian, he must prove it by living like a Christian. According to 1 John 3:7-10, what proves a person is a true believer?

"Wisdom is too high for a fool."
PROVERBS 24:7

✧ ✧ ✧

A fool wants his own way.

There's no question in my mind that we live in a world of fools. In fact, everyone born into this world comes in with congenital foolishness—otherwise known as the sin nature. Proverbs 22:15 says, "Foolishness is bound up in the heart of a child." Since we live in a world of fools, let's look at a few of their characteristics.

A fool denies God. Psalm 14:1 says, "The fool has said in his heart, 'There is no God.' They are corrupt, they have committed abominable deeds; there is no one who does good." I call this practical atheism. A fool lives as if there were no God—denying God with his actions.

A fool becomes his own god. Proverbs 12:15 says, "The way of a fool is right in his own eyes." No man can live without a god. It isn't a question of, does he worship? It's a question of, whom does he worship? If a person doesn't worship the true God, he will worship a false god—which inevitably will be a reflection of himself. He becomes the one who determines truth and error, articulating his own standards for living.

A fool mocks sin. Proverbs 14:9 says, "Fools mock at sin." Since a fool makes his own rules, he wants to justify his own behavior to make sure he's going to be all right in the end. He attempts to eliminate sin along with its consequences.

A fool, then, begins by living as if there were no God, substituting himself as god and determining his own style of life. Then he denies the existence of sin because he cannot tolerate guilt.

When God saved you, you stopped your foolishness and became His wise child. Be encouraged, knowing God will continue to help you grow in wisdom through your understanding of and obedience to His Word.

✧ ✧ ✧

Suggestions for Prayer: Pray for the salvation of a family member, friend, or neighbor who is living foolishly.

For Further Study: Read Matthew 7:24-27. What is the difference between a wise man and a foolish man?

*"The tongue of the righteous is as choice silver,
the heart of the wicked is worth little."*
PROVERBS 10:20

✧ ✧ ✧

A fool desires to share his folly with others.

Proverbs 1:7 says, "The fear of the Lord is the beginning of knowledge; fools despise wisdom and instruction." Wisdom, as defined in the Book of Proverbs, is living by divine standards, which implies accepting divine truth. But a fool rejects that. First Corinthians 2:14 says that "a natural man does not accept the things of the Spirit of God; for they are foolishness to him." To a fool, foolishness is wisdom and wisdom is foolishness.

That a fool rejects God's wisdom is evident by the way he speaks. Proverbs 15:2 says, "The tongue of the wise makes knowledge acceptable, but the mouth of fools spouts folly." In other words, a fool is quick to air his opinions. Just as a bitter fountain produces bitter water, and a rotten tree produces rotten fruit, so also a fool produces foolishness—speaking on his own authority and generating his own opinions. The world is full of the opinions of fools—fools who have denied God in their living, who have become their own gods, and who mock the reality and consequences of sin.

A fool not only is quick to air his opinions but also propagates his foolishness to others. Proverbs 16:22 says that the instruction of fools is folly. The fool contaminates the rest of society with the same foolishness that damns his own soul. He leaves it as a legacy to his children, his friends, and all those who fall under the influence of his folly.

In contrast to fools, you as a believer are blessed to have the Spirit of wisdom indwelling you and illuminating your understanding of His Word. Your words to others are based on the wisdom of Scripture, not empty speculation. By bringing His Word to mind in every circumstance, you can speak words that are "like apples of gold in settings of silver" (Prov. 25:11).

✧ ✧ ✧

Suggestions for Prayer: Thank God for teaching us how we should speak—and not speak—through His Word.

For Further Study: What does Colossians 4:6 say about our speech? ✧ What further insight do each of these verses add: Matthew 12:36; Mark 9:50; Ephesians 4:29?

*"Therefore be careful how you walk,
not as unwise men, but as wise."*
EPHESIANS 5:15

✧ ✧ ✧

Living wisely will set you apart from the world.

Walking in wisdom is an element of the worthy walk that Paul has been describing since the beginning of Ephesians 4. He says in verse 1, "Walk in a manner worthy of the calling with which you have been called" and then proceeds to describe this worthy walk with the following characteristics: It's a *humble* walk (4:1-3), a *united* walk (4:4-16), a *unique* walk (4:17-32), a *loving* walk (5:1-7), an *illuminated* walk (5:8-14), and a *wise* walk (5:15-17). The point that Paul is making in describing the various elements of the worthy walk is that Christians are different from the world. The world can't be humble because everyone is fighting for his rights. The world can't be united because it celebrates and exalts differences. The world can't be unique because it's trapped in its own self-destruction. The world can't love because it doesn't have the life of God—the source of real love. The world can't know light because it lies in the system of darkness. And the world can't be wise because the wisdom of God is hidden from the mind of man. As Paul says in 2 Timothy 3:7, "always learning and never able to come to the knowledge of the truth."

Realize that being different from the world is an asset to your Christian witness, not a hindrance. When others see you obeying Scripture—when they see you walking in wisdom—they'll notice you're not like them. That difference can create opportunities to tell them about your Savior. Jesus said, "Let your light shine before men in such a way that they may see your good works, and glorify your Father who is in heaven" (Matthew 5:16). Keep walking in wisdom, and let others be attracted to the light of Christ!

✧ ✧ ✧

Suggestions for Prayer: Ask God to help you be a witness whose testimony shines brightly for Christ.

For Further Study: How does 1 Peter 2:12 say you are to live? Why?

> *"Therefore be careful how you walk,*
> *not as unwise men, but as wise."*
> EPHESIANS 5:15

❖ ❖ ❖

Every believer is responsible to walk wisely.

I believe the moment an individual becomes saved, God deposits enough wisdom in him to make him absolutely responsible for his behavior. Someone may say, "Wait a minute! How can a brand-new believer walk in wisdom? Doesn't he grow into that? Haven't wise Christians been saved for many years?"

Such questions miss the point of Ephesians 5:15. The first word in this verse takes us back to Paul's invitation to become saved in verse 14: "Awake, sleeper, and arise from the dead, and Christ will shine on you." In other words, Paul is saying, "Because you are saved, you are to walk in wisdom." When you received Christ, you simultaneously received wisdom and therefore are responsible to walk wisely. First Corinthians 1:30 says, "By [God's] doing you are in Christ Jesus, who became to us wisdom from God, and righteousness and sanctification, and redemption." At the moment of salvation you are made wise, righteous, and sanctified. You don't get redeemed first and receive those things later. Colossians 2:3 says, "In [Christ] are hidden all the treasures of wisdom and knowledge." You are in Christ, and all the treasures of wisdom and knowledge are in Him; consequently, "in Him you have been made complete" (v. 10).

If you're redeemed, you have wisdom. You don't have to wait till you've been saved five, ten, or forty years. You're no longer a fool— you're wise. And on that basis Paul says, "Walk as wise. Live according to the wisdom that you possess."

❖ ❖ ❖

Suggestions for Prayer: Thank God for blessing you with His great salvation so that you can walk wisely.

For Further Study: Read Ephesians 1:7-8. What did you receive at the moment of your salvation (v. 7)? ❖ In what two ways were the riches of God's grace lavished on you (v. 8)? ❖ According to Titus 2:11-12, what does God's grace teach you?

"Grow in the grace and knowledge
of our Lord and Savior Jesus Christ."
2 PETER 3:18

❖ ❖ ❖

Growing in wisdom
means growing in Christlikeness.

Perhaps you're asking, "Shouldn't believers acquire more wisdom?" Yes, we should. No matter how much of God's wisdom we have, we should always hunger for more. The Bible tells us that we have all the principles we need to walk in wisdom, and yet there's much more available to us. We should "grow in the grace and knowledge of our Lord and Savior Jesus Christ" (2 Peter 3:18), and we should be more and more conformed to the image of Christ by the transforming work of the Spirit of God. Our wisdom should increase, as should our godliness, but we are given the basic principles at salvation. Even though a person may not know all the truths in the Bible, God's Spirit, who is resident in him from the moment of salvation, will convict and convince him of righteousness and sin.

What do you do if you want more wisdom? First, *worship*. Proverbs 9:10 says, "The fear of the Lord is the beginning of wisdom." Make it your goal to have a worshipful heart throughout each day and to be faithful in attending the Lord's house regularly (see Heb. 10:25). Second, *pray*. James 1:5 says, "If any of you lacks wisdom, let him ask of God, who gives to all men generously and without reproach, and it will be given to him." Make it your continual prayer to ask God for more of His wisdom. Third, *receive instruction*. The apostle Paul encouraged "admonishing every man and teaching every man with all wisdom" (Col. 1:28). If you want more wisdom, one good way to receive it is to be instructed by someone who is wise. Finally, *study Scripture*. In 2 Timothy 2:15 Paul says, "Be diligent to present yourself approved to God as a workman who does not need to be ashamed, handling accurately the word of truth." Set up a regular Bible study time, and let the Holy Spirit teach you.

What about you? Are you growing in wisdom? If not, make it your priority.

❖ ❖ ❖

Suggestions for Prayer: Ask God to help you grow in wisdom.

For Further Study: Make it your daily goal to implement the four ways mentioned in today's lesson for growing in wisdom.

> *"Therefore be careful how you walk,*
> *not as unwise men, but as wise."*
> EPHESIANS 5:15

❖ ❖ ❖

Walking wisely is a step in the right direction.

Sometimes a soldier has the thankless task of clearing mine fields from enemy territory. If you're aware of the procedure, you know the work is both dangerous and tedious. To proceed in an orderly fashion, a soldier marks areas that are considered dangerous and areas that have been cleared. Above all, he makes sure he is careful where he's walking!

In the spiritual realm, Paul is telling believers in Ephesians 5:15 to walk carefully. The Greek term translated "careful" speaks of looking carefully from side to side and being alert to what is going on. We need to be extremely alert because the world we're walking through is a mine field of sin and temptation. Therefore, we must walk carefully, exactly, and accurately. The wise Christian carefully charts his course according to life principles designed by God. He doesn't trip over the obstacles that Satan puts in his path or fall into the entanglement of the world's system. He is "careful."

The Greek word translated "walk" means "daily conduct," "daily pattern," or "daily life." The daily pattern of our lives must reflect wisdom. The Greeks saw wisdom primarily as head knowledge. They tended to spin off theories that had no practical implications. To them, the wise people were the intellectuals and the philosophers. The Hebrew mind, however, defined wisdom only in terms of behavior. When a person becomes a Christian, it's more than a change in theory—it's a change in how he lives.

Paul is saying in verse 15, "If you used to be a fool, but you've been made wise in Christ, then walk wisely." In other words, we're to practice our position, to live in accordance with who we are. When we became Christians, we came out of foolishness into wisdom. Therefore, we need to act like it!

Be careful not to act foolishly and step on Satan's mines. Your spiritual transformation demands that you live your life with care.

❖ ❖ ❖

Suggestions for Prayer: Thank the Lord for helping you obey His Word and avoid Satan's destructive mines.

For Further Study: Read Titus 3:1-8. What are you to be careful to do (v. 8)? Why?

> *"Behold, I have played the fool."*
> 1 SAMUEL 26:21

❖ ❖ ❖

A Christian should not act like a fool.

I n Deuteronomy 32:6 Moses looked out at the belligerent children of Israel who had failed God so many times and said, "Do you thus repay the Lord, O foolish and unwise people?" The children of Israel were playing the fool. Sadly, God's people today continue to play the fool.

One way they do so is through *disbelief*. On the road to Emmaus, Jesus appeared to two disciples who didn't believe that He had risen from the dead. Jesus said to them, "O foolish men and slow of heart to believe in all that the prophets have spoken!" (Luke 24:25). To disbelieve God and His Word is to play the fool.

Another way believers play the fool is through *disobedience*. In Galatians 3:1 the apostle Paul says, "You foolish Galatians, who has bewitched you, before whose eyes Jesus Christ was publicly portrayed as crucified?" And in verse 3 he says, "Are you so foolish? Having begun by the Spirit, are you now being perfected by the flesh?" They started out well but were disobedient and got caught up in the works of the law.

Still another way Christians play the fool is through *desire for the wrong things*. First Timothy 6:9 says, "Those who want to get rich fall into temptation and a snare and many foolish and harmful desires." If you desire the wrong things, you play the fool.

Finally, you can play the fool through *doing the wrong things*. James 3:13-17 says that there are two kinds of wisdom. Godly wisdom produces "good behavior" (v. 13), but foolish wisdom produces "jealousy and selfish ambition" (v. 16). A self-centered person plays the fool.

It's sad to see so many Christians playing the fool. It doesn't make any sense. Why should Christians live as blind, ignorant, foolish people when they have the wisdom of God?

Paul says at the end of Romans, "I want you to be wise in what is good, and innocent in what is evil" (16:19). If you have to be a fool at all, be a fool (unknowing, unacquainted) about evil.

❖ ❖ ❖

Suggestions for Prayer: Make Paul's exhortation in Romans 16:19 your prayer.

For Further Study: Read Proverbs 2:1-22 as a reminder of what benefits you'll receive from following true wisdom instead of playing the fool.

"Bodily discipline is only of little profit, but godliness is profitable for all things, since it holds promise for the present life and also for the life to come."
1 TIMOTHY 4:8

✧ ✧ ✧

Godliness should be the believer's priority in life.

I'm amazed at how devoted people can be to what they believe is important. There are many people outside Christianity who live in rigid conformity to a lot of meaningless rules. People in totalitarian countries, for example, live in rigid conformity to rules predicated on a denial of biblical truth. They walk circumspectly and toe the mark.

Some cultists are so rigid and walk so circumspectly according to the principles dictated to them that if they're told they can't get married or can't be with their spouses, they conform. They're made to live in abstinence from physical relationships, follow strict diets, fast, and so on. Some attempt to attain spirituality through such self-disciplined acts as lying on a bed of nails or walking through hot coals.

Others, such as athletes, go through tremendous self-discipline through dieting, running, weight training, and other means that involve great sacrifice.

People disciplined in things that are ultimately meaningless may be lax in things that count. I know people who run three miles every day but will not bother to read the Bible regularly. I know other people who cannot discipline themselves to feed on the Word of God but stick rigorously to a diet. Many Christians worship physical fitness and health and are so conformed to the world's system that they're careless and lazy about conforming to Christ.

If you are a wise Christian, you'll be sure to discipline yourself for godliness. You'll know what pleases God, watch for Satan's traps, resist the Devil, defeat temptation, and be selective about your behavior. In other words, you'll not walk as a fool; you'll walk in wisdom—living by God's standards.

✧ ✧ ✧

Suggestions for Prayer: Thank God for His Son, the perfect example of spiritual discipline and godliness. Ask God to help you be like Him.

For Further Study: According to 1 Timothy 4:7, what is the purpose of spiritual discipline? ✧ According to 2 Peter 1:3, what has God's divine power granted us?

"Making the most of your time,
because the days are evil."
EPHESIANS 5:16

✧ ✧ ✧

God expects the believer to use his time wisely.

Many people never finish what they begin. There are unfinished symphonies, unfinished paintings, and unfinished sculptures (sometimes because the composer or artist died). There are relationships that never become all they could be, ministries that never come to fruition, dreams that always remain dreams, and hopes that always remain hopes. For a lot of people, life can be an unfinished symphony or a dream without reality. But it doesn't have to be that way. I believe the answer can be found in the phrase "making the most of your time" (Eph. 5:16).

If we are ever to turn our dreams into realities and our hopes into facts—to finish our symphonies, paint our paintings, and sculpt our sculptures—it will be only when we have made the most of our time. I believe that in eternity past, God prescribed the specific time that we are to live. And only as we maximize that time can we maintain its potential for fulfillment.

The apostle Paul knew firsthand the importance of redeeming his time. In Acts 20:24 he says, "I do not consider my life of any account as dear to myself, in order that I may finish my course, and the ministry which I received from the Lord Jesus." In other words, God has given us a time boundary, and within that time He has defined a course. Paul in effect said, "I want to finish the specific course and specific ministry in the specific time given to me." At the end of his life Paul could say, "I have finished the course" (2 Tim. 4:7). He completed the race because he made the most of his time.

I believe God has sovereignly given you and me a specific period of time. He knows the beginning and the end because He predetermined both. Be sure to finish your prescribed race by walking wisely and living for His glory.

✧ ✧ ✧

Suggestions for Prayer: Thank the Lord for sovereignly giving you a course to run in life. ✧ Pray for His perfect will to be reflected in your life as you run the course.

For Further Study: Read 1 Peter 1:17-19. According to verse 17, how are you to live "during the time of your stay upon earth"? Why?

> *"Making the most of your time,*
> *because the days are evil."*
> EPHESIANS 5:16

✧ ✧ ✧

Seize opportunities every day to glorify God.

In one of the cities of ancient Greece stood a statue carved by Lysippos, a famous Greek sculptor from the fourth century B.C. The statue had wings on its feet and a great lock of hair on its forehead and was bald on the back of its head. This is how it was described:

> *Who . . . was thy sculptor?*
> *Lysippos . . .*
> *And who art thou?*
> *Occasion [or opportunity], the all-subduer . . .*
> *Why hast thou wings . . . on thy feet?*
> *I fleet on the wings of the wind . . .*
> *And thy hair, why grows it in front?*
> *For him that meets me, to seize . . .*
> *And why is the back of thy head bald?*
> *Because none may clutch me from behind, howsoe'er he desire*
> *it, when once my winged feet have darted past him.*

That fictional character knew how to make the most of every opportunity. In real life, the apostle Paul is calling for you to take advantage of opportunities by "making the most of your time" (Eph. 5:16). The Greek word translated "time" isn't the Greek word *chronos*, which refers to time in terms of a clock or calendar. It's the word *kairos*, which means "eras," "epochs," or "periods." Making the most of your time is another way of saying you are to make the most of your opportunities—opportunities that can be grasped for God, for His glory.

The psalmist had the right perspective when he prayed, "Teach us to number our days, that we may present to Thee a heart of wisdom" (Ps. 90:12). Wisdom numbers the days, sees the limited time, and buys the opportunity. Don't be foolish—shun opportunities for evil, but seize opportunities for good.

✧ ✧ ✧

Suggestions for Prayer: Pray through Psalm 90:12 and apply it to yourself.

For Further Study: In Colossians 4:5, what does Paul tell the believers to do?

*"Making the most of your time,
because the days are evil."*
EPHESIANS 5:16

✧ ✧ ✧

Evil days call for good behavior.

The days we live in are certainly full of evil. Read any newspaper, and you'll know what I mean. Can you imagine how it breaks God's heart to create a perfect world, filled with every good thing, and then see it become as corrupt, debauched, and vile as it is today? Can you imagine how it must be for God to watch Christians who, in the midst of this evil world, are given opportunities to do good, yet bypass them without notice? The days are evil, and God gives us these opportunities to make things happen that matter—to fill up at least one moment of every day with something good, something righteous, something for Him.

"Because the days are evil," the apostle Paul says in Ephesians 5:16, it's important to walk wisely and make the most of our time. When opportunities for goodness do come, we should seize them. When God gives us an occasion to glorify Him (which in turn will bring a blessing on us), we must take the opportunity for His name's sake. We must seize it in the midst of an evil day.

When I think of how God's heart is broken over the evil of a world that He made for His own glory, I say to myself, *If God gives me one small opportunity in the midst of an evil day to do something good, something to honor Him, or something to glorify Him, I'm going to grab that opportunity*. Since the days are evil and it seems as though goodness is so scarce, you and I need to take every opportunity we can for manifesting goodness.

✧ ✧ ✧

Suggestions for Prayer: Ask the Lord to help you be aware of more opportunities that you can seize for manifesting goodness.

For Further Study: According to Genesis 6:5, what did the Lord see in the days of Noah? ✧ What effect did that have on God (v. 6)? ✧ According to Hebrews 11:7, what did Noah do? ✧ What effect did Noah have on the world?

"You have left your first love."
REVELATIONS 2:4

✧ ✧ ✧

A wise person loves Christ supremely.

Because the days were evil, the apostle Paul wanted the church at Ephesus to make the most of their time and walk wisely (Eph. 5:15-16). A little more than thirty years after Paul wrote his letter to the Ephesian church, the apostle John wrote more to them, saying, "You have left your first love. . . . Repent and do the deeds you did at first; or else I [Christ] am coming to you, and will remove your lampstand out of its place—unless you repent" (Rev. 2:4-5). But the Ephesians did not repent, and the lampstand was removed. Their time was shorter than they believed, because the evil was so great. Their church fell prey to the time in which they lived and, not sensing the urgency to return to its first love, eventually went out of existence.

I believe we need to have a sense of urgency in the evil days in which we live. I don't know what's going to happen to Christianity in America, but I've asked God that if it takes persecution to bring us to the place where we get a grip on what we ought to be, then let it happen. In many cases throughout history, the church has thrived better under persecution than it has under affluence. As the church father Tertullian once said, "The blood of the martyrs is the seed of the church."

I'm not specifically asking that the church be persecuted. I'm saying that sometimes we don't sense the urgency of our evil day because we are sucked into the world's system, and the lines of conviction aren't clearly drawn. It's an evil day in which we live, and the time is short. We need to realize that "evil men and impostors will proceed from bad to worse" (2 Tim. 3:13). The situation is not going to become better. The world is blacker and more expressive of its vices than ever before. We must have a sense of urgency and redeem the time.

✧ ✧ ✧

Suggestions for Prayer: In Psalm 145, King David expressed his love for the Lord. Make his psalm your prayer and an expression of your love to God.

For Further Study: Read in Revelation 2—3 what the Lord says to the seven churches in Asia, noting what He approves and disapproves.

> *"Making the most of your time,*
> *because the days are evil."*
> EPHESIANS 5:16

❖ ❖ ❖

Time will tell whether you're unselfish or selfish.

In 1842 Robert Murray M'Cheyne, pastor of St. Peter's Church in Dundee, Scotland, wrote a pastoral letter to an individual who was an unbeliever. The following is an excerpt from his letter:

> *I was reading this morning (Luke ii. 29), what old Simeon said when he got the child Jesus into his arms: "Now lettest Thou Thy servant depart in peace, according to Thy word: for mine eyes have seen Thy salvation." If you get a firm hold of the Lord Jesus, you will be able to say the same. . . . God is leading you to the very spot where the Redeemer is,—a lowly, despised, spit-upon, crucified Saviour. Can this be the Saviour of the world? Yes, dear soul; kneel down and call Him your Redeemer. He died for such as you and me.*

M'Cheyne lived unselfishly, caring for the spiritual welfare of both believers and unbelievers. Because of poor health, he died at age twenty-nine after ministering but a short seven and a half years. His spiritual legacy of passionate love for the Lord and pastoral love for people continues to serve as an inspiring example for believers today.

M'Cheyne's life illustrates what the apostle Paul was saying to the Ephesian believers: make the most of your time. In Ephesians 5:16 the Greek term translated "making the most of" means "buy up for yourself." That doesn't mean you're to hoard your time for your own use; rather, you're to buy up for yourself time that will give God glory. Every day brings new opportunities to be seized for God—opportunities for good, for righteousness, for holiness.

Like M'Cheyne, buy up opportunities daily for God's glory and the good of others. Be committed to minister to the spiritual needs of believers and unbelievers. By doing so, you will make your time count for eternity.

❖ ❖ ❖

Suggestions for Prayer: Ask God to help you be unselfish and serve others effectively by His grace.

For Further Study: Read the following verses: Galatians 6:10; 1 Corinthians 10:24; Philippians 2:3-4. How do they say you are to live?

*"Do not be foolish, but understand
what the will of the Lord is."*
EPHESIANS 5:17

✧ ✧ ✧

God's will is revealed in His Word.

How can a Christian walk wisely and know the will of God for his life? The will of God is explicitly revealed to us in the pages of Scripture. God's will is that we be:

Saved—"This is good and acceptable in the sight of God our Savior, who desires all men to be saved and to come to the knowledge of the truth" (1 Tim. 2:3-4; compare 2 Peter 3:9).

Spirit-filled—"Do not be foolish, but understand what the will of the Lord is. And do not get drunk with wine, for that is dissipation, but be filled with the Spirit" (Eph. 5:17-18).

Sanctified—"This is the will of God, your sanctification" (1 Thess. 4:3).

Submissive—"Submit yourselves for the Lord's sake to every human institution, whether to a king as the one in authority, or to governors as sent by him for the punishment of evildoers and the praise of those who do right. For such is the will of God" (1 Peter 2:13-15).

Suffering for His sake—"It is better, if God should will it so, that you suffer for doing what is right rather than for doing what is wrong" (1 Peter 3:17).

Saying thanks—"In everything give thanks; for this is God's will for you in Christ Jesus" (1 Thess. 5:18).

You may say, "Those are good principles, but they don't tell me where I ought to go to school or whom I should marry." But if you're saved, sanctified, submissive, suffering, and saying thanks, you can do whatever you want! That's what the psalmist meant when he said, "Delight yourself in the Lord; and He will give you the desires of your heart" (Ps. 37:4). Does that mean He fulfills the desire? Yes, but before He fulfills it, He puts it in your heart. If you are living a godly life, He will give you the right desires and then fulfill them.

✧ ✧ ✧

Suggestions for Prayer: Give thanks to God for revealing His will in His Word so that you can live wisely, not foolishly.

For Further Study: Christ acted only in accordance with His Father's will. Read the following verses, and note how that was so: Matthew 26:42; John 4:34; 5:30; 6:38.

> *"Although [Christ] existed in the form of God, [He] did not regard equality with God a thing to be grasped, but emptied Himself, taking the form of a bond-servant, and being made in the likeness of men. And being found in appearance as a man, He humbled Himself by becoming obedient to the point of death, even death on a cross."*
>
> PHILIPPIANS 2:6-8

✧ ✧ ✧

Christ is the perfect example of humility.

In his book *Miracles*, English scholar C.S. Lewis used this analogy to describe the incarnation of Christ:

> *One may think of a diver, first reducing himself to nakedness, then glancing in mid-air, then gone with a splash, vanished, rushing down through green and warm water into black and cold water, down through increasing pressure into the death-like region of ooze and slime and old decay; then up again, back to colour and light, his lungs almost bursting, till suddenly he breaks surface again, holding in his hand the dripping, precious thing that he went down to recover. He and it are both coloured now that they have come up into the light: down below, where it lay colourless in the dark, he lost his colour, too.*

That was how Lewis illustrated the Incarnation, the central miracle of Christianity, which is also addressed in Philippians 2:5-8. In those verses Jesus is shown to be the perfect model of humility—the perfect illustration of Paul's instructions in verses 3-4. He did nothing out of selfishness or conceit but regarded others as more important than Himself.

We are to imitate Christ's perfect example of humility. James 4:10 says, "Humble yourselves in the presence of the Lord, and He will exalt you." What about your life? Does it demonstrate a Christlike humility that God will delight to honor by exaltation?

✧ ✧ ✧

Suggestions for Prayer: Thank the Lord for Christ, whose life exemplifies the perfect pattern of humility for you to follow. ✧ Think of areas in your life where you are especially prone to exalt yourself at the expense of others. ✧ Acknowledge your sin to God and ask Him to help you be humble in those areas.

For Further Study: Read Isaiah 14:12-17 and Ezekiel 28:12-19, which tell of Lucifer's fall from his exalted position in the presence of God. Write down ways his attitude is opposite Christ's in Philippians 2:5-8.

"[Christ] existed in the form of God."
PHILIPPIANS 2:6

✧ ✧ ✧

Christ possesses the very nature of God.

In the second part of John Bunyan's *Pilgrim's Progress*, Christiana and her children travel toward the Celestial Country. During their pilgrimage, Interpreter introduces them to one of his male servants, whose name is Great-heart. When Christiana asks Great-heart to explain the nature of Christ's forgiveness, part of his answer is: "He [Christ] has two natures in one Person, easy to distinguish but impossible to divide. There is a righteousness that belongs to both of these natures, and each righteousness is essential to that nature, so that one might as easily kill that nature as to separate its righteousness from it." Bunyan was affirming through his character Great-heart what Scripture says of Christ: He is God.

The apostle Paul stated the same truth, saying that Christ "existed in the form of God" (Phil. 2:6). The Greek word translated "existed" (*huparcho*) is not the common verb for "being" (*eimi*). *Huparcho* stresses the essence of a person's nature—his continuous state or condition. It expresses what one is, unalterably and inalienably, by nature. Paul's point was that Jesus Christ is unalterably and continuously existing in the form of God.

Clarifying the meaning of the Greek word translated "form" (*morphe*) is crucial to a proper understanding of this verse. According to respected Greek scholars Moulton and Milligan, *morphe* "always signifies a form which truly and fully expresses the being which underlies it." The word describes essential being or nature—in this case the essential being of God.

In using the word *morphe* in Philippians 2, Paul was saying Jesus possessed the unchangeable, essential nature of God. That interpretation of the first phrase of verse 6 is strengthened by the second phrase, which says Jesus was equal with God. Being in the form of God speaks of Christ's equality with God.

Perhaps, like Great-heart, you know someone who needs to be grounded in the fundamental doctrines of God's Word. Just as Great-heart helped Christiana, so also you can help someone learn about the deity of Christ and other great truths of God's Word.

✧ ✧ ✧

Suggestions for Prayer: Pray for an opportunity to teach someone the basic doctrine of Christ's nature.

For Further Study: Memorize Colossians 2:9, a verse that proves the deity of Christ.

"[Christ] existed in the form of God."
PHILIPPIANS 2:6

✧ ✧ ✧

Scripture makes clear that Christ is God.

The deity of Christ is the heart of the Christian faith. Inevitably when people attack the Christian faith, they attack the deity of Christ. Scripture makes clear, however, that such attacks are unfounded. The apostle John said, "In the beginning was the Word, and the Word was with God, and the Word was God" (John 1:1). Under the inspiration of the Holy Spirit, he began his Gospel by affirming the deity of Christ. John further declared Christ's deity when he wrote, "All things came into being through [Christ], and apart from Him nothing came into being that has come into being. In Him was life; and the life was the light of men" (vv. 3-4). In John 8:58 Jesus said, "Before Abraham was born, I AM." Jesus appropriated to Himself the name of God, who said, "I AM WHO I AM" (Ex. 3:14).

In Colossians 1:15-17 the apostle Paul wrote of Christ's deity: "He is the image of the invisible God, the first-born of all creation. For by Him all things were created, both in the heavens and on earth, visible and invisible, whether thrones or dominions or rulers or authorities—all things have been created through Him and for Him. And He is before all things, and in Him all things hold together." Christ is God, the Creator. The writer of Hebrews says, "[Christ] is the radiance of [God's] glory and the exact representation of His nature" (1:3). Christianity begins with the recognition that Jesus Christ is in essence the eternal God.

Whenever someone confronts you by attacking the deity of Christ, be sure to defend the faith, "holding fast the faithful word which is in accordance with the teaching" (Titus 1:9).

✧ ✧ ✧

Suggestions for Prayer: At the core of defending God's Word is an accurate interpretation of Scripture. Ask Him to help you interpret His Word accurately (see 2 Tim. 2:15).

For Further Study: John 1:1 says, "In the beginning was the Word," which undoubtedly reminded John's readers of Genesis 1:1: "In the beginning God created the heavens and the earth." What do the following verses demonstrate about Christ: 1 Corinthians 8:6; Ephesians 3:19; Hebrews 1:1-2?

> *"[Christ] did not regard equality with God*
> *a thing to be grasped."*
> **PHILIPPIANS 2:6**

❖ ❖ ❖

Christ is equal with God but willingly yielded
His divine privileges for our sake.

At the time Christ lived, even His worst enemies, the apostate religious leaders, knew what Jesus claimed about Himself. John 5:18 says, "The Jews were seeking all the more to kill Him, because He not only was breaking the Sabbath, but was also calling God His own Father, making Himself equal with God." In Philippians 2:6 Paul affirms Christ's claim of equality with God. The Greek word translated "equality" (*isos*) describes things that are exactly equal in size, quantity, quality, character, and number. *Isomorph* (equal form), *isometric* (equal measures), and *isosceles* triangle (a triangle with two sides of equal measure) are all English terms that describe equality. Christ is equal to God, and He exists in the form of God. A literal English rendering of the Greek text is: "He did not regard the being equal with God"— a tremendous affirmation of the deity of Christ.

The first step in the humiliation of Christ was that He did not hold on to equality with God. Though He had all the rights, privileges, and honors of Godhood, Christ didn't grasp them. The word translated "grasp" originally meant "robbery" or "a thing seized by robbery." It eventually came to mean anything clutched, embraced, held tightly, clung to, or prized. Paul meant that though He was always and forever God, Christ refused to cling to His favored position with all its rights and honors. He was willing to give them up for a season.

The Incarnation expresses the humility and unselfish nature of the Second Person of the Trinity. Christ looked down on wretched sinners who hated Him and willingly yielded His privileges to give Himself for their sake. Let us follow His example by being humble and living unselfishly for others.

❖ ❖ ❖

Suggestions for Prayer: Thank the Lord for His example of humility and unselfishness.

For Further Study: Read John 10:38; 14:9. What did Christ say about His relationship with the Father? ❖ In John 20:28 how did Thomas address Christ?

> *"Although He existed in the form of God,*
> *[Christ] did not regard equality with God a thing*
> *to be grasped, but emptied Himself."*
>
> PHILIPPIANS 2:6-7

✧ ✧ ✧

Christ emptied Himself
without ever surrendering His deity.

ote the contrast in Philippians 2 between verses 6 and 7: Christ didn't think equality something to be grasped but instead emptied Himself. Paul used the contrasting connective "but" to show that being equal with God didn't lead Christ to fill Himself up but instead to empty Himself.

The Greek verb translated "emptied" (*kenoo*) is where we get the theological term *kenosis*—the doctrine of Christ's self-emptying as part of His incarnation. The verb expresses Christ's self-renunciation, His refusal to cling to His advantages and privileges as God.

What did Christ empty Himself of? Certainly not His deity. He coexists with the Father and the Spirit. For Him to become less than God would mean the Trinity would cease to exist. Christ could not become less than who He truly is.

Professor Paul Enns, in his *Moody Handbook of Theology*, explains the emptying of Christ this way: "The emptying was not a subtraction but an addition. The four following phrases (Phil. 2:7-8) explain the emptying: '(a) taking the form of a bond-servant, and (b) being made in the likeness of men. And (c) being found in appearance as a man, (d) He humbled Himself by becoming obedient to the point of death.' The 'emptying' of Christ was taking on an additional nature, a human nature with its limitations. His deity was never surrendered." Christ didn't exchange deity for humanity; He retained His divine nature.

In his hymn "Hark! The Herald Angels Sing," Charles Wesley correctly presented the truths of Christ's deity when he wrote:

> *Veiled in flesh the God-head see;*
> *Hail th' incarnate Deity,*
> *Pleased as man with men to dwell,*
> *Jesus, our Emmanuel.*

May those words be the song of your heart as well.

✧ ✧ ✧

Suggestions for Prayer: Thank the Lord for emptying Himself for your sake.

For Further Study: Read 2 Corinthians 8:9. Why did Christ become "poor"? ✧ Look at Romans 8:3. Why did God send "His own Son in the likeness of sinful flesh"?

> *"[Christ] emptied Himself."*
> PHILIPPIANS 2:7

✧ ✧ ✧

Christ renounced His divine privileges.

Although Christ never surrendered His deity, He did empty Himself in certain ways. One such way was to give up His *heavenly glory*. That's why in John 17:5 Jesus prays, "Glorify Thou Me together with Thyself, Father, with the glory which I ever had with Thee before the world was." Christ gave up the glory of a face-to-face relationship with God for the muck of this earth. He gave up the adoring presence of angels for the spittle of men.

Christ also emptied Himself of His *independent authority*. He completely submitted Himself to the will of the Father and learned to be a servant. Philippians 2:8 says He was obedient, and we see that illustrated when He said in the garden, "Not as I will, but as Thou wilt" (Matt. 26:39). He came to do His Father's will, not His own (John 5:30).

Another way Christ emptied Himself was by setting aside the *prerogatives of His deity*—the voluntary display of His attributes. He didn't give up His deity, but He did give up the free exercise of His attributes, limiting Himself to the point of saying that even He did not know the time of His second coming (Matt. 24:36).

Christ also emptied Himself of His *personal riches*. "Though He was rich, yet for your sake He became poor, that you through His poverty might become rich" (2 Cor. 8:9). Christ was poor in this world; He owned very little.

Finally, Christ emptied Himself of a *favorable relationship* with His Father. God "made Him who knew no sin to be sin on our behalf" (2 Cor. 5:21). As a result our Lord cried out on the cross, "My God, My God, why hast Thou forsaken Me?" (Matt. 27:46).

Though Christ renounced all those privileges, He never ceased to be God. At any moment He could have blasted His enemies off the face of the earth, but He didn't. He voluntarily emptied Himself for you and me.

✧ ✧ ✧

Suggestions for Prayer: Christ submitted Himself completely to His Father's will. Regularly ask for the Lord's perfect will to be reflected in your life as well.

For Further Study: Every now and then men glimpsed Christ's glory. Read Luke 9:28-36 as one example, reminding yourself that Christ emptied Himself of the continuous outward manifestation and personal enjoyment of heavenly glory.

"Taking the form of a bond-servant."
PHILIPPIANS 2:7

✧ ✧ ✧

Christ submitted Himself to the Father's will.

When Christ emptied Himself, He not only gave up His privileges but also became a servant. First, He was a servant by nature. Paul used the Greek word *morphe* ("form") again to indicate that Christ's servanthood was not merely external but His essence. It was not like a cloak that could be put on and taken off. Christ was truly a servant. The only other New Testament use of *morphe* is in Mark 16:12. There Jesus appears in a resurrection *morphe*—a form fully expressing the nature of a resurrection body. In Philippians 2 Christ is shown as a true bond-servant, doing the will of the Father. He submitted to the Father and to the needs of men as well. Jesus was everything that Isaiah 52:13-14 depicted—a Messiah who was a servant.

Second, Christ was a servant by position. As God, Christ owns everything. But when He came into this world, He borrowed everything: a place to be born, a place to lay His head, a boat to cross the Sea of Galilee and preach from, an animal to ride into the city when He was triumphantly welcomed as King of kings and Lord of lords, and a tomb to be buried in. The only Person ever to live on this earth who had the right to all its pleasures instead wound up with nothing and became a servant. Although He was the rightful heir to David's throne and God in human flesh, He had no advantages or privileges in this world. He owned little but served everyone.

Christ, the perfect servant, said to His disciples, "Whoever wishes to become first among you shall be your slave" (Matt. 20:27). What about you? Are you seeking greatness by wanting others to serve you, or are you being truly great by serving God and others? Make it your ambition to be a true servant.

✧ ✧ ✧

Suggestions for Prayer: Ask the Lord to help you be like Christ—a true servant of God.

For Further Study: What can you learn from Luke 2:41-52 about Christ's submission and humility?

". . . Made in the likeness of men."
PHILIPPIANS 2:7

✧ ✧ ✧

Christ was fully God and fully man.

I n his *Systematic Theology* theologian Charles Hodge wrote, "The
Scriptures teach that Christ had a complete human nature. That is, He had
a true body and a rational soul. By a true body is meant a material body which
in everything essential was like the bodies of ordinary men. . . . It is no less
plain that Christ had a rational soul. He thought, reasoned, and felt."

Hodge's assessment is correct, for Christ was given all the essential attributes of humanity. He was more than God in a body. He became the God-
man, being fully God and fully man. Like a man, Jesus was born and
increased in wisdom and physical maturity (Luke 2:52). Hebrews 2:14 says,
"Since then the children share in flesh and blood, He Himself likewise also
partook of the same." Christ had the same flesh and blood that we have. When
He came into the world, He came in normal human flesh that experienced all
the effects of the Fall. He knew sorrow, suffering, pain, thirst, hunger, and
death. He felt all effects of the Fall without ever knowing or experiencing the
sin of the Fall.

Hebrews 2:17 points out how Christ's humanity has a direct bearing on
your life: Jesus "had to be made like His brethren in all things, that He might
become a merciful and faithful high priest." For Christ to feel what you feel,
He needed to be made like you. He experienced all the tests and temptations
you do, but He never gave in to sin. That's why He is such a faithful and understanding High Priest. Be encouraged, for we "do not have a high priest who
cannot sympathize with our weaknesses, but one who has been tempted in all
things as we are, yet without sin" (Heb. 4:15).

✧ ✧ ✧

Suggestions for Prayer: Thank Christ for being your faithful High Priest.

For Further Study: What human characteristics did Christ show in the following verses: Matthew 4:2; 9:36; 23:37; John 4:6-7; 11:34-35; 19:30?

". . . Being found in appearance as a man."
PHILIPPIANS 2:8

✧ ✧ ✧

*Many people view Christ only
as a man, but He is God.*

After winning a gold medal at the 1924 Olympics in Paris, Scottish runner Eric Liddell served as a missionary in China; he died in a prison camp during World War II. The camp's prisoners loved Eric, for he served them so unselfishly. It was only at his funeral that they first learned he was an Olympic hero. They had had no idea of his full identity.

Most people didn't realize Christ's full identity either, for He was "found in appearance as a man" (Phil. 2:8). At first glance that phrase seems like a repetition of the end of verse 7, "being made in the likeness of men." We could paraphrase verse 8 to read, "He was discovered to appear as a man." The difference between that and verse 7 is a shift in focus. In verse 8 we view the humiliation of Christ from the viewpoint of those who saw Him. Christ was the God-man, but as people looked at Him, they saw the "appearance" (Greek, *schema*, "outward form") of a man. Paul was implying that though Christ appeared to be a man, there was much more to Him that could not naturally be seen.

For Christ to become man was humbling enough. For Him not to have been recognized must have been humiliating. He performed miracles and taught authoritatively, yet the typical responses were: "You are a Samaritan and have a demon" (John 8:48) and, "Is not this Jesus, the son of Joseph, whose father and mother we know? How does He now say, 'I have come down out of heaven'?" (John 6:42). Because their minds were darkened by sin, people recognized His humanity but could not see His deity. They could not recognize who He really was. They not only treated the King of kings as a man but as the worst of men—a criminal.

Unlike people who don't recognize Christ's true identity, let's honor Him through a life of worship and obedience.

✧ ✧ ✧

Suggestions for Prayer: Worship Christ for who He really is—the King of kings and Lord of lords. Praise Him for this truth in your prayer time.

For Further Study: Christ was not only fully man but also fully God. Read the following verses in which Christ Himself bears testimony that He is God: Luke 22:69-70; John 10:30, 37-38; 12:45; 14:7-10. What else should one find in these verses?

*"He humbled Himself by becoming obedient to
the point of death, even death on a cross."*
PHILIPPIANS 2:8

✧ ✧ ✧

*Instead of asserting His divine rights, Christ
submitted Himself to the cross.*

Even though the people did not recognize the deity of Christ and treated Him as a criminal, He did not fight back. Instead, He "humbled Himself." Consider His trial. He said not a word to defend Himself throughout unbelievable humiliation. They mocked Him, punched Him, pulled out His beard—yet He did not say a word. He was silent and accepted man's abuse through each phase of His phony trial. He did not demand His rights but "humbled Himself."

In humility Christ was "obedient to the point of death" (v. 8). At no time did our Lord say, "Stop! That's enough"—not in the middle of His trial, not when He was mocked, not when forced to walk half-naked through the city of Jerusalem with a cross on His back, not even on the cross. Christ was willing to descend into the muck and slime of death that He might bring us out of death into life.

Christ suffered not just death but death on a cross—the most excruciating, embarrassing, degrading, painful, and cruel death ever devised. The Jewish people hated crucifixion because of Deuteronomy 21:23: "Anyone who is hung on a tree is under God's curse" (NIV). The God who created the universe suffered the ultimate human degradation—hanging naked against the sky before a mocking world, with nails driven through His hands and feet.

Early nineteenth-century American preacher Gardiner Spring wrote, "The cross is the emblem of peace, but it is also an emblem of ignominy and suffering: it was so to the Saviour—it is so to his followers." Christ said that His disciples must take up their cross and follow Him (Matt. 16:24). In keeping with Christ's example, have you taken up the cross, living for His honor and glory no matter what?

✧ ✧ ✧

Suggestions for Prayer: Ask the Lord to help you follow His example of self-denial.

For Further Study: Read Matthew 27:11-50, noting Christ's obedience.

"Being found in appearance as a man, He humbled Himself
by becoming obedient to the point of death,
even death on a cross."

PHILIPPIANS 2:8

❖ ❖ ❖

Christ's humiliation displayed God's wisdom.

Somewhere along the path of Christ's descent, you'd think He would have said to Himself, *These people really aren't worth redeeming. This is too degrading and humiliating!* But the grace and love of God toward sinners was such that Christ stooped to die for you and me. At the end of Paul's doctrinal survey of salvation in Romans, he said, "Oh, the depth of the riches both of the wisdom and knowledge of God! How unsearchable are His judgments and unfathomable His ways!" (11:33). He was in awe of God's plan of salvation—a plan no man would have devised.

If we had planned the Incarnation, we probably would have wanted Christ to be born in a palace. His family would have been wealthy and prominent, and He would have been educated in the finest universities with elite teachers and the best tutors. We would have orchestrated events so that everyone loved, revered, honored, and respected Him. He would have been in all the prominent places and met all the prominent people.

We would not have had Him born in a stable to a poor family. He would not have spent His youth in a carpenter's shop in an obscure town. Rather than a ragtag band of followers, we would have made sure He had only the best people as His disciples, and they would have had to pass stiff qualifying tests for the privilege.

We would not have allowed Him to be humiliated. We would have imprisoned or executed anyone who spit on Him, pulled His beard, mocked Him, or hurt Him. Our plan for the Messiah would have been very different from God's plan, and, as a result no one could have been saved. It's no wonder the psalmist said, "Thy judgments are like a great deep" (Ps. 36:6). God's ways are unsearchable, His truths profound. And His plan to redeem us was accomplished by Christ's humiliation.

❖ ❖ ❖

Suggestions for Prayer: Daniel prayed, "Let the name of God be blessed forever and ever, for wisdom and power belong to Him" (Dan. 2:20). Like Daniel, worship the only wise God, who saved you.

For Further Study: Read 1 Peter 2:21-24. What did Christ leave you (v. 21)?

"Therefore also God highly exalted Him, and bestowed on Him the name which is above every name, that at the name of Jesus every knee should bow, of those who are in heaven, and on earth, and under the earth, and that every tongue should confess that Jesus Christ is Lord, to the glory of God the Father."

PHILIPPIANS 2:9-11

❖ ❖ ❖

God will exalt the humble.

Having plumbed the depths of Christ's humiliation (Phil. 2:5-8), Paul now soars to the heights of His exaltation (vv. 9-11). Like Paul, the apostle Peter affirmed that the great theme of Old Testament prophecy was the sufferings of Christ and the glory to follow (1 Peter 1:11). Regarding Christ, the writer of Hebrews says that "for the joy set before Him [He] endured the cross, despising the shame, and has sat down at the right hand of the throne of God" (Heb. 12:2). Christ understood His sufferings in light of His exaltation.

Paul's purpose in Philippians 2 was not simply to detail the humiliation and exaltation of Christ but to use those truths as a practical illustration. He was calling for unity produced by humility (vv. 2-4), with Christ as the preeminent example of humility (vv. 5-11). But beyond the humiliation of Christ, Paul also affirms that He was exalted. The implication is that when we willingly humble ourselves as Christ did, God will lift us up. As James 4:10 says, "Humble yourselves in the presence of the Lord, and He will exalt you."

It is true that the man who humbles himself is the one whom God exalts, and the man who exalts himself is the one whom God will humiliate. In the divine economy, it is by giving that one receives, by serving that one is served, by losing one's life that one finds life, and by dying to self that one lives. These principles follow one another as surely as night follows day.

Like Christ, you will be exalted in Heaven one day. Meditate on that truth, and be encouraged by it as you go through your earthly trials.

❖ ❖ ❖

Suggestions for Prayer: Thank the Lord for the exaltation that awaits you in Heaven.

For Further Study: Read the following verses: Matthew 23:12; Luke 14:11; 18:14; 1 Peter 5:6. What principle do they all teach?

"God highly exalted Him."
PHILIPPIANS 2:9

❖ ❖ ❖

Christ followed the path to glory
so that we could follow Him.

Because Christ humbled Himself, the Father wonderfully exalted Him. His exaltation includes the elements of both His *resurrection* and His *coronation*—His exaltation to the right hand of God. The apostle Peter said Jesus was "raised up again" and "exalted to the right hand of God" (Acts 2:32-33). Peter and the other apostles preached, "The God of our fathers raised up Jesus. . . . He is the one whom God exalted to His right hand as a Prince and a Savior, to grant repentance to Israel, and forgiveness of sins" (5:30-31). Thus, the New Testament affirms both the resurrection and coronation of Christ (see also Eph. 1:20), as well as the forgiveness of sins that comes with Christ's *intercession* for His people.

Paul described Christ's coronation as placing Him "far above all rule and authority and power and dominion, and every name that is named, not only in this age, but also in the one to come" (v. 21). The final element is described in Hebrews 4:14: "We have a great high priest who has passed through the heavens, Jesus the Son of God." That alludes to the *ascension* of Christ. He "always lives to make intercession for [believers]" (7:25).

Christ's exaltation was thus fourfold: resurrection, ascension, coronation, and intercession. He rose from the dead and ascended into Heaven. Then He was seated on the throne of God to intercede as High Priest of His people.

As a believer, you will follow Christ in His exaltation. You will rise from the grave and ascend to Heaven. There you will experience coronation, for you will sit with Christ on His throne. You will no longer need our Lord's intercessory ministry, for the work of transformation will be complete.

❖ ❖ ❖

Suggestions for Prayer: Thank Christ for establishing the path to glory so you can follow after Him.

For Further Study: Meditate on Revelation 22:1-5. What in this passage helps you think about your future glory?

"God highly exalted Him."

PHILIPPIANS 2:9

✧ ✧ ✧

Christ's resurrection and ascension
were the first two steps of His exaltation.

The first step on Christ's progress from humiliation to exaltation was His resurrection. In Acts 13 Paul preached on the resurrection of Christ, declaring: "[God] raised up Jesus. . . . And as for the fact that He raised Him up from the dead, no more to return to decay, He has spoken in this way: 'I will give you the holy and sure blessings of David.' Therefore He also says . . . 'Thou wilt not allow Thy holy one to undergo decay.' For David, after he had served the purpose of God in his own generation, fell asleep, and was laid among his fathers, and underwent decay; but He whom God raised did not undergo decay. Therefore let it be known to you, brethren, that through Him forgiveness of sins is proclaimed to you, and through Him everyone who believes is freed from all things, from which you could not be freed through the Law of Moses" (vv. 33-39). Christ's death and resurrection provided forgiveness and freedom from sin, the law, and death.

Acts 1:9-11 records the second step in the exaltation of Christ. After Christ finished His final instructions to His disciples, "He was lifted up while they were looking on, and a cloud received Him out of their sight. And as they were gazing intently into the sky while He was departing, behold, two men in white clothing stood beside them; and they also said, 'Men of Galilee, why do you stand looking into the sky? This Jesus, who has been taken up from you into heaven, will come in just the same way as you have watched Him go into heaven.'" Acts 2:33 says that the result of His ascension was exaltation to the right hand of God.

Just before He ascended, Christ spoke these final words to His disciples: "You shall be My witnesses" (Acts 1:8). Until He comes again, let's be witnesses who maintain a positive testimony for the sake of the gospel.

✧ ✧ ✧

Suggestions for Prayer: Praise God "who according to His great mercy has caused us to be born again to a living hope through the resurrection of Jesus Christ from the dead" (1 Peter 1:3).

For Further Study: According to John 16:7, why is the ascension of Christ to your advantage?

"God highly exalted Him."

PHILIPPIANS 2:9

✧ ✧ ✧

Christ is the Sovereign of the universe and a faithful High Priest.

C hrist was exalted not only in His resurrection and ascension, but also in His coronation. Mark 16:19 says, "When the Lord Jesus had spoken to [the apostles], He was received up into heaven, and sat down at the right hand of God." In Scripture the right hand is a symbol of power and authority. What is the extent of Christ's authority? Ephesians 1:20-22 says, "[God] seated Him at His right hand in the heavenly places, far above all rule and authority and power and dominion, and every name that is named, not only in this age, but also in the one to come. And He put all things in subjection under His feet, and gave Him as head over all things to the church." Christ is the Sovereign of the universe.

Besides His coronation, Christ is exalted in His intercession for believers. He stands before the Father as the High Priest of His people. His first act was to send the Holy Spirit (Acts 2:33). Our sympathetic High Priest "has been tempted in all things as we are" (Heb. 4:15), and "He is able to save forever those who draw near to God through Him, since He always lives to make intercession for [us]" (7:25). Christ's intercessory work grants us faith, repentance, and forgiveness (see Heb. 4—9).

Puritan minister Thomas Watson said, "Had you a friend at court, who, when you were questioned for delinquency or debt, should plead with the judge for you, and bring you off your troubles, would you not love that friend? How often does Satan put in his bills against us in the court! Now Christ is at the judge's hand; he sits at his Father's right hand, ever to plead for us, and to make our peace with God. Oh, how should our hearts be fired with love to Christ!"

How intense is your love for Jesus Christ, our faithful Advocate?

✧ ✧ ✧

Suggestions for Prayer: "Draw near with confidence to the throne of grace, that [you] may receive mercy and may find grace to help in time of need" (Heb. 4:16). Pray for a fresh appreciation of this today.

For Further Study: What do 2 Corinthians 5:21 and Hebrews 2:17 say about Christ as our High Priest?

> *"When [Christ] had made purification of sins,*
> *He sat down at the right hand of the Majesty on high."*
> **HEBREWS 1:3**

❖ ❖ ❖

God has exalted Christ above everyone and everything.

C hrist in His majestic glory is "heir of all things" (Heb. 1:2). That's why it is His right to have the title deed to the earth, spoken of in Revelation 5:1-7. There He opens that deed and takes possession of what is rightfully His as heir of all things.

Hebrews 1 further describes Christ as "the radiance of [God's] glory and the exact representation of His nature. . . . When He had made purification of sins, He sat down at the right hand of the Majesty on high; having become as much better than the angels, as He has inherited a more excellent name than they. For to which of the angels did [God] ever say, 'Thou art My Son, today I have begotten Thee'? And again, 'I will be a Father to Him, and He shall be a Son to Me'? And when He again brings the first-born into the world, He says, 'Let all the angels of God worship Him'" (vv. 3-6; compare v. 13). Because Christ is the unique Son of God, the angels are called to worship Him.

The Father said of the exalted Christ, "Thy throne, O God, is forever and ever, and the righteous scepter is the scepter of His Kingdom. Thou hast loved righteousness and hated lawlessness; therefore God, Thy God, hath anointed Thee with the oil of gladness above Thy companions" (vv. 8-9). Christ is the eternal, righteous God. He is also the Creator who lives forever and remains the same (vv. 10-12).

If you see Christ in His majesty the way the writer of Hebrews did, you'll want to make the words of Charles Wesley's hymn "Rejoice—The Lord Is King!" your own:

> *Jesus the Savior reigns, the God of truth and love;*
> *When He had purged our stains He took His seat above:*
> *Lift up your heart, lift up your voice!*
> *Rejoice, again I say, rejoice!*

❖ ❖ ❖

Suggestions for Prayer: Both angels and the redeemed worship the exalted Christ. Use Psalm 103 as the basis of your prayer of worship.

For Further Study: Hebrews 1:10 shows Christ to be the Creator. Based on this and Psalm 148, what honor is He owed?

"God highly exalted Him."

PHILIPPIANS 2:9.

✧ ✧ ✧

The Father exalted the Son as the God-man.

A question that often springs to mind regarding the exaltation of Christ is how Jesus could be exalted since He is already God. We find the answer in Jesus' High-Priestly prayer in John 17, where He asked the Father to restore to Him the glory He had with the Father before the world began (v. 5). Christ's request shows that He gave up something that God would give back to Him. Christ gave up His glory in the Incarnation. Beyond glorification, in His exaltation Christ would receive more than He had before.

How is that possible? God has it all. Christ didn't become any more God or any more perfect; He was already the Most High God—King of kings and Lord of lords. But as the God-man, a new state of being for Him, He suffered things and was given things He would not otherwise have had if He had not become the God-man. For example, He never would have had the privilege of being the interceding High Priest for His people if He had never been touched with the feelings of their infirmities—tempted in all points like them. If He had not become the God-man, He would never have become our substitute by bearing our sins in His own body on the cross. As God He was incapable of elevation, but as the God-Man He could be lifted up from the lowest degradation to the highest degree of glory. So in a sense He received from the Father privileges He didn't have before—privileges He gained because of His incarnation.

At His ascension Christ was seated at the Father's right hand. He was elevated to that position as the God-man—a state of being that was His only because of His incarnation. Thus He entered upon the rights and privileges not only of God as God, but of God as the God-man. His exaltation was not with regard to His nature or eternal place within the Trinity but with regard to His new character as the God-man.

✧ ✧ ✧

Suggestions for Prayer: Thank the Father for exalting His Son to His rightful place in Heaven.

For Further Study: According to Acts 5:31, in what two ways did God exalt Christ to His right hand? Why?

> *"God highly exalted Him, and bestowed on Him*
> *the name which is above every name."*
>
> **PHILIPPIANS 2:9**

✧ ✧ ✧

Christ is exalted as Prophet, Priest, and King.

Jesus' exaltation was the reversal of His humble incarnation. He who was poor became rich; He who was rejected became accepted; He who had learned obedience returned to a position of power that calls all others to obey Him. Commentator William Hendricksen wrote, "As king, having by his death, resurrection, and ascension achieved and displayed his triumph over his enemies, he now holds in his hands the reins of the universe, and rules all things in the interest of his church (Eph. 1:22-23). As prophet he through his Spirit leads his own in all the truth. And as priest (High-priest according to the order of Melchizedek) he, on the basis of his accomplished atonement, not only intercedes but actually lives forever to make intercession for those who "draw near to God through him." And God was the source of Jesus' exaltation.

In Philippians 2:9 the apostle Paul says that God "bestowed on Him the name." The Greek word translated "bestowed" means "to give graciously" or "wholeheartedly." Christ so fully and completely accomplished God's plan of redemption that God wholeheartedly and graciously poured out on Christ the gifts of exaltation. Though He could not be made more than God, He now enjoys all the privileges of God as well as all the privileges of the God-man, which He now is.

Puritan minister Thomas Watson wrote in his *Body of Divinity*, "Christ's exaltation is our exaltation. . . . As sure as Christ is exalted far above all heavens, so sure will he instate believers in all that glory with which his human nature is adorned. John xvii 22." Be encouraged, for one day Christ will also exalt you!

✧ ✧ ✧

Suggestions for Prayer: First Corinthians 15:24-26 shows that God has exalted Christ as Sovereign over everything. In keeping with that theme, use Psalm 99 as the basis of your own prayer to praise Christ as Ruler over all.

For Further Study: According to Romans 14:9, why did Christ humble Himself? ✧ What has the Father given to the Son as part of His exaltation (John 5:22)?

> *"God highly exalted Him, and bestowed on Him*
> *the name which is above every name."*
> PHILIPPIANS 2:9

❖ ❖ ❖

God exalted Christ by giving Him a new name.

In today's verse a question that arises is, What is the name that is above every name? To be consistent with Scripture, it has to be a name that goes beyond merely distinguishing one person from another. It has to be a name that describes Christ's nature—revealing something of His inner being. Only such a name would cause Him to be clearly ranked above all others. Paul wasn't referring to a comparative name, but a superlative name—one that would set Christ above and beyond all comparison.

Change of name in Scripture indicates the commencement of a unique relationship. When God established His covenant with Abram, He changed his name to "Abraham" (Gen. 17:5). When God entered into a unique relationship with Jacob, He gave Him the name "Israel" (Gen. 32:22-32). In the New Testament, Jesus called a man named Simon to follow Him, then gave him a new name: Peter (Matt. 16:18). Those names were given to mark a definite stage in a person's life. God has done that throughout redemptive history. Philippians 2:9 affirms that God gave Christ a name. He already had many names—Jesus, Christ, Son of Man, Son of God, Messiah—but He received a new name.

Some assume that the new name is Jesus because verse 10 says, "At the name of Jesus every knee should bow." But that wasn't a new name; it was bestowed at birth (see Matt. 1:21). Nor is the name Jesus above every other name (there have been a lot of people named Jesus). The only name mentioned in Philippians 2:9-11 that is above every name is Lord. In verse 11 Paul says, "Every tongue should confess that Jesus Christ is Lord." That is the only name God gave Christ that is above every name. Whoever is Lord is in control.

Let us exalt Christ our Lord by offering Him praise and living a holy life.

❖ ❖ ❖

Suggestions for Prayer: Thank Christ for being Lord of the universe as well as Lord of your life.

For Further Study: Read Psalm 2. What are the key aspects? ❖ Is everyone happy about Christ's position?

*"God highly exalted Him, and bestowed on Him
the name which is above every name, that at the name of Jesus
every knee should bow . . . and that every tongue
should confess that Jesus Christ is Lord."*
PHILIPPIANS 2:9-11

✦ ✦ ✦

Christ's name shows Him to be sovereign ruler.

The name "Lord" is a New Testament synonym for Old Testament descriptions of Yahweh (the Old Testament name of God), which show God as sovereign ruler. It signifies rulership based on power and authority. Though it was always evident that Christ was the living Lord, it was in His exaltation that He was formally given the name Lord—a title that is His as the God-man. On earth He was known by many names, but now He bears the name that is above every name: Lord.

Philippians 2:10 doesn't say at the name Jesus every knee should bow, but at the name *of* Jesus. The name of Jesus immediately bestowed by the Father was "Lord." It is not the name Jesus that makes people bow—that's the name of His incarnation—but the name *Lord*.

That the name mentioned in verse 9 is Lord is confirmed by Paul's allusion to Isaiah 45:21-23, which says, "Is it not I, the Lord? And there is no other God besides Me, a righteous God and a Savior; there is none except Me. Turn to Me, and be saved, all the ends of the earth; for I am God, and there is no other. I have sworn by Myself, the word has gone forth from My mouth in righteousness and will not turn back, that to Me every knee will bow, every tongue will swear allegiance." God said through Isaiah that He is sovereign—the Lord of all. That is what Paul was referring to when he said that every knee would bow and every tongue confess (or admit) that Jesus Christ is Lord. Only God is Lord.

✦ ✦ ✦

Suggestions for Prayer: In his prayer in Ephesians 1:17-23 Paul mentions that Christ's name is above all other names (vv. 20-21). Use his prayer as a model when you pray for other believers.

For Further Study: Read the following verses: Luke 2:11; John 13:13; Acts 10:36; Romans 14:9-11; 1 Corinthians 8:6. What do they say about Jesus' lordship?

> *"God highly exalted Him, and bestowed on Him*
> *the name which is above every name . . . that every tongue*
> *should confess that Jesus Christ is Lord."*
> PHILIPPIANS 2:9, 11

❖ ❖ ❖

The Jesus who is Savior cannot be separated
from the Jesus who is Lord.

S cripture never speaks of any human being's making Jesus Lord. It is God who made Him Lord (Acts 2:36). Yet we often read statements such as this: "It is imperative to trust Christ as personal Savior and be born again. But that is only the first decision. Trusting Christ as Savior and then making Him Lord are two separate and distinct decisions. The two decisions may be close or distant in time. Salvation must always precede lordship. But it is possible to be saved without ever making Christ Lord of your life." In effect that is saying Christ isn't Lord unless we give Him permission—a completely unbiblical assertion. To be saved you must confess Jesus as Lord.

Jesus is called Lord throughout the New Testament. To omit the lordship of Christ from invitations to salvation would result in the elimination of numerous passages of Scripture. Peter's sermon in Acts 2—"Everyone who calls on the name of the Lord shall be saved" (Acts 2:21)—would need to be modified. Paul and Silas' method of presenting the gospel—"Believe in the Lord Jesus, and you shall be saved" (Acts 16:31)—would need to be corrected.

The centrality of the lordship of Christ is clear in the New Testament gospel. The Jesus who is Savior cannot be separated from the Jesus who is Lord. God cannot be separated from His authority, dominion, rulership, and right to command. When we acknowledge that Jesus is God, we mean He is all that God is.

❖ ❖ ❖

Suggestions for Prayer: Worship the Lord Jesus Christ, using Psalm 8, a Messianic psalm, as the basis of your prayer.

For Further Study: Jesus is called Lord over 700 times in the New Testament. Use a Bible concordance as a handy way to check some of these many references to Christ as Lord.

> *"God highly exalted Him, and bestowed on Him*
> *the name which is above every name . . . that every tongue*
> *should confess that Jesus Christ is Lord."*
> PHILIPPIANS 2:9, 11

❖ ❖ ❖

To receive Christ as Savior
is to submit to His authority as Lord.

I s Jesus Lord? According to the declaration of the Father, He is. We cannot know Him any other way than as Lord. That's why the first creed in the history of the church, given in Philippians 2:11, says, "Jesus Christ is Lord." Every Christian must acknowledge that. It is the foundation of the Christian faith, the very substance of what we believe. We don't make Him Lord after salvation. Every time I hear someone say, "You need to make Jesus Lord," it is as repellent to me as hearing fingernails scraped down a blackboard. We never make Jesus Lord—God has already done that.

Jesus Christ is Lord and Savior, and those who would receive Him must take Him for who He really is. Puritan John Flavel put it this way: "The gospel offer of Christ includes all his offices, and gospel faith just so receives him; to submit to him, as well as to be redeemed by him; to imitate him in the holiness of his life, as well as to reap the purchases and fruits of his death. It must be an entire receiving of the Lord Jesus Christ."

In a similar vein, A.W. Tozer said, "To urge men and women to believe in a divided Christ is bad teaching, for no one can receive half of Christ, or a third of Christ, or a quarter of the Person of Christ! We are not saved by believing in an office nor in a work." Jesus is Lord, and if you refuse Him as Lord, you cannot call Him Savior. If you have truly received Him, your life will be characterized by submission to His authority.

❖ ❖ ❖

Suggestions for Prayer: Take time to acknowledge the lordship of Christ in your own life.

For Further Study: Read Romans 10:9-13. What is a sinner to confess if he is to be saved? ❖ According to 2 Corinthians 4:5, what message did Paul preach?

> *"That at the name of Jesus every knee should bow . . . and that
> every tongue should confess that Jesus Christ is Lord."*
> PHILIPPIANS 2:10-11

❖ ❖ ❖

The proper response to Christ's exaltation is to worship Him.

P hilippians 2:10-11 gives the only proper response to Christ's exaltation: everyone is to bow before Him and acknowledge Him as Lord. Verse 10 begins with the Greek word *hina* ("that"), which indicates purpose or result. God's express purpose is that Christ's exaltation will result in our worshiping Him. We might translate the sentence, "He was given the name that is above every name in order that at the name of Jesus every knee will bow and every tongue confess that Jesus Christ is Lord." The reason Christ was given the name Lord was to put Him in authority and cause everyone to bow to Him. The subjunctive mood ("every knee should bow") implies that every knee *will* bow.

Christ is to be acknowledged as Lord because He is God. By God's grace some are enabled to acknowledge Christ's lordship by choice. Others will bow to Him because they are forced to do so. The phrases "every knee should bow" (v. 10) and "every tongue should confess" (v. 11) are taken from Isaiah 45:23. Isaiah 45—46 clearly establishes that God is Lord and sovereign. He is in charge. In Philippians, Paul affirms the same truth about Jesus Christ— every knee will bow, and every tongue will confess that He is Lord of all.

We know Christ as the Lord, and we know Him as Jesus—the names of His exaltation and humiliation. But He must be known as both in order to be known at all. One receives the gift of salvation by receiving both the humiliated Savior and by bowing the knee to a majestic, sovereign God.

❖ ❖ ❖

Suggestions for Prayer: Psalm 89 focuses on the rule and reign of Christ. Bow before Him as the exalted King by using verses 8-18 as the basis of your own prayer of worship.

For Further Study: Read Revelation 5:11-14. What is Christ worthy to receive? ❖ In verse 13 who is speaking? ❖ What was the response of the four living creatures and elders (v. 14)?

*"That at the name of Jesus every knee should bow, of those
who are in heaven, and on earth, and under the earth, and that
every tongue should confess that Jesus Christ is Lord."*
PHILIPPIANS 2:10-11

✧ ✧ ✧

All rational beings will acknowledge Christ as Lord.

Philippians 2:10-11 affirms that the whole intelligent universe is called to worship Christ. They are specified as those "in heaven, and on earth, and under the earth" (v. 10). *"Those who are in heaven"* consist of two groups: God's holy angels and the spirits of the redeemed believers (who await the resurrection of their bodies). Those who are in Heaven already acknowledge that Jesus is Lord. Throughout their time in Heaven they've been worshiping the Lord of glory.

"Those . . . on earth" (v. 10) also consist of two groups: the obedient and the disobedient. The obedient refers to us. By God's grace, we have submitted to Christ as Lord and Savior (cf. Rom. 10:9). The disobedient will also bow before Jesus Christ—by compulsion (cf. 2 Thess. 1:7-9). When Jesus returns to subdue the earth, He will remove the wicked from the earth, cast them into Hell, and establish His kingdom.

"Under the earth" (Phil. 2:10) refers to Hell, the place of eternal punishment, which is occupied by all the damned—both demons and unsaved people. They will also acknowledge the lordship of Christ—not by enjoying His reign, but by bearing the unending expression of His wrath.

Jesus Christ is Lord of the universe. Therefore, "every tongue should confess that Jesus Christ is Lord" (v. 11). To confess means "to acknowledge," "affirm," or "agree." By "every tongue" Paul didn't mean every physical tongue in every mouth but every language. Another way to express the idea is to say that all rational beings will acknowledge His lordship.

History is moving toward the day when Jesus will be acknowledged by all as the supreme ruler of the universe. He already sits in that seat of power but has not yet brought the universe fully under His authority. We live in days of grace, during which He brings men and women to acknowledge Him as Lord willingly rather than by force. Rejoice that He still provides that opportunity.

✧ ✧ ✧

Suggestions for Prayer: Pray for lost relatives and friends to submit to Christ willingly.

For Further Study: In Psalm 2:12, what warning does the Lord give?

> *"God highly exalted Him . . .*
> *to the glory of God the Father."*
> **PHILIPPIANS 2:9, 11**

✧ ✧ ✧

When the Son is glorified, so is the Father.

The purpose of Christ's exaltation is to glorify God. Philippians 2:11 says Jesus will be acknowledged as Lord "to the glory of God the Father." In Isaiah 45:5 God says, "I am the Lord, and there is no other; besides Me there is no God." None can be compared to God. He does not ask anyone for advice. He knows all and does exactly what He wants to do. All His purposes come to pass.

In light of who God says He is, one might assume that it would be blasphemous for everyone to bow to Jesus Christ and confess Him as Lord. To so honor Christ would seem to put Him in competition with the Father.

But the mystery of the Trinity is that when the Son is glorified, the Father is glorified. Perfect glory given to the Son is perfect glory given to the Father. John 5:23 says the Father has given all judgment to the Son "that all may honor the Son, even as they honor the Father. He who does not honor the Son does not honor the Father who sent Him." That's why the Father said of Jesus, "This is My beloved Son, with whom I am well pleased; hear Him!" (Matt. 17:5). When you believe in Jesus Christ and confess Him as Lord, you exalt not only the Son but also the Father. There is no competition within the Trinity. The Father is exalted by what He accomplishes in the Son. They are one.

What a joy to know that our confessing of Jesus as Lord glorifies God. Let's continue to glorify Him as Lord by bearing spiritual fruit in our lives (see John 15:8).

✧ ✧ ✧

Suggestions for Prayer: Jesus said, "Whatever you ask in My name, that will I do, that the Father may be glorified in the Son" (John 14:13). Whatever you ask in Christ's name, do so by acknowledging His sovereignty and desiring that God be glorified.

For Further Study: What do Romans 9:5, 1 Corinthians 15:28, and John 13:31-32 show about the glory of the Father and the Son?

"[Christ] is the image of the invisible God, the first-born
of all creation. For in Him all things were created, both in the
heavens and on earth, visible and invisible, whether thrones
or dominions or rulers or authorities—all things have been
created through Him and for Him. And He is before all things,
and in Him all things hold together. He is also head of the
body, the church; and He is the beginning, the first-born
from the dead; so that He Himself might come to have first place
in everything. For it was the Father's good pleasure
for all the fulness to dwell in Him."
COLOSSIANS 1:15-19

✧ ✧ ✧

A believer should defend the faith.

Despite the diligent labors of Epaphras, the Colossian church was in jeopardy. A serious heresy had arisen, and Epaphras was so concerned that he traveled to Rome to visit Paul in prison. The Colossian church had not yet been infected by that heresy, and Paul warns them against its dangers.

The heretics, denying the humanity of Christ, viewed Him as one of many lesser, descending spirit beings that emanated from God. They taught a form of philosophic dualism, postulating that spirit was good and matter was evil. Hence, a good emanation like Christ could never take on a body composed of evil matter. The idea that God Himself could become man was absurd to them. Thus, the false teachers also denied His deity.

Christ was also not adequate for salvation, according to the heretics. Salvation required a superior, mystical, secret knowledge, beyond that of the gospel of Christ. It also involved worshiping the good emanations (angels) and keeping Jewish ceremonial laws.

By far the most serious aspect of the Colossian heresy was its rejection of Christ's deity. Before getting to the other issues, Paul makes an emphatic defense of that crucial doctrine. In Colossians 1:15-19 Paul reveals our Lord's true identity by viewing Him in relation to God, the universe, and the church.

Perhaps you've met people who deny Christ's deity, but you weren't sure what to say to them. In the next few days, let Paul be your guide in showing you how to confront cultists in a biblical manner. By following his example, you'll be able to defend our precious faith.

✧ ✧ ✧

Suggestions for Prayer: Ask the Lord to teach you from His Word how to refute false teaching.

For Further Study: In verse 3 of Jude, what exhortation does Jude give to believers?

> *"[Christ] is the image of the invisible God."*
> COLOSSIANS 1:15

❖ ❖ ❖

In Christ, the invisible God became visible.

Sometimes I listen to different preachers on the radio or watch them on television, and I get tremendously frustrated. That's because so many of them present a confusing picture of who Christ really is. Since there are so many who distort the Christian faith, there should be in every believer a desire to defend it. The apostle Paul certainly had that desire. Since the heretics at Colosse viewed Jesus as a lesser spirit who emanated from God, Paul refutes that with a powerful description of who Jesus really is.

Paul describes Him as "the image of the invisible God" (Col. 1:15). The Greek word translated "image" (*eikon*) means "likeness." Although man is also the *eikon* of God (1 Cor. 11:7), he is not a perfect image of God. Humans are made in God's image in that they have rational personality. Like God, they possess intellect, emotion, and will, by which they are able to think, feel, and choose. We humans are not, however, in God's image morally: He is holy, and we are sinful. We are also not created in His image essentially, since we do not possess His divine attributes.

Unlike man, Jesus Christ is the perfect, absolutely accurate image of God. He did not become the image of God at the Incarnation but has been that from all eternity. Hebrews 1:3 says Christ "is the radiance of [God's] glory and the exact representation of His nature." Christ reflects God's attributes and is the exact likeness of God. That is why Christ could say, "He who has seen Me has seen the Father" (John 14:9).

By using the term *eikon*, Paul emphasizes that Jesus is both the representation and manifestation of God. He is the full, final, and complete revelation of God. He is God in human flesh. That was His claim (John 8:58), and it is the unanimous testimony of Scripture (cf. Col. 2:9; Titus 2:13). To think anything less of Him is blasphemy and gives evidence of a mind blinded by Satan (2 Cor. 4:4).

❖ ❖ ❖

Suggestions for Prayer: Thank the Lord for removing your spiritual blindness so that you could "see the light of the gospel of the glory of Christ, who is the image of God" (2 Cor. 4:4).

For Further Study: According to Romans 8:29, what has God predestined for all believers?

"[Christ] is . . . the first-born of all creation."
COLOSSIANS 1:15

✧ ✧ ✧

Christ is the preeminent inheritor
over all creation.

Puritan minister Thomas Manton once said, "Heresies revolve as fashions, and in the course of a few years antiquated errors revive again, and that by their means who did not so much as know them by name." He was right: false doctrines keep repeating themselves through the ages, only to reappear under different names. From the Arians of the early church to the Jehovah's Witnesses of our own day, cultists have sought to deny our Lord's deity. One of the favorite verses of such cultists is Colossians 1:15, which refers to Christ as the "first-born." They argue that it speaks of Christ as a created being and hence He could not be the eternal God. Such an interpretation completely misunderstands the sense of *prototokos* ("first-born") and ignores the context.

Although *prototokos* can mean first-born chronologically (Luke 2:7), it refers primarily to position or rank. In both Greek and Jewish culture, the first-born was the son who had the right of inheritance. He was not necessarily the first one born. Although Esau was born first chronologically, it was Jacob who was the first-born and received the inheritance. Jesus is the One with the right to the inheritance of all creation (cf. Heb. 1:2).

The context of Colossians 1:15 also refutes the idea that "first-born" describes Jesus as a created being. If Paul were here teaching that Christ is a created being, he would be agreeing with the central point of the Colossian false teachers. That would run counter to his purpose in writing Colossians, which was to refute them. Moreover, Paul had just finished describing Christ as the perfect and complete image of God (v. 15). In the following verses he refers to Christ as the Creator of all things (v. 16) and the One who "is before all things" (v. 17). Far from being an emanation descending from God, Christ is the preeminent inheritor over all creation. He existed before the creation and is exalted in rank above it.

✧ ✧ ✧

Suggestions for Prayer: Use Psalm 93 as the basis of your prayer to worship Christ, who is preeminent in rank over all creation.

For Further Study: Read Revelation 4:8-11. According to verse 11, what is Christ worthy to receive? Why?

> *"In [Christ] all things were created, both in the heavens and*
> *on earth, visible and invisible, whether thrones or dominions*
> *or rulers or authorities—all things have been*
> *created through Him and for Him."*
>
> COLOSSIANS 1:16

✧ ✧ ✧

Christ created everyone and everything.

The sheer size of the universe is staggering. The sun, for example, could hold 1.3 million planets the size of Earth inside it. The galaxy to which our sun belongs, the Milky Way, contains hundreds of billions of stars. And astronomers estimate there are millions, or even billions, of galaxies.

Who created this awesome universe? According to the false teachers at Colosse, it was not Christ. They viewed Him as the first and most important of the emanations from God; they were convinced it had to be a lesser being who eventually created the material universe. Believing matter to be evil, they argued that neither the good God nor a good emanation would have created the universe.

But the apostle Paul rejected that blasphemy, insisting that Christ made all things, both in the heavens and on earth, visible and invisible. When he mentions thrones, dominions, rulers, and authorities (v. 16), he is referring to the various ranks of angels. Far from being an angel, as the false teachers taught, Christ created the angels (cf. Eph. 1:21). Jesus' relation to the unseen world, like His relation to the visible world, proves He is God, the Creator of the universe.

Man is certainly interested in knowing about the universe that Christ created. That is evident, for example, by his exploration of space. Manned space capsules photographing the earth rising over the lunar horizon and satellites beaming pictures to us of planets at the outer edges of our solar system leave us in awe and wonder. Even more amazing is, not that man has gone into space, but that God came to Earth. In Christ, the invisible God who created everything and everyone became visible to man. How sad that while man looks into space, He refuses to look at the One who came to Earth.

✧ ✧ ✧

Suggestions for Prayer: Worship Christ for His awesome work of creation.

For Further Study: Read Psalm 19:1-6. What testimony does this passage give of the Creator?

> *"[Christ] is before all things, and in Him*
> *all things hold together."*
> COLOSSIANS 1:17

✧ ✧ ✧

The eternal Christ sustains His creation.

When the universe began, Christ already existed. The apostle John spoke of Christ's eternal existence this way: "In the beginning was the Word, and the Word was with God, and the Word was God. He was in the beginning with God. All things came into being through Him; and apart from Him nothing came into being that has come into being" (John 1:1-3). Christ Himself testified of the same truth when He told the Jews, "Before Abraham was born, I AM" (John 8:58). He was saying that He is Yahweh, the eternally existing God. The prophet Micah said of Him, "His goings forth are from long ago, from the days of eternity" (Mic. 5:2). Revelation 22:13 describes Him as "the Alpha and Omega, the first and the last, the beginning and the end." Christ has preeminence over all creation because He "is before all things" (Col. 1:17). He already existed when the universe began because He is the eternal God.

Having created the universe, Christ sustains all He has created (v. 17). He maintains the delicate balance necessary to life's existence. He is the power behind every consistency in the universe and the One who keeps all the entities in space in their motion. He is the energy behind the universe.

Christ, however, will not always sustain our present universe. One day in the future He will dissolve the heavens and earth. The apostle Peter describes that day, when "the heavens will pass away with a roar and the elements will be destroyed with intense heat, and the earth and its works will be burned up" (2 Peter 3:10). Until that time, we can be thankful that Christ continues to sustain it.

How encouraging to know that the eternal God who sustains the entire universe is also watching over you. No detail of your life is too small for His concern; no circumstance is too big for His sovereign control.

✧ ✧ ✧

Suggestions for Prayer: Thank the Lord for caring for the details of your life while He controls the universe.

For Further Study: According to Hebrews 1:3, what does God uphold? How?

> *"[Christ] is also head of the body, the church; and He is the beginning, the first-born from the dead; so that He Himself might come to have first place in everything. For it was the Father's good pleasure for all the fulness to dwell in Him."*
>
> COLOSSIANS 1:18-19

❖ ❖ ❖

Christ has preeminence in everything.

The apostle Paul presents four great truths in Colossians 1:18 about Christ's relation to the church. The first is that Christ is the *head of the church*. This concept looks at the church as a living organism, inseparably tied together by the living Christ. He controls every part of it and gives it life and direction (cf. 1 Cor. 12:12-20).

Christ is also the *source of the church*. The Greek word translated "beginning" (*arche*) is used here in the twofold sense of source and primacy. The church has its origins in Jesus. God "chose us in Him before the foundation of the world" (Ephesians 1:4). As head of the Body, Jesus holds the chief position or highest rank in the church. As the beginning, He is its originator.

Another truth is that Christ is the *first-born from the dead*. Of all those who have been raised from the dead or ever will be, Christ is the highest in rank. Furthermore, it is Christ who will cause the resurrection of others (John 5:28-29; 6:40).

Finally, Christ is the *preeminent One*. As a result of His death and resurrection, Jesus has come to have first place in everything. Paul states that truth to drive home as forcefully as he can that Jesus is not merely another emanation from God.

Paul then summarizes his argument by saying that all the fullness of deity dwells in Christ alone (Col. 1:19). It is not spread out in small doses to a group of spirits, as the false teachers were saying. Rather, in Christ, and Him alone, believers are "complete" (2:10).

What should be your response to the glorious truths about Christ in Colossians 1:15-19? Be encouraged to meditate on the glory of Christ as revealed in this passage. Doing so will help you be transformed into Christ's image and will prepare you to behold His glory in Heaven.

❖ ❖ ❖

Suggestions for Prayer: Thank the Lord for each of the four truths discussed above.

For Further Study: According to John 1:16, what have you received?

THROUGH THE BIBLE

Daily Readings

Covering the Entire Bible in a Year

Publisher's Note: This reading schedule has been adapted from a publication of the National Association of Evangelicals. Copies may be ordered in quantities of 25, 50, and 100 or more. Write to: National Association of Evangelicals, P.O. Box 28, Wheaton, IL 60189.

JANUARY

Day		Book and Chapter
☐	1	John 1:1-18
☐	2	Gen. 1-4
☐	3	Gen. 5-8
☐	4	Gen. 9-12
☐	5	Gen. 13-16
☐	6	Psalms 1-3
☐	7	Gen. 17-19
☐	8	Gen. 20-22
☐	9	Job 1-4
☐	10	Job 5-8
☐	11	Job 9-12
☐	12	Job 13-16
☐	13	Psalms 4-7
☐	14	Job 17-20
☐	15	Job 21-24
☐	16	Job 25-28
☐	17	Job 29-32
☐	18	Job 33-36
☐	19	Job 37-39
☐	20	Psalms 8-11
☐	21	Job 40-42
☐	22	Gen. 23-26
☐	23	Gen. 27-30
☐	24	Gen. 31-34
☐	25	Gen. 35-38
☐	26	Gen. 39-42
☐	27	Psalms 12-14
☐	28	Gen. 43-46
☐	29	Gen. 47-50
☐	30	Ex. 1-3
☐	31	Ex. 4-6

FEBRUARY

Day		Book and Chapter
☐	1	Ex. 7-9
☐	2	Ex. 10-12
☐	3	Psalms 15-17
☐	4	Ex. 13-15
☐	5	Ex. 16-18
☐	6	Ex. 19-21
☐	7	Ex. 22-24
☐	8	Ex. 25-27
☐	9	Ex. 28-30
☐	10	Psalms 18-20
☐	11	Ex. 31-33
☐	12	Ex. 34-37
☐	13	Ex. 38-40
☐	14	Lev. 1-3
☐	15	Lev. 4-6
☐	16	Lev. 7-9
☐	17	Psalms 21-23
☐	18	Lev. 10-12
☐	19	Lev. 13-15
☐	20	Lev. 16-18
☐	21	Lev. 19-21
☐	22	Lev. 22-24
☐	23	Lev. 25-27
☐	24	Psalms 24-26
☐	25	Num. 1-3
☐	26	Num. 4-6
☐	27	Num. 7-10
☐	28	Num. 11-12

MARCH

Day	Book and Chapter
☐ 1	Num. 13-15
☐ 2	Num. 16-18
☐ 3	Psalms 27-29
☐ 4	Num. 19-21
☐ 5	Num. 22-24
☐ 6	Num. 25-27
☐ 7	Num. 28-30
☐ 8	Num. 31-33
☐ 9	Num. 34-36
☐ 10	Psalms 30-32
☐ 11	Deut. 1-3
☐ 12	Deut. 4-6
☐ 13	Deut. 7-9
☐ 14	Deut. 10-12
☐ 15	Deut. 13-15
☐ 16	Deut. 16-18
☐ 17	Psalms 33-35
☐ 18	Deut. 19-21
☐ 19	Deut. 22-24
☐ 20	Deut. 25-27
☐ 21	Deut. 28-30
☐ 22	Deut. 31-34
☐ 23	Joshua 1-3
☐ 24	Psalms 36-38
☐ 25	Joshua 4-6
☐ 26	Joshua 7-9
☐ 27	Joshua 10-12
☐ 28	Joshua 13-15
☐ 29	Joshua 16-18
☐ 30	Joshua 19-21
☐ 31	Psalms 39-41

APRIL

Day	Book and Chapter
☐ 1	Joshua 22-24
☐ 2	Judges 1-3
☐ 3	Judges 4-6
☐ 4	Judges 7-9
☐ 5	Judges 10-12
☐ 6	Judges 13-15
☐ 7	Psalms 42-44
☐ 8	Judges 16-18
☐ 9	Judges 19-21
☐ 10	Ruth 1-4
☐ 11	1 Sam. 1-3
☐ 12	1 Sam. 4-6
☐ 13	1 Sam. 7-9

Day	Book and Chapter
☐ 14	Psalms 45-47
☐ 15	1 Sam. 10-13
☐ 16	1 Sam. 14-16
☐ 17	1 Sam. 17-19
☐ 18	1 Sam. 20-22
☐ 19	1 Sam. 23-25
☐ 20	1 Sam. 26-28
☐ 21	Psalms 48-50
☐ 22	1 Sam. 29-31
☐ 23	2 Sam. 1-3
☐ 24	2 Sam. 4-6
☐ 25	2 Sam. 7-9
☐ 26	2 Sam. 10-12
☐ 27	2 Sam. 13-15
☐ 28	Psalms 51-53
☐ 29	2 Sam. 16-18
☐ 30	2 Sam. 19-21

MAY

Day	Book and Chapter
☐ 1	2 Sam. 22-24
☐ 2	1 Kings 1-4
☐ 3	Prov. 1-3
☐ 4	Prov. 4-6
☐ 5	Psalms 54-56
☐ 6	Prov. 7-9
☐ 7	Prov. 10-12
☐ 8	Prov. 13-15
☐ 9	Prov. 16-18
☐ 10	Prov. 19-21
☐ 11	Prov. 22-24
☐ 12	Psalms 57-59
☐ 13	Prov. 25-27
☐ 14	Prov. 28-31
☐ 15	S. of Sol. 1-4
☐ 16	S. of Sol. 5-8
☐ 17	1 Kings 5-7
☐ 18	1 Kings 8-11
☐ 19	Psalms 60-62
☐ 20	Eccl. 1-4
☐ 21	Eccl. 5-8
☐ 22	Eccl. 9-12
☐ 23	1 Kings 12-14
☐ 24	1 Kings 15-17
☐ 25	1 Kings 18-20
☐ 26	Psalms 63-65
☐ 27	1 Kings 21-22; 2 Kings 1
☐ 28	2 Kings 2-4
☐ 29	2 Kings 5-7

| ☐ | 30 | 2 Kings 8-10 |
| ☐ | 31 | 2 Kings 11:1-14:25 |

JUNE

Day		Book and Chapter
☐	1	Jonah
☐	2	Psalms 66-68
☐	3	2 Kings 14:26-29; Amos 1-3
☐	4	Amos 4-6
☐	5	Amos 7-9
☐	6	2 Kings 15-17
☐	7	2 Kings 18-21
☐	8	2 Kings 22-25
☐	9	Psalms 69-71
☐	10	1 Chron. 1-3
☐	11	1 Chron. 4-6
☐	12	1 Chron. 7-9
☐	13	1 Chron. 10-12
☐	14	1 Chron. 13-16
☐	15	1 Chron. 17-19
☐	16	Psalms 72-74
☐	17	1 Chron. 20-22
☐	18	1 Chron. 23-25
☐	19	1 Chron. 26-29
☐	20	2 Chron. 1-3
☐	21	2 Chron. 4-6
☐	22	2 Chron. 7-9
☐	23	Psalms 75-77
☐	24	2 Chron. 10-12
☐	25	2 Chron. 13-15
☐	26	2 Chron. 16-18
☐	27	2 Chron. 19-22
☐	28	Joel 1-3; Obadiah
☐	29	2 Chron. 23:1-26:8
☐	30	Psalms 78-80

JULY

Day		Book and Chapter
☐	1	Isaiah 1-3
☐	2	Isaiah 4-6; 2 Chron. 26:9-23
☐	3	2 Chron. 27-29
☐	4	2 Chron. 30-32
☐	5	Isaiah 7-9
☐	6	Isaiah 10-12
☐	7	Psalms 81-83
☐	8	Isaiah 13-15
☐	9	Isaiah 16-18

☐	10	Isaiah 19-21
☐	11	Isaiah 22-24
☐	12	Isaiah 25-27
☐	13	Isaiah 28-30
☐	14	Psalms 84-86
☐	15	Isaiah 31-33
☐	16	Isaiah 34-36
☐	17	Isaiah 37-39
☐	18	Isaiah 40-42
☐	19	Isaiah 43-45
☐	20	Isaiah 46-48
☐	21	Psalms 87-90
☐	22	Isaiah 49-51
☐	23	Isaiah 52-54
☐	24	Isaiah 55-57
☐	25	Isaiah 58-60
☐	26	Isaiah 61-63
☐	27	Isaiah 64-66
☐	28	Psalms 91-93
☐	29	Hosea 1-3
☐	30	Hosea 4-6
☐	31	Hosea 7-9

AUGUST

Day		Book and Chapter
☐	1	Hosea 10-12
☐	2	Hosea 13, 14; Micah 1
☐	3	Micah 2-4
☐	4	Psalms 94-96
☐	5	Micah 5-7
☐	6	Nahum 1-3
☐	7	2 Chron. 33-34; Zeph. 1
☐	8	Zeph. 2-3; 2 Chron. 35
☐	9	Hab. 1-3
☐	10	Jer. 1-3
☐	11	Psalms 97-99
☐	12	Jer. 4-6
☐	13	Jer. 11, 12, 26
☐	14	Jer. 7-9
☐	15	Jer. 10, 14, 15
☐	16	Jer. 16-18
☐	17	Jer. 19, 20, 35
☐	18	Psalms 100-102
☐	19	Jer. 25, 36, 45
☐	20	Jer. 46-49
☐	21	Jer. 13, 22, 23
☐	22	Jer. 24, 27, 28
☐	23	Jer. 29, 50-51
☐	24	Jer. 30-33
☐	25	Psalms 103-105

☐	26	Jer. 21, 34, 37
☐	27	Jer. 38, 39, 52
☐	28	Jer. 40-42
☐	29	Jer. 43-44; Lam. 1
☐	30	Lam. 2-5
☐	31	2 Chron. 36:1-8; Daniel 1-3

SEPTEMBER

Day		Book and Chapter
☐	1	Psalms 106-108
☐	2	Daniel 4-6
☐	3	Daniel 7-9
☐	4	Daniel 10-12
☐	5	2 Chron. 36:9-21; Ezekiel 1-3
☐	6	Ezekiel 4-6
☐	7	Ezekiel 7-9
☐	8	Psalms 109-111
☐	9	Ezekiel 10-12
☐	10	Ezekiel 13-16
☐	11	Ezekiel 17-20
☐	12	Ezekiel 21-24
☐	13	Ezekiel 25-28
☐	14	Ezekiel 29-32
☐	15	Psalms 112-114
☐	16	Ezekiel 33-36
☐	17	Ezekiel 37-40
☐	18	Ezekiel 41-44
☐	19	Ezekiel 45-48
☐	20	2 Chron. 36:22-23; Ezra 1-3
☐	21	Ezra 4; Haggai 1-2
☐	22	Psalms 115-117
☐	23	Zech. 1-3
☐	24	Zech. 4-6
☐	25	Zech. 7-9
☐	26	Zech. 10-12
☐	27	Zech. 13, 14
☐	28	Ezra 5-7
☐	29	Psalms 118:1–119:16
☐	30	Ezra 8-10

OCTOBER

Day		Book and Chapter
☐	1	Esther 1-3
☐	2	Esther 4-6
☐	3	Esther 7-10
☐	4	Neh. 1-3
☐	5	Neh. 4-6
☐	6	Psalms 119:17-72
☐	7	Neh. 7-9
☐	8	Neh. 10-13
☐	9	Malachi
☐	10	Matthew 1-3
☐	11	Matthew 4-7
☐	12	Matthew 8-10
☐	13	Psalms 119:73-120
☐	14	Matthew 11-13
☐	15	Matthew 14-16
☐	16	Matthew 17-19
☐	17	Matthew 20-22
☐	18	Matthew 23-25
☐	19	Matthew 26-28
☐	20	Psalms 119:121-176
☐	21	Mark 1-4
☐	22	Mark 5-8
☐	23	Mark 9-12
☐	24	Mark 13-16
☐	25	Luke 1-4
☐	26	Luke 5-8
☐	27	Psalms 120-122
☐	28	Luke 9-12
☐	29	Luke 13-16
☐	30	Luke 17-20
☐	31	Luke 21-24

NOVEMBER

Day		Book and Chapter
☐	1	John 1-3
☐	2	John 4-6
☐	3	Psalms 123-125
☐	4	John 7-9
☐	5	John 10-12
☐	6	John 13-15
☐	7	John 16-18
☐	8	John 19-21
☐	9	Acts 1-4
☐	10	Psalms 126-128
☐	11	Acts 5:1-8:3
☐	12	Acts 8:4-11:18
☐	13	Acts 11:19-14:28
☐	14	James
☐	15	Galatians
☐	16	Acts 15-17:10
☐	17	Psalms 129-131
☐	18	Philippians
☐	19	1 Thess.
☐	20	2 Thess.; Acts 17:11; 18:11

☐	21	1 Cor. 1-3
☐	22	1 Cor. 4-7
☐	23	1 Cor. 8:1-11:1
☐	24	Psalms 131-134
☐	25	1 Cor. 11:2-14:40
☐	26	1 Cor. 15-16
☐	27	2 Cor. 1-5
☐	28	2 Cor. 6-9
☐	29	2 Cor. 10-13
☐	30	Acts 18:12-19:41; Eph. 1, 2

DECEMBER

Day	Book and Chapter
☐ 1	Psalms 135-137
☐ 2	Eph. 3-6
☐ 3	Romans 1-3
☐ 4	Romans 4-6
☐ 5	Romans 7-9
☐ 6	Romans 10-12
☐ 7	Romans 13-16
☐ 8	Psalms 138-140

☐	9	Acts 20-22
☐	10	Acts 23-25
☐	11	Acts 26-28
☐	12	Colossians
☐	13	Heb. 1-4
☐	14	Heb. 5-8
☐	15	Psalms 141-144
☐	16	Heb. 9-11
☐	17	Heb. 12-13; Titus
☐	18	Philemon
☐	19	1 Tim.; 2 Tim.
☐	20	1 Peter
☐	21	1 John
☐	22	Psalms 145-147
☐	23	2 Peter; 2, 3 John; Jude
☐	24	Rev. 1-3
☐	25	Rev. 4-7
☐	26	Rev. 8-10
☐	27	Rev. 11-13
☐	28	Rev. 14-17
☐	29	Psalms 148-150
☐	30	Rev. 18-20
☐	31	Rev. 21-22

SCRIPTURE INDEX

25:40	1/13	2:52	12/8
25:41	2/8	5:4-9	9/5
25:45	1/13	5:8	10/3
25:46	2/9	5:18-25	2/22
26	4/2	6:11	9/16
26:2	4/1	6:22-23	5/19
26:30	9/17	6:32	2/17
26:33	4/2, 13	6:35	2/18
26:35	4/13	6:36	2/22
26:36	4/3	6:38	8/2
26:38	4/4	8:2-3	4/20
26:39	1/22; 3/21, 27; 4/5; 6/16; 12/6	9:23	3/2
26:40-41	4/6, 13	9:28-36	2/28
26:47	4/7	9:29	2/28
26:48-50	4/8	9:32	2/28
26:51-52	4/13	12:7	2/15
26:52	4/9	12:15	8/21
26:53	4/9	12:15-21	8/5
26:56	4/10	12:16-21	8/9
26:59	4/11	12:18	8/12
26:64	4/12	12:20-21	8/5
26:65-66	4/12	12:30	1/16
26:69	4/13	14:26	5/7
26:75	4/13	15:11-32	3/5
27:12-14	3/24	15:18-19	3/5
27:3	10/7	15:20	3/5
27:3-5	8/7	16:9	8/2
27:45	4/17	16:11	8/22
27:46	4/18; 12/6	18	10/5
27:54	4/19	18:13	3/1
27:55	4/20	19:10	4/15
28:19-20	2/11; 7/12	19:41	4/3
28:5-6	4/21	22:3-6	4/8
		22:24	1/22
Mark	**Date**	22:27	3/22
		22:31	4/2
1:15	10/19	22:31-32	9/24
2:17	10/5	22:33	4/2
4:41	3/9	22:36	4/9
6:19ff.	6/17	22:44	4/4
8:31	4/21	22:45	4/5
8:36	8/5	22:61	4/13
8:38	5/28	23:34	1/19, 22; 2/22; 4/14
9:14-29	9/5	23:40-41	4/15
10:21	3/2	23:42	4/15
10:22	3/2	23:43	4/15
10:45	3/12	24:25	11/23
12:29-30	2/4	24:39	2/3
14:57-59	4/11		
14:72	3/7	**John**	**Date**
15:32	4/15		
15:39	4/19	1:1	12/3
16:12	12/7	1:1-3	12/30
		1:3-4	12/3
Luke	**Date**	1:12-13	9/22
		1:14	2/28; 10/24
2:7	12/28	1:16	2/19
2:14	2/28	1:29	4/1, 15
2:29	11/29	1:47	6/1
2:34-35	4/16	2:19	9/25

3:3-6	5/20
3:5-10	9/2
3:6	9/21
3:16	1/24; 2/18; 7/2, 6
3:19	10/2
3:33	2/24
3:36	2/23; 4/12
4:23	3/5
4:24	2/3; 9/12
5:8	12/3
5:18	12/4
5:23	12/25
5:24	9/7
5:28-29	2/13; 12/31
5:30	12/6
6:35	9/25
6:40	2/14; 12/31
6:42	3/23; 12/9
6:44	1/8
6:53-57	9/25
7:37-39	9/6
8:12	9/25
8:31-32	10/19
8:34	10/19
8:44	6/17; 10/2
8:48	12/9
8:58	12/27, 30
10:10	7/10
10:18	4/1
10:27-28	5/28
10:30	2/4
10:37-38	4/12
11:25-26	10/16
11:33-36	2/22
11:35	4/3
12:32	4/19
12:42-43	1/1
13:3-11	3/10
13:35	1/12, 7/16, 26
14	9/24
14:6	7/19; 10/4, 21
14:9	3/21; 12/27
14:15	11/8
14:16	7/19; 9/24
14:16-17	9/4
14:16-20	9/1
14:17	2/24, 9/4
14:19	4/25, 9/4
14:21	9/4
14:26	7/18; 9/4, 25
14:26-27	5/24
14:27	5/13
15	5/2
15:1	10/23
15:5	2/14; 9/4
15:8	12/25
15:13	1/24
15:15	2/29
15:16	1/8

TOPICAL INDEX